ITALIAN FOREIGN POLICY
UNDER MUSSOLINI

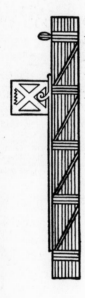

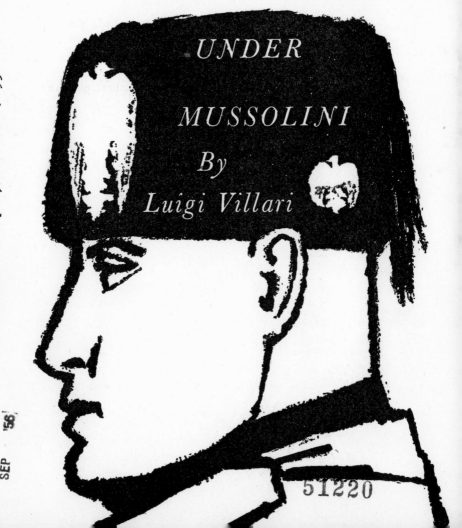

ITALIAN

FOREIGN POLICY

UNDER

MUSSOLINI

By

Luigi Villari

The Devin-Adair Company, New York, 1956

PUBLISHER'S PREFACE

This book is published as a serious contribution to the task of correcting the record on an important sector of contemporary history. The publisher has no special partiality with respect to Italy, Mussolini, or the latter's diplomatic activities. Dr. Villari's volume is offered to the public because of the unique need for the revision of the current and accepted version of Italian foreign policy under Il Duce.

Much has already been published in the United States to correct the biases produced by passion, rivalry and war with respect to the prewar policies and wartime diplomatic behavior of Britain, France, Russia, Germany and the United States. But virtually nothing has appeared in the English language to question or modify the hostile interpretation of Italian foreign policy under Mussolini which became generally accepted after the Italian invasion of Ethiopia, the Spanish Civil War, and Mussolini's entrance into the second World War in June, 1940.

No other country or leader has been more unfairly treated in the books written, read, or both, in Britain, France and the United States than Italy and Mussolini, especially in relation to foreign policies. These books and their interpretations have reflected the views and biases of leftwing radicals, pro-French and pro-British liberals, and imperialistic British conservatives. Even most of those American conservatives who were, in the years following 1929, demanding an "American Mussolini" to solve our depression problems "soured" on Il Duce and turned against him after his conquest of Ethiopia in the mid-1930's, or his entry into war in 1940.

This trend was aided and abetted by the shrewdest of all Communist diplomatic and propaganda *coups* before the outbreak of the second World War. Maksim Litvinov, the superbly shrewd and capable Russian representative at the League of Nations in Geneva, completely "sold" the liberals, particularly the French and British, on the notion that the only threat to democracy, liberty and peace came from the totalitarianism of the Right—Fascism and Nazism. Propaganda to this effect was stepped up in volume and frenzy after the establishment of the Popular Front Government in France in 1936, and the outbreak of the Spanish Civil War. Liberals in the United States were deeply affected by this Russian propaganda and its espousal by French and British liberals. Communists and fellow-travellers throughout the western world eagerly poured fuel on the flames.

This overt distortion of the historical record has been especially unfortunate if one wishes to establish the truth with respect to the total responsibility for the coming of the second World War. The extreme pro-French and pro-British versions of Italian foreign policy constitute almost the reverse of the truth relative to the more important events and issues involved, even if one fully concedes all the weaknesses and blunders which can be truthfully and fairly laid at Mussolini's door.

Particularly notable is the fact that Mussolini's foreign policy has rarely, if ever, been appraised on its merits or defects as *foreign* policy. Liberals and radicals in the Western world, while admiring the more drastic Communist totalitarianism, have bitterly hated the Fascist totalitarian system and have never been able to overcome their prejudices sufficiently to give Mussolini credit for sincere efforts to preserve peace, however obvious and realistic his suggestions and policies may have been. Conservatives, other than British imperialists after 1935, tended to support his foreign policy because they admired the Fascist success in suppressing Communism and other forms of radicalism.

It is generally agreed that the main cause of the second World War was the refusal thoroughly to revise the mistakes and follies of the Treaty of Versailles and the related pacts that followed the first World War. Even before he took charge of Italy as the Fascist leader, and throughout the period after 1922, Mussolini constantly urged a peaceful revision of these treaties and predicted a second European war if this was not done. No other European leader did this until Hitler arose and proceeded to revise the Versailles *Diktat* by violent means which, as Mussolini clearly foresaw, endangered the peace of the whole Continent.

To restrain this and other threats to European peace, Mussolini suggested and drafted a preliminary plan for a Four-Power Pact to eliminate the more important causes of conflict between the European nations and to restrain those who threatened to violate the public order and good-will of Europe. He threw all his energy and enthusiasm into the perfection of such a pact in 1933, but it was rejected by France, Britain and the pro-French Little Entente. Thus perished the only really adequate proposal for the preservation of European peace between the two World Wars—a project far more comprehensive and realistic than the Geneva Protocol, the Locarno Pact, or the Briand-Kellogg Treaty.

British, French and American liberals and radicals have denounced Mussolini beyond all else for his conquest of Ethiopia. But in this he was only following feebly and belatedly the patterns of international behavior by means of which Britain, France and Belgium had previously gobbled up most of Africa. Mussolini seized only a small sector of African territory, and the Italian need for land on which to settle its large surplus population and to provide food for Italians was very great and urgent. Even more, it is highly probable that, but for British recalcitrance, greed and encouragement of Ethiopia, an arrangement could have been made which would have averted war and preserved the formal independence of Ethiopia. Indeed, after the Ethiopian War and the British effort to enforce League sanctions against Italy, European peace might have been assured if Britain and France had been willing to heal the diplomatic wounds and cooperate with the Duce in maintaining the independence of Austria and preventing Hitler's expansion eastward.

Mussolini was very reluctantly driven by Franco-British hostility into the Rome-Berlin Axis, the dangers of which he realized, knowing full well that it embodied no such assurance of peace or protection to Italy as the rejected Four-Power Pact. Mussolini was alarmed at Hitler's aggression both on the eve of the Munich Conference and again at the time of his ultimatum to Poland in August, 1939. He was aghast and dismayed when he learned of Hitler's insane intention to attack Russia in June, 1941. He labored vigorously to bring about peace after the conquest of Poland, and entered the war in 1940 mainly because, during the preceding months of the war, Britain had, by unneutral raids and restraints, all but ruined Italian external trade. Even then, he did not enter the war as an arbitrary act of his own. There was strong pressure by both the royal and court circles and by the people urging him to enter the conflict, lest Italy be left out of the benefits of a victory won by the Germans alone.

Luigi Villari is the best equipped scholar now living to undertake the task of correcting the historical record by presenting a frank and straightforward Italian version of the diplomatic developments and international relations between the two World Wars and during the course of the second conflict. He is a great scholar, he is a widely travelled student of world affairs, and he has been in lifelong personal contact with European diplomacy and the Italian Foreign Office.

Sound historical writing demands that both sides of any controversial epoch should be presented. Until, in the aftermath of the second World War, we entered the quasi-Orwellian era in which opposing views are blacked out or suppressed, historians had welcomed the presentation of all relevant information even though some of it might conflict with their own prior dogmas or convictions. This was the essence of good historical research and writing as it had been described by the great master, Leopold von Ranke.

There is no pretense on the part of the publisher that Dr. Villari's book is completely objective history. It is a superbly capable and vastly informed exposition of the Italian position. Any thoroughly objective historian who approaches the theme of Italian diplomacy from 1919 to 1945 will make use of both the apologies for British and French policies toward Italy, which already exist in such profusion, and Dr. Villari's book. It is not likely that the Italian version will ever again be presented in a single volume with such adequacy, honesty and authority. The opinion may be hazarded that the putative objective historian of the future will find Dr. Villari's account closer to the facts than the Franco-British versions which have hitherto passed as unvarnished truth. If this book contributes notably to promoting truth and to exposing error and bias with regard to a vital segment of recent world history, the purposes of the publisher in making it available to the American reading public will have been fully justified and amply vindicated.

ABOUT THE AUTHOR

Luigi Villari was born in 1876, the son of a distinguished father, the eminent historian, Pasquale Villari, author of notable biographies of Savonarola and Machiavelli, of a famous history of the barbarian invasions of Italy, and numerous other important historical works. Luigi's mother was English, born Linda White. She too was a writer, with several books to her credit, and a translator of her husband's works. From youth Luigi spoke English as well as Italian, and the fact that he had an English mother helps to account for his familiarity with and frequent visits to England and the United States.

Villari took his doctorate in jurisprudence at the University of Siena, and then travelled extensively in all parts of Europe, including the Balkans, Turkey and Russia. In this period, he contributed extensively to newspapers and periodicals in Italy, England and the United States.

In 1906, he entered the Italian Foreign Office, and his familiarity with the English language and American journalism led to his immediate appointment as Italian Vice-Consul in New Orleans, followed by a similar post in Philadelphia, and later as Consul in Boston. He was chiefly concerned with Italian immigration problems, then a very delicate and heated issue.

After serving as a cavalry officer in the first World War, Villari carried out military and political missions in Asia Minor. As soon as the League of Nations was established at Geneva, he joined its staff, and he also attended the numerous post-war international conferences.

In 1923, Villari left the League staff to resume his duties in the Italian Foreign Office. Three years later, he was sent on a cultural mission to England and the United States. He delivered many lectures in both countries on Italian politics and culture. In the United States, he lectured before such important forums as the Williamstown Institute of Politics and the Institute of

Public Affairs at the University of Virginia. He made another extensive lecture trip about a decade later. No Italian publicist or scholar was better or more favorably known in the United States before the second World War. He retired from the Foreign Office in 1938, but kept in close contact with foreign affairs.

For his diplomatic and military services to Italy and the Western nations, Villari was awarded many honors, including the Chevalier of the Legion of Honor, the French *Croix de Guerre* (with palms), the British Military Cross, Grand Officer of the Crown of Italy, Officer of the Order of St. Maurice and St. Lazarus, and the Italian *Croce di Guerra*.

Villari has been a prolific writer and is the author of numerous important books, including one on the history of contemporary Italy in the *Modern World Series*. But his most notable scholarly and interpretative work has been in the field of international relations and diplomatic history. Equipped by specialized education, wide travel and observation, vast scholarly knowledge, and virtually a lifetime of close personal contact with the Italian Foreign Office, no other living person is as well prepared as Luigi Villari to tell the story of Italian foreign policy and international contacts during the Mussolini epoch. There is scarcely a chapter in this book on which he had not previously written an article, a series of articles, or an entire volume.

CONTENTS

PART IV *THE SECOND WORLD WAR AND THE FALL OF FASCISM*

LIST OF ILLUSTRATIONS

PART I

HISTORICAL BACKGROUND AND
FUNDAMENTAL PROBLEMS

CHAPTER ONE

Before the Triumph of Fascism

To understand the spirit of Italy's foreign policy under the Fascist regime, we must first review the period immediately preceding the first World War, for the events of that time undoubtedly helped to mold not only Mussolini's attitudes in the field of foreign relations, but also those of a very large number of Italians, regardless of party.

Italy had intervened in the War for two main reasons. The first was the desire to complete its unity by adding to the territory of the Kingdom the Italian provinces still held by Austria-Hungary. The second was the hope of securing colonial outlets for its superabundant population. The Pact of London of April, 1915, whereby Italy agreed to enter the war in alliance with Great Britain, France and Russia, promised satisfaction for the first objective; colonial aspirations were here provided for in somewhat vague language, but they were more definitely dealt with in the St. Jean de Maurienne agreement concluded in April, 1917, between Italy, Great Britain and France.

The Pact of London, largely owing to President Wilson's objections, led to protracted disputes and bitter wrangling at the Peace Conference both between Italy and its Western Allies and between Italy and Yugoslavia.

The four Cabinets which succeeded that of Orlando (who had been in office at the end of the war), *i. e.* those of Nitti, Giolitti, Bonomi and Facta, had been unable to arrive at a settlement of the country's outstanding international problems. The Brenner frontier was accepted by the Allies without dispute; it gave Italy the territory south of the Alpine watershed with the 400,000 Italians of the Trentino and some 200,000 German-speaking Tyrolese. The situation on the northeastern frontier was more complicated, for in many districts Italians and Slavs were intermingled, and the new Serb-Croat-Slovene state of Yugoslavia claimed the whole of that territory.

The Italian hope for new colonial territory needed for expansion and the relief of population pressure was entirely unrealized after the war. The St. Jean de Maurienne agreement, which conferred on Italy a portion of Asia Minor wrested from Turkey, including the Smyrna area, was flatly repudiated by Lloyd George's Government. All the colonial territories taken from Germany and several Turkish provinces were partitioned between Great Britain, France and Belgium, all three already rich in colonies, but Italy, which needed a breathing space more than any other country, got nothing.

This situation aroused great bitterness in all Italian classes and parties. The Nationalists were particularly incensed, but many other groups were hardly less indignant with the Allied Powers and with the Italian Government that had failed to uphold the country's aspirations, for which over 600,000 Italians had fallen in war.

There was much irritation with Yugoslavia for its claims on the Adriatic territories of Austria-Hungary, and annoyance with France, Great Britain and the United States. Here, ill feeling was more particularly concentrated on President Wilson, whose apparently anti-Italian attitude was regarded as his own personal prejudice, rather than that of the American people.

These events gradually led to a change in Italian public opinion on international affairs in general. After 1870, in addition to the traditional contrast between the Italian and the Germanic mentality,[1] there were many Italians, especially in Lombardy and Venetia where memories of Austrian oppression were still alive, who were still hostile to the Hapsburg Empire.

As that Empire was at the time dominated by the German element, the feeling against Austria extended to Germany. Subsequently, French hostility to the new United Italy had lessened this anti-German feeling and, eventually (1882) led to Italy's joining the Triple Alliance, which for 30 years was to be the basis of the nation's foreign policy. In the field of culture and science, German influence was also very strong.

The first World War revived anti-German feelings, but a distinction was then made between Germany and Austria, and hostility to Austria, which still held the Italian-speaking provinces on the northern and northeastern frontiers, was much more pronounced than that towards Germany. After the War, the treatment of Italy by her Allies aroused intense resentment against them, and the conditions imposed on defeated Germany seemed to many Italians not only harsh and unjust but highly dangerous to world peace. It was felt that 70,000,000 highly civilized persons could not be outlawed and made *taillable et corvéable* for all time. Sympathy was aroused also for the other defeated states, the poverty-stricken Austrian Republic, Hungary, deprived of half her territory and of many millions of purely Magyar citizens, and Bulgaria.

We have here the beginnings of Italy's revisionist attitude, independent of, but associated with, dissatisfaction over its own unrealized ambitions. As far back as 1921 Benito Mussolini had said: "The dilemma is this: treaty revision or a new war." The American Secretary of State, Robert Lansing, had said that "the Versailles treaty menaces the existence of civilization," and two successive Popes had likewise stigmatized that nefarious settlement.

At the same time an active Russian propaganda had influenced large numbers of Italians, not only among the working classes but even among a part of the bourgeois capitalists, who, fearing for their own safety and property, were inclined to wink at a felony and to profess sympathy with Communist aims. Strikes, riots, political murders and disturbances of all kinds, paralyzing the life of the nation, became endemic. The authorities were too weak and pusillanimous to cope with the situation, especially when Nitti was Prime Minister, for he was ever ready to give way to the most outrageous demands of

the seditious elements for the sake of a quiet and peaceful life
—which he failed to get.

The Government and the ruling classes thus found themselves faced by two currents of hostility: the Nationalists or
rather the patriots on the one hand, and the extreme Reds on
the other—both of them, while bitterly opposed to each other,
contributing to weaken the action of the Government.

All these facts gravely disturbed Italy's international position
and prevented its Government from being listened to with
comprehension and friendliness by other Powers, which regarded it as a hopelessly decadent nation. I well remember,
while in England at that time, hearing many Englishmen, including some who were not at all unfriendly to Italy, express
the opinion that it was down and out and destined to precipi-
tate decline into chaos.

To all the complaints of Italians concerning the alleged
unfairness with which their country had been treated at the
Peace Conference, British spokesmen and to a lesser extent
Frenchmen replied that the League of Nations would rectify all
injustices. But it soon appeared to many Italians and to many
non-Italians that the League was an organ created chiefly to
maintain intact the *status quo*. This was particularly favorable
to some countries but very unfavorable to others. Italians
could not, therefore, be induced to regard the League with the
sort of religious fervor that inspired men like Viscount Cecil
or Professor Gilbert Murray, who saw in the League something
pure and holy, to question the sacrosanctity of which was to
brand oneself a cynic, a militarist or an unreasoning nationalist. Italians believed, rightly or wrongly, that the British League
of Nations enthusiasts, chiefly inspired by the interests of the
British government, advocated the League idea only because it
was in harmony with those interests. There may have been
some exaggeration in this, since at least a few of those enthusiasts did sincerely believe in the League; but the British Foreign
Office often undoubtedly exploited their good faith for its own
selfish purposes.

This lack of confidence in the League and the suspicion of
it were very widespread in Italy, regardless of party, but there
was this difference to be borne in mind. The Nationalists and

later the Fascists expressed their sentiments openly, whereas others deemed it advisable to profess some belief in the Geneva institution and its possibilities. As we shall see, Mussolini for a time thought that the League might be made use of for Italy's legitimate aspirations and for world peace through treaty revision. But he was to be disillusioned before very long.

Benito Mussolini was born on July 29, 1883, at Dova di Predappio in Romagna. He was christened Benito, in memory of the Mexican Nationalist revolutionist, Benito Juarez. Brought up in a revolutionary atmosphere, he became an elementary school teacher, joined the Socialist Party at an early age and was chosen secretary of a local Socialist club.

On emigrating to Switzerland, he soon got into trouble owing to his connection with the internationalist extremists there, including Lenin, and was eventually expelled from the Confederation. In Italy he was arrested more than once, and in 1908 he emigrated to Trento, then under Austrian rule, and there edited a local Socialist weekly *L'Avvenire del Lavoro* and contributed to the daily paper *Il Popolo,* edited by Cesare Battisti, an ardent Trentino Irredentist.[2]

It was in the burning Italian Irredentist atmosphere of the Trentino that Mussolini's nationalistic education began. Indeed, this blending of Italian nationalism with a deep interest in social reform was destined to be one of the predominant characteristics of his whole public career.

He was at that time a youth of middle height, somewhat thin, with black hair, keen penetrating eyes and a vigorous jaw. "A highly educated young man," he was described by Irredentists, "he knows the German language perfectly, to the great advantage of our movement." He soon got into difficulties with the Austrian authorities because of his Irredentist sentiments, and he was arrested several times. He was finally expelled from the Empire (September 26, 1909) on account of an unmailed letter to the editor of the *Alto Adige,* found in a police search, denouncing as idiotic a phrase recently pronounced by the Austrian public prosecutor that "Italy ends at Ala." [3]

On returning to Italy, Mussolini again took up his work in the Socialist movement, opposed the Libyan campaign (1911-

1912) and in December, 1912, became editor of the official Socialist organ in Milan, *Avanti!* A born journalist, he edited the paper in a thoroughly personal manner, and was able to make it popular, independently of its political tone, raising its circulation to 100,000. He had now become a figure of national importance, and advocated a social upheaval that would radically alter the unsatisfactory political and economic situation of Italy and raise the standard of living of the masses. But he soon began to realize that it was not possible to improve the economic condition of the proletariat unless that of the whole nation also was raised, and that a fairer distribution of wealth was of little use if there was too little wealth to distribute.

On the outbreak of the first World War, Mussolini for a time was a vigorous advocate of Italian neutrality. His Irredentist feelings made him an uncompromising opponent of intervention on the side of Austria-Hungary, with which Italy was still nominally associated in the Triple Alliance, but he expressed his approval of the gesture of the one-time French antimilitarist, Gustave Hervé, who had volunteered to fight for his country. Mussolini, thus, became gradually more and more estranged from the timid materialism of his own party, which ended up by allying itself with the conservative neutralists, including the followers of ex-Premier Giolitti, and thus became almost pro-German and even pro-Austrian in its attitude toward entering the war.

The dilemma for Italy between neutralism to the end and intervention on the side of the Entente created a crisis in the conscience of Mussolini. He still believed in social revolution, a belief which in a sense never left him, but he was convinced that a social upheaval could not be brought about by a war unless the whole nation took part in it, spiritually as well as materially. At the same time, he felt that intervention was necessary to safeguard Italy's complete independence from foreign influences.

Little by little he came to regard the war from a purely national point of view. He had no sympathy with the Anglophile and Francophile sentimentalism of the Radicals and Freemasons,[4] who saw the conflict as a crusade for democracy and the "Immortal Principles," and he did not condemn Germany as solely responsible for the war—this matter of war guilt did not interest him. The great bulk of his fellow Socialists, owing to their unyielding anti-militarism and anti-nationalism, were uncompromising neutralists, and they regarded the Irredentist yearnings of the majority of Italians as mere bourgeois prejudice or greed.

Finally, Mussolini made a definite break with his party, resigned the editorship of the *Avanti!* and founded a new paper of his own, *Il Popolo d' Italia* (November 15, 1914). This had on its masthead a motto of Blanqui and one of Napoleon—"He who has steel has bread," and "Revolution is an idea which has found bayonets." His former comrades were bitterly incensed against him, and although they were convinced of his rigid honesty, they accused him of having been corrupted by French gold. On November 4, 1914, they expelled him from the Party.

He now openly joined the interventionist camp. Although he had not yet formulated a definite program of foreign policy, he was convinced that war was necessary to improve the conditions of the workers through national security and territorial expansion by obtaining the "Italia irredenta" and lands fit for Italian colonization.

While D'Annunzio's interventionist propaganda appealed to the intellectual classes, Mussolini's fiery oratory affected a large part of the working classes and thus helped to make interventionism a mass movement.

On Italy's declaration of war (May 24, 1915) Mussolini at once volunteered for military service, although as a newspaper editor he was entitled to exemption. In February, 1917, while serving in the front line, he was severely wounded by the explosion of a trench mortar bomb, and, after a long period in the hospital, he returned to his editorial desk in Milan.

The violent agitations of the Socialists and Communists after the end of the War made Mussolini realize the necessity for a strong nationalist trend, though he did not forget his former Socialist inspiration. Georges Sorel said of him: "He has an extraordinary capacity for understanding the Italian people and has invented something which is not in any book, the union of the National with the Socialist spirit." [5]

As a result of his discernment of the immediate needs of the Italian nation and economy at the time, Mussolini founded the Fascist Party on March 23, 1919. It rested primarily on that combination of national spirit and social welfare policies which Sorel mentioned. It brought together a number of the outstanding new trends in social and political theory: expert leadership of the élite, the psychological inspiration of national patriotism, pluralism in politics, the basic importance of interest-groups in the economic order, and the implementation of the new order through the corporative state.

At the general election of November, 1919, Mussolini stood as a Fascist candidate, but although he had many influential supporters—the great conductor Toscanini, subsequently a rabid anti-Fascist, was on his same list—he secured only 4,000 votes, and the *Avanti!* published a sarcastic account of his political defeat as if he were already dead.

At the election of 1921, however, he was returned by a large majority (124,918 votes) with a strong nucleus of other Fascists. In his first speech in the Chamber of Deputies, while he devoted most of it to domestic policy, he scathingly attacked the Government for its failure to defend Italian interests abroad. He asked why the independence of Montenegro, guaranteed by treaty, had not been respected. The country had been annexed to Serbia, in consequence of a bogus plebiscite held under Serbian terrorism supported by French bayonets. He took up the cause of the Arabs in Palestine, inveighing against the Balfour declaration in favor of a Zionist state and showing himself very well informed even on that question.

On another problem, of an international as well as of a domestic nature—relations with the Vatican—he showed respect for the Church, although he was not a professing Catholic. Quoting from the German historian, Theodore Mommsen, who had said years ago, when the Italian Kingdom occupied Rome in 1870, that one does not remain in Rome without a universal idea, he declared: "I believe and affirm that the only universal idea existing in Rome today is that which radiates from the Vatican." [6] Throughout his whole career Mussolini always had Rome and its greatness in mind—the Rome of the Caesars, the

Rome of the Popes, the Rome of united Italy, the Rome of the Fascist regime.

In a subsequent speech in the Chamber on December 1, 1921, he dwelt on the necessity for internal pacification, without which Italy could never hope to play an important part in world affairs. It was necessary, he said, that the attention of the ruling classes and of public opinion in Italy should be projected beyond the frontiers, the dilemma being "either a new war or treaty revision." He realized that the peace treaties of 1919-1920 were unfair and intolerable, not only for Italy but also for many other countries. This demand for treaty revision was to be another keynote of his whole foreign policy; disregard for its necessity was to be the cause of a second World War.

One of the main items in the platforms of the Socialists and Communists was the alleged success of the Russian revolution, and they yearned for a similar movement in Italy and other countries. But Mussolini from the very first maintained that revolution, far from bringing relief to the poverty-stricken masses of Russia, had only produced an appalling famine, and that the same thing would happen elsewhere if there was a similar uprising. In an article published in his *Popolo d'Italia* (December 23, 1921) he pointed out that 30,000,000 people in Russia were starving, and that the relief supplied by the various international organizations reached only a small percentage of the victims. The Italian masses, he added, were blinded by propaganda and knew nothing of all this. Statements of this kind at the time were regarded as heresy by most persons of Leftist views, even if they were not actually Communists.

Another point on which Mussolini saw further ahead than most political figures of his time was the inevitable revival of Germany;[7] for even if the mask of that nation was republican and pacifist, its soul was not, and the French attempt to strangle Germany economically was bound to prove an utter failure.[8]

In one of his last speeches before coming into power, delivered at Udine, on September 20, 1922, Mussolini stated that Italian unity would not be complete as long as her just claims in the Adriatic did not receive satisfaction.[9]

In summary, the fundamental points of Mussolini's outlook on international affairs as they shaped up on the eve of Fascist triumph were: (1) a demand for treaty revision, especially to adjust Italy's claims on the Adriatic; (2) skepticism of the pretensions of Soviet Russia; (3) anticipation of Germany's recovery; and (4) opposition to the more extreme French measures to enforce and prolong the subjection of Germany.

---

[1] Illustrated, among others, by Pasquale Villari in his essay, *La civiltà latina e la civiltà germanica,* published in 1862.

[2] On the outbreak of the first World War Battisti had volunteered for service in the Italian army and was taken prisoner by the Austrians and hanged as a traitor.

[3] Ala was then the frontier station between Austria and Italy.

[4] The Italian Freemasons held definite political principles: anti-clericalism, almost to the point of atheism, and political radicalism.

[5] Quoted by Giorgio Pini, *The Official Life of Benito Mussolini* (English edition, London, 1939), p. 104.

[6] *Scritti e discorsi di Benito Mussolini,* Milan, 1934, Vol. II, pp. 209-226.

[7] *Il Popolo d' Italia,* January 25, 1922.

[8] Article in *Gerarchia,* March 23, 1922.

[9] *Scritti e discorsi,* Vol. II, p. 307.

CHAPTER TWO

Mussolini in Power

The story of the March on Rome (October 28, 1922) and of Mussolini's advent to power belongs to Italy's domestic policy, but the repercussions of that event also extended to the field of foreign policy.

The manner in which Mussolini and the Fascist Party gained possession of the government was regarded in most foreign circles as an illegal act of violence. That may have been the case, technically, but it should not be forgotten that this action was the outgrowth of a widespread feeling among the majority of Italians that the chaos to which the country was then a prey under a succession of cabinets incapable of dealing with it had to be handled with a strong hand, and that the nation's international position must be adequately safeguarded.

Moreover, Mussolini had been summoned by the King to form a government, a procedure in strict harmony with the Constitution; and on November 18, 1922 (less than a month after his seizure of power) he secured a vote of confidence of 306 to 116 in a Chamber of Deputies that had been elected eighteen months before under the regime of Giolitti. On the 25th, after several important measures had been enacted, full powers were conferred on him by 275 votes to 90, and from

the Senate, only half a dozen of whose members had been nominated on his recommendation, he obtained an almost unanimous vote of confidence.[1] According to the text of the Constitution, Mussolini's Government was thus strictly legitimate.

In approaching the international reactions to Mussolini's
advent to power, it should be borne in mind that, according to
a widespread belief, especially in Anglo-Saxon countries, the
establishment of a despotic or totalitarian regime in any country
is directly and inevitably conducive to a policy of aggression.
As Mussolini's Government was widely regarded as having that
despotic character, its war-mongering spirit was often taken for
granted without further question or investigation.

Although many aspects of Mussolini's domestic policy actually differed radically from the picture of them presented in
the English-speaking press, the main point to be considered
here is the nature of his foreign policy, whether it was aggressive and bellicose, and whether it contributed to bring about
that great disaster to humanity, the second World War.

If it can be proved that his policy did not lead to that result,
he should be acquitted of the major crime, whatever one may
think of his domestic legislation and policy. If the contrary
view proves right, he deserves to be condemned before the bar
of history, however meritorious his measures of internal policy
may have been. But the great majority of the foreign judgments
on Mussolini's policy are based on ignorance of the facts about
Fascism, and also on both dislike and ignorance of his domestic
policy. Besides, they are often inspired by the extremely dynamic personality of the man, which either dazzled or repelled
most observers and prevented them from appreciating facts and
circumstances in their true light.

On assuming office, Mussolini took over, along with the
premiership, not only the Ministry of the Interior, as nearly
all his predecessors had done, but also the Ministry of Foreign
Affairs, which he continued to hold for the greater part of his
career. At the Foreign Ministry he had a succession of Undersecretaries who dealt with routine work, while he himself, as
the Duce of Fascism, handled all the major foreign problems.

Many statesmen on setting up governments of a new type are
prone to make wholesale changes in the permanent personnel

of the civil service. But Mussolini retained nearly all the former officials, particularly the members of the diplomatic service. Although many of them did not see eye to eye with him on various questions, Italy continued to be represented abroad in the main by career diplomats of long standing. The new Minister of Foreign Affairs considered this more important than blind doctrinal conformity, and the veteran diplomats and consuls continued to serve their country faithfully and efficiently, even though the new trend of foreign policy differed considerably from that of the past.

One of the few exceptions was Count Carlo Sforza, Ambassador in Paris at the time of the March on Rome. Whether disappointed at not having been re-appointed Minister of Foreign Affairs[2] or for some other reason, he sent in his resignation. But he stated that he "wished to avoid every difficulty and to facilitate the work of the Government," and "to perform an act of deep personal regard" for Mussolini, whose tenure of office he hoped "would be long and happy, because if it were to be of short duration it would signify disaster." He added that he wished to coöperate with the Government to the best of his ability, and that he was "prepared to undertake to represent Italy at the conference to be held on the Near East [the Lausanne Conference for peace with Turkey to be held in 1922-23] if your Excellency so desires." Later on, he concluded, "I should again take on a permanent post with you." Thus, while resigning from one appointment, Sforza asked for two.[3]

Sforza's wishes were not granted; he was placed on the retired list. From this time onward he devoted himself to unceasing propaganda activity abroad hostile to Mussolini's Government and to Italy in general, doing his best to arouse ill-feeling against his own country in Great Britain, France and the United States.

In his first speech in the Chamber as Minister of Foreign Affairs, on November 16, 1922, Mussolini laid down the main lines of his foreign policy. "The Peace Treaties," he said, "good or bad, once they are signed and ratified, must be carried out. A state which respects itself cannot have any other doctrine. But treaties are not eternal, they are not irreparable: they are chapters of history, not epilogues of history. To carry them out signifies to try them out . . . We want a policy of peace but not a policy of suicide . . . With the United States our relations are excellent, and it will be my task to perfect them, above all in the field of a desirable intimate collaboration of an economic nature." [4]

That same day he said in the Senate: "This Italy has blazed forth before those who represent other nations and who must henceforth realize, whether they like it or not, that Italy does not intend to follow the cart of others, . . . but means to claim with dignity all her rights and intends with no less dignity to defend all her interests." [5]

Almost from the first day of his premiership, Mussolini undertook a series of measures calculated to improve the country's financial situation and to raise the value of the lira; in fact, signs of progress soon began to appear. But the French occupation of the Ruhr upset the European financial situation, and of course Italy, as well as other countries, was unfavorably affected. In particular, Italy faced serious problems due to the difficulty of importing coal from Germany. This fact made Mussolini realize more clearly than ever the necessity of a more stable and satisfactory situation in that country.

His first visit abroad as Prime Minister had been to the Lausanne Conference, but he remained there only a few days. After his return to Rome he went to London in December to deal with the question of reparations and inter-allied war debts. Here he realized that the only real solution was the complete cancellation of both. This policy was ultimately accepted and put into practice, but not until after many years of bitter recrimination and undignified wrangling. Had it been accepted in 1922, Europe would have been spared innumerable quarrels, complicated by preposterous arrangements incapable of execution, by insistent demands for incredible reparations and by financial and economic crises.

The next international question to be dealt with was the ratification of the Washington Naval Treaty, concluded early in 1922, whereby France and Italy agreed to a construction policy for tonnage of large warships at the ratio of 1.67 for each, as compared with 5 each for the United States and Great Britain, and 3 for Japan. In his message to the Chamber announcing its ratification (February 6, 1923), Mussolini stated that his country was quite right in agreeing to this treaty, although he did not believe that it implied perpetual peace—he doubted if even Kant believed in such an idyllic possibility. He said that he thought the great philosopher had the title for his book suggested to him by an inn sign, and that the sign was a cemetery, where alone perpetual peace is possible. We have here an expression of skepticism, then regarded as immoral, which future events were, alas, amply to justify.

Another serious difficulty for Italy was its relations with Yugoslavia.[6] The frontier situation had been more or less unsatisfactorily settled by the Rapallo Treaty of 1920, and Mussolini at once grasped the need for some form of revision. In his speech in the Chamber on February 16, 1923, he stated that the treaty was open to many objections, that it could only be applied in its integrity or denounced; but, since denunciation would mean reopening the whole of the Adriatic settlement, loyal application by Italy and Yugoslavia was the only solution. At the same time there was no reason for claiming that the Rapallo arrangement was eternal and unchangeable, or that its future revision could not be considered.

The Rapallo Treaty was duly ratified, but Mussolini was already contemplating a new settlement with Yugoslavia. In a Senate speech on the same day he defined the existing instrument as "a lamentable compromise, the result of a difficult domestic situation and of a foreign policy that is not remarkable for an excessively independent spirit." He added significantly that "a foreign policy of dignity, style and firmness cannot be conducted if the nation does not constantly give evidence of an iron discipline." Here is the keynote of the Duce's whole attitude—strict discipline at home, firmness and dignity abroad.

The then existing Adriatic situation was an inheritance from the Peace Treaties, the solution adopted having been a series of compromises: Trieste, Gorizia, Istria and Zara were assigned to Italy, the rest of Dalmatia to Yugoslavia. This meant that the East coast of the Adriatic, into which innumerable deep inlets penetrate and which is guarded by rocky islands and constitutes a whole series of potentially formidable naval bases, might be placed at the disposal of any Great Power hostile to Italy, even if Yugoslavia itself then had no navy. On the other hand, the opposite Italian coast was almost defenseless, having no good naval port between Venice and Brindisi. The majority of the Dalmatian people were Croats, but all the cultural elements of the population spreading inland from the sea coast and indeed all traces of true civilization in the province were Latin— Roman, Venetian, Italian. "Each of these havens," as the English historian Professor Edward Freeman wrote, "with the cities which from early days have sprung up on each, has always been an isolated centre of civilization in a backward land." [7]

The Yugoslavs, even before the formation of their new state, had aspired to possess all the former Austrian Adriatic terri- tories assigned to Italy by the Pact of London and the Peace Conference. None of the territories in question had ever be- longed to Serbia or to any other Slav state, and in Trieste, Gorizia and Istria the great majority of the population was Italian, although during the preceding fifty years Austria had imported many thousands of Slovenes and Croats into these districts with the object of de-Italianizing them. The Yugoslav extremists even hoped to annex some territories within the borders of the Italian Kingdom, on the pretext that they con- tained trifling Slav minorities.

After many protracted disputes Italy had renounced at Ra- pallo even the part of northern Dalmatia assigned to it by the Pact of London, except the city of Zara, in exchange for Yugo- slavia's agreement to recognize the Italian city of Fiume as an independent city-state.

Mussolini had no wish for a conflict with Yugoslavia, and he hoped to reach an understanding with her on a more satisfactory basis, calculated to provide for friendly political and economic intercourse between the two countries. In the autumn of 1923 negotiations were begun; they were concluded on January 27, 1924.

The "free city" arrangement for Fiume had proved anything but satisfactory. In modern times, free city-states have never proved stable and are bound to lead to international conflicts.[8] At Rapallo, moreover, Italy had agreed to let Yugoslavia have

Porto Baros, which is an integral part of the port of Fiume.[9]
Fiume as a free city proved incapable of maintaining itself.
After D'Annunzio had occupied it for a time, Italy had to keep
troops and police there to maintain order and to supply the
population with funds and food, for the blockade imposed on
it by Yugoslavia during D'Annunzio's occupation had not been
removed and the city's economic life was strangled.

By the terms of the new treaty the Fiume city-state disappeared, for Yugoslavia recognized Italy's sovereignty over it.
But Yugoslavia now had Porto Baros as well as other Dalmatian
territories previously assigned to Italy, with some minor frontier
modifications. It was now hoped that a new era in Italo-Yugoslav relations had dawned. As Mussolini said afterwards, relations between two neighboring countries cannot be indifferent
—they must be either friendly or hostile.

Even before the Italo-Yugoslav negotiations had commenced,
other events in Italy's international relations were maturing.
The question of Russia was both an international and a domestic problem for Italy, as well as for other countries, inasmuch as
the Soviet Government and its subsidiary organs were ever
promoting and financing seditious agitations abroad with the
object of disseminating the new Communist creed and facilitat-
ing Russia's imperialist expansion. Italy's pre-Fascist governments had always been indecisive about Russia, not daring to
put a stop to its interference in Italian domestic affairs, to
establish commercial relations with it, or even to recognize it
officially.

Mussolini took a bolder view of the question. As far back as
November 16, 1922, he had stated that Italy must consider relations with Russia independently of that country's domestic
political institutions. One might well hate Bolshevik methods
without refusing to trade with Russia. He studied the possibility
of concluding a normal commercial agreement, discussing the
matter with Krassin and with Vorovski, who had been sent
to Rome as the semi-official representative of Soviet Russia.

An agreement was concluded on November 30, 1923, and
then Parliament granted Russia *de jure* recognition. To this
Mussolini had agreed, in exchange for a favorable commercial
treaty concluded in 1924.

But the Duce was not inclined to tolerate any activity on the part of Russian propaganda in Italy, and the Moscow Government was given very clearly to understand that the first attempt by Russian agents to promote agitation and strikes in Italy or to inspire the action of any Italian political party or group would be followed by the immediate expulsion of Russia's official, semi-official or other representatives and the rupture of all relations with Moscow.

The results of the commercial treaty were not altogether satisfactory for Italy, as Italian imports from Russia were much larger than exports to that country, and in any case the total amount of the trade proved very small.

In that same year, 1923, an incident brought about a clash between Italy and the League of Nations and proved the first of a series of disputes with Great Britain.

Italy's relations with Greece had been traditionally friendly. Italian volunteers had fought and died for the cause of Greek independence in 1825, and others imitated their example in the Greco-Turkish war of 1897. But during the Balkan wars of 1912-1913 there were disputes between the two countries, for Italy supported the cause of Albanian independence, while Greece wanted to annex a part of Southern Albania.

After the first World War, Great Britain and France had repudiated the St. Jean de Maurienne agreement[10] and had granted to Greece a large part of Asia Minor previously promised to Italy. This aroused much bitterness between Italy and Greece, but still more between Italy and Great Britain, which continued to back up Greek claims in the Near East, probably with a view to dominating that area by means of a vassal Greece.

When the Albanian State was created in 1913, its frontiers were defined at the Florence Conference that same year, but the outbreak of the war suspended the work of delimitation *in loco*. During the first World War there were other disputes between Italy and Greece in connection with the Macedonian campaign and in Albania. After the end of hostilities and the Peace Conference, the Conference of Ambassadors in Paris took over the Albanian question and appointed a Commission to delimit the

Greco-Albanian frontier with the Italian General Enrico Tellini as its president.

The Commission found its task far from easy, for the Greek authorities placed every obstacle in its way, objecting to the assigning of certain districts to Albania and accusing the Commissioners of unduly favoring Albanian claims. A violent campaign was started in the Greek press against Italy because the President of the Commission was an Italian, and the Epirot committees were particularly virulent in this propaganda. On August 27, 1923, General Tellini and the other members of the Commission were ambushed and murdered near the Greco-Albanian frontier, and there is every reason to believe that the outrage had been organized with at least the connivance of certain local Greek officials.

Mussolini and Italian public opinion generally were deeply incensed at the outrage, and the next day the Rome Government sent a vigorously worded protest to the Greek Ministry of Foreign Affairs, demanding full apologies, exemplary punishment of the guilty and ample reparations.

The Greek Government expressed its regret for the occurrence and offered apologies and reparations, but it did not fully accept all the Italian demands, saying that if its reply were not considered satisfactory, it would submit the dispute to the League of Nations. The reply was not considered adequate by Italy, and Mussolini said that an appeal to the League of Nations was improper, inasmuch as the Tellini mission was an outgrowth of the Conference of Ambassadors, and hence that body alone was competent to deal with the dispute.

On August 31st, an Italian naval force appeared before Corfu, and the admiral demanded the surrender of the island. The commander of the garrison having rejected the demand, a few blank shots were fired. When the Greek flag even then was not lowered, some shells were fired on the fortress. The Greek authorities had failed to inform the Italian admiral that refugees were lodged there, and a few of them were killed or wounded. The island was then occupied by an Italian force. On September 1st, the Greek Government submitted an appeal to the League Council, which was then sitting, but it dealt only with the question of the reparations demanded by Italy and did not mention the occupation of Corfu.

Until that moment the dispute had been one between Italy and Greece. But now a new element intervened—the League of Nations and its more fanatical advocates. The League on this occasion was personified by the British delegate Lord Robert (afterwards Viscount) Cecil, who, in his speech to the Council, after a casual allusion to the massacre of the Tellini mission as a matter of slight importance, poured the vials of his wrath on what he regarded as the iniquity of the Italian occupation of Corfu. He seemed eager, above all, to get the League to intervene, whether it was entitled to do so or not, lest its prestige should suffer from inaction. Possibly he regarded the occupation as prejudicial to British naval interests. He secured support for his views from the delegates of some of the smaller nations, who detected in Italy's action the possible menace of a great power against a small one.

In the meantime the question was being dealt with by the Conference of Ambassadors, and the Greek Government had declared its readiness to accept the decision of that body, while also appealing to the League. It is a generally recognized legal principle that two tribunals cannot be invested with the same case, but the Greek Government and, above all, its sponsors, maintained that the Conference was competent to deal with the massacre of the mission only, whereas the occupation of Corfu should be entrusted to the League. But according to the terms of the League Covenant a dispute which could not be settled by diplomatic action should be submitted to arbitration, and only if both diplomacy and arbitration failed should it be referred to the League Council (Article 13). Italy, therefore, refused at that moment to accept the League's competence, as the proceedings before the Conference constituted the first phase, i.e., diplomatic action.

The Conference declared itself competent in the matter, but Cecil and other League partisans made every effort to get the matter declared to be within the province of the League, in order to make the League appear to be doing something, even at the risk of failure. A part of the British press was very bitter in its attacks upon Italy for its refusal to submit the matter to the

League, but it was evident that these attacks were inspired less by League principles or sympathy for Greece than by hostility to the Fascist regime. This made the papers in question forget all about the real origin of the dispute, which was the massacre of the Tellini mission. Particularly violent were the *Daily Chronicle,* then the property of the Greek financier, munitions-dealer and mystery-man, Sir Basil Zaharoff, and the Labour Party's organ, the *Daily Herald.* The *Morning Post,* which had always been friendly to Italy, wrote that the anti-Fascists could forgive the Italians for Corfu, but not for castor oil! [11]

Finally the Conference of Ambassadors decided that the Greek Government must offer ample apologies to Italy with full military honors, that a Commission of delegates of the four Great Powers should be set up to inquire into the outrage and control the inquiry conducted by the Greek authorities into the circumstances of the case, and that the Greek Government should deposit a sum of 50,000,000 lire (the sum demanded by Italy) as a guarantee for the indemnities, the exact amount of which was to be fixed by the Hague Court. Italy had undertaken to evacuate Corfu when the reparations decision had been carried out, and in any case, not later than September 27th. This fact constituted a complete refutation of the charge made by Cecil and others that Italy intended to remain at Corfu indefinitely.

The League Council accepted the decision of the Conference, Greece carried out her undertakings, and the Hague Court awarded 50,000,000 lire to the Italian Government, which, after having paid indemnities to the families of the victims of the massacre of August 27th, offered the rest of the sum to the families of the refugees killed in the bombardment of the Corfu citadel. The Commission of Inquiry set to work, but those responsible for the outrage were never discovered.

The incident was thus closed, but it was significant for the relations between Italy and the League. As I have said above, Italian public opinion had never had much confidence in the Geneva institution, believing it to be mainly an instrument of the British and French governments to be used for their own interests, and partly a piece of hieratic and somewhat hypocritical sentimentalism. Its extreme advocates seemed to be men who, for the sake of promoting perpetual peace, were ever ready to plunge the world into war.

Mussolini's distrust of the League was intensified by the events connected with the Greek episode, which he believed had been inspired by jealousy of Italy in certain foreign countries and by indignation at seeing it finally conducting a vigorous foreign policy of its own. In a speech delivered in the Senate the Duce declared: "The battle at the League of Nations in Geneva was very bitter and difficult, because it was complicated by two elements. There were many sincere but more or less fanatical individuals, and there were others agitated by Italy's gesture of autonomy from a national point of view. All the shady world of semi-Socialistic and plutocratic democracy is furious because Italy is ruled by a Fascist Government." The League, he went on to say, "is an Anglo-French duet; each of these two Powers has its satellites and its clients, and Italy's position in the League was until yesterday one of absolute inferiority." [12]

Nevertheless, Mussolini did not propose that Italy should withdraw from the League; instead he promoted a more active Italian participation in its activities, trusting that it might be made a useful instrument for international diplomatic procedure. For the next few years, in fact, the Italian Government made every effort to operate through the League, and it succeeded in achieving some satisfactory results through the League's instrumentality.

But the League's foundations were never really solid. Many all-important questions, such as Franco-German relations and the reparations problem, were excluded from its jurisdiction, and it deliberately abstained from discussing treaty revision, provided for in Article 19 of the League Covenant, whereas that problem should have been one of its chief functions.

A lack of confidence in the League was by no means limited to Italy or to Mussolini. In most French circles similar feelings prevailed, and a story told of Clemenceau is typical of his attitude. It was reported that every night, before going to bed, he looked at himself in the glass, and said: "Georges Clemenceau, you *must* believe in the League of Nations." Every morning, on getting up, he again looked at himself in the glass, and said: "Georges Clemenceau, you *do* believe in the League of Nations."

Mussolini's feelings were not very different from those of "the Tiger," and he never pretended that they were—this was perhaps a serious defect on his part. A touch of hypocritical pretense might have gone a long way toward satisfying the fanatical enthusiasts of the League.

[1] The members of the Senate under the existing Constitution were then nominated by the King from a list submitted by the Prime Minister, who selected them from certain categories of citizens specified in that same Constitution.

[2] He had held that office in the Giolitti Cabinet (1920-1921).

[3] Text in *Corriere della Sera*, November 2, 1922.

[4] *Scritti e discorsi*, Vol. III, pp. 9-13.

[5] *Ibid.*, pp. 35-36.

[6] After the close of the first World War Italy's Adriatic claims were contested by France, President Wilson, and some British publicists.

[7] Edward Freeman, *Sketches from the Subject and Neighbour Lands of Venice*, London, 1881.

[8] Danzig, for example.

[9] When Sforza was asked in the Chamber of Deputies if he had promised Porto Baros to Yugoslavia, he strenuously denied it. But soon afterwards the Yugoslav delegate Trumbich produced a letter from Sforza in which he actually made such a promise.

[10] See Chapter I.

[11] During the early days of the Fascist régime some of the younger and more ardent Fascist extremists had forced Communists and other opponents to drink large doses of castor oil.

[12] *Scritti e discorsi*, Vol. III, pp. 268ff. Mussolini's views on the League of Nations, the "rash" of international conferences after the first World War, and popular diplomacy, based on fanfare and maudlin publicity, were much like those expressed in recent times by Sisley Huddleston in *Popular Diplomacy and War*, West Rindge, New Hampshire: Richard R. Smith, 1954; and Sir Harold Nicolson, *The Evolution of Diplomatic Method*, New York: Macmillan, 1955.

CHAPTER THREE

Italy, Yugoslavia and France

After the conclusion of the Rome treaty of 1924 the Yugoslav Government professed to accept the new situation, and it may indeed have been sincere in this attitude. But various Slav organizations, more or less under government auspices and control, or at least supported by individual members of the government, by generals or by high officials, attempted to promote Irredentist movements in the frontier territories assigned to Italy. It was claimed in certain Yugoslav circles that these agitations were the consequence of Italy's Italianization policy towards the non-Italian minorities, and the Yugoslav people could not help taking a sentimental interest in the Slavs living beyond the frontier. This may have been true, but the chief motive force of the agitation was ever the same—a desire to annex yet more territory to the Yugoslav state, an aspiration not limited to the districts containing Slav minorities.

The policy of Italianization, which at times assumed exaggerated aspects after October 1922, was due to those very agitations, fomented and financed from beyond the frontier, even though the conduct of some of the Italian officials, especially those of local origin, inspired by a half-century of struggle to maintain the Italian character of the districts in question, may have been open to criticism.

But the Italian conflict with Yugoslavia would not have assumed such a serious aspect had it not been for French intervention in connection with it. The constant anxiety of France ever since the end of the first World War had always been, perhaps not unnaturally, the fear of a revival of Germany and of the possible attempts by Germany to recover its lost position at the expense of France. French statesmen were ever seeking allies against a new German aggression long before the advent of Hitler. They believed that the support of the lesser states of Central and Southeastern Europe, built out of the ruins of Germany or of its old ally, the Austro-Hungarian Empire, as potential enemies of a resuscitated Germany and of its probable allies, offered the best guarantees of French security. This policy, however, involved France in the quarrels and aspirations of its allies and drew France into supporting them, even in disputes in which it had no direct interest. France thus found itself putting its approval on some very unreliable and dangerous combinations. One of the states whose support it sought for French policies was Yugoslavia, viewed as a potential enemy of Austria, Hungary and Bulgaria, all three potential allies of Germany. This policy at once brought France into conflict with Italy whenever the latter happened to be in a dispute with Yugoslavia, independently of such immediate differences as France itself might have with its trans-Alpine neighbor. France thus came to regard Yugoslavia's quarrels with Italy almost as its own.

As I have hinted, other incidents, having their origins in questions of domestic policy, brought France and Italy into conflict. On June 10, 1924, the Italian Socialist deputy, Giacomo Matteotti, disappeared mysteriously from Rome, and it was afterwards discovered that he had been kidnapped in a car by a group of four men. He was found dead some weeks later buried in a deserted spot in the Roman Campagna. The kidnappers were apprehended and condemned to various terms of imprisonment.

Matteotti, a wealthy landowner from Rovigo, had long been an influential member of the Socialist Party, and during the

first World War he had almost espoused the cause of the Central
Powers, enemies of the Italian Government of the time. Ever
since the advent of the Fascist Party to power he had been its
uncompromising opponent. Hence, his murder was consequently
attributed to some of its members and even to Mussolini himself. But neither at the trial of the kidnappers nor at any subsequent period was there any evidence incriminating any
member of the government. It was proved, instead, that the
kidnappers had acted on their own responsibility, and that they
had intended not to murder Matteotti but only to frighten him
into ceasing to support anti-Fascist activities in Italy and in
France.[1] He had died from a tubercular hemorrhage and heart
failure brought on by the struggle in the car, his precarious
physical condition being unknown to the kidnappers.

Although the kidnappers had served their sentences, those
who still survived at the end of the second World War, namely,
Amerigo Dumini, who had been the driver of the fatal car, and
Cesari Rossi, head of the Fascist Press Bureau and accused of
indirect complicity, were tried again by an anti-Fascist court in
1947. Rossi was acquitted, but Dumini received a life sentence
for purely political reasons since no fresh evidence was produced against him.

The Matteotti affair caused an immense sensation and provided abundant political capital for Mussolini's opponents both
at home and abroad. In France the reaction was particularly
virulent. Even before the Matteotti affair a number of Italian
anti-Fascists had found asylum and support in France, and some
of those who committed murders and other outrages against
Fascists in France were treated with great leniency by the police
and the courts. Among other cases, the journalist, Nicola Bon-
servizi, had been murdered by an anti-Fascist restaurant waiter,
and many Fascists, including Dumini, were convinced, rightly
or wrongly, that Matteotti had organized that crime and others
of the same kind.[2]

The reasons for the French attitude in this connection were
two-fold. In the first place, the French authorities were normally
inclined to be lenient in dealing with crimes committed by
foreigners against other foreigners on French territory; and
secondly, several French Cabinets had had Leftist tendencies—

Radicals, Freemasons,[3] Socialists—and therefore they sympathized with the opponents of the Fascist regime even if they were guilty of murders and other acts of violence committed against Italian Fascists. Such crimes were not proceeded against at all, or the culprits received only very mild sentences.[4]

This conduct on the part of the French authorities aroused Mussolini's violent indignation; and large numbers of Italians, including non-Fascists, saw in this attitude and procedure mainly evidence of French hostility to Italy and the Italian nation, and several of them returned French decorations that had been conferred on them. The feelings aroused in consequence of these events made it very difficult to settle amicably political disputes between the two countries, even when they were not of a serious character.

The French press was full of outbursts against Italy on account of her domestic regime as well as her foreign policy, and the Italian press responded in kind with no less bitterness.

But it was not only the French press that indulged in this attitude. A large part of the British press was hardly less bitter, and certain London and provincial papers, dealing with Italian internal affairs as if they directly concerned Great Britain, dictated to the Italians what they ought to do and indulged in outbursts of virtuous, if somewhat hypocritical, indignation at the alleged iniquities of Mussolini, of the Fascists and of the Italian people generally. Their contributors were ready to accept any story, however preposterous, told by Italians having a personal grudge against the Mussolini regime, or by British journalists who were ignorant of Italian affairs and even of the Italian language and who were misled by seditious Italians. Several of these journalists were British only in name.

These attacks were of three kinds: (a) charges of cruelty and oppression by the Italian authorities; (b) statements calculated to prove that the Italian economic and financial situation was disastrous and tottering on account of the government's policy; and (c) the claim that Italy was preparing vast plans of aggression against this or that country. Many of these statements were so absurd that only illiterates or half-wits could swallow them without serious mental indigestion.[5] Those under (b) and (c) were particularly insidious and were often inspired by persons eager to effect a depression in the value of Italian securities and consequently to arrange profitable flutters on the Stock Exchange. As a matter of fact, the economic and financial situation of Italy was never so satisfactory as at that time. Foreigners competent in this field and uninspired by political fanaticism were not much impressed by this form of misinformation, although it did have some effect on the mass of the public.

Mussolini, being a born journalist, attached great and perhaps exaggerated importance to these anti-Italian press campaigns. In some cases they contributed to mold his policy or at all events his attitude towards this or that country.

Another cause of Italo-French friction was the Tunisian question. Throughout the 19th century a steady stream of Italian emigration had flowed into Tunisia, consisting of enterprising business men, merchants, professional men, industrial workers and farmers, who had created the wealth and progress of the country. By 1881 the Italian community was estimated at anything up to 30,000 persons (no regular census had ever been taken). The immigrants were on excellent terms with the local authorities and with the inhabitants generally, and it was hoped and expected that sooner or later some form of Italian protectorate would be established over Tunisia. In the meantime the status of the Italian residents was regulated by the treaty of 1868 between the Italian Government and the Bey of Tunis, which had supplanted earlier arrangements between the Bey and the various pre-Risorgimento Italian states.

At the Berlin Congress of 1878, when France was particularly incensed against Great Britain over the Cyprus Convention,[6] the British delegate, Lord Salisbury, suggested that the French should occupy Tunisia as a sort of *fiche de consolation,* and Bismarck himself was not opposed to the plan, hoping that the occupation would make the French forget Alsace-Lorraine. The French Government was pleased at the prospect, though its Foreign Minister repeatedly assured his Italian colleague, who had got wind of the matter, that France was not dreaming of anything of the kind. Nevertheless, in 1881, an incursion of the Krumir tribe into the adjoining Algerian territory was suddenly fomented, Tunisia was occupied by French forces, and the Bey was obliged to sign a treaty recognizing a French protectorate.

This aroused great indignation in Italy, and the Cabinet was bitterly attacked for its failure to defend Italian interests. The Italian community in Tunisia continued to maintain its rights under the 1868 treaty, which France was bound by international law to respect, Tunisia having become not a French colony but only a protectorate. But the French local authorities made every effort to Gallicize the Italian settlers, conducted a campaign of propaganda against Italian institutions, forbade the building of new Italian schools or the enlarging of the existing ones, in spite of the steady increase in the Italian school population, placed obstacles in the way of the exercise of the professions by Italians and discriminated against Italian workers —all with a view to forcing them to apply for French nationality and thus increase the number of French citizens in the Protectorate.

The Italians resisted vigorously, and by 1930 their numbers had risen to 90,000, hardly any of whom had applied for French citizenship.

In 1895 the French Government forced the Bey to denounce the treaty of 1868, a measure against which Italy strongly protested. After protracted discussions a *modus vivendi* was arrived at, whereby existing Italian institutions were to remain unaltered under the *status quo*. But toward the end of the first World War, when the Allied victory appeared certain and France no longer needed Italian help, the French Government denounced the *modus vivendi*, which was succeeded by a new convention to be renewed every three months. This measure was regarded in Italy as grossly unfriendly, especially in view of the moment chosen for it; and time after time the Rome Government proposed a new agreement to last for a reasonable time—five to ten years—but France always opposed a *fin de non recevoir*, and the pressure and chicanery on the Italian community were steadily intensified. The reason was the same: the number of French citizens was far smaller than that of the Italians, and every means, fair or foul, was being resorted to in order to alter the proportions. Poles, Yugoslavs, Czechs, Jews and Maltese were imported by thousands and granted French citizenship, so as to increase the number of Frenchmen. Ultimately, those claiming French citizenship became slightly more

numerous than the Italians, although only a small proportion of
them were really French.

The Tunisian question continued to remain a festering sore
in Franco-Italian relations. It was one of the troubles that Mussolini inherited from his predecessors on coming into power.
Although he did not succeed in securing a permanent convention or *modus vivendi,* the increased prestige then enjoyed by
Italy under his rule reacted favorably on the situation of the
Italian community in Tunisia, which was better respected and
appreciated by the French authorities than ever before.

[1] There were different accounts of this episode. Matteotti was believed in some
quarters to have instigated a series of outrages against Italian Fascists in France.

[2] Amerigo Dumini himself dealt with the matter in a book entitled *Diciassette
colpi* (Milan, 1950), written while he was in prison. Under the amnesty decree of
December, 1953, he was set at liberty. From all the records and proceedings at
both trials it is clear that his responsibility in the Matteotti affair was of a
very secondary nature.

[3] Freemasonry in France, as in Italy, was a political organization with definitely
radical and anti-clerical tendencies.

[4] If such crimes had been committed in France by Italian Fascists, they would
no doubt have been dealt with quite differently. But no such offenses were
committed.

[5] In 1941 I published a book in Italian entitled, *L'Italia come non è* (*Italy
as She Really Isn't*) Rome, Tosi, in which I collected and published a large
number of such stories. Today it seems incredible that they could have been
published or circulated.

[6] The Cyprus Convention had been concluded secretly between Great Britain
and Turkey in spite of the agreement among the Powers participating in the
Congress that they would not deal separately or individually with any question
entrusted to that body.

CHAPTER FOUR

The Locarno Pact

Mussolini fully grasped the need for a settlement of the Franco-German question if a lasting peace in Europe was to be established, and he was ever ready to coöperate with Great Britain to this end.

Italy's relations with the Weimar Republic had always been correct if not intimate, and Mussolini strongly advocated the policy of treating Germany on a footing of equality. He was convinced that Germany would be much less likely to cause trouble through an attempt to secure by force the revision of the more oppressive clauses of the Versailles Treaty, if it was treated fairly, than if it was kept in a state of perpetual inferiority. Nor did he ever cease insisting on the necessity of linking up inter-allied debts and reparations with a view to the eventual cancellation of both.

In the course of the year 1925, a conference was proposed to settle the Franco-German dispute and to give France a guarantee against possible German aggression. Mussolini at once agreed to participate in the meeting, which was held at Locarno in the autumn of the year. Great Britain was represented by Austen Chamberlain, France by Aristide Briand, Germany by Hans Luther and Gustav Stresemann, and Italy by the famous

jurist, Vittorio Scialoja, and the Undersecretary for Foreign
Affairs, Dino Grandi. Although Mussolini from the first had
given his full support to the conference, he did not attend it in
person until the day before the signature of the treaty. Italy
had never asked for any *quid pro quo* for its adherence; and on
the first day of the meeting Scialoja stated that no guarantee
for the Brenner frontier would be demanded.

The Locarno Conference was the outcome of a change in
public opinion with regard to Germany and of an intuition,
always felt by Mussolini, that the Versailles settlement was not
all that could be desired for assuring peace.

The Italian premier arrived at Locarno on October 15, 1925,
and the Pact was signed the 16th. Chamberlain at a public dinner in London some years later said that Mussolini's contribution to the conclusion of the agreement had been extremely
valuable.

The most important clause of the treaty was the collective
agreement for the maintenance of the territorial *status quo*
and for the disarmament of Germany's Rhine frontier. Great
Britain, France, Italy and Germany all undertook to intervene
by force of arms against any of the said powers that should
attack that frontier.

In many quarters the conclusion of the Locarno agreement
was regarded as the definite consolidation of world peace. Mussolini, more realistic, was not so full of optimism, although he
did believe that it was an improvement on the previous situation. He subsequently expressed himself pleased "both with the
results of the Conference and with the methods employed—
methods of mutual confidence which have brought its labors to
an end in an atmosphere of friendliness. I believe, if the spirit
and the words of the treaty which we have signed become, as
they must, a living reality, that a new epoch in the relations
between peoples will begin." But his *sine qua non* condition
was: if the spirit and the words of the treaty are realized.

One important point was that Germany undertook to apply
for admission to the League of Nations, and that the treaty should
not come into force until Germany became a League member.
Germany did make its application and was admitted soon afterward.

The reason Italy had refused to ask for a guarantee of its Brenner frontier was that this frontier was with Austria and not with Germany. Mussolini at that time refused to contemplate the absorption of the Austrian Republic by the Reich. The Italian Government deemed it preferable in regard to frontier problems to count on Italian forces alone; and for the Brenner in particular on Article 80 of the Versailles treaty, whereby Italy was guaranteed against the annexation of Austria by Germany. Under the terms of this clause, Germany undertook to respect Austrian independence with the frontiers as established by the treaties between Austria and the Principal Allied and Associated Powers, and it recognized those frontiers as unalterable save with the consent of the League Council. Article 88 of the St. Germain Treaty stated the same thing, adding that "Austria undertakes to abstain, save with the consent of the League Council, from any act calculated to compromise her independence directly or indirectly, in any way." [1]

In his speech on the signing of the Locarno treaty Scialoja said that if it had been merely an agreement between certain states, "Italy would have had nothing to do with the undertaking. But when she saw that it was intended to lay the foundations of a great coöperative work for the preservation of European civilization, she wished to take her share and participate in the defence of the general interests of Europe. . . . Italy has declared that her sons may be called upon to fight not only for the protection of their own country but for the peace of the world."

At Locarno, Italy entered into a general agreement of a European character, but its relations with Germany in particular had other aspects which deserve mention.

The Treaty of St. Germain had given Italy a northern frontier along the Brenner watershed. The area thus assigned to Italy consisted of the Trentino, inhabited by a purely Italian population of some 400,000 persons, and a more northern district, which came to be known as the Alto Adige, containing 225,000 inhabitants, of whom some 200,000 were Germans. That frontier had been decided on as a natural and geographical line of demarcation, the Germans to the south of it having migrated from beyond the Brenner several hundred years previously. The district had always been an intermediate zone between Italy and Germany, and its chief city, Bolzano, was a busy market for Italo-German trade. The German inhabitants of this area were known in Italy as the Altoatesini.

Immediately after the first World War the Germans of the Alto Adige tended to regard the settlement as a purely provisional arrangement and refused to admit Italy's right to rule them, to introduce the Italian language into the schools and to apply Italian laws. Their aspirations were of a somewhat confused nature. Being devout Catholics and very conservative, they felt little sympathy for the new Austrian Republic, which they regarded as atheistic and semi-Socialist, while its economic conditions were far worse than those of Italy. The Austrian Government itself did not profess much interest in the matter, having other far graver problems to deal with. Germany also was then in no position to trouble herself about the aspirations of the Altoatesini. The question was chiefly interesting to the inhabitants of North Tyrol remaining under Austria because the relinquishing of the trans-Brenner districts represented a serious economic loss for them.

The Italian authorities under the successive regimes of Nitti, Giolitti, Bonomi and Facta were very incompetent in handling the situation, especially when the worthy but feeble and pusillanimous Luigi Credaro was prefect (the Trentino and the Alto Adige were then a single province).

Nevertheless, the Italian element in the Alto Adige began to increase rapidly, as the many new hydro-electric power plants and other large industries attracted more and more Italian workers. The population of Bolzano alone grew from 25,000 to 50,000 (today it is over 80,000), the increase being almost wholly the result of Italian migration. Not all the Italian officials sent to the district were of the best type, and the conduct of some of them left a good deal to be desired.

Later on, when the situation of Germany became more consolidated after the Locarno treaty, an agitation broke out in certain circles of the Reich concerning the Alto Adige Germans, in spite of the fact that Italy had been the first power to sign a commercial treaty with Germany after Versailles.

Mussolini, on assuming power, at once began to adopt a

policy calculated to strengthen the Italian position in this frontier district. He was determined that the Altoatesini, being
Italian citizens, should accept Italian institutions without question and learn the Italian language. The principles of this
policy were sound, even if it was sometimes carried out
harshly and unwisely.

An anti-Italian propaganda was instigated, the origins of
which were not in the Alto Adige itself or even wholly in
Germany. It was inspired less by a desire to lend support to the
German Altoatesini than to undermine Italy's international
position in general, and the most fantastic stories concerning
Italian policy were systematically spread about. Some of these
stories were repeated by Herr Held, President of the Bavarian
Government in the Munich Diet on February 5, 1926. To his
remarks Mussolini replied in the Chamber of Deputies on
February 6, 1926. "In the Alto Adige," he said, "we are conducting with the German-speaking inhabitants an Italian policy.
We consider them Italians, and we apply our laws. If we did
not do so, we should have an *imperium in imperio* within our
frontier."

Three days later the German Foreign Minister, Gustav Stresemann, supported Held's diatribes, and to him Mussolini retorted on February 10th, pointing out that Stresemann had
really confirmed Mussolini's own statements, including one,
"according to which, whereas millions of Germans had been
absorbed by France, Czechoslovakia and Poland and were far
more harshly treated, it was only for those of the Alto Adige
that an agitation had been aroused." He flatly denied Stresemann's statement that Italy had demanded a guarantee for the
Brenner frontier, adding that if the threatened German
boycott of Italian goods were proclaimed, Italy would retaliate
by a similar measure against German goods. Stresemann, he
pointed out, had confused denationalization of the Germans,
which Italy had not carried out, with the mere enforcement of
Italian laws in the Alto Adige as in all other Italian provinces.
Above all, Mussolini refused to allow any interference in the
question by a power which had never ruled over the Alto
Adige.[2]

What was particularly surprising to the Italians was that in

Great Britain, where hostility to Germany still persisted to a far greater degree than in Italy, a movement had been started to support the demands of the Germans of the Alto Adige, and that the preposterous stories against the Italian authorities were repeated in many British papers of Leftist tendencies, particularly the *Manchester Guardian* and the *New Statesman*. As an instance of this attitude I might mention an article by the Rome correspondent of the *Guardian* who had visited the Alto Adige; after repeating some of the usual charges, he added that he had not visited any of the schools as it was the holiday season, and that in any case he feared that if he had done so he might have seen something favorable to Italian rule! I also remember a conversation with the editor of the *New Statesman,* who at the time was in a veritable fury against Mussolini for his reply to Stresemann, saying that he regarded it as a direct threat of war.

These attacks in the British press caused intense irritation in Italy, even in circles not particularly Fascist. The Italian press retorted with extreme and sometimes exaggerated violence.

The agitation in Germany produced some reaction even in Austria, and the Innsbruck Provincial Diet called upon the Vienna Government to bring the Alto Adige question before the League of Nations.[3] But the impression in Italy was that the German Government lent support to this anti-Italian attitude mainly because it provided a rallying point between the Rightist parties hostile to Locarno and those of the Left hostile to Fascism.

After Mussolini's speech of February 10th there were no further replies from Germany. The Austrian Chancellor, Rudolf Ramek, did make a speech criticizing Italy's Alto Adige policy; at Mussolini's request, explanations were afterwards given, but not published. This marked the end of the polemics on the subject between the Italian Government and those of the two German States.

The attacks continued for some time longer in the British press and at the meetings of the Federation of League of Nations Societies. They were put forth by certain ultra-sentimental Englishmen, possibly inspired by circles hostile to

Italy in general, who found in the Alto Adige question a useful stick with which to beat Mussolini and Fascism. It is significant that after the advent of Hitler to power in Germany those same circles lost all interest in the matter.

[1] Carlo Schanzer, *Il mondo fra la pace e la guerra,* Milan, Treves, 1932, pp. 170-171.

[2] That province and the Trentino had been under the rule of Austria-Hungary, but never under that of Germany.

[3] Under the terms of the Peace Treaties, the League was not authorized to deal with minority problems related to territories annexed to France or to Italy.

CHAPTER V

Other Aspects of Italian Foreign Policy in the Mid-1920's

The Eastern Mediterranean had always attracted the keen interest of Mussolini as an area where Italy's political and commercial activities might be fruitfully developed. His attitude towards Turkey was uniformly friendly, although Mustafa Kemal was naturally somewhat suspicious of all the Great Powers of Europe. With Greece too, after the Corfu incident had been settled, Italian relations had become more cordial, for the Greeks understood that the dispute had been largely exploited by other nations for purposes which had little to do with Greek interests.

But even a show of friendliness between Italy and Greece was seized upon as an argument for disseminating suspicion. The visit to Rome of Roufos, Greek Minister of Foreign Affairs, in March, 1926, set tongues wagging about an alleged Italo-Greek treaty (which had never been signed or even planned), anticipating an attack on Turkey; and the replacing of the Italian battalion in Rhodes, which took place every year, added fuel to the flame. There was talk in London and elsewhere about the concentration of large Italian forces in the Aegean Islands for sinister purposes. These rumors were flatly denied by the Italian Embassy at Ankara and by the

Greek Government; but, like the reports of Italy's disastrous financial conditions, they were profitably exploited for Stock Exchange purposes.

It should not be forgotten that the attacks on Italy's foreign policy had their real origins in two main sources: shady financial activities, and the hostility in Leftist quarters, chiefly in Great Britain and France and to some extent in other countries, to Mussolini's domestic policy, which was regarded as constituting a sin against popular democracy.

These incidents did not, however, at that time affect political relations between the Italian and British governments, even if they did help to pave the way for future disputes. In the past there had been much talk about traditional British-Italian friendship. But in recent years this tradition had become somewhat fly-blown. During the Libyan War the insulting British attacks on Italy's policy and the Italian army had aroused a great deal of ill-feeling in Italy. At the end of the first World War and during the Peace Conference there had been much wrangling between the two countries. But Italian public opinion was inclined to attribute British hostility on that occasion chiefly to Lloyd George's anxiety to secure for his own policies the support of President Wilson, whose personal fanaticism and ignorance of European conditions were regarded as chiefly responsible for the trouble. Therefore, Italian feeling against the British nation as a whole was not very hostile.

After the Peace Conference Italians tended to regard Great Britain as the most moderate and level-headed of the Great Powers, and when Mussolini became head of the government he was eager for collaboration with Britain, as there appeared to be no serious reasons for disagreement. This attitude continued for many years. In his speech in the Senate on June 3, 1928, he said that "when we say that friendship between Italy and Great Britain is traditional, this is no mere commonplace but expresses a factual reality . . . At Locarno the two nations renewed their close political coöperation with a view to promoting European peace." This situation, he added, was not altered by the changes in the (British) Foreign Office, for "it was in harmony with higher considerations."

With Sir Austen Chamberlain Mussolini's personal relations were especially cordial. "I have had," he continued,
"the pleasure and honor of meeting Sir Austen Chamberlain
in December, 1925, at Rapallo; in September, 1926, at Leg-
horn. You remember, gentlemen, the polemical and journalistic ravings around those two meetings. The eminent statesman
in charge of the Foreign Ministry of the British Empire was
even accused of having encouraged Fascist imperialism, and
later on certain events were explained as a kind of authorization which Chamberlain had conferred on Italy's policy. Nothing could be more fantastic. The Italy of today has no need
to ask for anyone's authorization for her policy. She is perfectly autonomous in her foreign relations. I add that one of
the bulwarks of this policy is friendship with Great Britain.
This friendship requires no special protocols in order to be
fortified and protected. To this end the efforts of the Fascist
Government tend."

Sir Austen Chamberlain did, indeed, feel a particular regard
for Mussolini, which was cordially reciprocated.[1] Other prominent Britons were of the same way of thinking, both in the
political world and among men of letters. Others, especially
the liberals, were shocked at the Duce's somewhat outspoken
contempt for democracy, and even if they themselves did not
sincerely and completely believe in it, they felt that they must
pretend that they did and speak like true democrats—lest they
be dubbed reactionaries. British Laborites and Leftists generally, like men of the same views in other countries, disliked
Mussolini because they had a profound if unconfessed conviction that they alone were entitled to dominate the political
scene. Even when not in power, they considered that all the
ruling classes *must* conform with their principles. Consequently,
any government that rejected those principles was in their eyes
condemned to eternal damnation. That Mussolini's economic
and social measures improved the material and moral conditions of the workers, promoted and increased agricultural and
industrial production, eliminated malaria and reduced unemployment to negligible figures, were matters of little account in
comparison with his rejection of democracy (with a capital D).
It is noteworthy that these same Liberals, Leftists, and the

like, had only the most favorable attitude during this period for the totalitarian system in Soviet Russia which accomplished far less for the common man and violated far more drastically all democratic and liberal principles.

Further, some Liberal and Laborite Britons saw in the Fascist regime mainly a counterpart to the policy certain extreme British Conservatives favored adopting. An observant American journalist said to me that no British Liberal or Laborite dared to admit that there was anything good in Fascism lest he be associated with that arch-reactionary, the Duke of Northumberland.

As a matter of fact, however, Winston Churchill visited Mussolini in January, 1927, and praised the Duce and his work. In an interview published in the London *Times*, January 21, 1927, Churchill said: "If I had been an Italian I am sure that I should have been wholeheartedly with you [Mussolini] from start to finish in your triumphant struggle against the bestial appetites and passions of Leninism." As late as September 26, 1935, Churchill referred to Mussolini as "so great a man and so wise a ruler."

A fresh outburst of indignation in Italy against France was the result of an attempt against Mussolini's life September 11, 1926, by a man named Lucetti. This would-be murderer was born in France and had spent many years in that country, imbibing the subversive doctrines prevalent in many French circles, although he himself was an individualistic Anarchist. The outrage, while it failed to injure Mussolini, wounded several passers-by, and the French authorities were regarded as responsible for the atmosphere that made such acts possible. A demonstration was held outside the Palazzo Chigi where the Prime Minister's offices were then located, and the Duce in a short speech, delivered from the balcony of the palace to the assembled crowd, said very firmly: "There must be an end to such culpable and unheard-of tolerance beyond the frontier if any value is really attached to the friendship of the Italian people, which episodes of this kind might fatally compromise . . . The Italian nation, which is working strenuously because such is its duty, its privilege, its hope and its glory, cannot, shall not be disturbed by a group of criminals." [2] These words sounded an uncompromising warning to France, of which he only demanded that murder plots, not merely against himself, but against other Italian citizens, should not be freely hatched there with the connivance of the French authorities.

Widespread anti-French demonstrations followed in various Italian cities, and on September 16th the Order Sheet of the Fascist Party published a statement declaring that France offered asylum to all who were engaged in manufacturing and spreading libels against Italy: "We wish for friendship with France," it continued, "but if France desires the friendship of the Italian people, it must alter its present policy. It is merely a question of banishing some twenty scoundrels, blackmailers and thieves."

With East-Central Europe, Italy's relations were somewhat delicate. It was in that area that the territorial results of the Peace Conference appeared most visible. Three of the countries in question, Czechoslovakia, Rumania and Yugoslavia, by means of a series of bilateral treaties dating from 1920 and 1921 had contracted an alliance known as the Little Entente, principally with the object of safeguarding the signatories against any attempt by Germany, Austria, Hungary or Bulgaria to alter the territorial arrangements laid down in the Paris treaties.

This combination enjoyed a wide measure of support on the part of France, which saw in it a useful instrument against any attempt by Germany to call into question the clauses of the treaties calculated to provide for French security. The French Government never concluded any agreement with the Little Entente as a whole, but did so with its individual members.

Mussolini had no particular liking for the Little Entente as such. He was friendly to Rumania on account of its Latin civilization and culture, less so toward Czechoslovakia, which appeared to him (and to many others) a rather cheap imitation of French Masonic democracy, combined with the less desirable jetsam and flotsam of the old Austro-Hungarian Empire, and still less so to Yugoslavia, with which Italy had, as we have seen, many causes of conflict. The alliance of the three states seemed dangerous to world peace, for the only real link between its members, the very origin of the whole contraption, was uncompromising opposition to treaty revision, without which

Mussolini believed that no true European peace could be made secure.

Nevertheless, Mussolini was determined to try to establish better relations with at least one member of the French-dominated Little Entente. Yugoslavia, in spite of the 1924 agreements, was always suspected of anti-Italian activities and intrigues. Czechoslovakia was so closely associated with French Radicals, Socialists and Freemasons, and its vast war industries were so completely dominated by French capital and by the French Government, that an understanding with Italy would be very difficult. In Rumania, on the other hand, Italy enjoyed a wide measure of sympathy and prestige. The Latin language and origins of the Rumanian people were its patent of nobility, differentiating it from others of the Balkans. Before the first World War and immediately after it French influence had been predominant in the country in spite of its German dynasty, and the army had been re-organized by the French General Staff. But on the fall of the Bratianu ministry, the new Premier, General Alexander Averescu, educated at the Military Academy of Turin, had Italian sympathies, and while he did not wish to antagonize France, he hoped to secure Italian friendship.

One problem agitated Rumanian public opinion above all others, the question of Bessarabia. That province, inhabited by a predominantly Rumanian population, had been seized by Russia, partly in 1812 and partly in 1878.[3] But at the end of the first World War the population had voted a referendum in favor of re-union with Rumania, and Rumanian sovereignty had been recognized by France, Great Britain and Japan. It could not come into legal force, however, until recognition was ratified by all the four signatories, and Italy's signature was still lacking. Although Rumania occupied and governed Bessarabia, the Soviet Government refused to recognize the situation and demanded that it should be returned to Russia.

On September 15, 1926, Averescu visited Rome to conclude a treaty of coöperation and friendship with Italy, which was signed on the 17th. Bessarabia was not mentioned in the instrument, but in a letter attached to it Italy undertook to ratify the Bessarabian agreement at an opportune moment and agreed to lend Rumania 200,000,000 lire in exchange for oil concessions. On January 25, 1927, negotiations for an Italo-Rumanian commercial treaty were begun, and on March 8th it was announced that Italy had ratified the Bessarabian treaty, which thus came into force. This event aroused great enthusiasm in Rumania in favor of Italy, and a street in Bucharest was named after Mussolini.[4] It was, indeed, a triumph for the Duce's diplomacy to have secured Rumania's friendship while still retaining that of Hungary, with which Rumania was on bad terms on account of the Transylvanian question. In this way Mussolini established a close link with one member of the Little Entente, thereby weakening that combination and rendering it less likely to lend full support to France. Future events were to demonstrate to the French how utterly unreliable the Little Entente would ultimately prove to be.

[1] Sir Austen's widow, Lady Chamberlain, shared these views and she gave expression to them on the occasion of the Ethiopian War.

[2] *Scritti e discorsi*, Vol. V, pp. 389-391.

[3] At that time what is now known as Rumania was divided into the two principalities of Wallachia and Moldavia, and Bessarabia formed part of the latter.

[4] Mussolini would not permit any Italian town to name a street after him. This was in marked contrast to the situation in Germany under Hitler.

CHAPTER SIX

The Albanian Problem

Italy's relations with Albania had been very intimate long before the latter country had risen to independence. After the death of the Albanian national hero, George Skanderbeg, in 1467 and the conquest of the country by the Turks, a number of Skanderbeg's followers had fled to the Kingdom of Naples and had been given lands whereon to settle. Their descendants to this day number over 200,000, and many eminent Italians, including one of Italy's greatest statesmen, Francesco Crispi, were of Albanian origin.

Ever since the creation of the Kingdom, Italy had followed Albanian affairs with keen interest, and before the first World War Albania had been a source of political, economic and educational rivalry between Italy and Austria-Hungary. Italians feared that the control of the Albanian coast by Austria would strengthen the power of that empire to an extent dangerous to Italy's security. During the Balkan Wars of 1912-1913, Serbia and Greece wished to partition Albania between themselves, but Italy, on this occasion with Austrian concurrence, advocated the creation of an independent Albanian state, which in fact did materialize, with Prince William of Wied as sovereign.

On the outbreak of the first World War Russia, as the protec-

tor of the Balkan Slavic States, demanded that Northern Albania
be assigned to Serbia and Montenegro; and Great Britain and
France, recognized as the protectors of Greece,[1] advocated the
annexation to Greece of Southern Albania. Italy was forced by
the terms of the Pact of London (1915), on condition that its
own aspirations in the Trentino and the Venezia Giulia received
satisfaction, to acquiesce in these mutilations of Albanian territory. In that case, only a small central Albanian state would
have been created and endowed with a precarious independence.[2]

During the War the northern districts of Albania were occupied by Austro-Hungarian forces, and those of the south were
held by the Italians, who achieved great popularity by saving
a large part of the local population from starvation. At the end
of the conflict the Albanian state, after many vicissitudes, was
reconstructed; but, although it was larger than the small central
Albania provided for in the Pact of London, it by no means
comprised the whole of the Albanian population. About one
million Albanians were contained within its borders, but another million or more were assigned to Yugoslavia in the north
and to Greece in the south.

At the first Assembly of the League of Nations in 1920
Albania applied for membership and, with Italian support,
achieved it. In the subsequent disputes with Yugoslavia the
Albanian question was one of the left-overs of the Peace Treaties, and the country was entrusted to the Conference of Ambassadors, which, in turn, gave it over to Italy as a sort of *de
facto* protector of Albania.

Sundry attempts were made by Yugoslavia to annex further
parts of Albania, a policy largely inspired by the Serb element
in the Yugoslav state. At that time the Belgrade government
feared that sooner or later Croatia would break away, thereby
depriving Yugoslavia of the Dalmatian seaboard. In order to be
sure of having an outlet on the Adriatic, the Albanian coast
was considered essential as a substitute. But by this time all
the Great Powers were agreed on the maintenance of Albanian
independence.[3]

Albania went through yet further vicissitudes, including
several rebellions, probably fomented by Yugoslav agents. In

the autumn of 1924 an Albanian chieftain of the Mati tribe, Ahmed Zogu, with Yugoslav help made himself master of the country, and in 1925 he was elected President of the Albanian Republic. But, once in power, he refused to play Yugoslavia's game any longer. Convinced that he had better prospects in the support of Italy, which, unlike Yugoslavia, had no aspirations to annex Albanian territory, he entered into a close understanding with the Italian kingdom.

The first practical act in Italo-Albanian relations was the conclusion at Tirana on November 27, 1926, of a Pact of Friendship and Security between the two countries. This instrument aroused great indignation in Belgrade and in some foreign countries, especially in British "pacifist" circles, where it was regarded as part of Mussolini's general policy of "aggression." But actually it was only putting into effect the mandate conferred on Italy by the Conference of Ambassadors. Indeed, Italy was doing no more with regard to Albania than carrying out the obligations all members of the League were supposed to execute with respect to any other member state menaced by aggression. It was claimed in some quarters that Italy by the Tirana Pact guaranteed the then existing Albanian government against any attempt to subvert it from within. But all that Italy did actually undertake was to protect the Albanian state against revolutions plotted from outside under the auspices of foreign governments and organizations; such was the case of the bogus Mirdit revolt, which was a purely Yugoslav *coup,* and of other similar subsequent agitations.

After the conclusion of the Tirana Pact, the text of the Franco-Yugoslav Pact of Friendship was published; it had been initialed some time previously and contained no provisions to which objection could be taken. But the moment chosen for its publication gave it the appearance of a not too courteous retort to the Italo-Albanian Pact. Both in Italy and in Albania it was believed that France had given the Belgrade government a free hand for any action it might undertake against Albania or even against Italy, in exchange for future Yugoslav aid against Germany or Germany's probable allies. Albania had tried to conciliate Yugoslavia; and, as Mussolini had declared, the Rome government had informed Ahmed Zogu that it would not object to the conclusion of an Albanian-Yugoslav agreement on the same lines as the Tirana pact. But the Yugoslav government rejected Albanian proffers of friendship, being determined sooner or later with French or other help to absorb the whole or part of Albania into its own dominions.

The answer to the Franco-Yugoslav Pact was the conversion of the Tirana Pact into a regular defensive treaty of alliance, the terms of which were purposely made to coincide with those of the Anglo-Portuguese-Dutch treaty of alliance of May 16, 1702. Its conclusion produced considerable popularity in Albania, for it supplied a firmer guarantee against aggression than the Pact of Friendship or the general provisions of the League Covenant.

Italy's Albanian policy was a purely passive one, for Italy did not wish to occupy any part of Albania but was only anxious that no other power should do so, the Albanian coast being only a few hours by steam from that of Italy. Meanwhile Italy accorded very generous help to Albania, which now for the first time was able to begin a truly civilized existence. It had until then been in a more primitive state than any other part of Europe, with no railways, no real ports, practically no roads, hardly any schools, no industries and an extremely backward agriculture.

Italy began to transform the country in every way. Its policy, however, was of a dual nature. The Italian diplomatic representatives wished above all to develop the economic resources of the country, whereas the Italian officers, with General Alberto Pariani at their head, who were sent to reorganize or rather to create the Albanian army, wished to establish a strong patriotic Albanian movement for protection against any possible future trouble with Yugoslavia or Greece. In the end, it was the diplomatic and economic program that prevailed, and some years later Pariani was recalled.

Italy, however, by no means monopolized Albanian development. A British company obtained a concession for the oil-producing area, and certain industries were in the hands of British capitalists. To the existing native gendarmerie a British general, Sir Jocelyn Percy, and a dozen other British officers were attached as inspectors. But a gendarmerie was not in itself

Benito Mussolini at the time of his advent to power

Mussolini and the Austrian Chancellor, Engelbert Dollfuss

sufficient for guaranteeing security, as it must necessarily be scattered all over the country with very small detachments in each place, and it could not be hastily concentrated at any particular point where aggression might be attempted or threatened.

For this reason, one of Italy's first tasks was to create a small but efficient Albanian army under Italian and native officers with General Pariani in command. Roads were then built, the port of Durazzo was adequately equipped, numerous schools of all grades were opened, agriculture was improved, the marshes were drained, and efficient health services were introduced to combat the terrible scourge of malaria. The economies of Albania and Italy were complementary, for Albania had the oil wells and iron mines whose products Italy needed, and Albania was a market for Italian manufactured goods.

A Bank of Albania was instituted, a company for the internal development of the country (the S.V.E.A.) was put into operation, and a loan of 50,000,000 gold francs was granted, the bulk of the sum to be spent on public works.

That an Albanian army was necessary was proved by the events of 1928, when *komitadji* (guerrilla) bands, officered, armed and financed by the Yugoslav frontier authorities, concentrated on the borders of Albania. Italy did not send any of its own forces into Albania, but limited itself to calling the attention of the other Great Powers to the danger, and their action induced the Belgrade Government to abstain from aggression for the time being.

The internal political situation was not altogether satisfactory. On August 25, 1928, at the suggestion of the Italian Government, Ahmed Zogu was proclaimed King Zog I, but he was none too popular. He was a strong supporter of the Italian connection, from which he had received great benefits, but he had made many enemies in the course of his adventurous career, and thus was the object of vendettas. His own tribe, the Mati, which alone was unswervingly faithful to him, was regarded with intense dislike by the other tribes. More than one attempt on his life had been made, and he seldom left his palace at Tirana except when he went to his summer residence at Durazzo for sea bathing, and he never moved without being closely guarded by his picturesquely attired bodyguard of Mati tribes-men.

The Albanian public services were very unsatisfactory, and although there were several able and honest men in various departments, corruption was generally rampant in spite of the attempts of the few Italian and some native officials to introduce order and honesty. A retired British officer, Colonel Stirling, was appointed by the King to be Inspector of the Ministries, but his efforts met with great opposition and obstruction on the part of the native officials and of the King himself, who resented any outside interference.

Nevertheless, in course of time, Albania might have been raised to better conditions. Its people are intelligent, and in the days of the old Ottoman Empire many Albanians had risen to the highest positions, including those of commander-in-chief, of ambassador and even of grand vizier. Had it not been for the second World War and its aftermath, Albania might well have achieved an honored place in the European community.

[1] From the foundation of Greek independence guaranteed by them in 1832.
[2] Harold Nicolson, in his volume *Peace-Making*, London, 1933, states that Italy had insisted on this arrangement. Actually, Italy had agreed to it most unwillingly under British, French and Russian pressure.
[3] Decision of the Conference of Ambassadors on November 9, 1921.

CHAPTER SEVEN

Progress of Italy's International Situation

By 1928 Italy's position as one of the great world powers was consolidated. Six years after Mussolini had become chief of the government Italian relations with most other countries were based on a network of treaties—political, commercial and cultural. The war debt situation with the United States and with Great Britain had been satisfactorily settled by Count Giuseppe Volpi, Italy's very able Minister of Finance, who also concluded a treaty of conciliation and arbitration with the United States in April, 1928. With Great Britain an agreement had been arrived at concerning the territory south of the river Juba in East Africa, which was at last handed over to Italy as provided for in the Peace Treaty—the only colonial concession granted to it under the terms of that instrument.

No political treaty was concluded with Poland, but relations between the two countries were very intimate, and favorable commercial arrangements had been made whereby Italy was to secure large supplies of coal from Poland in exchange for Italian manufactured goods.

With reference to Germany, Italy continued to insist that the excessively onerous character of the conditions imposed on that country by the Versailles treaty was an impediment to the consolidation of peace. While Mussolini demanded that for reasons of national pride a fair share of German reparations be awarded to Italy, he never believed in their justice or that they would materialize; and he was ever more convinced that the cancellation both of war debts and reparations was the only sound solution.

With France the Duce always hoped for the possibility of an agreement, for, as he said in the Senate on May 5, 1928, the importance of a general understanding between the two countries "is so obvious that every word intended to prove it seems to me superfluous." Nevertheless, although most of the specific points of difference were capable of peaceful solution, Franco-Italian relations were not cordial. Italians were alarmed at France's persistent hatred and fear of Germany, which kept all Europe in a state of jitters.

The condition of Hungary, with half the nation's territory and nearly half of the Magyar inhabitants wrested from it, constituted a running sore, poisoning the whole atmosphere of central Europe. Hence Mussolini supported Hungary's revisionist demands; but here, too, he found himself always faced with the hostility of France (which did not wish its protégés to be unfavorably affected), and he was handicapped by the indifference of the British government despite the interest taken in the Hungarian question by many prominent Britons and by a part of the London press.

Bulgaria, another victim of the Peace Treaties, constituted yet another danger point. The annexation of the Bulgarian-speaking peoples of Macedonia by Yugoslavia and Greece, particularly by the former, had aroused bitter discontent among the people of the Bulgarian kingdom. Scores of thousands of Macedo-Bulgarians had been forced to flee from their old homes to escape persecution and forcible Serbification, and most of them had taken refuge in Bulgaria. Their presence not only constituted a serious economic problem for so poor a country, but the feuds of Macedonian revolutionary organizations, created to resist Yugoslav oppression, were transferred to Bulgarian territory and often led to political murders by the various factions. Along the Yugoslav-Bulgarian frontier raids, plunder and murder were of daily occurrence, each side accusing the other of provoking these outrages; but the real responsibility rested with the authors of the Peace Treaties, who had drawn up these frontiers regardless of national conditions and aspirations.

In August, 1928, the British and the French governments proposed to that of Bulgaria that it should suppress the Macedonian Internal Organization, which was particularly active against the Yugoslav authorities. They invited the Italian Government to join them in this step and thus bring stronger pressure to bear on Sofia; but Mussolini refused, as he was opposed to the idea of advising the Bulgarian Government to embark on a dangerous struggle with the Macedonians solely in the interests of Yugoslavia. France had wished to help Yugoslavia for the usual reason—eventual support against Germany's eventual allies; and Great Britain, with the all too frequent subservience of its Foreign Office to French wishes, had taken the same line.

The result of Mussolini's refusal was that Great Britain and France dropped their attempted imposition on Bulgaria. This fact strengthened the ties of friendship between that country and Italy.

In spite of Italy's attempts at a settlement, the difficulties with Yugoslavia were intensified by the activities of the secret terrorist Yugoslav organizations operating in the Venezia Giulia. During the Italian general election on March 24, 1929, a band of Yugoslavs in Istria opened fire on a party of voters on their way to the polling booths, killing one and wounding others. Various persons were arrested and tried in Trieste, the ringleader of the gang was condemned to death for murder, and others received severe prison sentences. The trial provoked violent indignation in Yugoslavia, and there were anti-Italian demonstrations in various towns. The man executed was hailed "a martyr to Fascist tyranny." [1]

Italy was also extending its political and commercial activities to the Far East, and its relations with Latin America were becoming ever closer. Italy had now acquired an international position such as it had never had before, and if in some foreign quarters anti-Fascist sentiments still persisted, mainly on account of the domestic legislation of Mussolini's Government, the great improvement in the general economic and social conditions of the country and the progress achieved in many fields aroused the admiration of nearly all those who visited Italy, including some of the most eminent foreign statesmen, beginning with Winston Churchill. Those foreigners who were most strongly opposed to Fascist Italy did not as a rule visit the country; they based their views on hostile hearsay evidence.

The country's new situation also affected the great mass of Italians living abroad, who for the first time felt that they enjoyed the effective support of their own government, and were proud of being Italians. Never before had modern Italy enjoyed such a position of international prestige.

Italy was not, however, as yet strong enough to impose its views with regard to the general international situation on other powers. It never ceased to suggest certain measures, calculated in the opinion of its rulers to promote international peace and good-will by removing intolerable grievances. Mussolini constantly repeated his assertion that the Peace Treaties could not be regarded like the laws of the Medes and Persians, as many foreign statesmen professed to believe, although actually many of the treaty clauses, as he said in his Senate speech on June 5, 1928, had never been enforced, and others were only partially applied or tacitly altered. "The Peace Treaties," he asserted, "are the result not of divine justice but of human intelligence, subject, at the end of a gigantic war, to influences of an exceptional nature. Will any man dare to claim that the Peace Treaties are a perfect achievement? There are in them certain accomplished facts that remain and that none of us would dream of abrogating or even of subjecting to discussion. But there are territorial, colonial, financial and social clauses that are open to discussion, revision and improvement, with the object of rendering the treaties more durable and of insuring a longer period of peace."

Referring to a previous speech delivered in 1927, wherein he had stated that between 1933 and 1940 Europe would reach a very interesting and delicate moment of her history, he went on to say: "That statement or forecast—indeed it was an easy one to make—should not be interpreted pessimistically. The fact is that at that period, in view of the evolution of the Peace

Treaties themselves, certain conditions will have arisen determining a new and important phase in the situation of various European states. Particular problems will arise that may be settled by the governments in a peaceful manner, as I myself sincerely trust."

He then went on to dwell at some length on the reparations question, insisting, as usual, on his old point of view that reparations and inter-Allied debts must be dealt with jointly, and claiming that if the whole question were definitely settled, European and world economy would derive immense benefits.

On the problem of disarmament, he called attention to the importance of the Soviet proposal of November, 1927, for a general, immediate and total disarmament; and he alluded to the conflict between the French view that disarmament should be subordinated to security and the German view demanding general disarmament in conformity with the Treaty of Versailles and with the League Covenant. The attitude of the Italian delegation was based on the thesis that armaments should not merely reflect the *status quo,* and that the limits of Italian armaments could not be permanently fixed. They must be proportionate to the total armed forces of other countries, especially implying parity with the most heavily armed Continental power, namely, France. Italy, Mussolini insisted, was ready to accept as a limitation of its own armaments any figure, however low, provided that those of no other Continental power rose above it, and provided that the method for securing limitation should be as simple as possible and not imply the necessity of outside control.

With reference to the League and to the oft-repeated charges that Italy was hostile or at least lukewarm in its sympathies for the League, he stated: "The Italian Government does not attribute to the League—at least not in its present historical period—the almost mythological virtues with which certain worthy idealists endow it. But placing the Geneva institution in its proper light, in view of the historical conditions in which it arose and of its real possibilities, does not signify hostility or indifference." [2]

He finally dealt with the many League questions in which Italy had played an active and useful part, adding that the merit of these activities was largely due to Senator Vittorio Scialoja, who represented the country at many of the Geneva meetings.

The figure of Scialoja deserves some mention. The most eminent jurist in Italy, he was one of Mussolini's closest and most valuable collaborators on international questions and on many others. He had never been a registered member of the Fascist Party—he had actually said, "Fascism means discipline, and I am essentially undisciplined"—but he rendered great services to the Duce and the Government through his thorough knowledge of intricate legal problems, his wide general culture and his keen and often biting wit. As a chairman of committees he had no rival, and often with a *bon mot* he completely demolished a rhetorically bolstered but untenable argument and pierced the empty talk-balloons and humbugs that infested the Palais des Nations at Geneva.

One of Mussolini's collateral interests in the international field was the dissemination of Italian culture abroad. The Dante Alighieri Society, in existence for many decades, now received full support. It dealt chiefly with teaching the Italian language in foreign lands. Italian cultural institutes of various kinds were set up in many countries, not only for teaching Italian but also for creating Italian libraries and centres of various Italian cultural and artistic activities where permanent and visiting professors lectured on Italian subjects. Institutes of this kind were created in France, Switzerland, Germany, Austria, Hungary, Rumania, Bulgaria, Poland and other countries. Mussolini, himself a voracious reader, had a keen sense of the importance of culture in all its branches, and he devoted particular attention to these activities.

Many foreign critics regarded all this work as subtle Fascist propaganda, although the eminent Italians whose work was emphasized in the Italian institutes abroad—Dante, Petrarch, Manzoni, Carducci, Leonardo da Vinci and others of the same categories—had lived a long time before Fascism was born or even anticipated.[3] It should be noted that Great Britain had begun to do the same thing during and after the first World War, some years before Mussolini's advent to power, with the creation of the British Institute in Florence, and later with similar institutes in other countries. France had the *Instituts*

français in many lands long before that war. On the outbreak
of the second World War, the British Council set up branches
with similar objects in many Italian and other cities, and since
the end of the conflict the United States Government has been
doing the same thing with the various U.S.I.S. libraries all over
the world.

This was one of the cases in which Mussolini's foreign critics
began by saying: "What dreadful things he is doing!" and
ended up by saying: "Let us now go and do the same thing."

While Mussolini wished to promote extensive and friendly
cultural relations with other countries, he was determined to
keep Italy free from financial subservience to foreign banking
interests. After a Morgan loan of $100,000,000 to meet a special
emergency, Mussolini declined to negotiate or accept any more
foreign loans. He made Fascist Italy a going industrial, commercial and financial concern. This may well be contrasted
with the situation after the second World War. At the end of
the year 1954, the total economic aid given to Italy by the
United States since the end of the War amounted to $3,712,-
494,000, along with an unrevealed sum which was regarded as
secret "classified" information. The total would surely be in
excess of four billion dollars, an amount equal to the total
Federal budget of the United States in pre-New Deal times.
This was the appalling price paid to bolster the wobbly Italian
Government, keep it from going Communist, and maintain its
subservience to Anglo-American foreign policy.

[1] The murderers of the Archduke Franz Ferdinand and his wife at Sarajevo
in June 1914 also were hailed as national heroes, and tablets were erected in
their honor.

[2] *Scritti e discorsi*, Vol. VI, pp. 175-228.

[3] As an instance of this prejudice and narrowmindedness we may cite one episode. An eminent American professor of classical languages had been invited to
give a lecture at a mid-Western university dealing with the Augustan Exhibition
held in Rome on the bimillenary of Augustus. But he was told at the last moment
by the president of that university that the exhibition in question only served
to exalt the Fascist regime in Italy and "that the less we hear about it, the
better pleased we shall be." The invitation was, therefore, cancelled.

CHAPTER EIGHT

Peace with the Church

Relations between Church and State, although primarily a matter of purely internal policy, have often had world-wide consequences, and in the case of Italy they have affected its relations with many foreign powers.

On September 20, 1870, when Italian troops entered Rome and the Temporal Power of the Papacy came to an end after 1600 years, all official connection between the Italian Government and the Vatican was broken off, and the moral position of the average Italian, who wished to be both a good Italian citizen and a good Catholic, became extremely difficult. The Vatican claimed that it could not fulfill its spiritual functions without the temporal power, and on various occasions it endeavored to secure the support of foreign Catholic nations, especially France and Austria, for the restoration of its earthly dominions. This frequently led to friction between the Vatican and the Royal Italian Government, and between the latter and the foreign nations that lent secret and sometimes open support to the Papal claims.

Many attempts had been made to arrive at a settlement of the conflict. On more than one occasion success had been all but achieved when at the last moment some unexpected obstacle arose. Often, although not always, this was a result of the intervention of some foreign government which feared that to have the Head of the Universal Church in Rome on friendly terms with Italy would confer too much prestige on that country.

It was this attitude on the part of France (where clerical and ultramontane influences were often very strong until after 1900) that helped to induce Italy to join with Germany and Austria in forming the Triple Alliance in 1882. But even Austria, although a signatory of that instrument, often showed itself anything but friendly to Italy over the Vatican question, owing to the strong clerical tendencies of the Hapsburg monarchy and its governing classes.

With the passing of years the Roman Question, as it was called, became less acute, and the breach between Church and State tended to become closed. But successive Popes continued to maintain and re-assert their protests against the usurpation of their rights by "him who detains." [1]

In the first World War the sympathies of the Vatican were to some extent on the side of the Central Powers, for Austria was then the only wholly and uncompromisingly Catholic nation, and in Germany the Catholic Center Party was very influential. But the Vatican did not attempt to exploit the conflict in order to secure a solution of the Roman Question satisfactory to itself. The Papal Secretary of State, Cardinal Gasparri, said that "the Holy See expects a settlement of its situation in Italy not by means of foreign arms but through the sense of justice of the Italian people."

At the Paris Peace Conference an attempt was made to reach a settlement at a meeting (May 1919) between the Italian Premier, Vittorio Orlando, and Cardinal Bonaventura Cerretti, arranged by Monsignor Francis C. Kelley.[2] But the plan fell through with the resignation of the Orlando Cabinet in June, and although it was taken up again, it did not lead to any practical result.

Mussolini, although not a practicing Catholic, had always felt a deep respect for the Church; and on his advent to power he at once undertook a revision of Italian ecclesiastical legislation. On the occasion of great religious festivals, especially those of the Holy Year 1925, special protection and official recognition were accorded to Church personages. Nevertheless on February 18, 1926, the Pope again repeated his protest against "the iniquitous conditions" imposed on the Holy See.

On August 5th of that same year, a prelate suggested to the Italian Councillor of State, Professor Emilio Barone, the possibility of initiating negotiations for a settlement. The idea at once appealed to Mussolini, who had long been meditating some such solution. He realized the great importance of the Catholic Church as an Italian institution and an international force and the consequent advantages of reaching an understanding between it and the Italian Government.

On October 4, 1926, after some conversations with Professor Barone, Mussolini sent a private message to the Vatican inquiring on what conditions it would be prepared to arrive at a friendly settlement of its relations with the Italian State. A reply was received on the 24th. As its tone was considered satisfactory, semi-official negotiations were opened.

On December 31, 1926, the conversations became official, but they were held in strict secrecy. Cardinal Pietro Gasparri acted on behalf of the Vatican and Professor Barone on that of the Italian Government. On the sudden death of Barone, his duties were taken over by the Minister of Justice, Professor Alfredo Rocco, acting under the direct instructions of Mussolini. Certain difficulties that subsequently arose delayed matters until the latter part of 1928, when the discussions were once more resumed.

Finally, on February 11, 1929, the agreements were signed in the Lateran Palace by Mussolini himself and Cardinal Gasparri. There were three separate instruments jointly constituting the so-called *Lateran Pacts:* (1) a political treaty whereby the Vatican State was created, consisting of the Vatican palaces, the Cancelleria and the Papal villa at Castel Gandolfo,[3] its citizens being only the persons residing within those buildings; (2) a financial convention under the terms of which the Italian State was to pay to the Holy See 750,000,000 lire in cash and 1,000,000,000 lire in government bonds; and (3) a *Concordat* regulating the status and the rights of the Catholic clergy, recognizing Church marriages and providing for religious teaching in the schools.

This was a remarkable achievement, for with no sacrifice of Italian sovereignty or authority, it settled relations between Church and State on a definite basis satisfactory to both parties. It had widespread repercussions abroad, where it was wholly unexpected; and in many foreign quarters it caused intense annoyance. The event was regarded rather generally as a triumph for the Italian nation, for the Fascist regime, and for Mussolini personally, and of great value for the Holy See. In Italy it was hailed with enthusiasm by practically all classes of the population.

One of the conditions that had been insisted on from the very beginning of the negotiations both by the Pope and by Mussolini had been that the matter should be conducted in the most absolute secrecy. Indeed, the result was a rehabilitation of the much maligned "secret diplomacy." If even a rumor had been spread about the negotiations, there would have been such an outcry on the part of foreign circles hostile to Italy, of the extreme anti-Clericals everywhere, and of the radical anti-Clericals and Freemasons in Italy and France, especially, that success would have been practically impossible.

I may add a personal reminiscence reflecting the secrecy of the negotiations. In the summer of 1928, several British journalists, who, like everybody else, had no inkling of what was going on in Rome, had been publishing articles on the relations between Church and State in Italy that were full of very obvious inaccuracies. Some of them presented the Holy See and the Catholic Church, in general, as victims of persecution by Fascist atheists; and others made out that the Fascist Government was completely dominated by the Vatican. Both these statements could not be true, and anyone with even an elementary knowledge of the situation in Italy knew that both were equally fantastic.

I was in England at the time, and I thought an article in some important British periodical on the actual state of affairs, as far as I knew it, might be timely. But, as Church and State relations were a very delicate matter, before undertaking to write anything I waited until I returned to Rome and could ask Mussolini's opinion about the advisability of such an article. When he received me at the Palazzo Venezia with his usual cordiality, he approved of my suggestion, adding casually that

I might usefully consult a recently published book on the subject by Dr. Giacomo Emilio Curatulo.[4] As it happened, I had
read the book, and while it did not add anything new to what
was common knowledge, it did contain at the end a scheme for
a possible solution.

I then proposed an article on the question to the editor of
the London *Quarterly Review,* who at once accepted my suggestion. In the article I began with a summary history of the conflict, followed by a presentation of the problem as it stood at
the time. In conclusion, I suggested a possible solution, based
on the lines of Curatulo's book.

The article was published in the January, 1929, issue of the
Quarterly Review, which appeared at the beginning of February and, as it happened, on the very day that the London
press announced that negotiations had been going on for some
months and that a settlement had been virtually arrived at. The
conclusion of the agreements was announced the next day, and
their texts appeared a day or two later. The basis of the Lateran
Pacts proved very similar to the suggestion made in my article
and in Dr. Curatulo's book.

The Duce had thus given me a hint of what was brewing
without saying a word about the negotiations. Readers of the
article naturally thought that I had had access to inside information, whereas I had been as much in the dark as anyone else.

The Lateran Pacts did not put an end to all disputes between
the Vatican and the Italian Government, and the questions of
Fascist youth education and of the activities of the Catholic
Action association gave rise to further and somewhat bitter con-
troversies. These were, however, settled soon after, as a result
of conversations between the Papal nuncio and Renato Ricci,
President of the Opera Balilla (the Fascist Youth Organization).[5]

The settlement arrived at finally put an end to an international conflict between the Italian State and a foreign Power
that had lasted 60 years, and that had often affected Italy's relations with many countries.[6]

---

[1] The King of Italy.
[2] Afterwards Bishop of Oklahoma.

³ It then became what it had been in the past, namely, the Pope's summer residence.

⁴ *La Questione romana da Cavour a Mussolini,* Rome, 1928.

⁵ Afterwards Minister of Corporations.

⁶ Even the present Government of Italy, which is seeking to destroy every trace of the measures enacted between October 28, 1922, and April 25, 1945, has left the Lateran Pacts unaltered. It has, indeed, incorporated them into the terms of the new Italian Constitution, although endeavoring to make the Italian people forget that Mussolini had anything to do with them. On the occasion of the celebration of the 25th anniversary of the Lateran Agreements in 1954, Mussolini's name was not mentioned in any of the official speeches and statements on the subject.

CHAPTER NINE

Emigration and Colonial Expansion

One of the underlying facts of Italy's economic and social life which has constantly affected its political situation as well has long been and still is the superabundance of her growing population.

The number of inhabitants of the country (including territories annexed in later years) had risen from 26 millions in 1861 (the date of the foundation of the Italian Kingdom) to 36 millions in 1911 and to 41 millions in 1931. This population had to find sustenance on a territory of 119,000 square miles (a little larger than the state of Colorado), of which only a part is fertile. Large areas are barren mountains, and many of the plains have for centuries been malarial owing to ill-regulated water courses. Land reclamation, begun only a few decades ago, was carried out in an incomplete fashion. The subsoil is poor, coal and iron are extremely scarce, copper is practically nonexistent, and oil has only recently been discovered; mercury and sulphur are the only minerals of which there is a fairly large quantity.[1]

It is only by intensely hard work—and no people on earth work harder than the Italian peasants—that a scanty living at low wages can be eked out of this unkindly soil. With the rapid growth of the population even these low earnings could not be secured for all.

Since the middle of the 19th century an ever-increasing number of Italian workers have been forced to emigrate abroad, to find more work and earn higher wages than could be obtained at home. Emigration did supply a safety-valve, a temporary solution of the problem, and from 1876 to 1900 some 200,000 Italians emigrated every year. From 1900 to the outbreak of World War I, the annual exodus increased to an average of 700,000, and in the year 1913 alone it had actually reached 873,-000. In all, about ten million Italians had left the country in fifty years. Of these about two-thirds ended up, sooner or later, sometimes after many journeys to and fro, by finally repatriating, and the remaining third settled definitely in some foreign country.

These migrants sent home remittances for a considerable aggregate amount, estimated before 1914 at about 500,000,000 lire per annum. But large as this sum was, by far the greater part of what Italian emigrants produced went to benefit the country to which they had migrated. Taking the United States alone, Italy contributed some 25 to 30 per cent of the 27,000,000 able-bodied workers brought up and educated to their productive age at the expense of the country of their birth. The 500,-000,000 lire represented only a small part of the value of what these men produced, the bulk of which remained in the country in which they were working. The same is true of Italian and other emigrants in other lands.

The solution through emigration, from the Italian point of view, was, thus, only a makeshift—and by no means a wholly satisfactory one. In the first place, the emigration movement always took "the pick of the basket," depriving Italy of its best and strongest workers, for the weaklings and the unhealthy did not wish to emigrate, or if they did, they were rejected by the immigration countries.

Emigration was, moreover, a very uncertain form of relief, for it was in danger of being held up at any moment by restrictive measures inspired by economic depression in immigration countries, by the fear that the influx of foreign workers would create fatal competition with native labor and reduce wages, or (in some cases) by waves of xenophobia and by the fear that the new immigrants might corrupt the virtues and pure blood of the native population.

The exodus not only meant the loss to Italy of large numbers of its most efficient workers. Many of these men subsequently returned home ruined in health by the hard conditions of life and climate in many immigration countries, or maimed by industrial accidents, for which often they could get no compensation and had later to be supported in their home country by public or private charity.

Others who ended by settling permanently abroad assumed the citizenship of the immigration country, where, however, they were still often regarded as only second-class citizens. During the first World War many thousands of emigrants repatriated and served under the Italian flag. After the War and still more after the establishment of the Fascist regime they felt prouder of their old country than ever before.

It was suggested in some foreign quarters, especially in Anglo-Saxon countries, that the Italian population problem might be solved by means of birth control. Mussolini's Government was severely called to task because he encouraged the growth of large families in various ways; but these critics evidently had no notion of the real nature of the population problem, and the following answers to their suggestions were offered by many Italians:

1. It remains to be proved that birth control can ever effect such a reduction of population as to secure the expected results. In any case no important reduction could be attained until after two or more decades; in the meanwhile the existing population would have to be provided for, and in due course there would be an ever-increasing proportion of old persons incapable of work to be maintained by a decreasing number of younger workers.

2. The immense majority of Italians are Roman Catholics, and the Church is definitely opposed to all forms of birth control as a sacrilegious interference with the laws of God and nature.

3. A growing population is held by many experts to imply national health and vigor, whereas a stationary or declining one

reflects deterioration and degeneration; to apply a policy tending to such a result is a sign of weakness and defeatism.

4. There had been much misconception about the unique-
ness of the measures enacted by Italy in favor of large families.
Similar measures have been taken in Great Britain, Germany,
and France, even to a larger extent than in Italy. Moreover, the
rate of increase of population in Italy has been tending to
decline in the 20th century as compared with the 19th.

5. Mussolini's main inspiration in this connection was the
idea of at least retarding the tendency of the white races as a
whole to decline in numbers, as compared with the rapid increase of the colored races, who, unless the former maintain
their existing proportions, will end by overwhelming and
swamping the whole of our common white civilization.

Mussolini realized from the first the drawbacks of emigration,
having been himself an emigrant. In his introduction to the
report on emigration for 1924-1925 he stated:

Our demographic exuberance will not exhaust itself because we
cannot change our natures and do not intend to do so. In order to
maintain it, it is our duty to exploit all the resources of our soil.
That is what we are doing. But as this task requires time, the emigration phenomenon will continue; it may even assume a more
accelerated rhythm and be as large as it was in past years. . . . We
may admit, as I do myself, that emigration is an evil, as it deprives
our people of active forces which go to consolidate the red corpus-
cles of anaemic foreign lands. But it will be a lesser evil if it is
trained, selected, financed, and organized.

The American quota law of 1924, which reduced Italian immigration to the United States to trifling proportions, Mussolini
did not regard as wholly objectionable, inasmuch as the majority of those who migrated to that country ended by settling
there altogether, and were thus lost to Italy. "They are," he
said, "foreigners to us. We only hope that they are proud of
their origins." Indeed, no attempt was made by the Italian
Government to induce that of the United States to mitigate its
restrictive measures.[2]

Emigration to countries on the European Continent was
neither encouraged nor discouraged. If Italians found opportuni-

ties for securing work at high wages, so much the better. But what Mussolini was definitely opposed to was the attitude of regarding emigration as an undoubted benefit to Italy and the policy of trying to induce the largest possible number of Italians to emigrate. This policy had been promoted in the past by the steamship companies and their agents, by certain contractors and industrial concerns in foreign countries, and by a whole host of intermediaries, sharks, and traffickers of all kinds who exploited the needs and the ignorance of the emigrants. At best, emigration was, as he saw it, a makeshift, not a solution of the population problem.

The reduction of emigration after the first World War resulted in a disconcerting increase of unemployment, and desperate attempts were made to cope with it.

A solution might have been found in the acquisition of colonial territory, as had been possible in the case of other European countries, and Italy had contemplated this possibility long before the War of 1914. But all the richer colonial areas, capable of supporting large numbers of white settlers, had gradually been seized or ear-marked by other powers at a time when Italy was concentrating every effort on making itself a free national unit. Therefore, when Italy too entered the colonial field, it had to be contented with the scraps left over by others.

The first Italian colonies, Eritrea and Somaliland, were not capable of supporting more than a small number of Italians. They were, however, gradually built up into model and well-administered colonies, making slow but steady progress, and their inhabitants became devoted to their Italian rulers and served them as excellent and faithful soldiers.

Libya, occupied after the Italo-Turkish war of 1911-12, became a prosperous and progressive colony by dint of intensively hard work and the investment of a large amount of capital, especially in the 1930's, and it was capable of supporting a considerable number of Italian farmers and their families. These men drove back the desert sands and transformed the land beyond all recognition. It was hoped that in time some hundreds of thousands of Italians would settle and prosper there.

But the solution had not yet been found, and the desire for colonies was not mere greedy imperialism, as unfriendly critics made out, but a compelling necessity for the Italian people, an alternative to unemployment and starvation.

With Italy's intervention in the first World War, it was hoped that at least a partial solution of the problem might be found. But even on this occasion, after the sacrifice of over 600,000 lives in the dread struggle, Italy saw the doors locked and barred against colonial expansion. The territories wrested from Germany and Turkey after the war were partitioned between the wealthier victors—Great Britain and France—already gorged with colonial territories for which they had no longer any emigrants. Even little Belgium, which possessed the immensely rich Congo area, got its share, whereas Italy got nothing at all except a small strip of desert land beyond the river Juba south of Somaliland, which was only grudgingly granted to Italy several years after the close of the war.

Then there was the question of raw materials. If Italy could have obtained a sufficient quantity of these, its industries might have been more fully developed, thus providing work for the growing population. But a plea to the first League Assembly in 1920 that no embargo should be placed on the export of those commodities by the countries well provided with them was laughed out of court. The British Government at that time, when Italy and other European countries were longing for coal for post-war reconstruction, had imposed an export duty on it which made its price prohibitive. In the end, the measure reacted unfavorably on the British coal trade, for other countries made every effort to secure their supplies elsewhere and to develop hydro-electric power, the use of oil engines, etc., instead of coal.

This fact contributed from the very first, even before the Corfu incident, to weaken Italian confidence in the League of Nations as an organ for international justice.

A further attempt to solve Italy's economic difficulties was made in another direction. Large-scale agricultural improvements—the draining of marshes in a systematic and scientific manner, irrigation, more and better agricultural machinery, adequate housing, etc.—provided work for numbers of the agricultural population, and industry was developed in various ways.

Despite all this, however, certain measures of fiscal protection were necessary in the hope of reducing the imports of foreign goods and the exports of currency to ease the financial situation. These measures were known collectively as *autarchy*, and they were condemned abroad—on the one hand as immoral and wicked and on the other as quite useless. As a matter of fact, they were merely the answer to the closing of the doors to Italian emigration, to the refusal to allow Italy to secure colonies and to the excessively high tariffs imposed by other countries on imports from abroad. Moreover, these same measures, when applied in Great Britain and elsewhere, were merely called "economic self-sufficiency," which sounded legitimate and respectable, whereas *autarchy* was dreadful—a real "smear" word.

All these economic difficulties should be borne in mind if we wish to understand the motives and character of Italy's foreign policy, whether under the Fascist regime or any other party.[3]

[1] The existence of methane or natural gas in large quantities has only been discovered within the last few years, and the same is true of the recent discovery of petroleum.

[2] The United States Government consented to participate in the Rome conference on emigration in 1924 only on condition that the American restrictive measures would not be discussed.

[3] Successive post-Fascist governments in Italy have enacted measures of an even more drastically "autarchic" nature. (See Professor Felice Guarneri, *Battaglie economiche*, Rome, 1953.)

PART II

FAILURE OF MUSSOLINI'S EFFORTS
TO PRESERVE PEACE IN EUROPE

CHAPTER TEN

Franco-Italian Relations and International Conferences

In July, 1928, a naval disarmament compromise between Great Britain and France was agreed upon along lines that had been rejected by both the United States and Italy. Considerable annoyance was aroused in Italian circles by the plan, but it was very soon dropped as impracticable, and in August the Briand-Kellogg Pact for outlawing war was concluded by France, the United States, Great Britain and Italy. Afterwards it was adhered to by Russia and other powers.

In the two Anglo-Saxon nations it was regarded by many as "a great moral gesture against war," but in Italy few believed that an instrument so vaguely worded and so devoid of any means for its enforcement could lead to practical results; it seemed indeed a gesture and nothing more, and future events were amply to prove the correctness of this estimate.

Independently of the Briand-Kellogg Pact, attempts were made at this time to improve Franco-Italian relations, which both governments evidently desired. But, as had so often happened before, events occurred to prevent the realization of this desire. The problems were so inflated that in some quarters it was believed that certain individuals and organizations were determined to sabotage anything effective. Attempts at rapprochement had been made on various previous occasions, but something usually occurred that actually intensified ill-feeling between the two nations.

On September 17, 1927, the honorary Italian Consul in Paris, Count Carlo Nardini, a kindly old man who had devoted himself to welfare work among the poorer strata of the Italian colony in the city, was murdered in his office by Modugno, an Italian Anarchist. The pretext alleged by the murderer was that he had applied to the Consulate for a permit enabling his wife, then in Italy, to join him. The Consular officials had done their part in forwarding the application to the home authorities, and had then told Modugno that it was up to him to get the matter speeded up in Italy. Although he did nothing himself, evidently not being very keen on the matter, he returned to the Consulate several months later and shot Nardini dead.

The trial of the assassin took place the following year, in November, 1928. The prisoner did not attempt to deny his guilt, but the court allowed a number of well-known and self-exiled opponents of the Fascist regime, such as Francesco Nitti and Gaetano Salvemini, and the radical French labor leader, Léon Jouhaux, who knew absolutely nothing about the case, to give evidence, not on the murder, but on the alleged iniquities of the Italian Government, so that the proceedings assumed the aspect of a debate on Fascism rather than the trial of a murderer. Modugno was sentenced to two years imprisonment, but, as he had already been in detention for 18 months, he had only six months more to serve; he was fined 200 francs (about $6).

This outrageously light sentence aroused an outburst of indignation throughout Italy. There were demonstrations in various cities, and a vote of sympathy was passed in the Italian Chamber of Deputies. But Mussolini issued strict orders that no insults should be offered to the French flag, and in Rome troops were called out to prevent indignant crowds from reaching the neighborhood of the French Embassy. But in the Cabinet Council he said:

The whole nation has in the last few days been seriously outraged by the verdict of the Paris jury, which has practically acquitted the murderer of an old man and a faithful servant of the State, our Consular representative. The Government understands the indignant emotion of the Italian people, and is glad to observe the spontaneous demonstration of students, which were, however, characterized by perfect discipline.

The French Cabinet issued a note stating that measures would be taken to prevent such intolerable abuses of French hospitality in future. Nevertheless, other outrages of the same kind continued, including the murder of an Italian priest by an Anarchist. Even Briand's friendly speech in the French Chamber did not improve the situation to any material extent.

On New Year's Day, 1929, the French police arrested three anti-Fascists suspected of plotting to murder the Italian delegates to the forthcoming session of the League Council in Geneva. The documents found on the arrested men led the authorities to believe that they had discovered a far-reaching conspiracy hatched in France, and they made further arrests on the Riviera of men suspected of complicity in the various bomb outrages committed the previous year. These measures produced a good impression in Italy as an attempt to improve relations between the two countries.

On the international situation in general Mussolini delivered the following speech in the Chamber of Deputies on December 9, 1928:

We are all for peace. We have signed the Kellogg Pact. I have called it sublime; it really is so sublime that it might almost be defined as transcendental. And if tomorrow other pacts were in sight, we should hasten to sign them. We certainly do not wish it to be said that the world would be flowing with milk and honey, that men would all become brothers, that this mediocre and divine planet which we inherit would be a paradise; but that all this, this beautiful feast, is spoiled by Fascist Imperialism.

But above, below, or by the side of these pacts, is a reality which we must not ignore if we do not wish to commit treason against the nation. The reality is this, gentlemen: The whole world is rearming!

Every day, the papers report the launching of submarines, of cruisers, and other peaceful instruments of war. We must have no illusions on the political state of Europe. When storms are brewing, it is then that there is talk of quiet and peace, almost as a deep yearning of the spirit. We do not wish to disturb the European

·equilibrium, but we must be ready. None of you will then be surprised, and no one in Italy will be surprised, if I ask the nation for another effort to place our forces on land, at sea, and in the air on a proper basis.

Fascist Italy is conducting a foreign policy which her very adversaries admit to be logical and peaceful. But the character of Fascist foreign policy consists in this, that the ill-omened era fraught with unhappy memories of "tours de valse" is over.[1]

There was no humbug about the meaning of this speech. A few weeks later, in an interview with the representative of the Anglo-American News Service, Mussolini made the following remarks:

I believe that by 1935 certain circumstances will arise necessitating a change in the European situation. The peace treaties are faulty, many problems created by the war must be solved by peaceful methods. I feel certain that they will be solved in time. There are nations which cannot continue in the state in which they find themselves at present; for example, Hungary. Something must be done to improve the position of that country. The problem of colonial expansion, so vital for Italy, must be dealt with, together with other problems so critical for the whole world. But you must understand me. What I say is not a threat of war, for treaties can be revised by peaceful means.

Here the Duce once more stressed the necessity for treaty revision and Italy's compelling necessity for expansion—the two keynotes of his whole foreign policy.

While Mussolini himself did not often visit foreign countries, he sent his different ministers and undersecretaries abroad to keep in touch with foreign governments and conclude or prepare agreements of various kinds. Dino Grandi, Undersecretary for Foreign Affairs from 1926 to 1929 (when Mussolini himself was Foreign Minister) and Foreign Minister from 1929 to 1932, visited Greece, Albania, Turkey, Hungary, Germany and other countries, and he represented Italy as chief delegate on many international conferences. A graduate in law of the University of Bologna, Grandi had had an excellent record in the first World War, had played an important part in the early days of the Fascist movement, was a man of tact, with a singular charm of manner and a good knowledge of French and English, and was able to win golden opinions and to acquit himself well in diplomatic debates. But he was inordinately ambitious, and although he had received every possible favor and honor from Mussolini, he was never satisfied. Suffering from a persecution mania, he was constantly discerning enemies and plots against himself where none existed.

The various debates on reparations were followed by Mussolini with keen interest, although he never deviated from his insistence on the necessity for cancelling them as well as war debts. To the international conference on reparations opened at the Hague on August 11, 1929, he sent a strong delegation that played an important part in the debates. The battle there was between the various Allies over their respective shares of this phantom treasure. On this occasion France and Italy found themselves in the same camp against Great Britain because the British Government refused to accept any reduction of its own share. The bitter tongue and undiplomatic language of Philip Snowden, the British delegate, certainly did not help to conciliate his French and Italian colleagues. An agreement of sorts was finally arrived at, and Great Britain's quota was made up by Italy's undertaking to collect from Czechoslovakia the sums owing on the Liberation Debt, to transfer them to Great Britain and to purchase 3,000,000 tons of British coal to offset the damage wrought to British trade through "reparations in kind."

In connection with this conference there was a typical example of the methods of a part of the British press. I remember seeing one day in London the posters of an evening paper announcing in huge headlines "Mussolini's No" to some suggested agreement. A day or two later, I happened to meet one of the Italian delegates to the conference who had just come over to London, and he assured me that there never had been any "No" from Mussolini or any Italian delegate on any point whatsoever. The episode had been an invention pure and simple by the paper's correspondent.

The question of a conference for the limitation of naval armaments was now raised in a definite form, and on September 17, 1929, the British Premier, Ramsay MacDonald, informed the governments of Italy, France, Japan and the United States, signatories of the Washington Naval Agreement of 1922, that he hoped to summon a meeting in London early in the following year to deal with the question.

Italy agreed at once without reservations; and, after a preliminary exchange of views, the Rome Government sent a note to that of Paris stating that it was, as usual, "prepared to accept and adopt as the limitation of Italian armaments any figure, however low, which should be not less than that of any other Continental Power. . . . The global figure stated by France should represent the maximum amount of tonnage up to which the two countries should be entitled to build, leaving them both free to decide if and when this limit should be reached, without deciding at the moment on any program constituting an obligation which might lead to the result of increasing armaments rather than of reducing them."

The French Government, however, would not enter into negotiations on this basis. It made counter-suggestions, but no conclusion was arrived at for the moment.

The Conference was opened in London on January 22, 1930, with the object of extending the limitation of naval armaments to those classes of ships that had not been covered by the Washington Treaty. Italy's chief delegate was the Minister of Foreign Affairs, Dino Grandi, who, from the first, made an excellent impression, with his personal charm and his good clear English.

On the very first day of the Conference, there was another example of certain journalistic methods then prevalent in a part of the British press. The reporter of a London paper, in his account of the opening meeting, stated that Grandi "was unable to speak English, so the bulk of the audience could not understand him." Being then attached to the press office of the Italian delegation, I rang up the editor and called his attention to this misstatement, asking him to rectify it in the next issue. He refused.

The main points of the Italian memorandum submitted to the Conference were the following:

1. Italy was prepared to postpone the construction of the battleships it was entitled to build under the terms of the

Washington Treaty in 1931-36, thereby renouncing 105,000 tons out of the 175,000 allowed it under that instrument.

2. Italy was ready to consider favorably the total abolition of battleships.

3. Italy would reduce its naval forces to any level not lower than that of any other Continental power.

4. Italy would notify in each case, as agreed at Geneva, at least six months before laying down the keel, all details concerning each warship it intended to build.

5. Italy was prepared to consider favorably the total abolition of submarines in connection with a general reduction of armaments.

This last point was a notable concession, as Italy had always regarded the submarine as a weapon peculiarly suited to a weaker naval Power such as it was; but Italy made this conditional on the abolition of battleships, whereas the British Government, while eager to see submarines abolished, rejected the idea of the abolition or even the reduction of battleships, in which the British navy was particularly strong.

There was much acrimonious wrangling at the Conference, especially between the Italian and French delegations. Grandi, as he himself told me, was constantly subjected to a "smoothing-out process" on the part of the British delegation, which was eager, for domestic political reasons, to reach a settlement— whatever it might be—so as to be able to face an election with "something achieved." Britain was quite ready to give way to France, for which the Foreign Office always had a soft place in its heart, at the expense of Italy. But Grandi stuck to his program, and after endless discussions the Conference broke up without having achieved anything at all.

In his speech in the Chamber, on May 10, 1930, on the estimates for the Ministry of Foreign Affairs, after a detailed report on the state of the reparations question, Grandi dealt with the London Naval Conference, stating that throughout the proceedings the Italian delegation had shown a conciliatory spirit, while valiantly supporting the cause of the reduction of armaments. He insisted, in spite of everything, that collaboration between France and Italy was essential if Europe was to recover from her long convalescence, and he expressed the hope that the naval conference would meet again.

In Paris, Italy's demand for naval parity with France was not popular, nor was Grandi's insistence on the duty of the Allies to implement their pronouncements in favor of an all-round reduction of armaments, although the press welcomed his reference to the need for a better understanding between the two countries.

In the speech quoted above, Grandi alluded to the proposals for modifying the League Covenant. After mentioning the important services already rendered by the League, he said that we must beware lest "subtle erosion should transform the purposes of its workings," and we must guard against the danger that "it should become an arena for rival interests and a competition for prestige." The League, he insisted, "was not intended to be an association of the victors against the vanquished." Only by a firm stand on realities and by equitable agreements would it be possible to establish the mutual confidence that could give rise to "the peace of justice" among all nations. It was evident that both Grandi and Mussolini still believed in the value of the League, provided that it was not exploited for purposes other than those for which its authors had ostensibly conceived it.

In May, 1930, Grandi met Briand at Geneva and suggested the resumption of naval negotiations between the two countries, as well as further discussions dealing with the frontiers of Libya and the status of Italians in Tunisia. On June 3rd he informed the Senate that the French reply was that negotiations on special Franco-Italian problems should now be conducted through the ordinary diplomatic channels, and that with regard to Italo-British-French naval problems "it was preferable to adjourn their consideration, while awaiting the outcome of the Franco-Italian negotiations."

On this point Mussolini delivered an important pronouncement in Florence on May 17th. He declared that in certain foreign circles Italy was regarded as a small weak country, and that its armaments program was believed to be a mere bluff. "But," he went on to say, "I affirm that that program will be

Victor Emmanuel III
King of Italy

Field Marshal Pietro Badoglio
Prime Minister of Italy
July 25, 1943 to June 8, 1944

realized ton per ton, that the 29 ships of the new program will be launched." Beyond the frontiers, he added, there were "groups, parties, men," who, being now organized in a "co-operative association for the exploitation of the 'Immortal Principles,' that is, of the greatest and most refined swindle which is now being operated at the expense of the people, think that they can isolate Fascist Italy, and who, although professedly pacifists and democrats, would not be averse, possibly through third parties, to launch a war against the Italian people, guilty of identifying themselves with the Fascist regime." [2]

This speech aroused a storm of obloquy in many quarters. It led to various absurd interpretations, which Mussolini answered in another speech delivered in Milan on May 24th in his usual hammer-and-tongs style, commemorating Italy's entry into the first World War: "Intervention," he said, "prepared Fascism. Intervention prepared the March on Rome. Today, the Italian people are absolutely masters of their own destinies. . . . An armed people, that means a people armed to defend its rights under the symbol of the lictors." [3]

Further Franco-Italian naval conversations were held in Paris in August, 1930, and resumed at the League Assembly in September. Italy, then ready to make even greater concessions to France, stood firm on the question of parity, which France continued to reject. Italy had no intention of building up a fleet equal to that of France, but Mussolini rejected the French insistence that Italy should agree *never* to do so.

Finally on March 1, 1931 an agreement was reached through British mediation, whereby Italy made still further concessions to France without sacrificing her own right to parity. But when the draft of the compromise was sent to Rome by the French Government on April 23, 1931, the basis of the March agreement appeared so radically altered that it was unacceptable to both the Italian and the British governments. They then proposed a fresh compromise, which went far to meet the French demands, but it was described in Paris as laughable. Yet, the hope was expressed that a solution might be found when the three Ministers of Foreign Affairs met in Geneva in the course of the month.

Italo-French relations were again put to a severe test by the murder of two Fascists in Paris in April 1931 and of two others in October. In both cases the murderers received trifling sentences.

There was trouble also with Yugoslavia. On April 29th nine Yugoslav terrorists, members of a secret Slovene terrorist gang, were arrested in Trieste on account of a bomb outrage committed there the previous February in the offices of the *Popolo di Trieste.* It had caused the death of one person and the wounding of others. The trial was held in the following September; four of the accused were condemned to death and the others to long terms of imprisonment. This sentence, as usual, provoked violent demonstrations in Yugoslavia, where the murderers were hailed as martyred patriots, the bomb outrage being ignored as a matter of no account.

The financial depression throughout the world that resulted from the crisis in the United States made the disarmament question still more urgent, for every country felt the necessity of effecting drastic economies. At last the intimate connection between reparations and war debts, which Mussolini had been urging for the last ten years, began to be recognized outside Italy.

On June 20, 1931, President Hoover proposed the postponement of all payments on government debts, reparations and relief debts, involving both principal and interest. After consulting with the ambassadors of the United States, Great Britain, France and Germany, Mussolini immediately telegraphed to Washington warmly accepting the plan and adding that he would shortly forward some suggestions for the practical measures to be taken for its application. He stated that Hoover's proposal "may mark the beginning of a period of useful coöperation between nations, which is so necessary in this moment of general difficulty and on the eve of the Disarmament Conference."

Italy was the first nation to accept the Hoover proposal. On June 30th the Italian Government informed all the creditor and debtor nations that it was ready to hold in suspense "the sums due to it on July 1," and that "it was depositing in the Bank of International Settlements on a provisional account the money it owed to other countries." Mussolini's action was

warmly welcomed in the United States, even in quarters usually
hostile to the Fascist regime. It was then decided that Secretary
of State Henry L. Stimson should visit Europe, commencing his
tour with Rome. There he had two interviews with Mussolini,
whom he found "cordial, frank and satisfactory" and entirely
living up to his expectations. "The object of my European
tour," said Stimson, "is to study the situation and meet the
statesmen. I have learned much in Rome."

In an interview granted to some American journalists Mussolini said that Stimson had given him one thought, "a great
thought, with which I entirely agree. It is that if Europe is
peaceful, we are following the path of certain European recovery . . . In her policy of peace Italy believes that to solve
the economic crisis it is necessary first of all to solve the political
crisis, which has already lasted too long. The success of the
Disarmament Conference is imperative if the peoples are to
retain confidence in their governments . . . We have found
ourselves in agreement with Mr. Stimson as to the road to be
taken—the road of peace."

On January 1, 1931, Mussolini addressed a wireless message
to the American people. After expressing his admiration and
sympathy for the United States, without whose formidable help
the war would not have been won, he added that "without the
action of the United States we shall not emerge from this post-
war period and shall not return to a period of prosperity." He
then went on to affirm that:

Neither I nor my Government, nor the Italian people wish to
prepare a war. I have fought in a war as a private soldier. I know
what war means. The terrible memories of that time, when red-hot
steel mowed down so many young generations, have not vanished
from my memory. A war today, even if it were to break out only
between two nations, would inevitably become a world war. Then
all civilization would be jeopardized. The war of tomorrow, with
the new discoveries of science, would be even more terrible than
the war of yesterday. Not only would the fighters risk death, but
whole populations would be endangered without the possibility of
efficient defence.

Italy, as I have said, will never take the initiative of a war. The
preparation of our youth aims at strengthening the race and at

conferring on it the aptitude for self-control, for a sense of responsibility and discipline. . . . Eight million men are gathered round
Fascism, all the human and efficient strength of the nation. No
regime in Europe has a more solid and vaster basis than ours. Americans must believe in our friendship for them and in our wish to
live in peace with all the peoples of the world. With the certainty
that peace will be maintained in the world and that a new period of
prosperity will not fail to materialize, I greet those who have listened
to my speech and present my cordial respects to the President of
your great Republic.[4]

It was decided to hold a general conference on disarmament
at Geneva, February 2, 1932. In the meantime at the meeting of
the League Assembly in September, 1931, Grandi addressed that
body on the 8th. He first dealt with the proposal for amending
the Covenant and bringing it into line with the Briand-Kellogg
Pact, but he stated that the League was still so new that he felt
some reluctance in accepting the idea of amendments until
there had been more experience with its operations.

With regard to disarmament he suggested that during the
period of preparation for the conference:

The states which have definitely undertaken to participate in it
might adopt provisional measures . . . My own feeling is that we
ought to try immediately to arrive at a really effective armaments
truce, at least for the period of the Conference, and I should like to
ask you seriously to consider my suggestion. A general and universal
agreement between states to suspend the execution of programs for
fresh armaments would not only set our peoples an example of
good-will, but would create a psychological and political atmosphere
of greater calm and confidence, which would do more than any
declaration of principles to further the work of the Conference and
lead to tangible results.

In this connection I may inform you that the King of Italy has
just signed the General Act for the pacific settlement of international disputes, and I have received from my Government instructions with a view to the attendance of Italy at the General Convention to strengthen the means for preventing war, should the
Convention be approved by the Assembly.[5]

It was immediately recognized that in the proposal for his
arms truce Grandi had, on behalf of the Duce, made a most

important contribution to the cause of disarmament, and that he had provided a test of the sincerity of the various governments on the whole question. He was supported in the Assembly by Viscount Cecil, who certainly could not be regarded as a friend of Fascist Italy. Briand, on the contrary, made no reference to the Italian proposal, as it had met with a bad reception in Paris.

The disarmament discussions dragged on painfully without reaching any definite conclusions, always owing to the alleged fear on the part of the French Government and people of a new German aggression.

[1] *Scritti e discorsi*, Vol. VI, pp. 283 ff.
[2] *Ibid.*, Vol. VII, pp. 204-205.
[3] *Ibid.*, p. 210.
[4] *Ibid.*, pp. 277-279.
[5] Quoted by Muriel Currey, *Italian Foreign Policy, 1918-1932*, London, 1932, pp. 314-315.

CHAPTER ELEVEN

Italy and Germany Tend to Join Hands

I have often mentioned Italy's attitude towards Germany and the change it underwent after the end of the first World War. Even during that War Italians, as I have said before, regarded Germany with less hostility than the Hapsburg Empire; and after the conflict they saw in the treatment meted out to the German nation by the Western Allies, independently of any moral consideration, a most unwise and dangerous political policy, for it created in every German of whatever party or class a sense of intense injustice that was certainly not conducive to promoting international peace.

The reaction in France to this attitude was very marked. In its subconscious sense of guilt for 1914 and 1919 and fear of German revival, France was outraged by the mere suggestion that any other power should treat with sympathy the hated German nation or should give Germany any encouragement. We have seen how this feeling affected Franco-Italian relations.

But Italo-German relations had many aspects. The idea of a possible union between Germany and Austria aroused in Italy somewhat mixed feelings.

On the one hand, such a union could not be regarded as unnatural, because Austria was obviously unable to stand on its feet unaided, and because if it was to receive outside support, it would obviously first turn to a people of its own race and language. After the ill-conceived breakup of the Dual Monarchy in 1919, the small Austrian rump state found itself with a wholly German population.

On the other hand, Italians were not too keen on seeing an excessive expansion of German territory and on having Germany as an immediate neighbor instead of Austria. Besides, such a union would have constituted a violation of the provisions of the St. Germain Treaty, which forbade Austria to unite with Germany without the consent of the League Council. And it would violate the Geneva Protocol, which enjoined Austria to take no measure calculated to compromise its financial independence.

As early as March, 1931, it had been announced that Germany and Austria intended to conclude a customs union. This aroused great excitement throughout Europe. In France the opposition to the plan was uncompromising; the British and Italian Governments limited themselves to agreeing that the matter should be submitted to Geneva.

At the May Council meeting of the League the proposed customs union was discussed, and the Italian delegate, while doubting whether the plan would be beneficial to either power, agreed to the British proposal that the Hague Court should be asked for an opinion, a view that was accepted. The Court expressed itself unfavorably to the union, and both Germany and Austria then announced that they had given up the plan.

Italians came to see ever more clearly that the Weimar Constitution, adopted under Allied pressure, was not suited to the German spirit and was never likely to operate satisfactorily. The French, who had been primarily responsible for imposing it, had done so with the sole object of weakening their *Erbfeind* (hereditary foe). Indeed, after the conclusion of the German armistice on November 11, 1918, Clemenceau, in announcing to various foreign representatives the penalties to be imposed on Germany—the loss of Alsace-Lorraine, West Prussia, Danzig and Posen, as well as all its colonies, the reduction of her armaments to an absolute minimum, the payment of reparations to an astronomical amount in money and goods—is reported to have added, as the harshest punishment of all: *"Et nous allons lui flanquer une bonne république."*

Germany had, in fact, been compelled to swallow a constitution allegedly in conformity with the "Immortal Principles" of Western democracy, but certainly not in harmony with the German mentality or tradition. Mussolini, who had always seen through the sham of the "Immortal Principles," fully sympathized with the German attitude toward them.

For these and other reasons—dissatisfaction with the Peace Treaties, the importance of Italo-German trade, etc.—a tendency had been developing in Italy in favor of closer relations with Germany, both politically and economically. The Alto Adige question had been the only cause of disagreement, but it had never radically affected relations between the two countries and after 1926 had been almost forgotten.[1]

In 1931 the German Chancellor, Dr. Heinrich Brüning, and the Minister of Foreign Affairs, Dr. Julius Curtius, visited Rome officially and were cordially welcomed. The communiqué issued on that occasion dwelt on the necessity for close coöperation between all governments to insure a successful outcome of the coming Disarmament Conference. At the official banquet in honor of the German guests Mussolini made the following statement addressed to Brüning:

At this moment, a particularly difficult one for Germany and in general for all the countries of the world, Italy fully understands the necessities of the situation and the duties incumbent on each country in the interests of all . . . The Italian people who have followed with keen sympathy the great efforts made by Germany in every field of human activity, feel certain that the German people will pursue its course with renewed vigor, fully conscious of the great forces it possesses. This is not only a hope, but a conviction, in which I am confirmed by the wise and energetic action which your Excellency is conducting to restore to the German people the most favorable conditions and to secure for it the future which it deserves.[2]

In his Naples speech of October 25th of the same year Mussolini set forth once more Italy's policy for treaty revision, debts, reparations and the reduction of armaments. After speaking of the domestic situation, he passed to foreign affairs, and went on to say:

Nine years have now elapsed since Fascist Italy set forth in London the problem of reparations and debts in the terms which are today generally accepted. But we ask ourselves: Must sixty very long years elapse before we can put the word *finis* to the tragic accountancy of income and expenditure, issuing from the blood of ten million youths who will no more see the sun?

Can it be said that legal equality exists between nations when on the one side we see standing forth those who are armed to the teeth, and on the other States condemned to remain disarmed? And how can we talk of European reconstruction if certain clauses of the Peace Treaties, which have driven whole peoples to the edge of the abyss and of moral despair, are not modified? [3]

And how much more time must yet elapse before we are convinced that in the economic apparatus of the world today something is being held up and perhaps cracking? . . . The world crisis which is no longer only economic, but is above all spiritual and moral, must not keep us in a state of listlessness or inertia; the greater the obstacles the more definite must be our will to overcome them. [4]

On the day on which this speech was delivered, Grandi reached Berlin to return the visit of the German Ministers to Rome. He was welcomed with exceptional warmth. In the toasts exchanged and in the communiqué issued, the friendship existing between the two nations and the identity of many of their tendencies and points of view on the chief international questions of the day were duly stressed. One of the reasons for German cordiality toward Italy was the admiration the German people felt for a country that had freed itself from many of the handicaps with which the Reich was still burdened. To the Germans, Mussolini appeared the one realistic and sincere statesman in Europe who dared to speak openly (contrasted with the host of cheap politicians who sought to camouflage the most egotistic imperialism under a veil of cheap sentimentalism and pseudo-humanitarian demagogy), and who had shown himself a true friend of their country.

We should not forget that Germany was then on the eve of Hitler's advent to power, and that a current of ideas and aspirations was spreading throughout the country that closely resembled what had happened in Italy.

Mussolini raised the German question once more in an article written for a group of American papers and reproduced in his own *Popolo d'Italia* (September 12, 1932), in which he stated that the most important event in the international chronicles of the day was Germany's official request to the British, French, Italian and other interested governments for arms parity. He noted that the press of France was almost unanimously opposed to the idea, that of Great Britain was reserved, and that of Italy sympathetic. After summing up the history of the problem, he said that Germany's disarmament was, in the words of the Versailles Treaty, to have been the preamble to a general reduction of armaments down to Germany's level, "a solemn undertaking not yet carried out." Speaking of the Disarmament Conference, he said that the printed reports on the subject had reached the height of the Empire State Building, out of which mountain only the small mouse of the Beneš resolution had emerged: "We are faced with von Schleicher's grave dilemma: either Germany's legal parity is recognized, or Germany will abstain from taking part in the new phase of the Conference. German abstention will mean the paralysis and adjournment *sine die* of the Disarmament Conference, and also a moral blow at the League of Nations organization, already so gravely compromised by the attitude of Japan and the reserve of Italy." [5]

We have here the beginnings of those intimate relations between Italy and Germany that might have remained merely a cordial friendship had not the blind policy of other powers converted them into the Axis Alliance. We should not forget that the advent of Hitler to power in January, 1933, was the result of the attempt to keep Germany in a state of perpetual inferiority, if not of actual bondage, originating in the Peace Treaties and never really eliminated. At a London dinner party held soon after the establishment of the National Socialist Government in Germany, one of the guests asked: "By the way, where was Hitler born?" "At Versailles," was Lady Asquith's prompt and cogent reply.

The radical change in Germany's political institutions, although it was not by any means wholly comparable to that

which had occurred in Italy, resembled it in many ways, and
Hitler considered himself a pupil of Mussolini. On the principle
that imitation is the sincerest flattery, Mussolini and the Italian
people in general could not help feeling a certain bond of sympathy with Hitler and the German people. Both countries and
governments tried to solve their own problems and difficulties
by two systems that had many points of similarity, and the differences between the two national mentalities were reflected
in the differences between the two methods. In any case, the
advent of Hitler and the Nazi Party to power did contribute to
strengthen the ties between Italy and Germany, even if many
Italians could not help feeling a certain amount of anxiety at
excesses of policy and zeal in which the new German regime
indulged.

In the summer of 1932 Grandi ceased to be Minister of
Foreign Affairs, as Mussolini himself decided to resume the
leadership of the country's international relations, with Fulvio
Suvich as Undersecretary for the department. Grandi was then
appointed Ambassador in London, to take the place of An-
tonino Bordonaro, who had died suddenly at his post in June
of that year. The death of Bordonaro was a real loss for Italian
diplomacy, for he had proved one of the best of Italian Ambassadors in London. He rendered invaluable services and made
himself extremely popular both with the British Foreign Office
and with public opinion in general. Grandi, too, was well received in London, and was to do well during both the sanctions conflict and the Spanish Civil War. But he had not that
exquisite tact and thorough knowledge of diplomatic procedure that had enabled his predecessor to present the Italian
case with uncompromising vigor, but in such a way that his
opponents did not always realize that he was hitting hard and
straight.

[1] In 1929 the Italian Consul in Innsbruck told me that his German colleague,
having been asked by his Government to draft a report on the question, begged
his Italian colleague to supply him with the necessary data.
[2] *Scritti e discorsi*, Vol. VII, pp. 303-304.
[3] These words might well have been pronounced in 1956.
[4] *Scritti e discorsi*, Vol. VII, pp. 317-318.
[5] *Ibid.*, Vol. VIII, pp. 102-103.

CHAPTER TWELVE

The Four-Power Pact and Its Fate

With the beginning of 1933 we have two new developments in Europe of two very different types, but both destined to bring about grave political changes and to affect Italy's international situation.

On January 30th, 1933, Adolf Hitler became *Reichskanzler* of Germany.

On February 5th of that same year the Little Entente changed its status. In a protocol agreed to by its several delegates at Geneva it defined itself as "a higher international unit" with a governing body for common policies. It thus claimed to be "the fifth Great Power of Europe."

France, counting on this latter development to counteract the effects of the former, was destined to be totally and tragically deceived. Both events contributed to encourage the Four-Power Pact.

Mussolini was not much impressed by the language of the Little Entente delegates. In an article written for the Universal Service Agency and re-published in the *Popolo d'Italia* of April 13, 1933, he pointed out that a protocol was not sufficient to create a great power. These three states, he declared, had really nothing positive in common with each other, neither race, nor language, nor religion, nor history, for they were made up of Slavs of different varieties, plus Germans, Magyars, Latins and other peoples, of Orthodox Christians, Roman Catholics, Greek Catholics, Moslems and Jews. Each member of the group comprised within its own borders large linguistic and religious minorities.

From a military point of view the Little Entente had not one army but three armies, each composed of heterogeneous racial elements, by no means blended into single units. The "fifth Great Power" was, he said, "only the Little Entente which had climbed on a green baize table to look taller."

Nor were the political interests of the three members by any means harmonious. Rumania had one long-standing quarrel with Russia, which continued to claim Bessarabia, and another with Bulgaria, which had never forgotten the Southern Dobrudja wrested from it in 1913. Yugoslavia was on bad terms with Italy, with Austria, with Albania and with Bulgaria. Would Rumania, being friendly to Italy, follow Yugoslavia in its anti-Italian policy? Czechoslovakia had a very large German minority and a smaller Magyar minority; hence, it was in a perpetual fear of a revived Germany and afraid of revisionist Hungary, but it was not interested in Bulgaria or Italy and was inclined to be friendly with Soviet Russia.

In the economic field there were further differences. The formation of an economic pact between the three members was bound to remain a dead letter, for Czechoslovakia and Rumania were more interested in securing trade with Italy than with each other.

The one common bond was the determination to safeguard their territorial *status quo* and prevent a Hapsburg restoration either in Austria or in Hungary. The anti-revisionist attitude, as Mussolini had said innumerable times, constituted a danger to any lasting peace. He, himself, particularly sympathized with Hungary's revisionist aspirations; but as he was also friendly with Rumania, he hoped he might some day act as an "honest broker" and conciliate the two rival states. This he actually tried to do during the second World War.

In this same article Mussolini asserted that the revisionist idea was on the march, and that the fragile bulwark of a protocol like the one that was supposed to unify the Little Entente could not obstruct it. It is on the march "because the world wants peace, a long period of peace, and feels that this immense yearning will remain sterile if peace is not accompanied by justice." [1] Revision of the peace treaties must be pushed ahead within the framework of the League, "as is indeed admitted and contemplated by the Covenant itself (Art. 19). Those who reject the idea of revision are therefore outside the spirit of the League of Nations, which cannot be reduced to the duties of a mere guardian of the 1919 treaties, but must be raised to the stature of a guarantor of justice between peoples." This then was Mussolini's idea of the functions of the League.

His views on the Little Entente were destined to prove absolutely correct. It merely became a source of jealousies and intrigues, conducive to unlimited international squabbles. When it came to a showdown in 1939, the combination utterly failed to save its members from invasion, devastation and wholesale massacre, ending up in slavery for all three under a bloodthirsty Communist regime, of the Stalinist variety in two of them, of a Titoist variety in the third, but both equally oppressive and abominable.

In view of the new regime instituted in Germany and of the probable troubles to which the Little Entente might lead, Mussolini became more and more convinced that unless an understanding between France and Germany could be achieved, no true peace was possible in Europe. Therefore, every effort should be made by the true peace-lovers to that end. He believed that, of the Great Powers of Europe, Italy and Great Britain were then the best balanced and the most moderate in their outlook, and that the initiative must be taken by them. The United States, whose immense influence might have proved decisive, was not a member of the League; and it was at that time determined to keep out of European quarrels. Russia was wholly out of the picture, due to the hostility of Hitler, encouraged by the British.

But a close understanding between Great Britain and Italy alone might arouse suspicions and jealousies in France. One between Italy and France would alarm Germany, then undergoing a radical political and economic transformation, and it would annoy Great Britain. The only sound solution would be a full agreement among all those four powers.

Mussolini had never been a believer in perpetual peace as many of the League partisans professed to be, but he was a thorough believer in the possibility and desirability of a temporary peace, to last as long as possible between the Great Powers, and to be achieved by means of a special Pact. The genesis of his scheme goes back to Locarno—and indeed to the Peace Conference of 1919.

In a speech delivered in Turin the previous year (October 23, 1932) Mussolini made the following statement: "If tomorrow, on the basis of justice, of the recognition of our sacred rights, consecrated in the blood of so many Italian generations, and of the premises necessary and sufficient for the collaboration of the four Western Powers, Europe could be peaceful from the political point of view, perhaps the economic crisis that torments us would approach its end." [2]

In the meantime, the Disarmament Conference was reaching a deadlock, and the situation was anything but promising. It was in this atmosphere that the idea of the Four-Power Pact first arose in Mussolini's mind. At a dinner on the occasion of the Volta Congress[3] in the autumn of 1933 dealing with the subject of Europe, Mussolini said to the diplomat, Francesco Jacomoni, after reading the minutes of the day's meeting: "This is Europe. Europe exists in so far as four great currents of energy exist which compose it and which, in their variety and emulation, determine its progress." It was a feeling for the need of an organization above that of the individual states, Jacomoni writes, that had ever been the keynote of the Italian mind, "its aspiration towards a function of balance and mediation, which for close on 2,000 years has been the privilege of the Roman Popes and which, perhaps, goes back to the thought of Caesar." [4]

In conversation with different persons, Mussolini was ever repeating that he had no wish for war. Deeply involved as he was in measures for social reform and the improvement of the country's economic conditions, a war was to him inconceivable unless the very existence and vital interests of Italy were menaced. He summed up his views on this point on December 18, 1932, when he inaugurated the new town of Littoria, which he had built in the heart of the reclaimed Pontine Marshes: "It is here that we have waged and are waging regular war operations. This is the war which we prefer. But all other nations must leave us employed in this work of ours." [5]

In a subsequent speech on Italy's armaments he went on to say: "It should be obvious that we are arming, materially and spiritually, to defend ourselves and not to attack." This referred to the special nature of the armaments Italy was building up, based essentially on measures of defense.

In view of the virtually negative results of the first phase of the Disarmament Conference (in the summer of 1932) and the stalemate early in March, 1933, when its apparent inability to achieve anything decisive in its second phase was becoming serious, the idea of a Four-Power Pact became fixed in the Duce's mind. He had been striving to arrive at an agreement with Great Britain and France in favor of treating Germany on a footing of equality of rights (*Gleichberechtigung*), but as yet without success. There were, indeed, at the time actually rumors of a preventive war against Italy, favored by the French General Maxime Weygand and encouraged by Russia. The Little Entente consistently opposed any idea of treaty revision such as Mussolini advocated. Poland, anxious about Danzig, the annexation of which it believed would be one of Hitler's first demands on coming into power, had concluded a pact with Russia.

At the Volta Congress (1933) Mussolini had various conversations with foreign statesmen and intellectuals, discussing with them the idea of European unity. The French Ambassador in Rome, Henri de Jouvenel, had so informed a correspondent of the Paris *Temps* of his own initiative. He told of four conversations between the Duce and several eminent Frenchmen. In an article for a German newspaper, the Duce had stated through the Italian delegation at the preparatory World Economic Conference at Geneva that "it was time to move on from the armistice to peace. The armistice had lasted for fifteen years, and we are up against the simple but terrible dilemma: to take up arms once more or to conclude peace." [6]

After meditating at his country home, La Rocca delle Caminate, on the urgent necessities of the world situation and the serious danger that menaced peace, Mussolini issued a first draft of the Four-Power Pact and handed it to the then Under-secretary for Foreign Affairs, Fulvio Suvich, a Triestine lawyer of singularly well-balanced mind, who was bound by ties of personal friendship to many of the leading statesmen of Europe. It reads as follows:

Art. 1.   The four Western Powers: France, Germany, Great Britain, Italy, undertake to carry out among themselves an effective policy of collaboration in view of the maintenance of peace, according to the spirit of the Kellogg Pact and of the "No force Pact," and undertake within the framework of Europe an action calculated to induce third parties also, if necessary, to adopt this policy of peace.

Art. 2.   The four Powers reaffirm, according to the clauses of the League of Nations Covenant, the principle of the revision of the Peace Treaties, in those conditions which might lead to a conflict between States, but declare that this principle of revision can only be applied within the framework of the League of Nations and through the mutual comprehension and solidarity of reciprocal interests.

Art. 3.   France, Great Britain and Italy declare that, should the Disarmament Conference only lead to partial results, parity of rights, recognized in favor of Germany, shall have an effective bearing, and Germany undertakes to realize this parity of rights in a gradual manner such as will issue from successive agreements to be concluded by the four Powers, through normal diplomatic channels.

Art. 4.   In all European and extra-European political and non-political questions the four Powers undertake to adopt, as far as possible, a common line of conduct, even with reference to the colonial sector.

Art. 5.   This political agreement of understanding and collaboration, which will be submitted, if necessary, within three months to the approval of Parliaments, shall have the duration of ten years, and will be considered as tacitly renewed for a similar period of time if it shall not have been denounced by one of the Parties one year before its lapse.

Art. 6.   The present Pact shall be registered at the Secretariat of the League of Nations.

As usual with Mussolini, insistence was laid on treaty revision, and Article 2 of this first draft gave teeth to Article 19 of the League Covenant, but he did not wish to operate outside the

League. Article 3 brought out the question of parity of rights for Germany, and Article 4 extended to the colonial sphere, which was of such great importance for Italy.

One of the negative aspects of the plan was that without it there was the danger that the four Powers might break up into two separate groups, more on behalf of the interests of their satellites than of their own—this referred particularly to France's policy of close coöperation with the Little Entente.

On March 3, 1933, the British Premier, Ramsay MacDonald, and his Foreign Secretary, Sir John Simon, then at Geneva, decided, in view of the unsatisfactory course of the Disarmament Conference, that it would be advisable to visit Mussolini in Rome and discuss the international situation with him. On hearing of this wish, the Duce extended a cordial invitation to them, and MacDonald, who had evidently some inkling of the Four-Power scheme, accepted the proposal and informed the press that it was desirable to form a group of powers inspired by good-will, in order to endeavor to clear up the complicated international situation.

The British Ambassador in Rome, Sir Ronald Graham, who had held his appointment for over ten years and had always collaborated closely as a good friend of Italy, was largely responsible for the visit.

MacDonald and Simon had their first interview with the Duce on March 18th and a second on the following day. The British Premier told the Italian journalists that he had found "a great spirit of understanding in Rome, a new energy and profound changes." An ample exchange of views took place between the Italian and the British ministers; and, as the communiqué states, "a plan of understanding on the main political questions had been prepared by the head of the Italian Government to promote the coöperation of the four Western Powers with the object of securing, in the spirit of the Kellogg-Briand Pact and the declaration of 'no resort to force,' a long period of peace in the world." At the Palazzo Venezia banquet on that same evening, Mussolini said that the meeting was "the result of ten years of order, of unity, of discipline, of constructive work in Italy."

MacDonald's expressions of admiration for Mussolini and

for the achievements of the Fascist regime were so expansive as to lead one of his colleagues to say: "There is nothing more for the British Prime Minister to do but to don the Black Shirt in the streets of London." MacDonald could not help noticing that the conditions of Italy were very different from those that irresponsible opponents and biased foreign journalists had depicted. Possibly, too, as a convinced Socialist, MacDonald was influenced by Mussolini's advanced social legislation and welfare institutions.

A few minor changes in the text were suggested by the British ministers in Rome, so as to stress more definitely the connection with the League and with existing agreements; and Mussolini raised no objection to the omission of all mention of colonial questions, inasmuch as these appeared indirectly covered by the undertaking to coöperate in the solution of economic difficulties.

In Berlin some objections were raised at first to what was regarded as a too decisive insistence on the Covenant in the matter of treaty revision, for Article 19 appeared insufficient to meet the case. But Mussolini's "brilliant conception" was applauded as opening a way out of present difficulties. A few days later Hitler declared that "Mussolini's magnificent plan is warmly welcomed in Germany" and that the German Government was "ready to collaborate loyally for the realization of this scheme of peaceful coöperation of the four great European Powers."

The French Government began by expressing its general approval, and it undertook to devote the closest attention to the plan.

President Roosevelt instructed his Ambassador in Rome to keep him fully informed about the plan, which MacDonald had defined as "the Peace Club."

On the other hand, violent opposition at once arose in Poland and in the Little Entente states, since it was feared in those quarters that treaty revision would apply chiefly to themselves and that the Pact would weaken their ties with France, which would also become less dependent on their support.

In the British Parliament, where Hitler's advent to power had produced a certain amount of anxiety, some members feared that the proposed Pact might imply close relations with Nazi Germany. While MacDonald defended the Pact very vigorously, Churchill in the House of Commons attacked it bitterly, and for a moment even Sir Austen Chamberlain was critical. In the House of Lords, Cecil was as hostile as Churchill, but other peers praised it warmly. Sir Austen himself ended by approving it.

In France, after the Government's general acceptance, much criticism arose and pressure was brought to bear on the ministers to "denicotinize" the plan. But the French Ambassador in Rome, de Jouvenel, appeared particularly keen for its acceptance. "Never," he stated, "have diplomatic negotiations been conducted with such loyalty. The Duce has always had in view the general interest. Every particularist idea was discarded, every form of bargaining absolutely ignored."

A French memorandum was then submitted to Mussolini, suggesting some further changes, and other amendments were proposed by Germany and by Great Britain. Later on still further obstacles arose in certain French quarters, although de Jouvenel always remained a fervent advocate of the plan to the point of informing his Government that, if it were not accepted, he would resign his post as Ambassador.[7]

In Germany it was hinted that a delay would be advisable, in view of the unsatisfactory course of the Disarmament Conference, although the probable complete failure of that Conference would have made the Pact even more desirable.

After a letter of April 3rd from MacDonald to Sir Ronald Graham proposing some minor alterations, the Fascist Grand Council expressed its full approval of the Pact. On April 9th de Jouvenel submitted a French counter-proposal to Mussolini, who let him understand that it was possible to continue the negotiations on the basis of the French suggestions. But these led to difficulties in Germany because, while the undertakings of Article 1 of the Anglo-Italian draft were confirmed, the French insisted that all the provisions of the Covenant must be respected, and that the four Powers should not compromise the rights of any state. In Article 1 an alteration was made in the sense that the four Powers should consult together and make efforts for a policy of collaboration. In Article 2 the principle of treaty revision was supplanted by the quotation of article 19 of the Covenant, together with Articles 10 and 16 (respect for the territorial and political independence of all League members, and the provisions for sanctions). In Article 3 the general undertaking to coöperate for a convention reducing armaments was supplemented by the mention of MacDonald's plan, accepted by Italy, for a convention for the reduction of armaments and a re-assertion of the old French thesis of associating parity of rights for Germany with "national security" (Article 5 of the Covenant).

Germany objected to this French proposal, especially to the changes in Article 3. But Mussolini brought strong pressure to bear on Hitler, and on April 22nd a German counterproposal reached Rome. In this, Article 3 was so drafted that the parity of rights for Germany should be made really effective and that the other powers should enter into a convention for a reduction of their own armaments, and German rearmament was to be carried out in five years instead of in ten. At the same time, Austria, Hungary and Bulgaria were to be re-armed.

De Jouvenel opposed this German draft, and the French press was extremely violent against it, under the inspiration of the Little Entente statesmen and especially of Eduard Beneš and Nicolae Titulescu. In the French Parliament, Edouard Herriot inveighed against it. On May 22nd, Marin said that if Edouard Daladier signed the Pact he would be defeated, to which Daladier replied: "I shall sign it if it is satisfactory." The opposition of the Little Entente was reduced by the French declaration of May 29th that "if questions of a territorial nature concerning the application of Article 19 of the Covenant arose, France would undertake to insist on the maintenance of the principle of unanimity in League declarations." Nevertheless, League suspicions remained, and Baron Pompeo Aloisi telegraphed from Geneva that Beneš, while renouncing his opposition to the pact, was prepared to boycott its application.

Some further objections were raised by Germany, but Hitler ended by saying (May 17th) that he again saluted the far-seeing and important plan of the head of the Italian Government, and that "my Government is prepared to give evidence of the greatest spirit of conciliation if the other nations are also ready to make a harmonious effort effectively to overcome all obstacles and difficulties."

Further conversations followed in Rome between Graham, de Jouvenel and Suvich. In Article 2, as a result of French insistence, mention of Article 16 of the Covenant was included. Article 4 of the draft of May 13th (omitted from that of the 30th) concerning economic reconstruction re-appeared. Article 3 remained unaltered.

On May 30th, the German Ambassador, Ulrich von Hassell, declared that he was authorized to initial the text. The opposition of the Little Entente then ceased and likewise that of Herriot—for the moment. Daladier said that his chief objective was to render Franco-Italian relations more cordial, and that he had often expressed the wish that the Pact be preceded by a special Franco-Italian agreement. Mussolini himself had said that "even if the Four-Power Pact is only a point of departure for the settlement of the main European problems, it will be tomorrow a fixed point for Franco-Italian relations."

On May 31st, the text agreed to on the 30th was sent to the Italian embassies in London, Paris and Berlin. The London *Times* lauded "the magnificent success of this great statesman Mussolini, one of the few reassuring aspects of the situation." Norman Davis, President Roosevelt's personal delegate, stated publicly that the Pact was a valuable contribution to the pacification of Europe.

A new text was drafted in Rome, taking the various suggestions by the other three governments into consideration. After some last difficulties had been overcome the final text was agreed to on June 7th, and initialed by Mussolini and the Ambassadors in Rome of the three other Powers. It read as follows (in the official text):

AGREEMENT OF UNDERSTANDING AND CO-OPERATION

The President of the French Republic, the President of the German Reich, H. M. the King of Great Britain, Ireland and the British Dominions beyond the seas, Emperor of India, and H. M. the King of Italy;

Conscious of the special responsibilities incumbent on them as possessing permanent representation on the Council of the League of Nations, where the League itself and its members are concerned, and of the responsibilities resulting from their common signature of the Locarno agreements;

Convinced that the state of disquiet which obtains throughout the world can only be dissipated by reinforcing their solidarity in such a way as to strengthen confidence in peace in Europe;

Faithful to the obligations which they have assumed in virtue of the Covenant of the League of Nations, the Locarno Treaties, and the Briand-Kellogg Pact, and taking into account the Declaration of the renunciation of force, the principle of which was proclaimed in the declaration signed at Geneva on the 11th of December 1932, by their delegates at the Disarmament Conference and adopted on the 2nd of March 1933 by the Political Commission of that Conference;

Anxious to give full effect to all the provisions of the Covenant of the League of Nations, while conforming to the methods and procedure laid down therein, from which they have no intention of departing;

Mindful of the rights of every State, which cannot be affected without the consent of the interested party;

Have resolved to conclude an agreement with these objects, and have appointed as their plenipotentiaries:

The President of the French Republic

H. E. M. M. Henri de Jouvenel, Ambassador of the French Republic, Senator;

The President of the German Reich:

H. E. Herr Ulrich von Hassell, Ambassador of the German Reich;

H. M. The King of Great Britain, Ireland and the British Dominions beyond the seas, Emperor of India; for Great Britain and Northern Ireland;

H. E. the Rt. Hon. Sir Ronald Graham, G. C. B., G. C. V. O. His Ambassador Extraordinary and Plenipotentiary at the Court of the Quirinal;

H. M. the King of Italy.

H. E. Cavaliere Benito Mussolini, Head of the Italian Government, Prime Minister, Minister of Foreign Affairs

Who, having exchanged their full powers, found in good and due form, have agreed as follows:

Article 1.

The High Contracting Parties will consult together as regards all questions which appertain to them. They undertake to make every effort to pursue, within the framework of the League of Nations, a policy of effective co-operation between all Powers with a view to the maintenance of peace.

Article 2.

In respect of the Covenant of the League of Nations, and particularly Articles 10, 16 and 19, the High Contracting Parties decide to examine between themselves and without prejudice to decisions which can only be taken by the regular organs of the League of Nations, all proposals relating to methods and procedure calculated to give due effect to these articles.

Article 3.

The High Contracting Parties undertake to make every effort to ensure the success of the Disarmament Conference, and, should questions which particularly concern them remain in suspense on the conclusion of that Conference, they reserve the right to re-examine these questions between themselves in pursuance of the present agreement with a view to ensuring their solution through the appropriate channels.

Article 4.

The High Contracting Parties affirm their desire to consult together as regards all economic questions which have a common interest for Europe and particularly for its economic restoration, with a view to seeking a settlement within the framework of the League of Nations.

Article 5.

The present agreement is concluded for a period of ten years from the date of its entry into force. If, before the end of the eighth year, none of the High Contracting Parties shall have notified to the others his intention to terminate the agreement, it shall be regarded as renewed and will remain in force indefinitely, each of the High Contracting Parties possessing in that event the right to terminate it by a declaration to that effect on giving two years' notice.

Article 6.

The present agreement, drawn up in English, French, German and Italian, of which the French text prevails in case of divergence, shall be ratified and the ratifications shall be deposited at Rome as soon as possible. The Government of the Kingdom of Italy will deliver to each of the High Contracting Parties a certified copy of the *Procès verbaux* of deposit.

The present agreement will enter into force as soon as all the ratifications have been deposited. It shall be registered at the League of Nations in conformity with the Covenant of the League.

Done at Rome, the 7th June, 1933, in a single copy, which will remain deposited in the archives of the Government of the Kingdom of Italy: certified copies will be delivered to each of the High Contracting Parties.

In faith whereof the above-mentioned plenipotentiaries have signed the present agreement.

Henri de Jouvenel—Ulrich von Hassell—Ronald Graham—Benito Mussolini

In his speech in the Senate on that same day Mussolini set forth the story of the negotiations, and on July 15th the instrument was signed in London. All that was needed was ratification.

If the final text differed from Mussolini's original draft and its force was somewhat attenuated in order to meet the objections of France, Article 19 of the Covenant (treaty revision) was mentioned as in the first draft; and if Articles 10 and 16 were also inserted, the main provisions of the agreement remained unaltered.

Mussolini's conception was most important. If it had been carried out, there is little doubt that a new era in European history would have dawned, on a basis of lasting peace. The Pact provided full possibilities for the peaceful settlement of all international questions between the four Great Powers on a footing of equality.

As Mussolini himself said, the agreement was not directed against any power, but was intended "to implement normal diplomatic relations through more or less periodic and frequent meetings, according to necessity, between the persons responsible for the foreign policy of the four great states." It would be a more flexible organ for international understanding than any other previously conceived.

Italy and Germany ratified the Pact, but France put off ratification time after time. Poland did not conceal its irritation, and the Little Entente opposed it in every way. At the Sinaia meeting of that body Beneš repeated the words he had pronounced at Geneva at the end of May, that if the signing of the treaty could not be prevented, it could at least be sabotaged. His opposition and that of his Yugoslav and Rumanian colleagues were due to the fear that, whereas at the League their pressure could always be brought to bear on the other powers —since votes counted at Geneva—under the Pact decisions might be taken without their intervention; but, above all, the very hint of treaty revision made their blood run cold. France, on the other hand, was inspired by the notion that, whereas at Geneva it could always rally the Little Entente, Poland and other small Powers to its support, under the Pact France would be only one among four.

The British Foreign Office was then, as often happened, very much under French influence, and the government therefore failed to ratify the Pact. France's uncompromising attitude at the Disarmament Conference on the question of the "token armaments" to be permitted to Germany and of the arms defined as aggressive and consequently forbidden to Germany under the terms of the Versailles Treaty, created an atmosphere of failure around the Pact, which thus ended up by remaining a dead letter. It was evident that France did not really wish to pledge itself to any plan calculated to limit its right to resort to force whenever it suited its convenience, and the British Government did not wish to do anything that might be too disagreeable to France.

The last mention of the Pact as a possible way out of international difficulties is found in a conversation between Italy's representative at Geneva, Baron Pompeo Aloisi, and the Secretary General of the League, Sir Eric Drummond (afterwards Earl of Perth), in which it was suggested that the disarmament problem be examined by Great Britain and Italy in order to study the manner in which they could jointly take up the matter diplomatically with France and Germany, summon a meeting of the four Powers and then transmit the results to the Disarmament Conference for a final decision. But nothing ever came of this constructive idea.

This scheme was defined by the official Vatican organ *L'Osservatore Romano* as "the loyal will, the active proposal for peace" of which the Four-Power Pact had attempted to make "a *praxis, a permanent initiative*," above the old jealousies between states, international tensions now overcome, and considerations of domestic policy.

The consequence of the failure to ratify the Pact was "to make of divided Europe a field open to aggressors." [8]

Independently of all other considerations, there is no doubt that the application of the Pact would have saved the world from the disasters of 1939-1945—and the members of the Little Entente themselves from the complete political annihilation they have since suffered, together with Poland and other countries as well. But perhaps the very reason why it was wrecked was that forces determined on war were already at work in many lands to hold up any attempt to consolidate peace.

Some time later Mussolini stated in an article written for the Universal Service Agency that, when the Pact failed, he had lost all hope for a peaceful solution of the problems tormenting Europe.

---

[1] These were almost the same words pronounced by Pope Pius XII during the second World War and equally in vain.

[2] *Scritti e discorsi,* Vol. VIII, p. 126.

[3] A gathering of scientists and experts from many lands held every few years at the Italian Academy to discuss leading problems of general world interest.

[4] Article by Francesco Jacomoni on the Four Power Pact in *Rivista di studi di politica internazionale,* January-March, 1951.

[5] *Scritti e discorsi,* Vol. VIII, p. 147.

[6] *Berliner Börsencourier,* March 5, 1933.

[7] Statement made to me by the then Undersecretary for Foreign Affairs, Fulvio Suvich.

[8] Jacomoni, *loc. cit.*

CHAPTER THIRTEEN

Italy, Austria and Germany

Italy had continued to remain on friendly terms with Austria both before and after Mussolini's advent to power. But the course of events in that country was by no means always peaceful.

On July 14, 1927, serious riots broke out in Vienna as a result of Socialist agitations, public buildings were burned down, and troops had to be called out to restore order. It was at once rumored that Italy was massing large forces on the border, preparatory to a miltary occupation of the country to crush the Socialists.

Mussolini, however, in addressing the Cabinet Council of August 1st, assured his colleagues that Italy was in no way concerned with the Vienna revolt: "It had given rise," he said, "to one of those habitual campaigns against the Fascist regime. . . . The Fascist Government never thought of interfering with the domestic affairs of the Austrian Republic. The Italian Minister in Vienna did not make a *démarche* of any kind. We did not concentrate troops on the Austrian frontier. From the very first moment, it seemed to me obvious that the revolt would wear itself out in a sterile manner without political results on the constitution of the state."

But due in part to the disastrous economic conditions of the country, the outbreak once more raised the question of Austrian independence. Austrian territorial integrity was menaced by two neighboring states. Czechoslovakia had a grudge against Austria as a Germanic nation. Yugoslavia, which had wrested vast territories from the old Hapsburg Empire, was not yet satisfied and demanded Carinthia as well, on the pretext that it contained a small Slovene minority.

Germany, then under the disarmed Weimar Republic, was less dangerous than the two smaller but heavily armed Slav states. But as soon as it commenced to revive economically, and still more after the advent of Hitler and the Nazis to power, Germany began to consider the possibility of absorbing Austria, for economic, ethnic and linguistic reasons, as a matter of practical politics. In Austria itself the very difficult economic situation fostered the growth of a local Nazi party and a yearning for some sort of union with Germany as the only means of economic salvation.[1] There was, indeed, at that time no party inspired by strong patriotic Austrian sentiments, and the great mass of the people merely struggled on, wondering how best to get along from day to day.

Italy, viewing the independence of Austria as necessary for the balance of power in Central Europe, had no wish to see Germany excessively enlarged by the absorption of Austria under the form of a *Gleichschaltung* (setting up a regime analogous to that of Hitler) or of an *Anschluss* (outright annexation).

When, after various political vicissitudes, Engelbert Dollfuss came into power on May 29, 1932, Mussolini at once felt great admiration and a keen personal friendship for this man, who seemed to be honestly struggling to create a real Austrian patriotism and a party capable of maintaining national independence. Commercial relations between Austria and Italy had always been very close, owing to the complementary character of their respective economies and products. But economic difficulties remained Austria's basic problem, and the tendency toward closer ties with Germany oscillated according to the improvement or the deterioration of Austria's conditions, union finding less support in times of prosperity than in those of depression.

By the autumn of 1933 there were signs of improvement; and although attempts were made to increase trade with Germany, any idea of political union was definitely rejected by Dollfuss's Government, which, indeed, took severe measures against the activities of the Austrian Nazi party, then in intimate relations with that of the Reich.

In February, 1934, another and more violent Socialist revolt broke out in Vienna and some other Austrian cities. Though the sympathies of the Italian Government were undoubtedly on the side of the Chancellor, the stories of consignments of Italian arms to Austria proved devoid of foundation. On the other hand, it was ascertained that large quantities of war material had been supplied to the Vienna Socialists from Czechoslovakia, whose semi-Socialist and rabidly anti-Austrian Government missed no opportunity of fishing in troubled waters, although it is not clear whether the material had been sent just before the revolt or at an earlier date.

Dollfuss acted with great energy and succeeded in crushing the outbreak very quickly, but not without considerable loss of life and property. The stringent measures taken against the revolutionaries, however, alienated the Austrian Socialists from him and thus weakened his power of resistance to Nazi pressure, whether of Austrian or German origin. Dollfuss could no longer count on their support, even if they disliked the Nazis more than his Government.

The British and French governments had repeatedly expressed their intention of giving the fullest support to Austrian independence against all outside interference, but they had never taken any practical steps to implement their platonic sympathies. After negotiations with Italy, the three Powers had, it is true, issued a joint statement on February 17, 1934, affirming "the necessity of maintaining Austrian independence and integrity in accordance with the relevant treaties." [2] Italy hoped that a common front on the question would materialize, but the two Western Powers continued to limit themselves to diplomatic support. At a meeting in Venice between Mussolini and

Hitler (June 14 and 15, 1934) the Austrian question was discussed, and a sort of gentlemen's agreement was arrived at whereby Germany undertook not to interfere in Austria's domestic affairs. A temporary decrease in Nazi activity followed, and a more satisfactory situation seemed about to materialize.

But suddenly on July 15th the Vienna *Putsch* took place as an attempt to overthrow the Dollfuss Government and set up a Nazi regime. Dollfuss was murdered, but the movement failed completely, and the leaders were arrested, tried and condemned.

The causes of the outbreak were many. Although the movement had received encouragement and perhaps inspiration from Germany, it was conducted almost wholly by Austrian Nazis.

The news of the *Putsch* and its probable German affiliations produced consternation in Italy, and the Duce was horrified by the brutal murder of his friend Dollfuss. He was indignant with Hitler for having at least countenanced the outbreak. Fearing a possible German occupation, Mussolini immediately took drastic measures to safeguard Austrian integrity. Italian troops were this time actually hurried to the Brenner, and the Italian press was very outspoken in its criticisms of German policy in Austria.

It is significant that in Cordell Hull's memoirs not a word is said about Italy's action to save Austrian independence, just as the Four-Power Pact is not mentioned. These omissions are, no doubt, due to the fact that the Secretary of State was writing at a time when it was considered bad form to say anything that might be interpreted as favorable to Italian foreign policy before 1945.

The action to safeguard Austria, in order to be effective, should have been international. Although the presence of Italian troops on the Brenner did save the situation for the time being, Great Britain and France should have coöperated closely with Italy for the purpose. The three Powers did state on September 27th that they agreed that the declaration of February 17th regarding the independence and integrity of Austria as necessary, in accordance with the treaties in force, "retains its full effect and will continue to inspire their common policy." [3]

But, since it seemed evident for the moment that a permanent *rapprochement* was very unlikely between Nazi Germany and Austria, other than the setting up of an Austrian Nazi regime in Vienna under German auspices, the two Western Powers hesitated to take any action. A secret military agreement between Italy and France signed by Marshal Badoglio and General Gamelin had been concluded with a view to joint action in the event of a German invasion of Austria, but Great Britain would not undertake any engagement. So, in the end, Italy was left unsupported. This fact forced the Italian Government to abstain from any further measures, for it could not act alone. Mussolini thus found himself left in the lurch, as he explained in an article in the *Popolo d'Italia*, February 13, 1935.[4]

The events connected with Austria, together with the non-ratification of the Four-Power Pact,[5] convinced Mussolini that he could not count on any collaboration of the Western Powers in his policy for European peace. France seemed too terrified of Germany, and Great Britain too eager to avoid any decisive action. Here were the origins of Mussolini's gradually and unwillingly formed conviction that a close understanding with Germany was Italy's only practical alternative. British and French indifference or hostility to his peace efforts and to his attempts to protect Austria from Nazi domination forced him reluctantly into the Rome-Berlin Axis.

---

[1] In September 1921 the Austrian Chancellor, Monsignor Ignaz Seipel, had proposed an economic union with Italy, but the Royal Government rejected the offer.

[2] Arnold Toynbee, *Survey of International Affairs*, 1934, London: 1935, p. 455.

[3] *Ibid.*, p. 485.

[4] *Scritti e discorsi*, Vol. IX, pp. 169-173.

[5] See Chapter XII.

CHAPTER FOURTEEN

Economic Relations with the Danube States: Italian-Yugoslav Conflicts Again

In March, 1932, the French Government had prepared a system of preferential tariffs to govern trade with the Danubian states. The plan also represented the views of Beneš, which were always regarded with suspicion both in Rome and in Berlin, where this Czechoslovak statesman was considered the personification of intrigue, camouflaged under the guise of pure democracy. It was, therefore, rejected by Italy and Germany at a conference in London, for it was regarded as implying nothing more than an extension of French influence in the Danube basin, without any corresponding benefit to the countries concerned.

Italy had at that time concluded commercial agreements with Austria (February 18, 1932) and Hungary (February 23, 1932), and the Rome Government believed that an Italo-Austro-Hungarian trade pact was the proper solution, inasmuch as it would help Austria to secure favorable commercial relations without depending too exclusively on German trade. The foundations of such an agreement were laid on the occasion of Dollfuss's visit to Italy, and the Hungarian Prime Minister, General Gyula Gömbös, visited both Italy and Austria. In September,

1933, Italy issued a memorandum on Danubian economic recon-struction with a series of draft bilateral agreements between the Danube states based on preferential tariffs. These were put forward as a basis for discussion between those states and the signatories of the Four-Power Pact. It was hoped that the Little Entente States also would join and that such a plan would en-able Austria to resist German pressure by removing the trade barriers separating Austria from its other neighbors. It was an attempt at a partial economic reconstruction of the old Haps-burg edifice, which, though a hopeless hodge-podge of diverse rival nationalities, was undoubtedly an important and vital economic unit.

Rumors were circulated in June, 1932, that Mussolini was con-templating a political union between Austria and Hungary under a Hapsburg prince. There were, indeed, strong tend-encies in favor of a Hapsburg restoration in both countries, especially in Hungary. But this did not involve a political union between them, and, in any case, such restoration plans were quite independent of Italian action. The Little Entente states were, as I said before, rabidly opposed to a monarchical restora-tion, fearing that it would be followed by demands for the return to Austria and to Hungary of other ex-Hapsburg lands. Their governments actually declared that they would regard a Hapsburg restoration as a *casus belli*.[1]

Early in 1934 the Italian Undersecretary for Foreign Affairs, Fulvio Suvich, visited Vienna and Budapest with a view to promoting a closer economic understanding with the two coun-tries, leaving open the question of coöperation with the ever uncertain Little Entente. Suvich was particularly suited for a mission of this kind, owing to his thorough knowledge of the Danube area, especially in the economic sector—he had been Undersecretary for Finance.[2] In March, 1934, Dollfuss and Gömbös were in Rome, and on the 17th of that month three protocols were signed. The first was a consultative pact, in which the two statesmen and Mussolini declared that they were "ani-mated by the intention to aid the maintenance of peace and the economic restoration of Europe on the basis of respect for the independence and rights of every State." They undertook "to act together on all the problems that particularly interest them and also on those of a general character," with the object of strengthening existing treaties of friendship. "To this end the three governments will proceed to common consultations each time that at least one of them may consider this course opportune." [3]

The second protocol provided for economic relations between the three countries in the spirit of previous arrangements and it stipulated that the new bilateral agreements were to be concluded before May 15th of that year. The third protocol, signed only by Mussolini and Dollfuss, provided for a new Austro-Italian commercial treaty to be concluded before the same date.

These arrangements led to a declaration by the Little Entente states that they were ready to settle the problem of Central Europe on the basis of the existence of an independent Austria, provided that there was no Hapsburg restoration or preponderance of any Great Power, and that there should be coöperation on the basis of existing treaties without any idea of their revision. This, of course, was flatly contrary to one of the chief pillars of Mussolini's conception of foreign policy.

In his speech before the second quinquennial assembly of the Fascist Party on March 18th the Duce stated that Austria could count on Italy to defend its independence, and that his Government would make every effort to improve the conditions of the Austrian people. Alluding to the three protocols, he said that Hungary, deprived of many purely Magyar territories, found in Italy absolutely full comprehension of its problems, and that Hungary asked only for justice and the maintenance of the promises solemnly made to it at the time the treaties were signed.

On May 14th the bilateral treaties between Italy and Austria, Italy and Hungary, and Austria and Hungary were signed.

The political aspect of the Austro-Hungarian agreements were implemented in the latter half of 1934; it was in no way altered by the murder of Dollfuss. On August 20th and 21st the new Austrian Chancellor, Kurt Schuschnigg, met Mussolini in Florence, and the two statesmen were reported to have reached a complete understanding for strengthening Austro-Italian relations in the spirit of the protocols. On November 6th Gömbös again visited Mussolini in Rome, and it was then announced that they had "established the unchanged and perfect community of principles inspiring the two governments, and their intention to continue and develop their collaboration with Austria." [4] That same month, Schuschnigg and his Foreign Minister, Egon von Berger-Waldenegg, visited Rome and an official communiqué stated that the policy of close understanding between Italy and Austria was confirmed. Further, an examination was made of the conditions necessary for enabling Austria, supported by Italy and Hungary, to resume its "true historic function as holding the equilibrium between the forces that converge on the basin of the Danube." [5] It was also announced that the tripartite agreements were open to all other states prepared to accept their fundamental conditions.

We have here a framework within which the Danube states and the Little Entente might have established a really sound basis for peaceful collaboration. If Great Britain and France had given their support, the arrangement would have been definitely consolidated. But that support failed, and at the next Geneva meeting the Little Entente states felt themselves authorized to reject the idea of guaranteeing Austrian independence. Czechoslovakia might perhaps have adhered to the tripartite arrangement, but the terms of the Little Entente statute precluded it from taking such a step independently. Yugoslavia, owing to its recurrent disputes with Italy, refused to agree. Once again, the Little Entente and its leaders proved an insuperable obstacle to any lasting peaceful settlement in Central and Danubian Europe for which the Italian Government had striven so hard.

In the meantime, the internal situation of Yugoslavia had been causing anxiety throughout Europe. In Croatia there was intense and growing hostility to King Alexander's dictatorial regime and his oppression of his non-Serb subjects.[6] Large numbers of Croats had fled abroad and were conspiring against the Belgrade government. Many of them were in Hungary, quartered in various refugee camps, chiefly at Janka Puszta, since 1931; and the Yugoslav Government alleged that they were plotting political outrages to be committed in Yugoslav territory. Others were in Italy, including Ante Pavelich, who was afterwards to become the head of the Croatian government during the second World War.

In October, 1934, King Alexander decided to visit France in the hope of securing French support for his international policy, thereby strengthening his internal situation as well. He was particularly alarmed at the prospect of a Franco-Italian understanding, since it had been arranged that the French Minister of Foreign Affairs, Louis Barthou, was soon to visit Mussolini in Rome. The King landed at Marseilles on October 9th and was murdered that same day by Croat terrorists. Barthou, who accompanied him, was wounded and died from loss of blood, no one having cared for him after he was shot.

The Yugoslav authorities attributed the outrage to the facilities accorded to the Croat revolutionaries in Hungary and Italy, and violent anti-Italian demonstrations broke out in various Yugoslav towns; the Italian press retaliated by publishing bitter attacks on the shortcomings of the Belgrade government. Many Yugoslavs were then so obsessed by bitter hatred of Italy that they actually welcomed German pressure on Austria, and called Hitler's regime "first and foremost a delectable thorn in Italy's flesh." Nevertheless, Mussolini sent a prompt and generously worded message of condolence to the Yugoslav people, and he gave orders that flags on public buildings in Italy should be flown at half-mast.

The Yugoslav Government then dropped its charges against Italy and concentrated them on the Hungarian Government. The dispute was transferred to the League of Nations, but the unanimously voted resolution of the Council exonerated the Hungarian Government from all responsibility, although admitting that some of its local authorities might have been insufficiently vigilant. No charge against Italy materialized; and at the trial in Aix-en-Provence of some of the accomplices in the Marseilles outrage (the actual murderer had been killed by a French policeman immediately after the fatal shot was fired), there was no hint at any responsibility on the part of the Italian authorities. Indeed, the chief responsibility, apart from the actual deed of the Croat terrorists, was the utter inadequacy of the protective measures taken by the French authorities, largely in consequence of the jealousy between the Marseilles police and the Paris *Sûreté*.

Relations between Italy and Yugoslavia continued to oscillate between violent tension and attempts at conciliation. The regency appointed on the death of King Alexander, the heir Michael being a minor, proved more moderate and reasonable than the late regime both in its domestic policy and its international action. The old bitterness against Italy subsided somewhat, largely on account of the improvement in Franco-Italian relations. Yugoslav hostility to Italy usually found widest expression when Belgrade felt that it could count on the support of the Quai d'Orsay.

[1] Toynbee, *op. cit.*, p. 501.

[2] When he first met Hitler the Führer said to him: We are sure to understand each other for we are both bad Austrians."

[3] Toynbee, *op. cit.*, pp. 499-501.

[4] *Ibid.*, p. 505.

[5] *Ibid.*

[6] The eminent American historian, the late Charles Austin Beard, who visited Yugoslavia at the suggestion of an American Yugoslav association, left the country after a short stay because of his disapproval of the persecution of the non-Serb minorities.

PART III

PRELUDE TO EUROPEAN WAR

CHAPTER FIFTEEN

African Prelude

Barthou's visit to Rome had been announced in October, 1934, but the French Foreign Minister himself was, as we have seen, one of the accidental victims of the Marseilles outrage. Conversations in Rome with a member of the French Government were thus adjourned, and a Cabinet crisis in France caused further delay, Gaston Doumergue having resigned the premiership. His successor, Pierre-Etienne Flandin, chose Pierre Laval for the Quai d'Orsay, and the new Foreign Minister was just as eager as his predecessor for a better understanding with Italy. As soon as the internal situation was cleared up, he departed for Rome and met Mussolini on January 5, 1935. At the Palazzo Venezia banquet on that evening Mussolini in welcoming Laval said that his visit was a clear sign of a Franco-Italian *rapprochement*, which both Laval and his predecessor and he, himself, had long ardently desired, "having in view certain common objectives transcending the sphere of Franco-Italian relations and rising to a higher significance in a European sense . . . It is not a question, with regard to Central Europe, of renouncing our respective friendships; we are to harmonize in the Danube basin the vital necessities and interests of individual states with those of a general nature, with a general pacification as our aim."

Laval replied in a similar tone, saying: "You are the head of a great country on which you have been able, with your authority, to confer the finest page in the history of modern Italy. Placing your prestige at the service of Europe, you will give an indispensable contribution to the maintenance of peace . . . Before the vestiges of ancient Rome let us swear not to allow humanity to fall once more into the obscurity that so many past centuries have known." [1]

During the visit an agreement between France and Italy was concluded (January 8th) dealing with Italian policy in East Africa and the position of Italian citizens in Tunisia.

Apart from other questions, Laval's visit cleared the air with reference to Franco-Italian relations in general. Italy obtained for Libya an extension of territory amounting to 114,000 square km. and another for Eritrea of 1,000 square km., but these were vast almost uninhabited sandy wastes of purely geographical import. Italy also secured an interest of 20 per cent in the Jibuti-Addis Ababa railway. On the other hand, Italy agreed to renounce the Italian citizenship of her settlers in Tunisia within 30 years, to allow the Gallicizing of the Italian schools in 20 years and to abandon all general claims over Tunisia.

In view of these important concessions, Laval had given Mussolini, so far as France was concerned, a free hand in Ethiopia, with which Italy's relations at that time had begun to be difficult. At a later date the British Foreign Minister, Anthony Eden, declared that Laval had assured him that he had spoken of "a free hand" only in the economic sphere. Laval, himself, in a letter sometime later, asserted that he had actually used the expression "a free hand" without any qualifications, so that it might be interpreted either in a political or an economic sense. It is not likely that Mussolini would have surrendered the rights of the Tunisian Italians on so large a scale unless he was convinced that he had secured an adequate *quid pro quo*.

Collaboration between France and Italy seemed at last to be assured—"the greatest service rendered to the cause of peace," as the eminent Swiss publicist Paul Gentizon wrote, "since the first World War." [2]

Immediately after the signing of the agreement Mussolini dwelt once more on its importance in a statement to a party of French journalists, ending with the following words: "The crucial year begins under the propitious auspices of the Franco-Italian agreements. Let us now set to work with intelligence and perseverance, so that they may prove to be what the world expects." [3]

Of the two authors of this attempt to settle an ancient quarrel in a real effort at European pacification, one was to die the victim of a foul murder, and the other, already a dying man, before a firing squad. There were—and are—too many men determined at all costs to prevent world peace and to punish as criminals all those who attempt to achieve it.

For the Ethiopian question, which had now come to the fore, we must go back a few years. I have already explained how Italy first attempted to achieve a measure of colonial expansion, imposed on her by the pressure of population. Her first colony, Eritrea, inhabited by tribes of various races, had been for long under a vague Turco-Egyptian suzerainty.[4] After the occupation of Assab and Massaua, Italian forces had begun to penetrate inland and came into conflict with Ethiopia. At Adowa in 1896 an Italian force had been attacked and defeated by Ethiopians four times as numerous. That defeat, followed by unspeakable atrocities committed upon captured Italian soldiers, had always remained a bitter memory for the Italians and had rendered relations with Ethiopia very difficult. In Italy the mass of the people were not yet colonial-minded like the British and the French, and for many years East Africa was almost forgotten, although the small colony remained and was intelligently developed.

Various conventions and protocols were concluded with Ethiopia and also with Great Britain concerning the frontiers of Eritrea. On December 13, 1906, an instrument known as the Tripartite Agreement, signed by Italy, Great Britain and France, reaffirmed the validity of the earlier instruments.[5] The three powers agreed to maintain the existing political and territorial *status quo* in Ethiopia, their various spheres were further defined, and a common line of action was laid down in view of probable changes in the internal situation of Ethiopia. The Lake Tana area was admitted to be within the Italian sphere, although British interests in its waters and in those of the Blue Nile were recognized by Italy, in view of Great Britain's position in Egypt and the Sudan.

Ethiopia did not recognize the validity of the Tripartite Agreement, and this kept open the whole colonial problem, of which that country was the main object. At that time, another agreement was concluded between the three powers for the repression of the arms traffic in the Red Sea area.

After the first World War Great Britain had begun to show signs of attempting political and economic penetration into Ethiopia. One British newspaper started a campaign to demand international action, or possibly British action alone, against Ethiopia to repress slavery which was rampant throughout the country, and it suggested that a mandate be conferred on Great Britain for the purpose.[6] This would have meant a British protectorate, and it was for this reason that in 1923 Italy very imprudently supported Ethiopia's application for admission to the League of Nations. The application encountered opposition in many quarters, but it was eventually granted on the condition that Ethiopia should abolish slavery and respect all international engagements on the control of the arms traffic. It is needless to say that Ethiopia carried out neither of these undertakings.

At the end of 1925 an exchange of notes took place between Great Britain and Italy for coöperation in questions concerning Ethiopia on the basis of the Tripartite Agreement of 1906, and these were communicated to the Addis Ababa Government. The Negus of Ethiopia lodged a protest with the League of Nations, but the Italian Government replied that the exchange of notes was purely a measure of procedure for coördinating the economic interests of Great Britain and Italy, that it could only be put into effect subject to its recognition by the Ethiopian Government, and that the British and Italian interests in question were in conformity with those of Ethiopia. The agreement was registered at the League on July 2, 1926. On September 4th, the Ethiopian Government wrote to the Secretary General of the League re-affirming its own point of view; but after that there were no further reactions in this connection.

On August 2, 1928, Italy concluded a treaty of friendship with

Ethiopia for the duration of 20 years, whereby the two governments undertook to promote reciprocal trade. It was completed
by a convention for the construction of a motor road between
Dessieh in Ethiopia and the Italian Eritrean port of Assab.

The frontiers between the other Italian colony of Somaliland and Ethiopia had never been delimited. An agreement had
been signed on May 16, 1908, which stipulated that "all the
territory belonging to the tribes *toward the coast* will remain
under Italian rule, and all the Ogaden territory and that of the
tribes *toward Ogaden* will remain under Ethiopia." [7] The two
governments undertook (Art. 5) to delimit the frontiers, but
the work did not begin until December, 1910; and even then
the Ethiopian delegates placed every obstacle in the way of the
Italians, so that the delimitation was never completed. At this
time the question was not important, for Italian Somaliland
was not yet fully organized. But, in 1923, the new Governor,
Count Cesare De Vecchi, proceeded to occupy the whole territory of the colony. He established a line of small military posts
along the presumptive frontier to give security to the tribes
under Italian protection against the frequent incursions of Ethiopian raiders, whose object was to carry off natives and enslave
them. These posts also served to protect the springs used by all
the inhabitants of the area, whether they were Italian or Ethiopian subjects, to water their flocks and herds in that very dry
country. One of the posts in question was Wal-Wal, around
which some small forts had been erected.

The raids continued because the internal conditions of
Ethiopia were chaotic, not only along the Somaliland border
but also along that of Eritrea. At the same time in spite of the
provisions of the 1928 treaty every obstacle was raised against
the activities of Italian traders and business men in Ethiopia,
and the building of the Ethiopian sector of the Dessieh-Assab
road was held up.

In November, 1934, large Ethiopian forces suddenly approached the Italian frontier post at Wal-Wal—an area which
had been under Italian rule for many years and to which
Ethiopia had never made any claims at all. About that time,
an Anglo-Ethiopian commission had been engaged in de-
limiting the frontier between Ethiopia and British Somali-

land; and on November 23rd it, too, appeared before Wal-Wal, with an escort of 80 men of the British Somaliland Camel Corps and another much larger force of Ethiopian warriors. The British and the Ethiopian commissioners sent a joint protest to the commander of the Italian frontier area, because they were not allowed to circulate freely "in Ethiopia, in the Wal-Wal area."

A conversation took place between the Italian commander, Captain Roberto Cimmaruta, and the British Commissioner, Lieut.-Colonel Clifford. Cimmaruta protested because the Ethiopian force was commanded by Samantar, a notorious bandit and criminal.[8] The Ethiopians were now strengthened by fresh bands until they were five times as numerous as the Italian force of native troops at Wal-Wal. Colonel Clifford obviously encouraged the aggressive attitude of the Ethiopians, assuring their commander that the territory belonged by right to Ethiopia and giving him to understand that the claims of Ethiopia were supported by the British Government. Addis Ababa was thus led to count on Great Britain; the Negus and his advisers evidently were unfamiliar with the history of the Schleswig-Holstein dispute in 1864.

Clifford, himself, however, now withdrew to Ado, so as to avoid direct responsibility for himself, while leaving his protégés to do what they wished.

On the night of December 4, 1934, the Ethiopians attacked Wal-Wal, but were beaten off after heavy fighting. As the Italians were only one-fifth as numerous as the Ethiopians, it is hardly likely that they would have been the first to attack, as the Addis Ababa Government asserted. Moreover, the only advantage which the Italians had over the Ethiopians was the possession of a couple of aeroplanes, but the attack took place at nightfall when the planes would have been of very little use. Cimmaruta, himself, not expecting the attack at that point, had moved to another post, and the native soldiers, with no Italian officer at Wal-Wal, would certainly not have taken any such initiative.

Protracted negotiations now took place at Addis Ababa, the Italian Government demanding satisfaction for the outrage and compensation for the families of the native soldiers killed in the attack. After various exchanges of notes, it was agreed that the matter should be referred to a committee of arbitration and conciliation.

In the meantime, behind the Italo-Ethiopian dispute British-Italian friction began to loom on the horizon. At first, it seemed limited to the activities of various official, semi-official and unspecified British representatives in Ethiopia, but it soon extended to the Government itself. The Cabinet was beginning to be eager, for electioneering reasons, to secure the support of the League of Nations Union.[9] The publication of the so-called Peace Ballot, got up by this organization, seemed to imply a very strong current of League feeling and of opposition to Italy, which was pictured as a lukewarm believer in League principles. France had up to that moment shown itself favorable to Italian policy, but there was reason to believe that if it were to find itself faced by the alternative of choosing between the sacrifice of British friendship and that of Italy, France would prefer to rely on the British in view of a possible German aggression.

Further frontier incidents occurred in East Africa, and many raids by irregular and even regular Ethiopian forces were made on Italian colonial territory.

The Wal-Wal incident was submitted in May to the League Council, where it was finally decided that the Arbitration Committee should meet in June, first in Milan and then at Scheveningen, Holland. The Italian Government insisted that the Committee's authority and responsibility should be limited to the Wal-Wal incident, whereas the Ethiopian Government demanded that the question of the legal rights to the disputed territory also should be discussed. Italy was quite ready to discuss the latter question—but independently of the Wal-Wal incident.

Ethiopia now began to concentrate ever larger forces on the frontiers of the two Italian colonies and to import quantities of war material, purchased or received gratis from foreign countries. Until February, 1935 (nearly three months after Wal-Wal) the Italian East African colonies had been left almost defenseless save for small native garrisons with a few Italian officers and N.C.O.'s, whereas Ethiopia brought forward a large and well-armed standing army. It was then that Italy began to think of reinforcing its African garrisons with home troops, which required a week's voyage to reach Eritrea and a fortnight to reach Somaliland.

When the possibility of warlike operations in East Africa began to be contemplated, the British Government suggested to that of Italy that it might be imprudent to embark on an African expedition, the presence of its forces in Europe being indispensable for the maintenance of world peace. To this attitude, Mussolini replied indirectly in the Senate on May 14, 1935, saying that if Italy was to be present in Europe and free from all anxiety, "we must have our rear positions completely secure in East Africa." He added that up to that moment more workmen had been sent to the colonies than soldiers.

The Arbitration Committee met for the first time on June 6th in Milan, then at Scheveningen, and finally on August 25th in Paris. It made a trip to Bern to examine Captain Cimmaruta and other witnesses, Italian and Somalis. It consisted of four arbiters, two for Italy and two for Ethiopia, but forming a single unit, plus an Italian and an Ethiopian agent as representatives of the two governments. It is significant that none of the Ethiopian members was a native of that country, one being a Frenchman and the other an American. As the Committee failed to come to an agreement, its members selected a fifth member as super-arbiter, and the choice fell on the Greek Minister in Paris, Nicholas Politis.

Politis declared that he wished to find a solution which would leave no ill feeling behind it on either side, giving satisfaction to Italy without humiliating the Negus, because, if he were humiliated, it would be impossible for Italy to secure such concessions in Ethiopia as would avert war. This was obviously an attempt at squaring the circle and at finding a solution not based on equity. Politis later expressed the view that the best plan would be to confer on Italy a mandate over all Ethiopia, and he undertook to try to induce the Negus himself to accept it. He claimed that Laval was of the opinion, we know not on what grounds, that the British Government would agree to this plan, as the only legitimate British interests in Ethiopia were those concerning the waters of the Blue Nile, which Italy had always been ready to respect. Had all this been true, the Italo-Ethiopian war might have been avoided, but evidently in Politis's mind the wish was father to the thought, without any real foundation in fact.

The League Council had met on July 31st and declared that the Committee was not to consider the question of ownership of the Wal-Wal district, but only the circumstances of the incident, which is what Italy had demanded. The Council invited the Committee to hand in its decision not later than September 4th, when the Council was to meet again to consider the general question of Italo-Ethiopian relations.

After a series of lively debates in Paris, where the Italian delegate, Count Luigi Aldrovandi, had proposed that the Committee should visit Wal-Wal to study the question *in situ*—a proposal flatly rejected by the non-Italian members—on August 31st Politis submitted his final report, which was accepted by the other four arbiters. Politis stated that he was prepared to dismiss all responsibility on the part of the Italians and to declare that the Italian version of the events was probably correct, though that he could not be sure of it. His conclusions were:

1. That no responsibility for the actual fact of the Wal-Wal incident can be attributed to the Italian Government or its agents *in loco;* the charges formulated against them by the Ethiopian Government are contradicted, particularly by the many precautions taken by them to avoid all incidents on the occasion of the concentration of the regular and irregular Ethiopian forces at Wal-Wal, and also by the absence of any interest on the part of the Italians in provoking the conflict of December 5th.

2. That even if the Ethiopian Government also had no interest in provoking this conflict, its local authorities, by their attitude, especially by the concentration and maintenance after the departure of the Anglo-Ethiopian Commission of numerous Ethiopian forces in proximity to the Italian line at Wal-Wal, may have produced the impression that they had aggressive intentions, which might render the Italian version plausible; but it is not proved that they can be regarded as responsible for the actual incident of December 5th.

This decision was neither satisfactory nor consistent. If all Italian responsibility was dismissed, how could there have been none on the part of the Ethiopians?

But the dispute had now gone far beyond Wal-Wal. Relations between Italy and Ethiopia were becoming more tense every day, and some general solution had to be arrived at. The question had been discussed in the Mussolini-Laval conversations in January, 1935, when the French Minister had assured the Duce of France's *désistement* with regard to Italian policy in East Africa. Mussolini, as we have seen, interpreted the word in a general sense, whereas later Laval was said by Eden to have meant it to apply only to economic activities.

As the British Government was beginning to show anxiety about Italy's possible action in East Africa, Mussolini invited it to a frank discussion of the respective interests of the two countries in the African Continent. The Foreign Office replied that, before expressing a definite opinion, it would have to examine the British position and consult its experts. On March 6th an inter-Ministerial Committee to go into the whole question was set up under the chairmanship of Sir John Maffey, Permanent Undersecretary for the Colonies. The Committee concluded its labors on June 18, 1935, but its report was never published. Several months later (February 20, 1936) the Rome *Giornale d'Italia* printed a long summary of it, which it had obtained in some manner not disclosed. Its conclusions were:

1. Italy will certainly do everything within the next few years to insure its control over all Ethiopia, even if for the present it intends to limit its activities to the lowlands bordering on Italian Somaliland.

2. There are no British interests such as to impose on H.M.'s Government resistance to an Italian conquest of Ethiopia. Italian control over that country would in some ways be advantageous to Great Britain (in the matter of security of the frontier districts); in others it would not be advantageous (in the matter of trade). In a general way, it would be indifferent to Great Britain whether Ethiopia remained independent or was absorbed by Italy.

3. From the point of view of imperial defense, an independ-

ent Ethiopia would be preferable, but the threat to British interests seems a distant one, and it would depend only on a British-Italian war, which now seems very unlikely.

4. Britain's chief interest in Ethiopia consists of Lake Tana and the Nile basin. Should Ethiopian independence cease, Great Britain should assume control of Lake Tana and consider connecting it with the Sudan.

5. If the Italians established themselves in Ethiopia, the British Government should take steps to safeguard British interests concerning the other tributaries of the Nile.

6. If the British Government failed to secure control of Lake Tana, it should take measures to safeguard British and Egyptian interests concerning that Lake and to obtain conditions less unfavorable than those stipulated with the Ethiopian Government in regard to the construction of a dam on the lake.

7. All grazing rights beyond the frontiers for the British-protected tribes must be safeguarded, either by annexing the territories in question or by obtaining Italian recognition of grazing rights in the territories, now Ethiopian, which will have become Italian.

8. If Italy absorbed Ethiopia, every effort should be made to make sure that British subjects continue to enjoy equality of treatment in that country by means of an open-door policy.

9. If possible, rectifications of the frontier should be made so as to incorporate in Kenya and the Sudan the places that have an economic affinity with those countries.

The report shows: (1) that an Italian occupation of Ethiopia would, in the opinion of the very competent members of the Committee, be of no serious prejudice to British interests; (2) that any such interests as might require measures to safeguard them concerned countries like the Egyptian Sudan, which Great Britain had seized with no more legal rights than Italy would have in her eventual occupation of Ethiopia; and (3) that in the event of such an occupation Great Britain should take the opportunity of securing more territories and economic advantages for herself. League of Nations principles were evidently not even considered by the authors of the report.

Although this document had been drafted in order to enable the British Government to answer the Italian proposal for a discussion of the interests of the two countries in East Africa, that answer was never given.

During this period Hitler had undertaken the cancellation of the more burdensome limitations imposed on Germany at Versailles. In March, 1935, he re-established compulsory military service and raised the nation's peacetime effectives to 36 divisions. These moves were not wholly approved by Mussolini. Although he had always been favorable to treaty revision, he did not consider that it should be effected unilaterally, and he still believed that Italy, Great Britain and France should collaborate to keep the peace in Europe.

France was eager that a meeting should be held in Italy between French, British and Italian representatives to deal with the situation generally and especially with the German problem. This scheme was discussed in Paris (March 24th) at a preliminary meeting between Laval, the British Minister for League Affairs, Anthony Eden, and the Italian Undersecretary for Foreign Affairs, Fulvio Suvich. From this conversation it was evident that the British Government was trying to avoid a meeting in Italy, so as not to offend the susceptibilities of the Liberal-Labor Opposition, which hated the Fascist regime. But at the same time the British Government sought to contact the even more totalitarian regimes of Germany and Russia, sending the Foreign Secretary, Sir John Simon, to Berlin and Eden to Moscow.

Having failed to arrive at any definite conclusions in either capital, the British Government agreed to the meeting in Italy, which took place at Stresa from April 11th to 14th and was attended by MacDonald, Simon, Flandin, Laval, Mussolini and various officials. From the first moment, MacDonald showed great consideration for Germany; and if Laval appeared more uncompromising, it was only because he hoped thus to arrive at a lasting arrangement with Hitler. Mussolini predicted that the Führer's next move would be the occupation of Austria, and he reminded his hearers of Italy's vigorous action to safeguard Austrian independence after the murder of Dollfuss, an action not supported by the Western powers.

A "Stresa front" was vaguely talked about and Great Britain

and France invited Italy join in a guarantee to keep Germany
in restraint. Yet, at this very same time they were also contemplating sanctions against Italy in regard to the Ethiopian affair.

While agreements were arrived at on various minor matters, nothing was concluded on the main point, a common and
definite line of policy toward possible German aggression.
The British delegates limited themselves to saying "Naughty,
naughty!" to Hitler.

The Ethiopian question, over which British public opinion
and, to some extent, the British Government were getting
excited, was not discussed at all by the delegates. It was only
casually talked about by some of the British and Italian officials.

Two months after Stresa, Great Britain, without consulting
France or Italy, concluded an agreement with Germany author-
izing the Reich to build a fleet including submarines, in flat
violation of the Versailles Treaty. Laval was very indignant with
the British, but the Foreign Office replied that Great Britain
would lend France support in the North Sea provided that
France undertook to support the British position in the Mediterranean—evidently against Italy. Laval brought this out at
the Pétain trial, where he also revealed that in 1934 secret military agreements had been concluded between France and Italy
in case of German aggression.[10]

It was only when the results of the Peace Ballot (a sort of
referendum organized by the British League of Nations Union)
were published and seemed to prove the existence of League
fanaticism in millions of British subjects (including infants,
and lunatics), that the Baldwin Cabinet decided that it must
adopt a 100 percent League policy if it was to win the next
election. No member of the Government seems to have realized
that the ballot was one of the most colossal frauds of modern
times. It is at this moment that the real quarrel between Italy
and Great Britain began, the British Government being convinced that it must uphold League principles at any cost, even
a world war.

In the spring of 1935 it was suggested in certain British
quarters that Italy might be given a position in Ethiopia similar
to that of Great Britain in Egypt. Mussolini replied that this
idea was by no means without merit. Perhaps a solution on that

basis might have been reached at that time, but Stanley Baldwin afterwards repudiated it, fearing that it would prove distasteful to the League of Nations Union. France, too, had suggested an Italian mandate over Ethiopia, and Italy would have considered this favorably before developments had reached a point of too serious tension.

The first definite proposal for a solution was presented on behalf of the British Government by the Minister for League of Nations Affairs in the Baldwin Cabinet, Anthony Eden, who visited Rome in June, 1935. But it was very different from the suggestions and assumptions of the Maffey report. Ethiopia was to give the Ogaden province to Italy, and Great Britain was to compensate Ethiopia by giving it Zeila and a corridor to that port, so that the Negus could have access to the sea.

The proposal did not prove satisfactory to Italy, for it would have provided Ethiopia with ample facilities for the traffic in arms from Europe and slaves from Arabia. These were the only real objects of the Ethiopian demand for access to the sea, its legitimate foreign trade being negligible. It would have opened the door for the direct intervention in Ethiopia of other countries—Russia, for instance. On the other hand, the permanent Ethiopian menace to the security of Italy's existing colonies would have remained unaltered. In exchange Italy would only have secured more waste lands to add to her already superabundant "collection of deserts," as Mussolini called it.

In Great Britain, even this plan was very unfavorably received. The idea of giving away even a small fraction of British territory was regarded by the imperialists[11] as intolerable; and that of making even a minimum concession to Fascist Italy seemed monstrous to Liberals, Laborites and League partisans.

In any case Mussolini rejected the plan as wholly inadequate, and this refusal had a profound effect on Eden, puffed up as he was with the fatuous vanity of a second-rate mind. He was unable to get over the idea that a proposal made by *him* could be turned down, and he never forgave Mussolini or Italy for this snub. Always after that time he devoted his every effort to get condign punishment inflicted on the Italian people and its chief statesman.

While the arbitration procedure was still developing over

Wal-Wal, it was decided at the Geneva Council meeting to summon the representatives of the powers signatory to the Tripartite Agreement of 1906 to meet in Paris and discover some new solution of the whole controversy. Accordingly, Eden for Great Britain, Laval for France and Aloisi for Italy met in the French capital on August 16th-18th, and Eden and Laval submitted another proposal to Aloisi. It, too, proved unacceptable, although it was of some interest, for it implicitly admitted the justice of the Italian view that Ethiopia was incapable of reforming or governing itself. According to the Eden-Laval proposal, Ethiopia should apply to the League of Nations for assistance in developing its own resources and reforming its administration. This aid and guidance were to be collective. Either the League Council would delegate a re-organization mission, the decision to be taken in agreement with the Ethiopian Government, or a treaty between Italy, Great Britain, France and Ethiopia would be concluded and communicated to the Council to supplant the 1906 Agreement. In either case, *all* the activities of the country would be subject to the League Commission, and only in theory would the sovereignty and independence of Ethiopia be respected. Italy's economic interests in the country's resources would be taken into consideration without prejudice to the special rights of Great Britain and France.

This plan again might have served as a basis for discussion and experiment had it been presented two months previously; but in the new political climate it appeared to be merely an attempt to humiliate Italy. Ethiopia's military power must be broken; otherwise it would always be a menace. "League formulae," the Italian reply stated, "throw much dust in Italy's eyes, but they would also leave the integrity of Ethiopia intact and indeed increase her prestige in a sort of quadruple alliance on a footing of equality with Great Britain, France and Italy."

The chief objection to the proposal was the extreme complications it would have created. It would have produced innumerable claims and counter-claims, none of them properly defined, but all calculated to give rise to disputes, divergent interpretations and future conflicts, not only between Italy and the other powers, but between Italy and Ethiopia, which might well exploit them whenever it had disputes with Italy in other fields. Addis Ababa would have become such a hotbed of international intrigues as would have made the Constantinople of the days of the Sultans seem an infant asylum by comparison.

Aloisi was requested to communicate the proposal to Mussolini, but he asked to have the text in writing. The French and British had prepared a note on the subject; but when Aloisi read it, he realized that its terms were even more unfavorable to Italy than those set forth orally. He merely communicated its general principles to Palazzo Chigi, and Mussolini's reply was negative. Laval expressed his regret at the failure of the proposal, adding that while Eden had declared that it was "the extreme limit of British concessions," he himself was sure that it was only a basis for further political concessions to Italy. But Eden's remark showed that he considered Ethiopia a British fief with which he could do what he liked.

We do not know exactly when Mussolini first contemplated drastic operations in East Africa and the occupation of Ethiopia, or a protectorate over it. He does not seem to have thought of it before the Wal-Wal incident, even though in a general way he was always obsessed by the compelling problem of finding some outlet for Italy's superabundant population. A more intensive development of Libya might have been a partial solution, and he did, indeed, undertake a large-scale scheme of that kind, which soon began to convert the North African colony into a prosperous domain. But the danger to the small Italian colonies in East Africa from Ethiopian raids and the possibility of settling a large number of Italians in Ethiopia itself, first through some understanding with the Negus, suggested to his mind the idea of a more drastic solution. Had it not been for the Wal-Wal episode, which convinced him that no satisfactory agreement could be reached with Ethiopia as it then was behaving, relations with that country might have remained peaceful, at least for a very long time.

If the Ethiopian Government had allowed Italian economic activities to develop freely, and if it had appointed a certain number of Italian experts in the various technical public services as it had undertaken to do under the terms of the treaty of 1928, Italian penetration might have developed peacefully without a war and with beneficial results to all concerned.

There were no Ethiopians capable of carrying out important technical work, and foreigners had to be employed. Yet even after the 1928 treaty, when large numbers of European advisers were actually appointed, only one of them (an electrical engineer) was an Italian. An Englishman was selected as adviser for internal administration, one Frenchman for public works, another for archeological research, and a third for foreign affairs (supplanted later by a Swede), another Swede for military affairs, other Frenchmen and Germans for aviation, a Swiss for legal affairs and an American for finance.

But the Wal-Wal episode and other subsequent acts of violence by Ethiopians had brought the relations between the two countries to a state of acute tension, which was rendered more serious by the intervention of the British Government, or at least by its agents, in East Africa who, openly or clandestinely, encouraged resistance to all Italian claims. There can be no doubt that it was these events that gradually brought Mussolini around to the idea of a plan for converting Ethiopia into an Italian colony or protectorate. The direct or indirect responsibility of British action for the events that followed is well established.

It is possible that Mussolini might have secured the results desired by indirect means through a system somewhat like that adopted by Great Britain in Egypt and elsewhere, which, as we have seen, had been suggested. He could have claimed to be acting on behalf of the *real* interests of the natives, camouflaging imperialistic ambitions under the guise of humanitarianism, of the defense of international law and so on. He might also have found plenty of arguments in support of his policy in the League Covenant.[12] Possibly, the methods he followed may have been faulty, too direct, too logical, too outspoken. He never concealed his plans or his policy, and indeed, he did in 1935-1936 only what Great Britain, France, Spain, Portugal, Holland, Belgium, the United States, not to speak of Russia, had done in the past. Moreover, he acted as he did at a time when Italy's need for a population outlet was greater than that of any other country.

Had not Hailé Selassié been encouraged by Great Britain, he might well have come to terms with Italy and secured for himself a position like that of the Khedive of Egypt under Great Britain or of the Bey of Tunis under France. Even now that he has been reinstated on his throne by the Allied armies, he is in the position of a poor relation dependent on the grudging good-will and the skimpy generosity of his British "protectors." He may, indeed, now regret that he did not come to terms with Mussolini when it was still possible. But, of course, all this lies now in the realm of the might-have-been.

The United States Ambassador in Rome, Breckinridge Long, was always very friendly to Italy. In connection with the Ethiopian question, he suggested in a dispatch to Secretary Hull on September 12, 1935, that a settlement might be arrived at if a part of the Ethiopian territory were awarded to Italy. But the idea did not appeal to Hull, and he does not even mention it in his memoirs.[13]

[1] *Scritti e discorsi*, Vol. IX, pp. 157-160.
[2] Paul Gentizon, *Défence de l'Italie*, Lausanne, 1950, p. 128.
[3] *Scritti e discorsi*, Vol. IX, p. 163.
[4] That area had never been under Ethiopian rule.
[5] See Luigi Villari, *I precedenti politici del conflitto*, Rome, 1937.
[6] *The Westminster Gazette*, January 18, 19, 20, 1922.
[7] Villari, *op. cit.*, pp. 67-68.
[8] He was also a fugitive from justice, having committed a murder in Italian territory.
[9] An association for promoting ideas favorable to the League of Nations, having a membership of nearly a million persons of all parties.
[10] This fact was also mentioned in General Roatta's trial in 1948.
[11] The British had not yet adjusted themselves to the loss of India, Ceylon, Burma, etc., which was to take place after the second World War.
[12] That instrument has been compared to the Bible in that you can find almost anything you like in it.
[13] Charles Callan Tansill, *Back Door to War*, Chicago: Regnery, 1952, pp. 193, 199-202, 208.

CHAPTER SIXTEEN

The Ethiopian War

It should be borne in mind that the idea of occupying and colonizing Ethiopia enjoyed very wide popularity in Italy. The compelling need for more land was keenly felt by all classes. It was not mere greed for colonies, but an urgent necessity. Even many of the opponents of the Mussolini regime were less hostile to the Ethiopian enterprise than to any other measure of the Fascist Government.[1] It was well known that the Ethiopian uplands contained far more land than the natives in their primitive conditions could possibly occupy or cultivate. There was, indeed, room for many hundreds of thousands of Italian families in the country without encroaching on the small area farmed by the Ethiopians.

Some months before hostilities broke out, Mussolini delivered one of his basic addresses on foreign affairs in the Chamber of Deputies. After summing up the various agreements recently concluded by his Government and the results of the Stresa conference, he stated that what might happen in East Africa would reveal to Italy who were its real (not its alleged) friends. "The menace to our frontiers in East Africa is not potential, but actual, in proportions which grow more serious every day, and such as to place the Italo-Ethiopian problem in the crudest and most radical terms." The treaty of 1928 had remained a dead letter because in 1929 Ethiopia began to reorganize its army with the help of European instructors, and after 1930 certain European industries had begun to supply it with modern war material on a large scale. "No one," Mussolini concluded, "must hope to make of Ethiopia a new pistol permanently pointed against us,[2] which in case of troubles in Europe would render our position in East Africa untenable. Let everyone realize that when it is a question of the security of our territories and of the lives of our soldiers, we are ready to assume all responsibilities, even the supreme one." [3]

On August 28th the Duce at a Cabinet Council at Bolzano, after the summer maneuvers, sketched out the attitude the Italian delegates were to take up at the League Council meeting in September. They would present the Ethiopian problem "in all its crude reality," submitting a memorandum on the political and diplomatic history of Italo-Ethiopian relations in the past fifty years and on Italy's conventional rights in East Africa. "Great Britain," he once more asserted, "has nothing to fear from what will be Italy's policy toward Ethiopia. . . . Italy has a dispute with that country; she has none and does not wish to have one with Great Britain, with which during the World War and later at Locarno and at Stresa collaboration of undoubted importance for European stability was effected." He then spoke of the possibility that sanctions would be applied against Italy, for they were already in the air. He said that "to talk about sanctions means placing oneself on an inclined plane that may lead to the gravest complications."

The League Council met in Geneva on September 4th, and the Italian delegate, Baron Aloisi, made a speech and submitted the memorandum alluded to by Mussolini at Bolzano. The delegate from Ethiopia, who was not an Ethiopian but a Frenchman, began by attacking not Italy's African policy, but the country's domestic regime, which obviously had nothing to do with the case in dispute.

The Geneva atmosphere was distinctly unfavorable to Italy, owing to the propaganda of the British delegates and officials and also of certain Italian anti-Fascists who had tried to intensify Italy's quarrel with Great Britain in the hope of provoking a British-Italian war and of returning to power in Italy under the protection of British bayonets.[4]

After various discussions, a Committee of Five (Great Britain, France, Spain, Poland and Turkey) was set up to examine the situation, and eventually it submitted a proposal to Aloisi for a settlement. The League would undertake to assist Ethiopia in all branches of the civil service, and the sovereignty of the country would thus be reduced to trifling proportions. But Italy would have no real influence since the consent of the Negus would be necessary for the choice of all foreign advisers, and he could refuse the appointment of any Italian. Ethiopia would thus be recognized as *non compos sui,* but Italy was to have no share in the guardianship. Some very inadequate territorial concessions were offered to Italy, but its economic interests would have no guarantees.

On September 19th Aloisi communicated this plan to Mussolini, saying that the dilemma was: either the League framework, in which British requirements for imperial defense, expansion and security might be conciliated, or determined British opposition to Italy by every means. In his first comment, Aloisi expressed himself as somewhat favorable to this proposal, but in all his subsequent communications he set forth Italy's case with extreme vigor.

Mussolini rejected the plan as inadequate, but he did not break off relations with Ethiopia. He demanded that Ethiopia should be deprived of the many territories recently conquered by force of arms which were inhabited by non-Amharic peoples and treated with great harshness, and that the Ethiopian army be disbanded.

Many of the delegates at Geneva—French, Polish, Turkish, Czechoslovak and Yugoslav—disliked Great Britain's League policy but dared not oppose it, lest they be subjected to retaliatory measures. Anyone who attempted to raise objections was soon brought to heel by the crack of Eden's whip.

In London Grandi conversed with the Foreign Secretary, Sir Samuel Hoare and with Sir Robert G. Vansittart, Permanent Undersecretary for Foreign Affairs, expressing his surprise that, in order to avert a colonial campaign, Great Britain should try to promote a European conflict. Vansittart, like most British

Foreign Office officials, had no real faith in the League, but he repeated Stanley Baldwin's dictum that "the League was the country's sheet anchor." Grandi reported that Hoare, by his speech at the League Assembly, had tried to maneuver the enemies of Fascism at the League into supporting his own anti-Italian policy.

In the meantime, early in September, the British Mediterranean fleet was being reinforced, and on the 19th, part of the Home Fleet was sent to join it, while half of the whole British army was concentrated in Egypt. Subsequently, many pretexts were produced to explain these movements. One of them was that they were intended to counteract the effect of Virginio Gayda's anti-British articles in the *Giornale d'Italia*. Gayda was certainly a brilliant and vigorous journalist, but it seems doubtful whether even his warmest admirers would agree that his articles could be countered only by dispatching a war fleet of 800,000 tons.[5]

The true explanation seems to be, according to a statement made by a British admiral to an Italian naval officer, that the British Ambassador in Rome had sent an alarmist telegram to London to the effect that a prominent Fascist personage (name not given) had told a high official of the South African Government (also anonymous) that Italy was about to attack the British Empire, bomb Malta, invade Egypt and do a lot of other dreadful things. The admiral admitted, indeed, that the fleet movement had been the result of a panic decision. It was not the first time that inaccurate information sent by the British Embassy in Rome contributed to poison British-Italian relations.[6]

Not all British statesmen were of the same idea, and Neville Chamberlain's speech at Floors Castle (Kelso) seemed to indicate that he was opposed to the application of sanctions against Italy.

On September 29th Winston Churchill told Grandi that the situation was due to election anxieties, as the Government, although under Conservative leadership, was a prisoner of the Liberal and Labor Opposition, and that some of its members were alarmed about the safety of the route to India.[7] Grandi's own view was that, while everyone in Great Britain was in favor of collective action and collective responsibility, the British fleet had been sent to the Mediterranean merely to control the enforcement of sanctions against Italy as soon as they should be voted by the League.[8]

At Geneva, Laval assured Aloisi that France would only agree to economic sanctions, but the general impression was that it would be impossible to draw the line between economic and military sanctions.

Long before sanctions were actually decreed, the British Foreign Office had studied the problems to which they would give rise, and the Admiralty had been instructed to prepare the means for enforcing them. Everything was to be in readiness so that the moment the delegates of the member states were jockeyed into decreeing sanctions, the button would be pressed and Italy blockaded. After this happened, it would be easy to concoct a pretext for declaring war against Italy. It was hoped that it would be forced into some action capable of being interpreted as aggression against a League measure, and then France and other powers would be forced into supporting anything Great Britain might decide.

Hoare told Grandi on September 30th that his Government did not want war, but that if the situation continued as it then was, war would be inevitable. The only concession Great Britain was prepared to make was that if Italy withdrew its reinforcements from Libya (they had been sent there *after* large British reinforcements had been sent to Egypt), the British Government would reconsider its decision to send yet *more* divisions to Egypt.

A few days earlier (September 26th) Eden had proposed at Geneva that, although the work of the Assembly was finished, the session should not be closed but merely declared adjourned. Aloisi pointed out that this was a breach of the rules of procedure, but no delegation dared disobey Eden.

Grandi explained to Vansittart the Italian proposal that Ethiopia should be expelled from the League for having defaulted on its undertaking to suppress slavery. Vansittart replied that the Covenant did not provide for the expulsion of a member state. Then Grandi quoted paragraph 4 of Article 16 that "any member of the League which has violated any of the undertakings of the Covenant of the League may be declared to be no longer a member of the League by a vote of the Council concurred in by Representatives of all the other Members of the League represented thereon."

Finally on October 2nd the Italian Government informed that of Great Britain that, in view of the total mobilization of the Ethiopian army, operations were about to commence. Italy, the note declared, was ever ready to demobilize in the Mediterranean, provided that Great Britain did likewise. On the 3rd operations in East Africa began, and from that moment the tension between Great Britain and Italy reached such a pitch that a new world war seemed almost inevitable.

Mussolini still thought that he could count on French support in the Ethiopian conflict. But on October 5th the 52 nations, including France, decided to apply sanctions against Italy. A lively struggle now began in France itself between the wish to support Italy and the fear of losing British support against Germany, a struggle that continued throughout the whole Italo-Ethiopian controversy.

It was decided at Geneva that if Italy rejected the proposals of the Committee of Five and initiated military action, Article 15 of the Covenant should be applied and, subsequently, Article 16 (imposing sanctions). For this purpose, another Committee to enforce sanctions was set up, that of the Thirteen (i.e. all the members of the Council except Italy).

The Council meeting was scheduled for October 3rd, and Laval again assured Aloisi that his Government would refuse to apply military sanctions, but being unable to act independently of Great Britain, it would be forced to apply economic sanctions. He hoped, however, to secure for Italy Ethiopia's "colonies," the territories recently annexed to that state. Laval reported a recent conversation between the President of the French Republic and the Prince of Wales (afterwards King Edward VIII and now Duke of Windsor), who had approved of this plan and had undertaken to talk about it to King George.

At the meeting of the Committee of Thirteen the British and French delegates maintained that Italy's action was flagrant aggression. At the Council, to which the report of the Committee was submitted, no delegate dared to resist British exhortations, although Aloisi pointed out that for years the Italian colonies had been subjected to constant Ethiopian aggression, and that Ethiopia itself was in a state of complete anarchy. The delegate of the Negus accused Italy of violating Articles 12, 13 and 15 of the Covenant and demanded the immediate application of Article 16 against her.

A third Committee of Six was now set up (France, Great Britain, Denmark, Holland, Rumania and Chile), to report on the future communications of the two parties to the conflict.[9]

Aloisi tried to persuade Laval that there had been at least a bilateral breach of the Covenant, but under British pressure the French Minister refused to accept a resolution to that effect.

French public opinion was generally averse to sanctions for economic reasons. Laval made a new attempt at conciliation by proposing a meeting of the powers signatory to the Tripartite Agreement of 1906; but Eden rejected the idea of any conciliatory measure being taken "outside the framework of the League"—because within that body he enjoyed a prestige which he did not have anywhere else.

In her Italophobe policy, Great Britain secured the full support only of Soviet Russia, which hoped to strike down Fascism by means of a war.

The Assembly met again in October, and on the 9th the President (Beneš), in conformity with Eden's orders, asked each delegation to express its approval or disapproval of the Council's decision in favor of sanctions. He did not propose a vote, because the British delegate feared that it might not be unanimous —Austria and Hungary would refuse to vote against Italy; and without unanimity the decision would be valueless. Nevertheless this illegal decision was taken and declared valid. At the meeting on the 11th, Aloisi pointed out that there had been no declaration by a competent League organ that Italy was in the situation contemplated under Article 16. The fact that fourteen states (including Ethiopia which was a party to the conflict) were in agreement on the situation did not, he maintained, pledge the League as a whole. But, again, it proved impossible to induce any of the delegates to resist British threats, blackmail and bribes.

The Assistant Secretary General of the League, Frank Walters, assured the Italian diplomat, Renato Bova-Scoppa, that Great Britain would never agree to territorial concessions for Italy in Northern Ethiopia, but might possibly admit that some be made in the Southeast in exchange for an Ethiopian outlet to the sea.

Grandi reported from London on October 17th that France's attempt at a moderating action had irritated the British Foreign Office, and that even Neville Chamberlain, who was not originally in favor of sanctions, had told a correspondent of the Paris *Soir* that if France failed to support the League (*i.e.* Great Britain), the British Government would consider itself free from the Locarno engagements. Grandi had told Hoare that he was convinced that Great Britain's aim was to make war on Italy and to crush Fascism; and Mussolini said the same thing to the British Ambassador in Rome on the 18th. Although both Hoare and Sir Eric Drummond rejected this view, British action seemed to bear it out.

The League Assembly now decided that the Council should appoint yet another Committee, composed of one delegate for each member of the League (except those of the two parties to the conflict), to coördinate measures for the enforcement of sanctions. The president of the new Committee was to be the Portuguese delegate, Augusto de Vasconcellos, who was a mere tool of British policy. The Committee proceeded to create an executive sub-committee of 18 of its own members, with the same Vasconcellos as chairman. It at once voted that all states should prohibit the export of war materiel to Italy, and on the 14th it formulated financial sanctions, forbade all imports into Italy and certain exports from Italy, and decided to grant assistance to such countries as might suffer loss from the suspension of trade with Italy. Eden's object was to starve the Italian people into submission, by preventing it from securing foodstuffs from abroad and by bringing about national bankruptcy.[10] He was convinced that if a large number of Italian women, children, sick and aged persons were starved to death, Italy would be unable to hold out.[11]

The measures to enable the poorer sanctionist countries to secure help from the richer ones to make good their loss of trade with Italy did not materialize. No claims for compensation were admitted except in one case: Great Britain undertook to buy from Yugoslavia the eggs which the latter would have sold to Italy—and this decision raised a violent outcry on the part of British poultry farmers.

When the Italian communiqué announcing the launching of military operations was issued, Vansittart expressed the hope to Grandi that the action would not go beyond the limits of security or assume such proportions as to preclude a solution on a new basis that the League Council might suggest. To this Grandi very properly replied that it was now solely for the military authorities to decide what measures were necessary to solve the Ethiopian problem in its entirety. "If guns are firing now," he added, "it is the fault of the British Government, which has tried to impose its own solution and prevented a reasonable settlement, even of a League character." He then quoted a passage from Stanley Baldwin's speech at Bournemouth, in which the British Premier had stressed his hostility to dictatorships and Fascism. Vansittart replied that he had not seen that passage in *The Times* or the *Daily Telegraph,* but Grandi showed him the report of the speech containing it in the *Manchester Guardian* and the *Evening News*. It had been deliberately suppressed in other papers. Grandi concluded by stating that Italy was fighting not only for the security of her own colonies, but also for that of other European possessions in Africa, those of Great Britain included.

While the British Parliament and most of the British press were shrieking about the iniquities of Italy and attributing lurid crimes to the Italian troops, a number of distinguished Britons expressed very different views. Among others, Field Marshal Viscount Milne[12] and Lord Lloyd [13] both regretted that Baldwin had rejected Mussolini's proposal for a joint demobilization in the Mediterranean; and the ex-Minister for India, Leopold S. Amery, told Grandi that he would do everything to prevent his country from being drawn into a critical situation with Italy, as Eden was trying to do. A member of the British Cabinet told the Italian Ambassador in confidence that those of his colleagues who like himself were favorable to a policy of neutrality in the Ethiopian conflict had been forced to accept the uncompromising policy of Eden within the Government and of Vansittart outside of it because of the intense pressure brought to bear on them.

Many eminent British authors such as Rudyard Kipling and Bernard Shaw were opposed to sanctions. The very last article that Kipling wrote began with the words: "Sanctions? What nonsense!"

Lord Mottistone (J. E. B. Seely) was also a strong anti-sanctionist, and although Hoare and Lord Stanhope tried to prevent him from speaking against sanctions in the House of Lords, even reminding him of his duties as Privy Councillor, he refused to be intimidated.

On the other hand, in the House of Commons Hugh Molson on October 22nd demanded that the Government should prevent even a drop of water from being sold to Italian troopships passing by Aden.

The City of London was anti-sanctionist, but the financial press was becoming hostile to Italy, owing to the influence of Walter (now Lord) Layton, editor of the *Economist* and an uncompromising partisan of the League.[14]

It is worth recording that the British telephone officials prevented Aloisi from broadcasting to America in favor of the Italian cause as he had been invited to do by the Columbia Broadcasting Company. Grandi protested to Vansittart, who first gave an evasive reply but finally admitted that the order had actually been issued by the Foreign Office. Guglielmo Marconi, the inventor of wireless, was prevented from speaking to America in the same way, but he afterwards succeeded in getting his message through indirectly.

British sanctionist pressure assumed many unexpected forms. For example, the British Minister at Prague threatened Czechoslovakia with reprisals if Dr. Kramarz, a former prime minister, was not forced to suspend his anti-sanctionist articles in the press. J. L. Garvin, editor of the London *Observer,* told Grandi on October 31st that the Government had threatened to hold up the candidacy of the son of Lord Astor (owner of the paper) for Parliament at the coming general election if Garvin's pro-Italian articles were not suspended.

On November 5th Mussolini had another conversation with Drummond, who assured him that Great Britain had no wish to go to war against Italy. The Duce thanked him but remarked that, as long as the Negus was convinced that he was supported by Great Britain, he would never come to terms with Italy. There is, indeed, every reason to believe that he had been prepared to offer a compromise solution but was prevented by British pressure from proposing it.

At the Lord Mayor's banquet a few days later, Hoare stated that the Government's policy would not even change after the elections, and he assured his audience that even the non-League Powers were ready to take part in sanctions. The latter statement, to put it mildly, must be defined as a "terminological inexactitude."

The British elections gave the Government 420 seats—a majority of 250. The support of the Liberals and a part of the Laborites had also been secured by the sanctionist policy.

Sanctions, which had been decided on by the League Council on October 7th, came into force on November 18th. The chief features of the situation were:

1. The intense pressure by the British Government to force all members and non-members to apply sanctions, the attempt to bring the United States into the sanctionist ranks being particularly vigorous, but unsuccessful.

2. A series of attempts by the British Government to get ever more restrictive measures enforced—"another turn of the screw" —was the usual expression in British sanctionist circles.[15]

3. The various degrees of resistance to this pressure by other States.

4. The nature of Italian reprisals.

The day before sanctions came into force the British Government attempted to force non-League countries to issue certificates of origin for all goods exported to Great Britain, so as to be certain that they did not come indirectly from Italy. The demand was, however, rejected by the governments concerned as an intolerable interference in their own affairs; and in the end considerable quantities of Italian goods were actually admitted into Great Britain *via* neutral countries. Cargoes of lemons, for instance, were landed in British ports as coming from Norway or Iceland. On the other hand, on one occasion, 100 Rolls-Royce motors for war aeroplanes were landed at Spezia for the Italian air force.[16] Sometimes, even under sanctions, business is business.

The League Powers other than Great Britain were not at all keen about sanctions and had only agreed to them under intense British threats. In France, Laval continued to maintain his strong opposition to them, although even he did not dare to irritate the British too much. He tried hard to work out some solution which might appear to have a League character, again suggested an Italian mandate over Ethiopia, and made other conciliatory proposals. But he always found the British uncompromising. At a public dinner some years later (June 29, 1939) he said: "It was in order not to break with Great Britain and the League that sanctions were applied. It was in order not to break with Italy and provoke a war, at that time practically certain, that sanctions were applied with moderation." [17]

French public opinion and most of the press were openly anti-sanctionist, and there were violent public demonstrations against sanctions. The British tried to stop the publication of pro-Italian articles in certain French newspapers, such as *Gringoire,* and the British Embassy protested indignantly against Henri Béraud's fiery attacks on British policy.

Officially, the United States did not take a definite stand on the Ethiopian question, but there were a good many opponents of Italy's policy, either inspired by League sympathies or by dislike of Mussolini's domestic policy. Secretary Cordell Hull, for instance, shows himself in his memoirs very critical of Italy's East African adventure, and he says not a word about her claims and grievances. The U.S. Government limited itself to imposing an embargo on the export of arms to both belligerents.[18] But when an oil concession in Ethiopia was granted by the Negus to an American firm (a subsidiary of the Standard Oil), an impression was created that the efforts to prevent Italy from occupying Ethiopia were dictated mainly by the desire to corner possible oil resources. Secretary Hull protested against such activities on the part of the American company, which was compelled to give up the concession. The Negus protested, recognizing that the withdrawal of the company had been due to United States pressure.

In view of the isolationist sentiments of the American people at that time, Hull let it be known that his Government would have nothing to do with sanctions, but he tried to hold up any increase in American exports of oil, copper, steel, scrap iron and motor trucks. In answer to a protest from the Italian Embassy, Hull asked Ambassador Augusto Rosso why Italy had not invested $100,000,000 in Ethiopia instead of waging a war which would cost it a great deal more. Rosso retorted that for forty years his country had attempted to carry out a policy of economic development and agricultural settlement in Ethiopia but with no practical result.[19]

We now come to the most extraordinary episode in the whole Ethiopian conflict—the Hoare-Laval plan.

Italian military operations having begun very successfully, the British Government, while trying desperately to enforce a solution by means of ever more severe sanctions, now had an inkling as to the advisability of trying a more conciliatory settlement in agreement with France, which asked for nothing better. A first proposal was suggested at Geneva by a British Foreign Office official to the Italian diplomat, Renato Bova-Scoppa, whereby some territorial concessions would be granted to Italy in exchange for an Ethiopian outlet to the sea. Italy's repeated military victories had convinced Laval that a solution really acceptable to that country must be found, and he invited Hoare to come over to Paris to discuss the matter with him. Hoare accepted the invitation, for he feared that, if the oil embargo against Italy then being discussed in League circles was applied, it might give Italy an excuse for attacking the British fleet in the Mediterranean. He was also anxious about the increase of the German navy that the British Government had authorized and about the possibility of an Italo-German agreement on Austria and other matters.

The Hoare-Laval meeting took place early in December 1935, to discuss the plan in strict secrecy; but there were soon "leaks" by two left-wing French journalists, *Pertinax*[20] and Geneviève Tabouis, and news also reached *The Times* of London. On December 8th the London *Observer* published a scheme whereby Italy was to receive the non-Amharic ("colonial") territories of Ethiopia, which Mussolini had claimed previously, a plan alleged to have the support of the British

Colonial Office, always less anti-Italian than the Foreign Office. But in League circles the mere suggestion of a conciliatory solution still aroused outbursts of hysterical indignation.

It was not known at the time that before leaving London Hoare had instructed Rex Leeper, of the Foreign Office Press Section, to prepare public opinion for lifting the sanctions. Leeper replied that this would require a month's work, but Hoare insisted that it must be done before the Geneva Council meeting scheduled for December 12th.

The plan arranged by Hoare and Laval was communicated to Mussolini by the British and French ambassadors in Rome, with the request that he should declare as soon as possible whether he was prepared to negotiate on that basis. The joint note proves that the plan was the proposal not merely of Hoare and Laval personally, but of the British and French governments. The idea was that Eastern Tigrai and other territories be ceded to Italy and that Ethiopia be given an outlet to the sea at Assab in Eritrea. In Northern Ethiopia, Italy then would have an area assigned to it for economic development and colonial settlement, but operating under a League scheme of assistance in which Italy would have a predominant but not exclusive share.

The plan was obviously very complicated and offered infinite possibilities for intrigue and disputes. But it was an improvement over all previous proposals, and it might have served as a basis for discussion, as the Italian Government admitted. In any case, it completely upset the League thesis, for, by admitting Italy's right even to a square mile of Ethiopian territory, it wiped out the charge of Italian aggression and violation of League pledges.

The Addis Ababa Government, to which the plan had been communicated, protested indignantly and demanded that the League Assembly be summoned to discuss it.

In the British House of Commons, as soon as some members got wind of the plan, there was an outburst of virtuous indignation. The horrified members of the League of Nations Union rose up in arms, and the Government was much perturbed and frightened. Baldwin did not wish to assume responsibility for rejecting the plan himself, as it was the joint proposal of his whole Cabinet, but he hoped that the League Council would reject it and save him from making himself ridiculous. In the meantime, the British Minister in Addis Ababa, Sir Sydney Barton, encouraged the Negus to reject the plan.

In France, in Government circles and in the country generally, it was hoped that the plan would be accepted. In some other countries, it was regarded with curiosity and with the hope that something might come of it to ease the general tension. In the United States, Secretary Cordell Hull was definitely opposed to it but took no action.[21]

In Rome, Mussolini studied the plan very carefully but would make no decision until he had consulted the Grand Council, which was to meet on December 18th, as that body had by law to be consulted on all questions affecting Italian territorial possessions.

The full text, published on December 13th, increased the indignation of British Liberal, Labor and some Conservative circles. A delegation of the League of Nations Union called on Baldwin to protest against the plan.

At Geneva the delegates of the smaller powers expressed strong disapproval, but for a different reason. After having been bullied and threatened into sacrificing their interests to suit a purely British policy, they were being let down by the British Government now that it suited its own interests to come to a settlement with Italy.

On the 19th Hoare issued a detailed defense of his action, and Clement Attlee, leader of the Opposition, inveighed against the plan as "a concession to the aggressor." Baldwin, fearing for his majority (which was in no danger whatever) and with a hypocrisy rare even in the politics of Great Britain, now said that he "had never really liked the plan," that on that fatal Sunday it had not been possible for the Foreign Office to communicate with Paris (though there was a quite efficient London-Paris telephone service), and that the outcry against the plan had greatly impressed him. The plan, he said, must be regarded as dead and buried. All this was typical of Baldwin: while posing as the plain, honest, simple English business man who knew hardly anything about politics, he was really a crafty politician who thought of little except manipulating votes and concocting clever intrigues. Hoare then felt obliged to resign from the Foreign Office, and the war-mongering Eden was appointed to succeed him. Hoare, who had on the whole been right, was thus forced to go; but Baldwin, who had been wrong, remained, and Eden, who had been still more wrong, came in.

Subsequently, an excuse for the British withdrawal of the plan was based on a speech by Mussolini at Pontinia, and this was the explanation given to me by a member of the British Embassy in Rome. All that Mussolini had said on that occasion was that "we shall not send the flower of our manhood to distant lands if we are not sure that they will be protected by the Tricolor." But Baldwin had anounced his intention of withdrawing the plan (which he "had never liked") on the same day and at the very hour that Mussolini had delivered the Pontinia speech.

The real explanation was that Baldwin feared that a considerable section of his own very large majority might go over to the Opposition, and that he might be forced to resign by a hostile vote—in his eyes a far worse calamity than a world war.

Hoare was an honest, well-intentioned and not unintelligent statesman, but somewhat weak and vacillating. The manner in which he anounced his resignation was dignified; not so was his defense of his action in the House of Commons or his letter to his constituents.

Instead of defending the plan, which was originally that of all the members of the two governments, he seemed eager to prove that it only offered "a very small concession to the aggressor." The late Sir Arnold Wilson, in talking to me about Sir Samuel Hoare, said that he seemed to have been descended from several generations of maiden aunts.

The United States did not take a definite line on the Ethiopian war. But on January 5, 1936, President Roosevelt told Congress that Italy and the other have-not Powers had failed to demonstrate "the patience necessary to attain reasonable and legitimate objects by peaceful negotiations or by an appeal to the finer instincts of world justice," and he somewhat sanctimoniously contrasted these grasping nations with peaceful and moral America. This statement provoked a sharp rejoinder from Mussolini.

Although the United States Government did impose certain partial restrictions on trade with Italy, in spite of Ambassador Long's remonstrances and the appeals to the Italo-Americans, the Government resisted the very intense British pressure and refused to take any part in sanctions.[22]

For some time there were no further attempts at a settlement, but there was no tightening up of sanctions such as Eden wished. Laval told Cerruti, the Italian Ambassador in Paris, that decisive Italian military success would be the best help toward a solution. But his own position was now compromised and his resignation imminent. On the eve of retirement, he wrote a letter to Mussolini saying that when (January 1935) he had spoken of a free hand for Italy in East Africa, he meant it only with regard to economic predominance, although this would really have signified in the long run complete Italian domination in every field. The British Secret Service in the meantime had been conducting an active clandestine campaign to get Laval ousted, and it had actually reached the point, as one of the French delegates at Geneva told an Italian colleague, of bribing certain French deputies. The game succeeded, Laval fell, and a *Front populaire* Government, hostile to Italy, came into power.

Italy's victorious progress led, however, as Laval had expected, to a new suggestion for a conciliatory solution. But at a meeting of the Committee of Eighteen on March 2nd Eden, to everyone's surprise, stated that his Government favored an embargo on oil against Italy, provided that all other countries adhered to it.[23] The new French Premier, Flandin, although less friendly to Italy than Laval, succeeded in avoiding an increase in the tension by proposing that the Committee of Thirteen be summoned to seek a new solution. The Thirteen did meet soon after and voted a resolution inviting both belligerents to institute negotiations "within the framework of the League and in the spirit of the Covenant." The Negus's acceptance arrived on the 5th and that of Italy on the 7th. This greatly upset the British sanctioneers, but other delegates intervened to seek a way out. The Spanish representative, Salvador de Madariaga, tried to act as an intermediary; but after various discussions Eden proposed on April 7th that if hostilities were not suspended at once, the Eighteen should be summoned again to intensify sanctions (another "turn of the screw").

An unexpected move was made by the delegate for Ecuador, Gonzalo Zaldumbide, who on that same day announced to the League Council that he had been instructed by his Government to declare that the continuance of sanctions was a menace to world peace, and that other means must be found to secure it. This was the first open challenge, presented by a small South American state, which thus gave a lesson to all other countries and an answer to Eden's bullying—the first sign that the sanctionist front was beginning to crack.

Eden now tried another tack; he accused Italy of having used poison gas in the Ethiopian campaign. Thereupon, it was decided, at Madariaga's suggestion, that a committee of three jurists be appointed to prepare a report on all the violations of the accepted laws of war by both belligerents that would be submitted to the Thirteen, who would study the procedure for a future inquiry. Italy had, in fact, often called the attention of the League to many such violations attributed to the Ethiopians. The League Secretary-General then asked the International Red Cross to supply him with all the information in its possession on that subject, but his request was rejected. Aloisi announced that Italy had used gas only in very few cases, that it had done so chiefly to block certain roads and to prevent their use by the enemy, and that in any case this had only been done several months *after* his Government had submitted a detailed report on the atrocities committed by the Ethiopians (the use of explosive and expanding bullets, etc.)—a report of which not the slightest notice had been taken.

Some officials of the League Secretariat in conversation with the Italians now reverted to the old proposal that Italy be granted in Ethiopia a position similar to that of Great Britain in Egypt —which, incidentally, was quite illegitimate from the point of view of international law. In any case, it was rather late in the day for such a suggestion.

On May 2nd, after an uninterrupted series of Italian victories, a solution was hastened by the sudden flight of the Negus for Palestine. He announced his intention of proceeding thence to

London at the invitation of various British associations. Even
then, it seems that he actually wished to come to terms with
Italy, which would certainly have treated him very generously
as a gallant defeated enemy; but the British authorities had
spirited him away to keep him in cold storage for future use.
There was nothing that was less desirable from a British-Eden
point of view than an agreement between Fascist Italy and
Hailé Selassié.

The Italian forces, after overcoming the last enemy resistance, reached Addis Ababa on May 5th. The news came as an
astounding surprise to many millions of newspaper readers in
Great Britain, who had been repeatedly assured for many
months by correspondents telegraphing from Ethiopia (or
from Khartoum or Cairo or Baghdad or Antofagasta) that the
Italians were being held up, that they were dying from disease
like flies, that they were being defeated, and that they were in
headlong flight.

On the 7th Mussolini, interviewed by the British journalist,
Ward Price (representing the Rothermere Press, which had
always supported the Italian cause), said that the League of
Nations must continue to exist, should not be entrusted with
tasks beyond its power, and should be made to operate in a
different spirit so far as concerned the needs and the position
of the peoples of Europe; and that his own policy was never
intended to cause prejudice to the interests of the British Empire.

On May 9th Mussolini announced the annexation of Ethiopia to Italy with King Victor Emmanuel III as Emperor.

A new series of debates now started at Geneva, where Eden
still rejected any idea of lifting sanctions. But in Great Britain
an ever-increasing number of political leaders declared themselves opposed to their maintenance. Baldwin, who always
sensed which way the political wind was blowing, admitted
the failure of collective security, attributing it to the absence
from the League of the United States, Germany, and Japan.

On May 28th even Eden was beginning to change his views.
He admitted that Mussolini's conciliatory attitude had in-
fluenced the dissension already manifest in Italo-British relations. His own Government, he now said, wished to eliminate

the crisis between Italy and the League. But the question now was whether the League could find a way out that would permit a formal if not an honorable liquidation of the past without compromising its existence. Eden ended by confessing —rather late in the day—that the sanctions experiment had failed signally, and that Italian collaboration was more than ever necessary for the system of collective security in Europe.

In London Vansittart told Grandi that sanctions must be lifted, that the League had proved entirely wrong about Italy, that its face must be saved—and that of Great Britain, too. Sanctions had failed, he finally admitted, because no power except Great Britain was really keen for them.

Count Galeazzo Ciano, Mussolini's son-in-law, who had been Undersecretary for Propaganda since 1934 and Minister in that same Department since 1935, was appointed Minister of Foreign Affairs immediately after the end of the war, on June 9, 1936, a post held until then by Mussolini himself. The choice was variously appraised, for although he was a man of undoubted abilities and a diplomat of experience, Ciano was regarded as too young for so responsible a position, and he had made himself unpopular in many quarters because of certain defects of character.

While the lifting of sanctions was now admitted to be imminent, another difficulty arose over the international recognition of the Italian Empire in Ethiopia. On June 16th Drummond assured Ciano that while the sanctions question was practically settled, recognition could not yet be admitted, and the same opposition arose on the part of some other countries.

The League Council met on June 28th and the Assembly on the 30th. The gathering was now attended by the Negus, where his presence gave rise to much excitement. After some wrangling and bitter disputes, on July 15th a resolution was voted for lifting sanctions, but the Ethiopian proposal that no annexation obtained by force should be recognized was not even put to the vote. The Ethiopian request for a loan of £10,-000,000 was rejected by 23 votes and 23 abstentions, with only one vote in favor of it—that of the Ethiopian delegate.

The application to Ethiopia of the same trickery as had been applied to Italy in October, 1935, provided the measure of the meanness and immorality of League methods. The President (the Belgian Paul van Zeeland) interpreted the Assembly's silence as consent to his thesis that the first Ethiopian resolution should not be put to the vote, just as President Beneš had interpreted in a sense hostile to Italy the silence of the Assembly the previous year.

Thus ended one of the most deplorable episodes in politico-diplomatic history: the unsuccessful attempt to starve a civilized nation of 40,000,000 people into surrender.

However we may judge Italy's policy in conquering Ethiopia, it will be admitted that in the few years during which it ruled the country, Ethiopia reached a higher level of civilization and prosperity than it had ever enjoyed before. Slavery was definitely abolished; roads, bridges, schools, hospitals, churches, public buildings, hotels arose rapidly everywhere; the old towns were transformed beyond all recognition, and new ones were built; law and order were established; many forms of welfare work were instituted; diseases formerly prevalent, such as leprosy, were attacked with success; agriculture improved to a remarkable extent; and new industries were set up. Scores of thousands of Italian farmers and industrial workers were settled in the country without in any way interfering with the rights of the natives, whose own conditions were actually improved in every way. At the same time, an efficient and thoroughly honest civil service—another startling novelty for Ethiopia—was instituted and had begun to function satisfactorily.

In one part of Ethiopia soon after the occupation an uprising broke out among the Amharic tribes that had previously dominated the whole country, but it was quickly quelled with little difficulty and small loss of life. The attempt on the life of the new Viceroy, Field Marshal Rodolfo Graziani (he had succeeded Marshal Badoglio), who had conquered Ethiopia from the South,[24] was the work of a handful of fanatical plotters, actually inspired by persons and organizations not indigenous to Ethiopia. Graziani was seriously wounded, and he resigned his appointment in 1937. He was succeeded by H.R.H. the Duke of Aosta. These were the only disturbances between May

9, 1936, and the occupation of Ethiopia by Allied forces during the second World War and the consequent re-instatement of Hailé Selassié under British tutelage.

The conquest of Ethiopia had solved to a large extent Italy's population problem, for the country now had room for many hundreds of thousand of families, and its agricultural possibilities and its mineral wealth would have supplied Italy with much of what she lacked; and Italian occupation would have increased the productive area for the world at large which had so pressing a need for increased output.

Mussolini should, perhaps, have considered all these advantages more thoroughly before he allowed himself to be involved with Hitler and the latter's rash diplomacy of 1938-1939, however much incitement was provided by the hostile attitudes of Britain, France and the Little Entente. The economic opportunities provided by Ethiopia probably were of greater moment than any military and diplomatic alliance with Germany, especially as the latter ultimately proved fatal to Mussolini and devastating to Italy. It can be said in extenuation that, at the time of the signing of the Rome-Berlin Axis (November, 1937), Mussolini could hardly have foreseen the rash and impetuous action of Hitler in 1939 that later involved Italy in a ruinous war.

The Western coalition since 1945 has succeeded in the task of holding up all progress in Ethiopia. Since the departure of the Italians, the country has reverted to its former primitive conditions, and the Negus himself appears to be anything but satisfied with his position as a satellite of Great Britain. It has been ironically said that the British brought Hailé Selassié back to Addis Ababa in order to bring the Russians into Berlin, Vienna and Port Arthur. Let us hope they are pleased at the result.[25]

[1] Ex-Premier, Vittorio Emanuele Orlando, and the Socialist deputy, Arturo Labriola, wrote to Mussolini in support of his Ethiopian policy, as did many other former opponents.

[2] This was an allusion to the assertion of a French politician after the occupation of Tunis that "Bizerta was a pistol pointed at Italy."

[3] *Scritti e discorsi,* Vol. IX, pp. 191-193.

[4] The attitude of these men is reminiscent of that of the defeated factions of the Italian city republics of the Middle Ages, ever ready to call in foreign

arms to get reinstated, of the advocates of the Neapolitan Bourbons after 1860, and of those of the Temporal Power of the Papacy after 1870.

[5] Gayda was killed in an air raid on Rome.

[6] This did not happen when Sir Ronald Graham was Ambassador.

[7] The route to India was regarded by many Britons as sacrosanct.

[8] A high official of the British Foreign Office admitted to me that nobody really understood the meaning or implications of collective responsibility or collective security.

[9] The Chilean delegate never took part in its labors, but it continued to be called the Committee of Six to distinguish it from the Committee of Five.

[10] I say Eden deliberately, for he was absolute master at Geneva.

[11] His attitude is reminiscent of that of the Inquisition which shrank from shedding blood but did not hesitate to hand heretics over to the secular arm to be burned to death.

[12] Formerly General Sir George Milne, commander-in-chief of the British army at Salonica.

[13] Formerly British High Commissioner in Egypt.

[14] In the British press, the *Morning Post* and the *Observer*, the Rothermere and Beaverbrook papers, were anti-sanctionist and friendly to Italy.

[15] Another reminiscence of Inquisitorial methods.

[16] This statement was made to me by an Italian naval officer who saw the motors being landed.

[17] Gentizon, *Défence de l'Italie*, 147.

[18] Cordell Hull, *Memoirs*, New York: Macmillan, 2 vols., 1948, Vol. I, p. 425.

[19] *Ibid.*, p. 432.

[20] Henri Géraud.

[21] Hull, *op. cit.*, p. 445.

[22] Tansill, *op. cit.*, pp. 231, 236, 240.

[23] The chief exporter of oil was the United States. Its government refused to take part in the sanctions policy.

[24] Marshal Badoglio had conquered from the North and had been named Viceroy for a very short time.

[25] Much of the material in this chapter is taken from my book, *Storia diplomatica del conflitto italo-etiopico*, Bologna: Zanichelli, 1943, which is based on the official documents and reports which I was able to consult.

CHAPTER SEVENTEEN

The Spanish Civil War

The many revolutions and pronunciamentos that have broken out in Spain during the last 130 years have been almost exclusively internal disturbances. But the rising of the Nationalist forces against the Republican Government in 1936 at once assumed an international character, affecting all Europe and even to some extent the United States. It all but brought about another general European war.

After the fall of the Monarchy in 1931 Spain had been again a prey to endemic agitation, often breaking out into anarchy accompanied by arson and murder. At the election of February, 1936, although a majority of votes had been cast for the Centre and Rightist parties, the Leftists, owing to the peculiarities of the Spanish electoral system, as well as to many acts of violence, terrorism and manipulation of votes, secured a small majority in the Cortes, and a "Popular Front" Government was set up with strongly marked Socialist and Communist tendencies. Murders of political opponents and acts of incendiarism increased to an alarming degree, including the burning of churches and convents and the raping of nuns.

A wholesale massacre of the opponents of the Republican regime was planned for May 1st but was later postponed.

Immediately after the election, a number of Russian experts in revolution flocked into the country, and whole shiploads of Russian war materiel were landed at the Spanish ports. Russia's aim was to set up a Communist base in Spain with which to operate against other European countries; Lenin himself had stated many years previously that, second only to Russia, Spain offered the most promising possibilities for a Communist revolution. Russian officers and N.C.O.'s also began to arrive, and further aid from the Leftist parties in France and other countries was forthcoming in ever-increasing quantities.

The anti-Republican National parties now began to plan a counter-offensive, and an uprising was scheduled for the late summer or early autumn. But the outbreak was precipitated by the murder on July 15th by policemen of the Red Government of Calvo Sotelo, a prominent Rightist member of the Cortes.

The National uprising began in Morocco. General Francisco Franco had arrived there from the Canaries, where he had been virtually exiled by the Madrid Government. While preparing to cross over to Spain he sent a mission to Mussolini to ask for assistance, knowing that the imminent setting up of a Communist outpost in the Western Mediterranean would gravely endanger Italy's position. The mission consisted of: the journalist, Luis Bolin, who had arranged the flight of Franco from the Canaries with the help of English friends; Saenz Rodriguez, the jurist of the Nationalist movement; and the diplomat, Federico Urrutia. Although they were unable to see Mussolini, they were received by Count Ciano. At first, no Italian assistance was forthcoming, except for a few volunteer airmen with five small planes that conveyed a handful of Franco's men across the Straits.

Once in Spain, Franco found support in the majority of the army and of the population in general, which was suffering under the oppression of Republican tyranny. The rapid advance northwards easily overcame such resistance as was offered. But on approaching Madrid, the Nationalists found themselves opposed not only by the Republican militia, with its improvised and incompetent officers, many of them keener on shooting unarmed citizens and on plunder, than on real fighting, but by large and ever-increasing foreign forces imported from France, under officers with World War experience and armed by the French authorities and by Russia. These men constituted the International Brigades, and it was mainly they who held up Franco's Nationalist army.

Day by day more men, guns, tanks and planes poured into Spain over the French frontiers or were landed in the Catalonian ports. The French *Front populaire* Government aided and abetted that of the Spanish *Frente popular* in every way. Committees were set up in France to organize help for Republican Spain from various countries, but it was Russia that maneuvered most of the international action. The Kremlin sent to Paris another expert in revolutions, one Piatnitzki, who had prepared the Communist risings in Estonia, Shanghai, Indo-China and elsewhere. He appointed a liaison committee between the Comintern, the Profintern (the union of international radical syndicates) and the Amsterdam International, and set to work to ensure coöperation between these various bodies for carrying on the Spanish War. The Committee met for the first time on August 25th to establish contact with the Madrid Government,[1] and the Russian Ambassador in that city, Rosenberg, was admitted to the meetings of the Cabinet and helped to shape its policy.

On August 3, 1936, the French Minister of Foreign Affairs, Yvon Delbos, proposed to the British, Italian, German, Russian and Portuguese Governments the formation of an international non-intervention agreement with regard to the Spanish War, whereby all should undertake to abstain from sending war materiel to either side in Spain. When (August 10th) the French Ambassador in Rome communicated the proposal to Ciano, the Italian Minister submitted to him a counter-proposal of a broader scope, extending the prohibition to raising money by public subscriptions, propaganda, and recruiting volunteers for either side. Ciano also showed the Ambassador documentary evidence proving the vast amount of French assistance given to the Spanish Reds. The German and Portuguese governments adhered to the Italian plan, but Great Britain and France re- fused to go beyond Delbos's proposal, saying that, as their governments were pure democracies, they could not possibly prevent their own citizens from volunteering or otherwise aiding the Spanish Republicans.

A Non-Intervention Commission was set up. It met for the first time in London on September 9th. Nevertheless, foreign help to Republican Spain continued unabated and in ever-increasing proportions. It was evident that world Communism, assisted by Socialists, Freemasons and other seditious organizations, was preparing a gigantic mobilization to insure Red predominance in Spain. For this reason Mussolini finally decided to lend Italian assistance to the Spanish Nationalist cause.

In the second half of December, 1936, the first detachment of Italian volunteers (ex-service men and Blackshirts), 3,000 strong, landed at Cadiz. They were at first brigaded with Spanish units, but when more men arrived, some wholly Italian units were formed. In February, 1937, there was one Italian division of three brigades and some smaller units in the mixed Italo-Spanish brigades. Eventually, the total number of Italians fighting in Franco's ranks under the command of generals and officers belonging to the Italian regular army reached 50,000 or 60,000. The first Italian commander-in-chief was General Roatta, succeeded later by General Gambara. The capture of Malaga, Santander and Bilbao, as well as many other important successes, were due to the Italian troops. The Italian air force proved of great value; by June, 1937, it had brought down some 300 Republican planes.

In addition to the Italians with Franco's forces there were some 10,000 Germans, mostly airmen, gunners, sappers and other specialists; a small number of Irish Catholics under General O'Duffy; and some British and other foreigners.

Mussolini's action in Spain was no doubt illegal from the point of view of international law. But it was the answer to the equally illegal actions committed by other countries. The chief difference between the two illegalities is that Mussolini acted openly, employing regular troops as well as volunteers, whereas the governments of other countries (except, of course, Russia) tried to cover up their tracks and pretended that they were doing nothing of the kind.

The foreigners on the Republican side consisted chiefly of French and Russians, but there were also Czechoslovaks, British, Americans, Swiss, Belgians, Mexicans, and some Italian anti-Fascists and German anti-Nazis. Their total number is difficult to establish, because the Republican authorities deprived all foreign volunteers of their passports and often conferred temporary Spanish citizenship on them. These passports proved very useful to the Communist cause; whenever a foreign fighter was killed, his passport was sent to Moscow, where a special office manipulated it and converted it to the use of some other person to be sent abroad on a Soviet secret mission. Evidence of this fact came out at the trial in Mexico City of Trotsky's murderer, who had obtained his passport in that way.

Of the foreign war materiel sent to the Republicans, the following may be mentioned: Schneider-Creusot batteries of '75's, Russian batteries of '124's, 1,214 aeroplanes from both countries from July, 1936, to August, 1937, including French Potez bombers of the latest type, 76 Dewoitine chasers, 35 Block bombers, 27 S.P.A.D.'s, 21 Nieuport chasers from the French national workshops, 237 Rata and Moskva monoplanes, Chatos biplanes and 232 Katushka and Natasha bombers from Russia.

The strong influence of Russia in Republican Spain, either directly or through her branch house in France (the French Communist Party), continued to the end of the war.

Various differences between the two foreign groups should be borne in mind. The Italians were valuable allies, but they represented only a small percentage of the total Nationalist forces; and if they included veteran officers, the number of excellent Spanish officers was far larger. On the other side, the foreigners constituted the backbone of the army and contributed most of the well-trained officers. Without this aid, the Republicans might have crumpled up in a few weeks.

Owing to the large quantities of war materiel sent to Spain by sea on ships flying many flags, it was natural that the few submarines available were used to prevent these vessels from reaching their destination, and not a few of them were sunk or damaged. The British press was constantly claiming that *all* the submarines on the Nationalist side were Italian, whatever flag they might be flying, although it was admitted that evidence on this matter was very hard to come by, and usually there was no evidence at all. What was much more doubtful was the nationality of the allegedly British merchant ships engaged in this traffic. The great majority of them belonged to Greek, Levantine, Jewish and other non-British owners, and their crews were of many nationalities, very few of the men being British. The owners mainly aimed at pocketing huge profits by selling supplies to the belligerents, and in many cases they actually had their heavily over-insured ships sunk.

At the instance of Eden an international conference was summoned at Nyon to deal with what he called "Italian piracy." The conference, attended by British, French, Italian and Russian delegates, met, but no evidence of the kind desired was forthcoming.

On March 24, 1937, Great Britain proposed an armistice in Spain to enable the foreign volunteers to be withdrawn from both sides, in conformity with the recommendations of the Non-Intervention Commission. The Nationalists at once accepted the proposal, but the Republicans rejected it, and the New York *Times* explained this refusal on the ground that the Republicans were then on the point of victory. The proposal thus fell through.

One of the charges against Mussolini's policy in Spain was that he never intended that the Italian forces should leave Spain at all, and that the Balearic Islands, Spanish Morocco and other places were to be permanently occupied by Italy. That he had no intention of the kind is proved by the rapid withdrawal of the Italian volunteers as soon as a decision to that effect had been taken by the Non-Intervention Commission. In that body when there was a discussion as to the best means for transporting the Italians from the interior to the ports, a British official informed his Italian opposite number that a quantity of suitcases had been secured for them, and he inquired if they would like porridge to be supplied for their breakfasts *en route*. The Italian officer replied by showing his British colleague a telegram just received announcing that the Italian volunteers from Spain had already reached Naples on Italian ships.[2]

After the war was ended, the Spanish Minister of Foreign Affairs, Ramón Serrano Suñer, stated at a banquet given in his honor in Rome that the only Italian soldiers left in Spain were the thousands who had fallen in action for the common cause.

The anti-Italian propaganda throughout the war in many foreign countries (particularly Anglo-Saxon) had been extensive and had reached an amazing degree of violence. The well-known British journalist, Sisley Huddleston, in his volume of reminiscences, *In My Time,* wrote that he was never so ashamed of his profession as on the occasion of the Spanish Civil War. Among other things, the Italians were called both (a) indispensable for the success of Franco's cause and (b) cowards who were defeated in every battle and hated by the Spaniards. Coherence and consistency are not necessary in propaganda. In order to horrify newspaper readers, it was constantly claimed that the Italian and German planes habitually bombed defenseless cities to terrorize the inhabitants, aiming particularly at women and children.[3]

One story refers to the operations on the Basque front (spring of 1937) in which the Italians played an important part. On April 30th the 2nd Italian Mixed Brigade (Italian and Spanish) known as the Black Arrows, was attacked by a Republican force six times more numerous. The Black Arrows not only held their ground but drove off the assailants with heavy loss, giving other Nationalist forces time to push ahead. The Black Arrows then seized further positions which were to lead to the capture of Bilbao on June 10th. But a part of the British press concocted a story of how a large Italian force had been put to flight by a far inferior Republican contingent, adding that a number of Italian legionaries had been thrown into the sea by Basque fishwives.

Another story is worth recording. While the Non-Intervention Commission was discussing the means of withdrawing foreign forces from both sides, a report emanating from the British Foreign Office went the rounds of the press in October, 1937, to the effect that 6,000 more Italian soldiers, fully armed and equipped, had just landed at Cadiz. For this statement there was the following explanation: a party had landed at Cadiz from Italian ships, but it consisted of only a few hundred; they were not Italians, nor even armed—they were Spanish children who were returning home after enjoying the hospitality of holiday camps in Italy.

On February 27, 1939, the British Labor M.P., Will Thorne,

asked Mr. Butler, the Undersecretary for Foreign Affairs, in the
House of Commons for details about the chocolate boxes alleged
to have been dropped from Italian planes on Spanish towns and
villages, which, when picked up by starving Spanish children
(starving of course on account of the Italian blockade), exploded, killing or maiming them. Butler replied that the statement had not been reported by British representatives on the
spot, but that some Spanish children had been injured while
playing with unexploded shells left behind by Republican
forces in retreat. Yet the story of the explosive chocolate boxes
continued to be repeated.[4]

On the other hand, there were many eminent British and
American writers who took a quite different view of the conflict
and strongly defended the Nationalist cause and Italy's policy.

The stories attacking Italian action in Spain and, above all,
the insults heaped on the Italian forces in the country filled
Mussolini with bitter indignation against the British and (to
some extent) the American press—and consequently against
Anglo-Saxons in general. We must not forget that he was a journalist to the core, and often attached exaggerated importance
to press campaigns. This spate of libellous statements undoubtedly contributed to prepare the way for the Berlin-Rome
Axis.

The real reason for Italian support of the Spanish Nationalist
cause was the fear that a Communist stronghold might be set
up in the Western Mediterranean, closing Italy off from the
Atlantic, or at least putting at the mercy of Soviet Russia all
Italian trade with countries beyond the Straits of Gibraltar.
Mussolini was convinced that, in supporting Franco's cause, he
was rendering a service to all the civilized countries of Europe,
for Soviet penetration from a Red Spain into France would
have been easy indeed, especially with a *Front populaire* Government in power. Even for Great Britain, it would not have
been exactly pleasant to see the hammer-and-sickle flag waving
over Calais and Dunkirk, and perhaps over Ostend and Ant-
werp.

The Spanish Civil War ended in the spring of 1939 with the
complete victory for what Professor Antonio Pastor[5] called
Spanish Spain. As Count de Saint Aulaire[6] wrote, we must not

forget that Italian action was a reply to that of Moscow, which, moreover, would not have taken place or assumed such vast proportions without the complaisance of the French *Front populaire* Government. "Let us not forget," he wrote, "that the latter favored the recruiting of the first foreign volunteers for Spain, the French and the Belgians who, since August, 1936, obstinately defended Spain against the Nationalists . . . If there were also Italian volunteers in Spain they were recruited by Russia and France—by Russia, which set the first example of foreign intervention in Spain, by France, which when at the beginning of the war Mussolini asked that the Powers should forbid the departure of volunteers, refused, alleging that democratic states could not, like the dictators, prevent their citizens from fighting for causes which they regarded as just." [7]

There is no doubt that whatever judgment from the point of view of international law one may pass on the Italian intervention in Spain, that action did contribute to saving at least one European country from falling under the rule of the Moscow regime and to establishing one bulwark of Western civilization against the extension of that rule. This is an achievement to Mussolini's credit that survives him.

The Spanish Civil War was destined to have reactions on future Italian public life. Several extremely prominent politicians of today, including at least two ex-members of the Cabinet, in addition to several members of the Senate and the Chamber of Deputies, had taken part in the war on the Republican side, even if they did not actually risk their lives in it but limited themselves to inducing others to fight and deriving various advantages from their action. They owe their present privileged position mainly to that action. To quote a few instances: Randolfo Pacciardi, formerly Minister of Defense, fought or at least was enrolled in the Italian anti-Fascist brigade in Spain. Pietro Nenni had been one of the founders of the first Fascist group in Bologna in 1919, and had aspired to be the leader of the party instead of Mussolini, but afterwards he became leader of the one Socialist group practically absorbed into the Communist Party and was at one time anti-Fascist Minister of Foreign Affairs. He was a political commissar to an

Italian Red unit in Spain and was attached to the military Junta in Madrid. But his activities were of a commercial rather than a military character. Luigi Longo, now the second in command of the Italian Communist Party, had been one of the organizers of the Italian Red units in Spain. The Spanish Civil War was actually a nursery for Communist and Leftist politicians, both in Italy and in many other countries.

One episode indirectly connected with the Spanish Civil War is worth recording, on account of its international reactions.

Carlo Rosselli, a wealthy Jewish intellectual from Florence, had been ever since the rise of Fascism one of its strenuous opponents. When Filippo Turati, then the leader of the Italian Socialist Party, believing (wrongly as it happened) that he was about to be persecuted by the Fascist authorities, decided to expatriate, Rosselli helped him to leave the country clandestinely without a passport, an offense punishable even under the pre-Fascist law. He was in consequence deported to the island of Lipari, whence he managed to escape and settled in Paris. There he became the leader of one of the dozen anti-Fascist groups, but exercised small influence.

On the outbreak of the Spanish Civil War, he went to fight in the ranks of the Republican army. There is good reason to believe that Anarchists (one of the many groups fighting in the ranks of the Red armies in Spain) had murdered his friend, Professor Camillo Berneri. Although an Anarchist himself, Berneri had, like Rosselli, accused the members of his own party of not having done their duty and of behaving in a cowardly and treacherous manner. This fact, and the other atrocities which Rosselli had witnessed in Spain, disgusted him with the conditions in that country and induced him to return to France.

While undergoing a cure at Bagnoles-sur-Orne, he was joined by his brother, Nello, who was not a Fascist but was on good terms with the Italian Government. Nello held a teaching appointment in Italy, and had also been sent to England to make historical researches in the Record Office. It was rumored, in fact, that he was the bearer of a message from the Italian authorities to his brother Carlo that he might freely return to Italy.

On June 9, 1937, the two brothers, while they were driving in a car some miles from Bagnoles, were ambushed and murdered.

At first, the news was spread about that the murderers were acting under the orders of the Italian Government, but this story was soon dropped by the French authorities and the press, and the crime was attributed to a French Rightist group known as the Cagoulards. But it was afterwards suggested in anti-Fascist circles that these men had been acting on behalf of the Fascist Government; and the Italian anti-Fascists in France claimed that the Cagoulards had committed the crime on account of a reward offered them of "facilities for the purchase of one hundred carbines." This explanation was preposterous: the Cagoulards were far too deeply involved in French domestic politics to expose themselves to the risk entailed in murdering two foreigners for so ridiculous a reward.

The story of Fascist complicity in the deed continued to be repeated, and Fillippo Anfuso, *Chef de Cabinet* to Mussolini's son-in-law and Minister of Foreign Affairs, Count Ciano, was accused, together with some officers of the Italian military information service, with Ciano and with Mussolini himself, of having engineered the crime.

On the fall of the Fascist régime, the story was brought up again, and proceedings were instituted against Anfuso and the military officers (Mussolini and Ciano were then both dead). Anfuso at that time was in prison in France, accused of the murder and of his connection with the Cagoulards, with one or two of whom he had had a few minutes' conversation in Rome some years previously.[8] But on February 3, 1948, he was fully acquitted on both charges by a French court and, on October 14, 1949, by an Italian Court of Assizes at Perugia. In both cases, no evidence was forthcoming of the connection or complicity of any Italian official or authority; and in the Perugia Court it was admitted that possibly the crime was the result of the internecine quarrels of the various anti-Fascist groups in France. There is reason to believe that either the Spanish or the Italian Reds decided to murder Carlo Rosselli, fearing that he might break away from them and perhaps return to Italy and make very embarrassing revelations, especially about Red activities in Spain. Nello Rosselli apparently was killed only because he happened to be in the company of his brother Carlo.

A great deal of party capital was made out of the affair by the anti-Fascists, and even the British press took up the case. On the eve of the Perugia trial the Rome correspondent of the London *Times* stated in a telegram to his paper that the Rosselli affair was one of the worst instances of Fascist gangsterism. After the decision of the Court had been announced, not a word about it appeared in the *Times*. I sent a letter to the editor, calling his attention to the verdict acquitting all the accused, but he refused to publish it. Evidently he did not wish to let down his Rome correspondent.

The Spanish Civil War, in conjunction with the Ethiopian War and its aftermath, completed the transformation of the League of Nations into a Communist-front organization and an anti-Fascist and anti-Nazi instrument. This trend had been begun by Maksim Litvinov when Russia was admitted to the League in 1934. It was furthered by the establishment of a Popular Front Government in France in 1936 and by the Peace Ballot movement in England in 1935. The idea of collective security against alleged aggressor nations was the key to the process. Litvinov and the Russians were able to convince the League and Western liberals generally that only Fascist and Nazi totalitarianisms were aggressive and the sole international evil, thus cleverly distracting attention from the threat of Soviet totalitarianism to democracy and peace. For just about ten years this threat was ignored—until the Cold War between the Western nations and Soviet Russia was forecast by Winston Churchill in his Fulton, Missouri, speech in March, 1946, and officially proclaimed by President Truman on March 12, 1947. For a decade, Western liberalism had enthusiastically aided in the process of raising Soviet Russia to a dominant position in the Old World.

---

[1] Francesco Belforte, *La guerra civile in Spagna,* Milan, 1938, Vol. II, pp. 63-65.
[2] This fact was communicated to me by one of the officials of the Commission.
[3] This was before the bombing of Dresden, Treviso, Frascati, Hiroshima and Nagasaki.
[4] Luigi Villari, *L'Italia come non è,* pp. 175-242.

[5] Formerly Professor of Spanish at the University of London.

[6] A former French Ambassador.

[7] *La renaissance de l'Espagne,* Paris, 1938, pp. 226-227, 240.

[8] As Chef de Cabinet to Ciano, he saw and talked with people and groups of all kinds and parties, both Italian and foreign.

CHAPTER EIGHTEEN

Propaganda and Superficial Journalism

Propaganda or emotional engineering has for many years played an active part in domestic and foreign politics in every part of the world. During the first World War all the belligerents had set up propaganda services of various kinds. But the system did not develop on a truly permanent scale until later. In Italy, governmental press and propaganda departments were set up in 1934, under Count Ciano. They became an undersecretaryship the following year and later on a ministry, still under Ciano, and then under Dino Alfieri, with the name of Ministry of Popular Culture. It dealt with a great variety of matters, internal and international, issued directives to the Italian press on all political questions, including those on foreign affairs, information to the foreign press, theatrical affairs, the cinema, wireless, etc. Press conferences were frequently held for Italian and foreign journalists, and Mussolini received periodic reports from the Minister on the state of public opinion on the more important questions. One section of the ministry exercised a censorship over book production.

Mussolini, being a journalist through and through, attached much importance to all press matters, but there was never a close censorship of the press, except what the editors themselves applied in conformity with the directives received from official quarters. The Italian foreign press service was not always well run, for some of the officials in charge of it had no journalistic experience and did not know how to issue or to withhold information skillfully. Often they answered questions by flatly refusing to say anything, which of course gave rise to rumors and suppositions of all kinds, sometimes fantastic.

Other countries had similar organizations, and although some appeared to be privately owned, they were often clandestinely spoon-fed and financed by government authorities.

Apart from press propaganda a number of books on international affairs have been published in Anglo-Saxon countries, which, whether indirectly inspired by official sources or not, did serve to spread over a wide public certain views and stories in harmony with the policies of particular governments or parties. Their authors professed (and still profess) omniscience on *all* the political, diplomatic and economic problems of the day. Some of these books have been eagerly read on both sides of the Atlantic by millions of persons who believe that, once they have read and inwardly digested their contents, they know all about everything that is happening in every part of the world.

If the authors of these works had no other intention than to produce salable yellow sensationalism, we might only deplore their productions as mere bunk, like that of the producers of gangster films, and we would pity those who enjoy such trash. But there is reason to believe that the real object of these writers or of those who inspire them goes much further. When we read the same exaggerations and misinterpretations of facts, the same blatant falsehoods and libels repeated in several books by different authors, possibly in different forms and languages but leading to the same conclusions, we can only infer that all these writings emanate from a common source and form part of a common plan—the promotion of international hatred and the disintegration of civilization by discrediting and destroying those forces and tendencies that support sound ideas and policies.

One of the most flagrant instances of this kind of literature is to be found in John Gunther's books, particularly his *Inside Europe*. When I read it in 1937, the copy I had was the 31st

Count Galeazzo Ciano
Minister of Foreign Affairs 1936-1943

Fulvio Suvich
Under-Secretary for Foreign Affairs, 1932-1936
Italian Ambassador to Washington, 1936-1938

edition, and there may have been others since then. I do not, of course, profess to be competent to discuss all the subjects dealt with in this book, but on those on which I do happen to know something I can attest to the utter unreliability or ignorance of the author.

In chapter XIII dealing with Italy he tells us that, because Mussolini's fingerprints were taken by the Swiss authorities when he was a working man in Switzerland, he had always hated that country. As a matter of fact, the very first treaty of conciliation and friendship concluded by his Government was that with Switzerland, an instrument that came to be regarded as a model of its kind and has been copied in many other such treaties. Moreover, Mussolini, throughout his career, never failed to express his sympathy with and admiration for the Swiss people.

Gunther further tells us that in the first World War Mussolini went to the front in December, 1916, and remained there for only 38 days. As I have said before, he was entitled to exemption from military service as a newspaper editor, but he waived his right and volunteered on the outbreak of hostilities, went to the front in December, 1915, and remained in the trenches until February, 1917, when he was severely wounded. This makes fifteen months, not 38 days. Gunther, wishing to prove that Mussolini was a coward, says that there were streets in Rome along which he never dared to pass. Yet if there is one quality that no one could deny to the Duce, as his whole career has proved, it was his exceptional physical courage.

According to the egregious Gunther, the Fascist regime was sustained only by the Morgan loans. Actually, the only Morgan loan issued to the Italian Government was of $100,000,000, a sum less than one-tenth of the annual state budget. Subsequently, Mussolini discouraged foreign loans to the Government for reasons with which I have already dealt. A few smaller loans were issued to the cities of Rome and Milan and some to certain limited liability companies.

About the Matteotti affair, Gunther tells us that the murder was the work of highly placed Fascists, whereas it was proved at both the Matteotti trials, one under Fascism and the other after its fall, that the kidnappers were irresponsible individuals, acting on their own initiative.

For many years, Mussolini lived in one of the houses belonging to Don Giovanni Torlonia in the Via Nomentana (Rome). Gunther claims that Torlonia offered him the villa because he could not afford to keep it up, whereas Torlonia was notoriously one of the richest men in Italy.

Gunther tells us that Mussolini "never forgave an enemy." He was, on the contrary, as everybody knows, extremely forgiving, and when a man condemned for political offenses applied to him for pardon or a remission of his sentence, he nearly always granted it. Perhaps if he had been a little less forgiving in certain cases, it would have been better for himself and for the country.

Gunther's whole book simply bristles with similar howlers of the most amazing kind.

Other literary compositions almost equally preposterous, insofar as they deal with Mussolini and the Fascist regime, are George Seldes' *Sawdust Caesar,* Pierre Van Paassen's *Days of our Years,* Douglas Reed's *Insanity Fair,* and Eugene Young's *Looking Behind the Censorships.* But Gunther remains preeminent in this bevy of bunk-makers, and there are literally millions of perfectly innocent and respectable people on both sides of the Atlantic whose only knowledge of foreign affairs is derived from the perusal of his light-hearted concoctions. It is difficult to overestimate the immense amount of harm wrought by these unscrupulous muckrakers and sensationalists.

Of course, this type of irresponsible defamation of Mussolini has not been limited to foreign writers. After the end of the Fascist epoch, radical and leftwing Italian sensation-mongers and partisans vented their spleen on the dead Duce. Their literary vilification is comparable to the garbage thrown on the corpse of Mussolini in the marketplace in Milan.

Perhaps even more violent have been the attacks of former Fascist propagandists who have done a flip-flop and sought to curry favor with the post-Fascist authorities by vicious attacks on the political system and leaders which they once adored and flattered. One of the best examples of this latter *genre* of vilification is the biography of Mussolini by an Italian journalist, Paolo Monelli, which was published in the United States in the summer of 1954. Monelli, in the heyday of Italian Fascism, was one of its most ardent apostles and propagandists.

He was one of the most active and vigorous Fascist journalists during the Fascist era, correspondent of the *Corriere della Sera,* the *Gazzetta de Popolo,* and other Fascist newspapers and periodicals. It was Monelli who, while working in Berlin, arranged for Mussolini's first visit to Germany. He was covered with favors and emoluments by Mussolini and the Fascist regime, all of which he accepted with eagerness and self-satisfaction. After the regime fell, Monelli sought safety in obscuring his Fascist past and by maligning the Duce. His biography of the latter was so slanderous and misleading that even the intensely anti-Fascist American magazine, *Time,* August 23, 1954, was compelled to call it little more than a caricature of Mussolini. Unfortunately, Monelli is only one of many such turncoats.

CHAPTER NINETEEN

British-Italian Relations and the Rome-Berlin Axis

After the actual Italian occupation of Ethiopia, British statesmen began to feel that it might be advisable to try to come to terms with Italy. Mussolini was ready to offer the hand of friendship, and in his speech of May 9, 1936, announcing the foundation of the Empire, he called it "an empire of peace, for Italy wants peace for herself and for all."

On July 8th the British Government, after agreeing to the lifting of sanctions, recalled the Home Fleet from the Mediterranean, and exchanges of notes and points of view followed. As Mussolini said in his speech of November 1, 1936, what Italy wanted was to discuss with Great Britain the bases of British recognition of the new Italian position in the Mediterranean and in East Africa, and to induce Great Britain to renounce its claim to absolute supremacy in that sea. "For the British," he said, "that sea is a route, a short cut for the British Empire; for us it is life." There could be but one solution—"a firm, sincere, swift understanding on the basis of mutual interests." He felt that he could now talk this language, not only on account of Italy's new position in Africa, but because of his understanding with Germany.

During the Ethiopian campaign Germany had steadfastly rejected the blandishments of the sanctioneers, thereby rendering a great service to Italy. Relations between the two countries, difficult in 1934, were becoming ever closer. For the first time, Mussolini spoke of a *vertical axis*. What he asked of Great Britain was, if not the immediate recognition of the Italian East African Empire, at least a position of equality for Italy in the Mediterranean. We find Eden speaking in the House of Commons (November 5, 1936) of a *rapprochement* with Italy and admitting that the Duce was right when he talked of the vital importance of the Mediterranean for his country. The British Government then withdrew its Indian bodyguard from the Addis Ababa legation and agreed to the resumption of commercial exchanges.

Mussolini's next move for a Mediterranean understanding was his second interview with the *Daily Mail* (November 9, 1936). "A gentlemen's agreement is what I have in mind"—not a solemn treaty, but an admission that British and Italian policies in the Mediterranean are parallel. The idea was accepted by the British Government, and in January, 1937, an agreement was concluded providing for free access to the Mediterranean and free circulation there, collaboration and understanding, but no British hegemony in that sea. This was followed by a further agreement to develop trade between Ethiopia and British Somaliland, which was to give new life to the derelict ports of Zeila and Berbera.

But fresh clouds soon arose. The venomous attacks of the British press on Italian policy in Spain had greatly irritated Italian public opinion, and Great Britain's heavy rearmament program and the concentration of large British forces in the Suez Canal area caused anxiety in Italy. These facts lessened the value of the gentlemen's agreement. The attempt on Marshal Graziani's life (February 19, 1937) was followed by some hundreds of arrests and by a very few death sentences; but the incident was enormously exaggerated in the British press and led to further outbursts against Italy, to which the Italian press retorted by reminding the British of the Amritsar atrocities, which had resulted in a far larger number of casualties with much less provocation.

It was then that the Duce suggested (May 27th) in an interview with the American journalist, W. P. Simms, that President Roosevelt should take the initiative in summoning a conference for the limitation of armaments; "for Italy," he said, "needs peace. She needs it for a long time to develop the resources which she possesses."

While the British were showing such spite toward Mussolini and even Italy in general, they were paying court to Hitler and Germany and showing great consideration for Germany's claims. Not content with concluding a naval pact with the Reich, in 1934, Lord Halifax was negotiating an air pact. These moves all contributed to drive Italy, too, ever nearer to Germany. On November 6, 1937, Italy joined Germany and Japan in the anti-Comintern Pact against Soviet Russia, and this placed Italy in a still stronger position to face British antipathy. In reply to Neville Chamberlain's speech expressing the wish for closer relations with Italy, a semi-official note in the *Informazioni diplomatiche* of November 10th stated that "Italy will not let herself be chloroformed or taken by surprise," and that if negotiations are to be undertaken, they should begin at once. The gentlemen's agreement must be extended to the Red Sea. Italy, in fact, now felt its shoulders protected to the north by Germany and to the east by recent agreements with Yugoslavia.

Ever since the imposition of sanctions Italy had been drifting further and further away from the League of Nations, which Italy considered practically impotent for promoting general peace in spite of the semi-divine aura with which it was surrounded, but capable of doing much harm. On December 11, 1937, in consequence of a decision of the Fascist Grand Council, the Italian Government broke off its connection with the League. This was another step in Italy's trend towards separation from her old Allies of the first World War. After only a year, the gentlemen's agreement had fizzled out, and Italo-German relations became still closer, for Mussolini was beginning to feel that Italy's real sin in British eyes was her geographical position—cutting across Britain's imperial route.

Italy's victory in East Africa had created an atmosphere very favorable to her in Berlin, as the German Ambassador told Ciano,[1] and on June 29, 1936, the Führer recognized the new

Italian Empire. A few days later the French Ambassador in Rome stated that his country considered the Mediterranean agreements between Great Britain and France and other powers still in force until the conclusion of a new general agreement to which Italy should also be a party.[2]

In the meantime Italy continued to devote itself to the task of developing its new possession, for which it spared no expense, without neglecting Libya, where it promoted intensive colonization by 20,000 families sent to cultivate and improve the land. But Italy could not fail to be anxious about the European situation; and if it could not find support in Great Britain or France, it had to count more and more on Germany. The foolish British refusal to recognize the *fait accompli* in East Africa aroused the ire of many people even in Great Britain, and Bernard Shaw suggested that Italy should retaliate by refusing to recognize King George V as Emperor of India.

Immediately after Germany's re-militarization of the Rhineland, Hitler had proposed (March 1936) a plan for a European understanding, with a new meeting of the Locarno Powers to be held at the latest after the French elections and under the leadership of Great Britain, for the conclusion of a non-aggression pact, to last for fifteen years, between Great Britain and France on the one hand and Germany on the other. Ciano, on being informed of the scheme, told the German Ambassador that he saw no reason why this honorary preference should be accorded to Great Britain, but von Hassell explained that the object was to draw Great Britain ever more closely into the anti-Soviet group of powers.[3]

Hitler's disarmament and non-aggression proposal of March, 1936, was the most drastic and far-reaching program for European peace between the two World Wars. It went even further than Mussolini's Four Power Pact. It is significant, in the light of all the charges of militarism and aggression levelled against the two "dictators," Hitler and Mussolini, that the two really comprehensive proposals for maintaining the peace of Europe came from them. The propagandists in the democracies have tried to belittle these plans on the ground that one could not trust either the Duce or the Führer. Surely, their reputation for probity and consistency matches up to the record of Chamberlain, Churchill, Roosevelt and Stalin. Witness Chamberlain's sharp reversal of policy after Munich, Churchill's numerous alterations of attitude toward Fascist Italy, Nazi Germany, and Soviet Russia, according to the shifting vicissitudes of his policy, dictated by ambition and expediency, the frank admission by even Roosevelt's admirers that he "lied the United States into the war," and the notorious mendacity of Stalin.

During this period, Italy kept in close touch with Austria and Hungary, and there still seemed to be some prospect for an agreement between Austria and the Reich. But Austrian statesmen were very anxious about Germany's persistent tendency to expand and about the danger of a definite split in Europe, for France was becoming ever closer to Russia, Czechoslovakia and Poland. Yugoslavia was an uncertain quantity, but Prime Minister Milan Stojadinovich wished to meet Schuschnigg and establish friendly relations with Austria.[4]

In any case Italo-German relations from 1934 to 1938 were dominated by the question of Austrian independence, to which Mussolini attached great importance, although the British and French had refused to support his policy except by good words. It was, indeed, the attitude of the two Western Powers on this point that had helped to drive Italy towards Germany, even before sanctions. The Swiss publicist, Paul Gentizon, wrote in his *Défense de l'Italie:* "The Rome-Berlin Axis was forged in Paris and London. It bears the trademark 'made in England.' " And before the Axis, the *Anschluss,* too, was made in France and Britain. Sumner Welles has held that Mussolini's most fatal error was the abandonment of his determination to maintain Austria as a buffer state between Germany and Italy; but he forgot that the basic fault lay with the Western powers. Italy was unable to act alone as the sole champion of Austrian independence, and some form of Austrian arrangement with Germany, not perhaps an *Anschluss,* but at least a *Gleichschaltung,* seemed inevitable.

Mussolini for a long time continued to hope that Austria might remain a second German state, Catholic and independent, a centre of intellectual and commercial attraction for the Balkans. But, after the Ethiopian war, the development and security of the new possessions became Italy's predominant consideration. If there had been no sanctions, or if the Western Powers had at least recognized the new Italian situation immediately after the end of the war, Mussolini would have continued to mount guard over Austria. Now, instead, his choice lay between complete isolation, with Great Britain and France unfriendly if not actually hostile, and Germany indifferent, on the one hand, or a close agreement with the Reich as a safeguard against the Western Powers, on the other.

During the year 1937 the Italian Government was much disappointed by the long delay over the renewal of the commercial treaty with the United States. The U.S. Ambassador in Rome reported that this delay would push Italy ever further into the eager arms of Hitler. But Hull refused to speed up matters, saying that "it would be unwise to bind our hands by entering into a treaty with Italy." This is another straw showing how Roosevelt and Hull were drifting ever nearer to an alliance with Great Britain and France—and, therefore, toward a European war.[5]

In November, 1937, we reach the Rome-Berlin Axis. Japan and Germany had, as we have seen, signed the anti-Comintern Pact on November 25, 1936. Nearly a year later (November 6, 1937) a protocol was signed at Palazzo Chigi, whereby Italy adhered to that agreement.

It now seemed that Hitler, if he could hold his own, would establish a pan-German domination over Central Europe. This was hardly satisfactory or comfortable for Italy, but, on the other hand, the country could now hope to secure coal and iron from Germany if difficulties arose about obtaining those commodities from the West. Italo-German trade had already increased considerably and would now develop to a still greater extent. The Spanish Civil War had strengthened the bonds between the two countries, while straining those between Italy and the Western Powers.

Having thus succeeded in securing a stronger Continental position through its understanding with Germany, Italy could also hope to negotiate more favorably with Great Britain and France for definite recognition of its new status in Africa.

The mere fact of the Italo-German agreement produced a

deep impression on Great Britain. Its first effect was to bring to a head the latent hostility between Neville Chamberlain and his Foreign Minister, Eden. Chamberlain had come to regard an understanding with Italy as desirable, but Eden was still bitterly anti-Italian. He could not forgive the rejection of his proposed settlement of the Ethiopian question in June, 1935, and there were other causes of dissent between the two statesmen.

Ciano wrote to Grandi on February 16, 1938, that the approaching Nazification of Austria signified a further advance of German power in general.[6] "We are now," he wrote, "between the fourth and the fifth act of the Austrian drama. This interval, and this interval only, may be used for negotiations between ourselves and London." The imminent annexation of Austria would make it very difficult to conduct such negotiations, for Italy would appear to be acting under the fear of Germany and therefore of "going to Canossa"[7] with Great Britain. It was not that Italy wanted to come to an agreement with Great Britain at any cost, but the agreement, he said, was desirable for both parties, and this was the best moment for it.

Grandi on the 18th sent a very long telegram to Ciano about his conversations that same day with Chamberlain.[8] Eden had unexpectedly asked the Italian Ambassador to meet him at the Foreign Office, but Grandi put off the visit, saying that he must await instructions from Rome; he requested Eden to understand that he did not wish to discuss matters with him at a moment when the situation was dominated by the Austrian crisis. Immediately afterwards, Chamberlain informed Grandi that he wished to see him; Grandi, accordingly, called on the Premier on the 18th. After a few words on the Austrian question, which, Grandi repeated, he would rather not discuss until he had received further instructions from Rome, Chamberlain said that he could not understand Italy's passive attitude on the problem. To this, Grandi replied that "Italy has done all she could to preserve Austrian independence, whereas the Western Powers have done nothing." At Stresa the Western Powers had declared themselves ready, together with Italy, to guarantee that independence; but soon afterwards they promoted and carried out sanctions in order to inflict on Italy a veritable military and political defeat. Italy had emerged victorious in East Africa, but Great Britain and France, instead of recognizing the accomplished fact and coming to terms with Italy, showed themselves now with one pretext and now with another definitely hostile to Italy. What was happening in Austria was the actual consequence of British and French policy during the last three years. "Great Britain and France are directly responsible for what is happening in Austria."

Eden, who was present at this meeting, then wished to speak, but Chamberlain proceeded to say that it was now a question of Italy's position in the general European situation. Grandi, thereupon, insisted on the urgency of reaching a definite agreement between the two countries; and he argued that for this purpose British recognition of Italy's Empire in Ethiopia was indispensable. He denied that there were any misunderstandings with Germany regarding a common policy in Europe, but he added that this did not refer to the future. On being asked by Chamberlain what would be a practical suggestion for reaching positive results, he replied: "the immediate initiation of official conversations in Rome."

Eden then intervened, saying that a general agreement could not be reached unless the Austrian question was first discussed and settled, and that there was also the Spanish question,[9] with reference to which Italy must undertake not to send any more volunteers to Spain. Grandi retorted by reminding Chamberlain that Italy both before and after the gentlemen's agreement had repeatedly urged that the Non-Intervention Commission should take measures to prevent the flow of volunteers to Spain for either side. He further reminded Eden that Eden himself had admitted that enormous quantities of supplies had been sent to Republican Spain from Russia, and that when Italo-British relations were beginning to improve, there had been an intensified campaign of anti-Fascism (both internationally and in Great Britain) that was designed to wreck all attempts at an understanding. Italy supported Franco for the same reasons as those that made Wellington support Spain against France in Napoleon's time.

Chamberlain then told Eden that Italy was asking Great Britain to recognize her position in Ethiopia, and that thereafter all matters relating to a general agreement between the two countries would be examined. Grandi agreed to this statement, but added that no previous conditions should be laid down. Eden retorted that he could not see how British-Italian conversations could be harmonized with the activities of the Non-Intervention Commission, and that, first of all, the volunteers must leave Spain.

Chamberlain, after reminding Eden that in the meantime new events had taken place in Europe, asked Grandi if he thought that a public declaration that conversations were officially opened would contribute to a swift conclusion of a general agreement between the two countries. Grandi replied definitely in the affirmative.

A second meeting took place that same afternoon, and Chamberlain undertook to ask his Cabinet to authorize him to announce that conversations had commenced, without the other questions having been solved. The conversations, he stated, would begin without waiting for a decision of the Non-Intervention Commission on the questions of recognizing General Franco as a belligerent and of withdrawing the volunteers. Grandi at once promised to submit this proposal to Ciano before the following Monday, when Chamberlain was to meet his Cabinet.

A long debate now followed about where the conversations should be held. Chamberlain suggested London, and Grandi insisted on Rome because the Non-Intervention Commission was sitting in London and might exercise a prejudicial influence on the conversations. He reminded the Premier that the British Government in two notes to the Embassy in Rome (August 6 and September 27, 1937) had stated that the conversations should be held in that capital. On Grandi's assertion that the decision in favor of Rome would have a favorable effect on the result, Chamberlain agreed to accept the proposal that the meeting be held in Rome.

In concluding his dispatch to Ciano, Grandi added that the rift between Chamberlain and Eden was obvious: Chamberlain wished to put the word *"finis"* to the Ethiopian conflict, but the vindictive Eden wanted at all costs to prepare for war against Italy. Chamberlain was mobilizing the City and all the Right and Centre forces in the country; Eden was relying on the mob, which saw in him the head of a future British Popular Front Cabinet. Winston Churchill, who was Chamberlain's personal enemy, was rallying the Leftist Conservatives to Eden's side.

On February 20th the British Cabinet met three times while the crowds in Whitehall were shouting: "No agreement with dictatorships! Send armies to Spain!" There was even an attempt to break into No. 10 Downing Street.[10] At 10:25 p.m., Eden's resignation was announced, and Lord Halifax became Foreign Secretary. The dropping of Eden at last opened the door, it was hoped, for a better understanding between Italy and Great Britain.

After further acrimonious disputes between the governments of Berlin and Vienna, German troops entered Austria on March 12, 1938. They encountered no resistance, being welcomed by a very large part of the population who saw no other way out of their intolerable economic difficulties than union with the Reich. The next day the *Anschluss* uniting Austria to Germany was proclaimed.

Mussolini and his Government were by no means pleased at the solution, nor was Italian public opinion in general. But the accomplished fact was accepted as inevitable. Neither Great Britain nor France raised any objections.

The conversations now began in Rome between Count Ciano and the British Ambassador, the Earl of Perth (formerly Sir Eric Drummond), who submitted on March 8th a list of the questions to be discussed. A second meeting took place on the 12th, and others followed. The final result announced on April 10th was the so-called Easter Pact. Unlike the gentlemen's agreement of January 1937, it covered all questions at issue between the two governments, from Gibraltar to Bab-el-Mandeb, from Palestine to Kenya. Until then Great Britain had regarded Italy as a sort of Portugal and the Mediterranean as a British lake. Now the two Powers reached an understanding on a footing of equality.

But Mussolini considered recognition of Italian sovereignty over Ethiopia as a *sine qua non* of the Easter Pact, and requested that the British Government should ask the League Council to bury the Ethiopian problem altogether, for Italy,

although no longer a member, wished the states that still belonged to the Geneva institution to recognize Italy's new status
in East Africa.

The League Council met on May 12th, and attempts were
made in various quarters to prevent recognition of Italian
sovereignty over Ethiopia. It was now up to Lord Halifax to
find a solution, and he began by saying that his Government did
not in any way approve of Italy's action in Ethiopia, but that
the Italian position must now be recognized. The French
Minister of Foreign Affairs said more or less the same thing,
adding that it was necessary to abandon a situation "which
threatens the peace of the world." Finally a resolution was
voted to the effect that all states were free to recognize Italian
sovereignty individually.

Italy was now in a position to play a really important part
in Europe. On the one hand, it had the support of Germany;
on the other, it had apparently disarmed British and French
hostility for the time being.

Two months after the *Anschluss* Hitler visited Rome and
was sumptuously and impressively entertained. At the Palazzo
Venezia banquet on May 4th Mussolini stressed the common
interests of the two nations, saying that both had cast aside the
"Utopias" to which Europe had entrusted her fate, to seek a
new system of international coöperation, "which should equit-
ably set up for all men efficient guarantees of justice, security and
peace. This can be attained only when the elementary rights
of every people to live, to work and to defend themselves are
loyally recognized, and when the political balance corresponds
to the reality of those historic forces which constitute and
defend it."

Hitler's reply was especially cordial. "You and I," he said,
"who have become immediate neighbors, trained by the experience of 2,000 years, intend to recognize the national frontier
that Providence and history have obviously planned for our
two peoples." This meant the definite recognition of the Brenner frontier and the elimination of the Alto Adige question.
The Führer concluded by insisting on the necessity for close
collaboration between Italy and Germany.

In the light of the fact that the destinies of Italy and Germany and of Mussolini and Hitler were to be interwoven until death claimed both of these leaders, it will be helpful to cite the brilliant contrast of their personalities and methods which has been set forth by the famed English journalist, Sisley Huddleston, who had an opportunity to observe them both at close quarters:

Plutarch wrote parallel lives of Greeks and Romans, showing how two men whose careers were not dissimilar resembled and differed from each other. Were it relevant to my theme, I, too, would write the parallel lives of Hitler and Mussolini. Although outwardly they seemed to resemble each other at many points, they were opposite in character. . . .

In my travels in Italy, in my encounters with the Duce, I never felt that the [Fascist] movement transcended the rational. . . . Mussolini was an exceptionally gifted administrator with a remarkable sense of showmanship, and a wonderful talent for maneuvering among the shoals and shallows of national and international affairs, rather than the mystical embodiment of the nation. He was a twentieth-century *condottiere,* of splendid intelligence, usually knowing just how much he could do, getting it done, and striking impressive dramatic postures. . . . It is impossible for the impartial historian not to admire his personal qualities when they were displayed at their best.

These qualities were in sharp contrast with those of Hitler, who was not so much intelligent as intuitive. He was a political "medium" in the spiritualistic sense. I realized the difference when I saw them meet at Venice. Hitler was modest in his demeanor, not choosing to put on airs, whereas Mussolini was the man of the theater, posturing, superb . . . One almost felt sorry for Hitler, shabbily dressed, shrinking, one might have supposed shy, beside his proud-strutting compeer. Mussolini cast himself deliberately in the rôle of Superman. Hitler was content to be the demi-God, revealing himself only when in action on the platform . . . Hitler was the madman with a mission, heedless of everything except what he conceived to be his mission. One had an unconquerable belief in himself; the other trusted implicitly in his Daemon. . . . When his Daemon deserted him, Hitler preferred to perish, like a Wagnerian hero, in the flames and havoc of a ruined world.[11]

In a speech at Genoa on May 14th Mussolini said that the agreement between Rome and London was one between two empires, and "as it is our interest to respect this agreement scrupulously, and as we believe that the rulers of Great Britain will do likewise, it may be hoped that this agreement will be a lasting one . . . You will allow me to be circumspect with reference to conversations with France, as they are now being carried on. I do not know if they will reach a conclusion because in one very actual fact, the Spanish war, we are on opposite sides of the barricade. They yearn for the victory of Barcelona, we on the contrary wish for the victory of Franco . . . We want peace, but we must be ready with all our forces to defend it, especially when we hear speeches, even from across the Atlantic, on which we must ponder. Perhaps we should accept the idea that the so-called great democracies are really preparing for a war of ideologies. In any case, it is well to let it be known that in that case the totalitarian states will constitute a solid block and will drive ahead to the end."

Mussolini realized instinctively that he could not count on a lasting understanding with the democratic powers. While he felt a warm personal sympathy for Neville Chamberlain, he had seen that at the recent British elections the Labor Party was gaining ground, and that opposition to the Conservative Government was very vigorous. The Easter Pact was concluded, but not yet carried out, and recognition of the Italian Empire had not yet been announced. He raised the dilemma of "Rome or Moscow," and hoped that Great Britain would understand.

Recognition was still delayed by a clause in the Easter Pact on which the British Government had insisted: that the Pact was not to come into operation until the withdrawal of all the foreign combatants from Spain had been carried out. When the Pact was signed, it seemed as if Franco's victory was imminent. But it was not yet to be, as the Republicans had been able to launch a last counter-offensive which delayed the end for some months more. For reasons of domestic policy Chamberlain delayed recognition until the Spanish question was settled. This attitude merely served to strengthen the ties between Italy and Germany. But France, after the recall of de Jouvenel, refused to send a new Ambassador to Rome because he would have had to be accredited to the King of Italy also as Emperor of Ethiopia. Finally, however, the new Ambassador arrived in October, 1938, in the person of André François-Poncet.[12] Great

Britain at last (November 17, 1938) agreed to recognize Italian sovereignty over Ethiopia.

The reason that induced the two Western Powers to take this step was Munich. But it was late—too late. Great Britain and France had been steadily driving Mussolini into ever closer bonds with Hitler.

The German philosophic historian, Hegel, once remarked that the main lesson we learn from history is that mankind seems unable to learn anything from the study of history. Never was this observation better confirmed than in connection with the political fate of Anthony Eden. More than any other Englishman, he was responsible for blocking any successful effort to attain relatively permanent peace between the two World Wars and for thus exposing England to an "unnecessary war" which "liquidated" the main portions of the British Empire, subjected Britain to many years of austerity after the War, and reduced it to the status of a second-rate world power. Yet, the Conservative Party groomed him to replace Churchill as Prime Minister, which he did in April, 1955. Even more striking and preposterous was the fact that, in the General Election which Eden called for May 26, 1955, he was returned with a comfortable majority as the popular choice of the English people.

Some English critics are inclined to throw all the blame for English disasters since 1939 on the shoulders of Winston Churchill. The English monthly magazine, *The European,* observed in an editorial in the issue of May, 1955, that Churchill "found a great Empire and left a small dependency." This is true, but Eden was more responsible than Churchill. But for Eden's blocking of peace moves before 1939, it is likely that there would have been no war in 1939 and Churchill could never have become Prime Minister to bring about the liquidation of the British Empire in large part. In short, Edenism from 1934 to 1938 was responsible for Churchill and the disastrous impact of the latter's policies on Britain, Europe and the world.

Anyone who thinks my estimate in this chapter of Eden and his part in British-Italian relations is biased should read a few pages in a book by Sisley Huddleston, probably the best informed and most distinguished journalist who wrote on world affairs between the two World Wars. He lists in "a record of failure from the British point of view . . . Mr. Eden piled up at the Foreign Office after the departure of Sir Samuel Hoare" a score (numbered from 1 to 20) of serious events "due to the protracted postponement of conversations with Italy." [13]

[1] Galeazzo Ciano, *L'Europa verso la catastrofe*, Milan: Mondadori, 1948, pp. 23-24.

[2] *Ibid.*, p. 25.

[3] *Ibid.*, pp. 45-46.

[4] *Ibid.*, pp. 63-71.

[5] Tansill, *op. cit.*, p. 516.

[6] Ciano, *Diario, 1937-1938*, Bologna: Cappelli, 1948, p. 114.

[7] It was at Canossa that Emperor Henry IV humiliated himself before Pope Gregory VII in 1077.

[8] Ciano, *L'Europa verso la catastrofe*, pp. 249-278.

[9] The Spanish Civil War was not yet ended.

[10] The British Premier's official residence.

[11] Sisley Huddleston, *Popular Diplomacy and War*, pp. 190-192.

[12] Until then Ambassador in Berlin.

[13] Sisley Huddleston, *In My Time*, New York: E. P. Dutton and Co., 1938, pp. 350-52.

CHAPTER TWENTY

The Jewish Question in Italy

The Jewish question in Italy was, of course, primarily a problem of domestic policy, but it had international repercussions that deserve examination.

The number of Jews in Italy has always been very small, and the great majority of them belong to the Sephardic branch, considered the most elevated and distinguished of the Jews. Most of them had migrated to Italy after their expulsion from Spain; others, also of Spanish origin, had come from the Balkans, Egypt or Tunisia. They were largely assimilated with the rest of the population, although retaining certain Jewish characteristics. Many had played a distinguished part in the *Risorgimento,* and not a few had held high places in Italian political, social and intellectual life, in the professions, in the public administration, in the fighting services, as well as in all forms of business. There was virtually no anti-Semitism in the country, because there were no masses of the proletarian and mainly non-Semitic Jews from eastern Europe who are those that usually tend to arouse such feelings among the non-Jewish population.

It is often claimed that Mussolini enacted his racial legislation only at the instance of Hitler. But although the Führer did, no doubt, bring pressure to bear on the Duce in that connection, this is not the whole story. Mussolini had always been suspicious of international organizations of all kinds, especially those dependent on authorities outside his own country. He had long regarded Jews as a community inspired by international considerations independent of their Italian citizenship. And like large numbers of other men all over Europe and in the United States, he believed that he discerned strong Jewish influences in the Bolshevik Government of Russia, to which as an uncompromising anti-Communist after 1917 he was definitely opposed.

In an article published in the *Popolo d'Italia,* as far back as June 4, 1919, he had written: "If Petrograd does not fall, if Denikin marks time, it is because the great Jewish bankers of London and New York so desire, linked up as they are by racial ties with the Jews who, in Moscow and Budapest, are revenging themselves on the Aryan race which for centuries has condemned them to dispersion."

In 1920 he was unfavorably impressed by the activities of certain Italian Jews in connection with the Zionist congress in Trieste, and he warned them "not to arouse anti-Semitism in the one country where it has never existed." [1] Later on he again referred to the Italian Zionist Federation,[2] asked why its delegates had attended the meeting of the Jewish Committee of Action at Karlsbad, and expressed his disapproval of Zionist policy in Syria and Palestine.

That Mussolini's fears relative to the possible international dangers inherent in Zionism were not groundless was later proved in the courageous book by the able American Jewish publicist, Alfred Lilienthal, *What Price Israel,* published in the United States in 1953, at a time when the full diplomatic and political impact of Zionism was beginning to become apparent. Nevertheless, however valid Mussolini's ideas may have been on this subject, there is no doubt that his attitude helps to explain the bitter hatred of British and American Zionist Jews toward him and the Fascist regime.

At the Rome Fascist Congress (November 8, 1921) Mussolini insisted on the importance of the racial question in a national sense. With his suspicion of all forms of internationalism, he was also openly hostile to Freemasonry, with its anti-Catholic attitude, its international affiliations and above all the dependence of the Italian lodges on the Grand Orient of France, which frequently acted as an instrument of French foreign policy in a manner hostile to Italy. Dislike of Freemasonry often went hand in hand with anti-Semitism in Italy, for large numbers of Jews were Freemasons. No professing Catholic could join the organization, whereas Jews were free to do so.

Soon after Mussolini's advent to power, a resolution that he proposed was voted by the Fascist Grand Council on February 12, 1923, declaring that Fascists could not be Freemasons, because Fascism admitted only one discipline and one loyalty. When a law was later enacted compelling all associations to publish their standing orders and their membership lists, Italian Freemasonry preferred to dissolve itself rather than reveal its secrets.

But it was chiefly the activities of international finance that actually prepared the way for racial legislation in Italy. An article in the *Popolo d'Italia* of March 17, 1932, attributed to Mussolini himself, emphasized the close alliance between international Jewry and certain German-American banking interests. Mussolini noted that Jewish finance was becoming ever more hostile to him and to his regime because of his opposition to international loans for Italy in which Jewish financiers were largely interested. His suspicion of such loans was due to the influence which they later often exercised on the policy of the countries to which they were issued. After the $100,000,000 Morgan loan he refused all foreign loans for Italy. Jewish international financiers were perturbed not so much by the prospect of losing the Italian loan market, which was not a very large one, as by the fear that Italy's example might be followed by other countries, which, indeed, actually happened.

Thus, a persistent campaign against Italy's financial and economic system was launched on a large scale by Jewish financial circles and by the papers controlled by them. The hostility of a large part of the American press to Fascist Italy was chiefly due to the Jewish influences that provided so much of the advertising in the newspapers. An English friend of mine told me that a well-known Boston paper had refused to publish an article of his, commissioned by the editor and favorable to Mussolini's regime, for fear of losing the advertising of the large Jewish-owned department stores. An American Jew, whom I met in New York and who had just returned from Italy, told me that he had written an article showing how well the Jews were treated there, as compared with other countries, but no American paper would publish it because anything favorable to Fascist Italy was taboo in the eyes of the powerful Jewish advertisers.

There is good evidence that the hostility shown toward Mussolini and Hitler by the international bankers, both Gentile and Jewish, in the years immediately before the War, was due more to the fact that the Führer and the Duce were developing a financial and commercial system which rendered them independent of foreign banking control than it was to any anti-Semitism, the suppression of political and intellectual freedom, or Hitler's aggressive diplomacy and territorial annexations. This probably accounts for the increasing hostility of the London "City" toward Hitler. Earlier, Montagu Norman and other great British bankers had been markedly friendly to Hitler and in favor of his repression of German Communism and radicalism.

The conquest of Ethiopia raised the problem of miscegenation—between whites and natives of Africa—which was considered undesirable from all points of view.

All these circumstances, in addition to Hitler's example and pressure, gradually led Mussolini to the racial legislation of 1938.

On August 5, 1938, the *Informazioni diplomatiche* (n. 18) published a note on the racial question in general. It there stated that in the next census Jews would be registered as such. The participation of Jews in the public life of Italy, it was claimed, should be proportionate to their actual numbers. In October, 1938, Mussolini declared that the Jewish question was only a part of the general racial problem, but he added that for the past sixteen years "world Jewry had proved an irreconcilable enemy of Fascism."[3] Jews of Italian citizenship, he said, "who show undoubted civil and military loyalty towards Italy and the regime will find comprehension and justice; as for the others, a policy of separation will be followed with regard to them."

Immediately afterwards, a series of measures concerning the Jews was enacted, based on the following principles:

1. The international concept of Israel is basic and obvious.

2. The Jewish problem must be solved by setting up in some part of the world—not in Palestine—a Jewish state.

3. The position of Jews is defined on the principle that they are foreigners in the countries in which they are settled.

In actual practice the chief measures taken against the Jews were their exclusion from all positions in the public administration, diplomacy, the fighting services, the teaching professions, the larger banks and other institutions of national interest and the Fascist Party. But a number of exceptions were made in the case of Jews who had rendered valuable services to the country, had been decorated for gallantry in the field, had become Christians for a certain number of years, and Jews who had one Gentile parent and had not been brought up in the Jewish faith, etc. Jews who had been employed in the leading Italian banks could secure positions in the foreign branches of those same banks; and in many cases Mussolini himself undertook to find employment for eminent Italian Jews in foreign countries, especially in the teaching profession.

The measures were not as a rule carried out in a rigorous spirit, and many loopholes were found to enable Jews to evade their application. Nor was there any general feeling of hostility to the Jews on the part of the Italian people such as existed in many other European countries and in the United States, and many non-Jews having had ties of personal friendship with individual Jews continued to maintain them.

The following incident is characteristic of the Italian attitude towards the Jews. An eminent Italian Senator and ex-Cabinet Minister went to call one day on the Undersecretary of the Interior, Guido Buffarini-Guidi, and, while waiting in his antechamber, he met another Senator, who had been a bitter anti-Semite long before the racial laws. The anti-Semitic Senator asked him what had brought him there. The ex-Minister replied, "Do not think ill of me, but I have come to plead the cause of a Jewish friend." To this the anti-Semitic Senator replied, "Do not think ill of *me*—I am here for exactly the same purpose."

It was only after the armistice of September 8, 1943, when the Germans were in occupation of the greater part of Italy that stricter measures were taken against the Jews, but they were enforced almost exclusively by the German authorities, and many Italians, including officials of high rank and Catholic prelates, helped Jews to avoid deportation or other penalties at the hands of the Germans. The Italian Embassy in Berlin was able to protect many Italian Jews who had been deported to Germany. Italian officials in France between the Armistice of 1940 and the "Liberation" of 1944, gave much protection and assistance to French and refugee Jews.

While the existence of a Jewish problem demanding some solution was generally admitted, the measures enacted by the Italian Government did not help to solve it, but they brought much odium on Mussolini and on Italy in general. They undoubtedly constituted one of the chief mistakes of the Duce, inasmuch as they were unnecessary and aroused a wide measure of disapproval even among many loyal Fascists. Their effect abroad was equally deplorable, even among persons who were not prejudicially hostile to Italy, to Fascism or to Mussolini personally. The activities of international Jewish finance, which were undoubtedly dangerous and do serve to explain Mussolini's attitude, might have been dealt with in other and better ways.

After the fall of the Fascist regime, the Jews who had been in hiding or had fled abroad re-appeared, save for a very small number who had been killed by the Germans or had died in German concentration camps. Many of those who returned were naturally very bitter against the past regime, and they took an active part in persecuting its former adherents, while many who had been protected by non-Jews did not show much gratitude to their erstwhile protectors. But this was not the case with all.

It must, indeed, be said that even during the brief period of racial discrimination many Italian Jews remained faithful supporters of the regime, although they were no longer allowed to be members of the Fascist Party. To quote one example, the former Italian Consul General in Boston, the late Dr. Guido Segre, who had been put on the retired list on account of his race, returned to Boston, where he had many friends, in order to find some means of support. He was offered a good appointment on condition that he declare himself an anti-Fascist. This he refused to do, saying that, although he could no longer be a member of the Party, he was still a believer in its principles and still faithful to Mussolini. As a result, he had to be content with giving private Italian lessons for a small honorarium.

[1] *Popolo d'Italia,* October 19, 1920.
[2] *Ibid.,* August 31, 1921.
[3] This referred to foreign Jews; many Italian Jews had rendered notable service to the Fascist régime in various fields of activity.

CHAPTER TWENTY-ONE

Munich and Its Aftermath

After the *Anschluss* the world was wondering if Hitler would again push ahead and, if so, in which direction. He certainly did not attempt to conceal his intentions, for very soon he raised the question of the German minorities in Czechoslovakia. Although it was not one that directly affected Italian interests, it did come within the sphere of Mussolini's revisionist ideas. He had constantly said, as far back as 1921, that the dilemma was: a new war or treaty revision. The American Secretary of State, Robert Lansing, had declared that "the Versailles Treaty menaces the existence of civilization," and two Popes had stigmatized that instrument. Benedict XV had condemned it for "the lack of an elevated sense of justice, the absence of dignity, morality or Christian nobility," and Pius XI in his encyclical *Ubi arcam Dei* (December 26, 1922) deplored an artificial peace set down on paper, which instead of arousing noble sentiments increases and legitimatizes the spirit of vengeance and rancor."

Czechoslovakia, like its very name, was one of the abortions of the Peace settlement. If the map of Europe was to have been recast on the basis of nationality, the creators of the Czechoslovak state surely did not contribute to that consummation. Of all the structures erected at Versailles, this was one of the most artificial. Several eminent Frenchmen asked themselves, whether for the sake of preserving "this medley of many nationalities, it was worth setting fire to the world." [1] Like the old Austro-Hungarian Empire, it was made up of many diverse peoples but was ruled by one alone, with an administration far less efficient and far more corrupt than that of the Hapsburgs. Seven million Czechs dominated three and a half million Germans, three million Slovaks, one million Magyars, half a million Ruthenes and 150,000 Poles. Had the new State been governed on the same lines as Switzerland, these various races might have managed to live side by side without too much friction. But it was erected as an artificially unified state, completely dominated by the Prague camarilla. The German inhabitants, known as the Sudeten,[2] the ablest, most hard-working and efficient element in the population, were concentrated mostly along the border lands of Bohemia adjoining the German frontiers, but others were scattered all over the country. With the political revival of the German nation under Hitler, they began to feel the attraction of the Fatherland and to resent the position of inferiority to which they were condemned under Czech rule. A movement arose among them for full autonomy, associated with the name of Conrad Henlein; but the *Anschluss* awoke in them aspirations of a more radical nature.

The Prague Government began to get alarmed. It hoped to secure outside support, possibly from Russia as the most powerful Slav nation, with which it had concluded a pact of mutual assistance. But Russia did not seem inclined to lend Czechoslovakia a helping hand at that moment. France had concluded two pacts with Czechoslovakia (in 1924 and 1925), but France was not prepared to risk a war with Germany for the sake of the Czechs. Great Britain had an alliance with France, and some of her most noisy publicists, such as Wickham Steed and R. W. Seton-Watson,[3] were closely associated with the dominant clique in Prague, but the Government was very doubtful about the rights and wrongs of the dispute.

Lord Runciman, who had been sent out by the British Cabinet to inquire into the situation, reported in favor of the Sudeten claims. When Hitler put forth a demand for the German annexation of the Sudetenland on the grounds of the self-determination of peoples, Neville Chamberlain was prepared to consider it favorably. But he wished, above all, to avert the danger of war. He visited Hitler in Germany, after which the British and French governments proposed a plan for a settlement that the Prague Government accepted. Then Hitler announced his intention of occupying the disputed territories by force before October, 1938, and thereafter holding a plebiscite in them. The Czech Government ordered a general mobilization, and Chamberlain again visited Hitler. The London *Times* suggested that the Prague Government should accept Hitler's demands.

In Italy public opinion on the whole supported the German case, but hoped that the matter would be settled amicably and that Czechoslovakia might be detached from France and Russia. But Italy did not wish to see German troops overrunning the country.

During his tour in northeastern Italy in September, 1938, Mussolini delivered a series of speeches in which he insisted on plebiscites for all the minorities of Czechoslovakia as the only means for averting a serious European crisis. Where these peoples form compact units, he said, they might become independent or join some other state to which they felt themselves more akin; where there were racial admixtures, autonomy should be conferred. While conducting a generally Germanophile policy, he hoped in this way to secure the friendship of the minorities.

Hitler's ultimatum to Czechoslovakia on September 27th filled the world with deep anxiety and with the fear of an outbreak of war if his threat of invading Czechoslovakia materialized. Great Britain had mobilized its fleet, France had commenced military preparations, Hungary and Poland were on a war footing. Italy alone took no special measures. Great Britain and France felt that they ought to declare war if Hitler carried his threats into effect, but neither country was really eager for war. A number of American scholars, notably Professor Charles C. Tansill and Dr. Frederic R. Sanborn, hold that it was the pressure exerted by President Roosevelt which led Chamberlain and Daladier to make the crucial decision to ab-

stain from military action. It is believed that Roosevelt felt
that a war at this time would lead to so rapid a defeat of Hitler
that the United States would not have time to enter hostilities.
When Chamberlain's attempt to restrain the Führer failed, it
was to Mussolini that the British Premier appealed to use his
influence in saving world peace.

Lord Perth informed Ciano that the British Premier was
about to invite Mussolini officially to obtain from Hitler a
suspension of his threatened operations. According to the
Times (September 16th), he had already telegraphed the Duce
from Berchtesgaden requesting his intervention. In fact, Mussolini in his speech at Treviso on the 21st had praised Chamberlain's action, saying that he was "piloting the little bark towards
the haven of peace."

Mussolini at once got into touch with his ambassador in
Berlin, Bernardo Attolico, instructing him to request Hitler
to suspend mobilization for a few hours and, if possible, to
abstain altogether from the use of force.[4] He further accepted
his British colleague's suggestion for a conference of the four
Great Powers on the Czech question. Hitler agreed, and the
conference met on the 29th in Munich. There, Hitler, Mussolini, Chamberlain, and Daladier, with their Ministers of
Foreign Affairs and their staffs discussed the situation during
many hours.

By agreement with Hitler, Mussolini submitted a plan which
was accepted as a basis for discussion. The French Ambassador
in Berlin, François-Poncet, paints a vivid picture of the meeting in his book: "The English converse but little among themselves, the Germans and the Italians a great deal. Mussolini is
deeply ensconced in his arm chair. His features, of extraordinary
mobility, are never for a moment in repose. His mouth opens
in a broad smile and contracts with a pout. His eyebrows rise in
astonishment and frown as if in threat. His eyes have an amused
and anxious expression and suddenly discharge flashes." [5] No
one presided and there was no methodical program; but toward
evening, the English drew from their file a type-written sheet.
Immediately the debate, which had wavered, was crystallized
round this projected agreement. Mussolini enjoyed the advantage over his colleagues of being able to speak French, English

and German fluently and correctly. His text, drafted the previous day, bore a close resemblance to the Franco-British proposal. The British and the French suggested certain alterations, and at 1 a.m. on September 30th Hitler accepted the plan.

It was agreed that the Czech troops should evacuate the Sudeten territory between October 1st and 10th, and that plebiscites be held in each district under international control. Mussolini supported the Hungarian and Polish claims—the former reasonable, the latter less so—as part of his revisionist policy, and the governments concerned were to be allowed three months to reach an agreement; and if this proved impossible, the settlement would be entrusted to a new conference of the four Great Powers.

Peace was thus secured outside the League of Nations, which had proved incapable of solving any of the really serious European problems. Credit for the Munich settlement was undoubtedly mainly Mussolini's. Both Chamberlain and Daladier contributed to it; but, as Hitler's intimate partner, Mussolini alone could play the rôle of a Bismarck as "an honest broker." The British Ambassador in Berlin, Sir Nevile Henderson, states that: "Peace was saved the moment Hitler, at Mussolini's request, put off his mobilization." [6]

Throughout Europe the general feeling was: "For this relief much thanks," and it seemed as if a new era in world history had begun. Mussolini was everywhere acclaimed as the great peace-maker. On returning to Italy he was received by enthusiastic crowds at every station, and in Rome there was a monster demonstration, for the Italian people really desired peace. For the time being at least the danger of war was averted. In Great Britain and France, too, the great majority of the people cordially welcomed their respective premiers.

But not all were pleased. Both in Great Britain and in France there were many who deplored that an opportunity had been lost to strike down one totalitarian nation, and that it was due to another that the chance had been allowed to slip by. Certain persons and papers actually maintained that Chamberlain and Daladier had been bribed to avoid war. Some time ago, an American journalist told me that a colleague of his, present at Munich, had declared that on leaving the *Führerhaus* Chamberlain and Daladier appeared deeply dejected, whereas Hitler and Mussolini gloated over their success, suggesting of course that the two latter had done in the former, who now realized that they had been done in. The manufacture of myths is evidently not yet a lost art.

Secretary Cordell Hull strongly disapproved of the Munich settlement.[7] Indeed, all through the spring and summer of 1938 large sections of American public opinion, especially in Leftist circles, reviled Chamberlain as a traitor to the cause of justice, democracy, etc., for having dared to adopt a policy of diplomatic adjustment, hereafter to be smeared as "appeasement," instead of at once going to war.

In Czechoslovakia the solution was deeply regretted, and Beneš and his followers saw it as an act of treachery on the part of the Western Powers, which is, of course, not surprising. But the real cause of the discomfiture of the dominant clique in Prague was the actual existence of Czechoslovakia, a monstrosity which should never have been hatched. The country's subsequent desperate fate was the result not only of its original sin, but also of the sins of the statesmen who were afterwards to deliver a large part of the Old World to Soviet Russia.

While the Munich settlement was maturing, I was on an Italian liner between New York and Naples, and I shall never forget the days of heart-breaking suspense which we all went through or the immense relief I felt, together with the other passengers and the members of the crew, when the wireless message came through: "Mussolini has appealed to Hitler and a conference of the four prime ministers will be held. Peace is saved!"

Munich marked the end of the League of Nations. It had been shattered by sanctions but was to survive for another year in an ever more anaemic state, until it definitely vanished with the second World War.

On September 30th Hitler and Mussolini signed a mutual declaration of non-aggression that brought the two countries yet closer together.

The opponents of the Munich settlement were at first carried away by the general wave of enthusiasm over the temporary removal of the immediate risk of war. But they soon plucked up courage. In Great Britain the extreme militarist Conservatives, led by Churchill, were operating arm in arm with the extreme Laborites. Under the guise of peace-lovers, both seemed determined on war against the totalitarian states, the Conservatives because they objected to new imperialisms, for Great Britain alone was entitled to be imperialist, and the Laborites because they objected to Italian and German social legislation, believing that no government had the right to promote the welfare of the working classes except through Fabian Socialism. In France the militarists disliked the militarism of Germany and Italy. That of Great Britain could not be avoided or destroyed; and in any case, they hoped to exploit it for purposes of French policy. The French Leftists took the same view as the British Laborites. In both countries the liberals were annoyed because the Munich settlement had been achieved by nations who wickedly disregarded the "Immortal Principles."

The French Government, however, now felt it advisable to attempt a reconciliation with Italy after coöperation at Munich, but it was somewhat late in the day. A new ambassador had been sent to Rome, and this implied recognition of Italian sovereignty over Ethiopia; but in Italy this was regarded merely as a just reparation for sanctions, and some further gesture of friendliness was expected. The violent outbursts of anti-Fascism continued in France, showing that hostility toward Italy had not really been altered.[8]

The progress towards a yet closer union between Italy and Germany continued. On October 28th von Ribbentrop came to Rome, not only to deal with the further developments of the Czechoslovak question but also to promote a veritable alliance with Italy. An alliance existed, he said, between Great Britain and France, both those powers were re-arming heavily, and the Franco-Russian pact was still in force. Hitler believed that in the United States isolationism was becoming ever stronger, and that it would increase still more at the slightest rumor of war. At that moment he wished to strengthen Germany's ties with Poland and hoped that Yugoslavia, Hungary and other countries would be more and more drawn towards the Reich. Russia was weak, he believed, and would remain so for many years. Consequently, Germany had to guard only against the

Commander Junio Valerio Borghese

Count Serafino Mazzolini
Under-Secretary for Foreign Affairs
1942-1945

menace from the West; and for this purpose Germany and Italy must coöperate.

Mussolini agreed to this, but he said that the alliance must define its objectives, that the situation had yet to mature, and that Italy knew where she wanted to go. But no particulars were given out.[9]

The Italo-German arbitration concluded in Vienna with regard to Czechoslovakia was another step along the revisionist path; Hungary recovered 400,000 square kilometres of its lost territories with a million inhabitants; and Czechoslovakia, or what remained of it, gravitated more and more around Berlin and Rome, as was admitted by its new Minister of Foreign Affairs, František Chvalkovsky.[10]

Then at last came Great Britain's recognition of Italian sovereignty over Ethiopia, but this was too late to be really effective. It materialized only when Italy's position seemed to be so greatly strengthened as to make its friendship worth while for Great Britain while Great Britain's friendship was now less vital for Italy.

Franco-Italian relations continued to be unsatisfactory, and there was little hope for improvement so long as the *Front populaire* remained in power. Under that government ratification of the January, 1935, agreement was not possible. That arrangement provided that a commission be set up to regulate the position of the Italians in Tunisia by a special convention. But such a convention was never concluded, although the Italian Government had declared itself prepared to make notable sacrifices in exchange for a friendly French attitude toward Italy's needs for expansion in East Africa. France's conduct with regard to sanctions hardly came up to that specification, and her policy in the Spanish Civil War intensified mutual ill-feeling.

Italy as a partner in the Axis was no longer alone and undefended, but it had not secured the same advantages as Germany out of the combination. Hence Mussolini now began to consider revision in reference to his own country.

On November 30, 1938, Ciano delivered an important speech in the Chamber of Deputies. Speaking of Italy's desire to consolidate peace, he declared: "This consolidation is and will be the high aim of our policy, and we shall pursue it with a tenacity and a realism not detached from that circumspection which is indispensable if we wish to safeguard with inflexible firmness the interests and natural aspirations of the Italian people." He did not specify those aspirations and interests, but several members of the Chamber, after applauding the speech, shouted aloud: "Tunis, Jibuti, Nice, Corsica!"

Ciano had not expressed any particular opinions on these subjects. In a letter to Grandi written on November 14th he had alluded to Tunisia and Jibuti merely to say that in the former territory an improvement in the conditions of Italian workers must be properly defined, and that the Jibuti-Addis Ababa railway should now be in Italian hands, and the port placed under a Franco-Italian administration. Otherwise Italy would deflect her trade with Ethiopia to other routes. The Suez Canal [11] was another Italian interest, as Italian shipping now occupied the second place (after Great Britain's) in the Canal traffic. Corsica and Nice he did not mention.

But the unexpected shouts of the deputies made a deep impression both in Italy and abroad, and in many quarters it was affirmed that the outburst had been carefully staged in advance. Ciano, in his *Diary*, definitely denies it, and Gentizon suggests that the Chamber acted like the chorus in a Greek tragedy which expressed what the protagonist felt. The semi-official press merely stated that the Munich spirit must continue to operate "to redress ancient and recent grievances and repair injustices." The only official statement was a note declaring that Italy now considered the agreement of January 7, 1935, to have lapsed, since it had never been ratified. The French Government was reminded that Article 13 of the Pact of London (1915) had never been carried out by France, and that everything must now be re-examined in view of Italy's new position in the Axis. Mussolini did afterwards allude to Nice, Corsica and Tunisia as Italy's necessities; but in a confidential speech before the Fascist Grand Council he concluded that he "had only followed 'the marching orders'," and that he would "impeach for high treason anyone who revealed wholly or partially what I have said." [12]

But the French Minister of Foreign Affairs, Georges Bonnet,

referring to the shouts of the Italian deputies, said that France would not give Italy an inch of French territory.

In spite of all that had taken place, Mussolini did not then wish his country to be too intimately and indissolubly associated with and tied to Germany. His ideal solution was a true collaboration between the two Western powers on the one side and Italy and Germany on the other, or else a complete understanding between Great Britain and Italy as a bridge between Germany and France—the Four-Power Pact again. But all attempts of the kind were rejected both by Great Britain and France.

At the end of 1938 Mussolini still believed that Great Britain might prove an intermediary between France and Italy. But unluckily the British Government had no real wish for an Italo-French understanding. It did not wish to see the two countries at war with each other, but neither did it want them to be too friendly. It was a case of "allegro, ma non troppo." Besides, Italy's aims on Tunisia had always aroused British anxiety, for an Italian Tunisia directly opposite and very near to Sicily might possibly jeopardize the sacred route to India.

Nevertheless an attempt to strengthen Italo-British relations was made once more. At Munich Mussolini had invited Chamberlain to come to Rome; and the visit, which had been finally agreed upon on November 28, 1938, when the Easter Pact came into operation, might, it was hoped, lead to better relations with France.

The visit took place according to plan. On January 11th, 1939, Chamberlain and Halifax arrived in Rome, and great hopes were entertained of the meeting with Mussolini and Ciano. But all that the British Premier could suggest was that Italy should come to a settlement with France, and all that was agreed to was a re-affirmation of the Easter Pact. "Nothing has been done," Ciano wrote in his *Diary* on January 12th. "The visit has been a flirtation without consequences." Chamberlain asked Mussolini if, when the Spanish War came to an end and normal relations were restored between Italy and France, he thought it would be possible to summon a new disarmament conference. Mussolini replied affirmatively but insisted that it be prepared through the ordinary diplomatic channels; otherwise it was bound to be a failure.

The Duce was not pleased with the situation. He had honestly believed that Munich meant peace and stability, whereas Hitler seemed determined to extend his power to ever wider areas, far wider than Mussolini himself had bargained for. The Czechoslovak Prime Minister, Emil Hácha, had gone to Berlin, where he had been induced by fear or force to agree to a German protectorate over what remained of Czechoslovakia, *i.e.*, Bohemia and Moravia. Slovakia had become independent, and a part of the Magyar districts had reverted to Hungary, so that the rump remnant was not self-supporting. German troops occupied it, and this breach in the Munich pact was by no means agreeable to Italy. Although Czechoslovakia had been admittedly a crazy construction, and its inhabitants did not offer the least resistance, the German occupation made all Europe uneasy as to where the next blow would fall. Italy, although Germany's ally, had not been previously informed. Mussolini himself, much as he disliked the whole Czechoslovak set-up, had not wished to see Bohemia and Moravia annexed to Germany.

In France Hitler's last move aroused angry feelings, and there was talk of vigorous counter-action. Laval, then not in office, said at a secret meeting of the Senate Foreign Affairs Committee (March 16) that the only way to restrain Hitler was for France to come to a close understanding with Great Britain and with Italy. An attempt in that direction had been made before Hitler's occupation of Prague, but the French Premier's answer had been unsatisfactory. Negotiations between France and Great Britain were speeded up; but their indecisive outcome served only to tighten the bonds between Germany and Italy.

On March 20th the German Ambassador in Rome presented to Ciano a letter from von Ribbentrop, stating that as Germany had absorbed Bohemia and Moravia, and as Italy had declared itself not interested in the matter, the Reich recognized Italy's exclusive rights in the Mediterranean. The Führer, the letter declared, has decided "that Germany in Mediterranean questions will never conduct a policy independently of Italy" and that Germany has no interests whatever in the Croatian question. "This decision of the Führer's will ever be an unchanging law of our foreign policy." [13]

Mussolini was partially satisfied with this statement, but he still hoped for an understanding with France as well. In his speech of March 26th at the Olympic Forum he said that above all he wanted peace, and peace for a long time; but, before taking any action for peace, Italy wished to see its own aspirations satisfied. In that connection, reconciliation with France was by no means impossible. Spain had been a barrier dividing the two countries, but now that Franco's forces were about to strike a decisive blow, that barrier could be regarded as demolished. He repeated that the only problems separating Italy from France were the situation of Italians in Tunisia, Italian participation in the Jibuti railway and an Italian share in the management of the Suez Canal. He concluded by stating that for Italy the Mediterranean is "a vital space."

These words offered France an opening for a reconciliation to dissipate all misunderstandings. But on March 29th Daladier replied that what Italy demanded was new rights in consequence of her conquest of Ethiopia. "I need not say," he continued, "that we cannot accept that argument . . . The claims that might be made on us would be practically unlimited . . . We shall not give up one hectare of territory nor a single one of our rights." [14]

In Rome Daladier's speech made a bad impression as confirming the usual uncompromising French attitude toward Italy, which had not demanded any French territory or wished to deprive France of any of its rights, but had expected only a share in certain activities to which Italy's new situation in East Africa entitled it.

In a conversation with Ciano on April 29th the Rumanian Minister of Foreign Affairs, Vasile Gafencu, told him that certain persons in France considered that their government should make a gesture of friendship towards Italy, whereas others believed that Italy should be left to convince itself of the necessity for a *rapprochement*. Ciano exclaimed that the former were undoubtedly right, but if France waited too long, it might be too late.

Gafencu also saw Mussolini, who told him that "the difficulties with France were serious, but not grave. They are in the colonial fields. It is not for these that we shall go to war." [15]

Cardinal Luigi Maglione, the Papal Secretary of State, assured Gafencu that neither Italy nor France wanted war, but neither was free to act as she wished. He begged the Rumanian statesman to bring pressure to bear on his friends in Paris to intervene as soon as possible in a peaceful direction.

With the capture of Madrid on March 28, 1939, the victory of Nationalist Spain was now definite, and the Civil War came to an end. This should have greatly contributed to general pacification. But unfortunately Neville Chamberlain gave a guarantee to Poland on March 31, 1939, that was equivalent to a blank cheque to be cashed whenever the Polish Government believed that the country was menaced, leaving Great Britain no freedom to decide if the menace was real and, hence, no freedom of action. Britain was now bound to intervene whenever the Polish Government demanded it. This was the most disastrous single diplomatic move yet made. It rendered the second World War almost inevitable, for a quarrel between Germany and Poland, even if capable of a peaceful settlement, might now be converted into Armageddon at the caprice of whoever happened to be in power in Poland at the time. This was just what happened in August, 1939. Chamberlain, by no means a war-monger, had evidently been driven into this act of madness by the followers of Churchill and the Laborites whose program was to make war inevitable, while Poland was being hypotized by assurances given by President Roosevelt's envoys who insisted that it should not even try to come to terms with Germany, whatever conditions the Reich might offer Poland.

It was only a little before this time that Roosevelt had proposed to the Italian ambassador in Washington a meeting with Mussolini, possibly in the Atlantic on the occasion of American and Italian naval maneuvers. Mussolini himself had never shown himself otherwise than friendly to the United States, and the idea of a meeting with the President appealed to him. But the course of events made it impossible. It is probable that Roosevelt, who, ever since 1937, had been contemplating another war,[16] was mainly eager to avert the possibility of any coöperation between Italy and Germany to the prejudice of Great Britain. It is, therefore, very doubtful that even if such a meeting had taken place, it would have led to any decisive result for the maintenance of peace.

In the years before the War, radical and ultra-liberal opinion in the United States, like that of the League of Nations Union in England, was overwhelmingly hostile to Fascism and Nazism, and the animosity grew after Hitler's anti-Semitic legislation, Mussolini's invasion of Ethiopia, and the Spanish Civil War. On the other hand, when the English were favoring the strengthening of Nazi Germany as a bulwark against Soviet Russia, the powerful conservative Eastern seaboard interests in the United States, always Anglophile after 1914, were very tolerant of Hitler's policies, even his diplomatic and political aggression. This attitude only changed as British conservative opinion shifted, due mainly to Hitler's financial policy of operating without the coöperation of foreign bankers.

The situation is well reflected by the writings of Walter Millis, one of the editors of the New York *Herald-Tribune,* the most influential American Anglophile newspaper. In 1937, Millis had written a book, *Viewed without Alarm: Europe Today.* Here he had stated that: "If the Nazis can create a going economic and social system in Central Europe, it will be—however unpleasant for the lesser nations which it swallows—not a menace, but a market and stabilizing force for the rest of the world." But, as soon as the British attitude toward Germany and Italy shifted and became bellicose, Millis changed his attitude and became one of the earliest and most vehement supporters of an early American intervention in the war.

One could be far more tolerant of the violent antipathy of British and American Liberals and Laborites toward the Fascist and Nazi totalitarianism if they had been consistent in their condemnation of all totalitarian ideas and practices which challenged "the Immortal Principles" of democracy and socialism. But, while vehemently denouncing the relatively moderate and conservative totalitarianism of Italy and Germany, they lauded the far more drastic and brutal totalitarianism of Soviet Russia and held it up as a model for the American and British liberals and democrats to imitate. At least this was true down to the Nazi-Soviet Pact of August, 1939. Even then, those who repudiated Russia did so mainly on the ground that it had come to terms with the hated Führer; not because of the brutal Soviet totalitarianism which had liquidated hundreds of thousands of deviants in the preceding three years, among them most of the best thinkers and generals in Russia.

[1] Gentizon, *op. cit.*, p. 227.

[2] From the name of the Sudeten mountain district which most of them inhabited.

[3] A popular gag was: "S.W. and W.S. have got the world in a hell of a mess."

[4] *Scritti e discorsi*, Vol. XII, p. 68.

[5] *Souvenirs d'une ambassade à Berlin*, Paris, 1946, p. 332.

[6] Quoted by Georges Bonnet in his book *De Washington au Quai d'Orsay*, Paris, 1946, p. 286.

[7] Hull, *op, cit.*, Vol. I, p. 592.

[8] That hostility to the Fascist regime was not really due to its arbitrary methods is proved by the extremely arbitrary acts, to put it mildly, of these same French democrats when they returned to power after the second World War. See Sisley Huddleston, *Terreur, 1944*, Paris, 1945; and *France: the Tragic Years, 1939-1947*, New York: Devin-Adair, 1955, Chaps. 18, 22, 23.

[9] Ciano, *Verso la catastrofe*, pp. 373-378.

[10] Gentizon, *op. cit.*, p. 244.

[11] The majority of shares were still in French hands.

[12] Ciano, *Diario, 1937-1938*, p. 302.

[13] Mario Toscano, *Le origini del Patto di Acciaio*, Florence, 1947, p. 37.

[14] At the end of the second World War, though it considered itself one of the victors, France was to lose more than "one hectare of territory."

[15] Grigoire Gafencu, *Les derniers jours de l'Europe*, Paris, 1946, pp. 170 ff.

[16] See F. R. Sanborn, *Design for War*, New York: Devin-Adair, 1951; and Viscount Elibank, "Franklin Roosevelt: Friend of Britain," in *Contemporary Review*, June, 1955.

CHAPTER TWENTY-TWO

Albania Again

Italy had continued to take an active interest in the affairs of Albania, which was making slow but steady progress under Italian guardianship. It was now fairly secure from any possible aggression on the part of its neighbors.

When the Albanian President, Ahmed Zogu, was proclaimed King Zog I at the suggestion of the Italian Government, he secured ever increasing support from Italy, which between the year of his proclamation (1928) and 1939 had spent 1,837,000,-000 lire on the country's development.

In the course of time, however, the new king's popularity tended to wane because he seemed more inclined to look after his own personal interests than those of his people, and the corruption in the public services did not diminish. There is evidence that he was beginning to intrigue with foreign powers to the detriment of Italy, especially after his marriage with a Hungarian noblewoman, and he was also getting into closer touch with Germany. As I said before, he had also made many personal enemies among his own subjects.

At the same time Italy was eager to strengthen its own position in the Balkans. Hitler had assured Mussolini on March 10, 1939, six days before his forces occupied Prague, that he had no objection to any Italian move of the kind. The German absorption of Bohemia-Moravia, the British guarantee to Poland and Britain's offer, together with that of France, of protection to Rumania and Greece finally led Italy to take a more direct part in Albanian affairs. This action was not taken at the suggestion of Germany.

King Zog in the uncertainty of his own situation was looking now toward this power and now toward that, hoping to strengthen himself by intrigues of various kinds. At one moment he had asked for a closer alliance with Italy, and negotiations to that effect had actually commenced. He had even requested that Italian troops be sent into the country, but afterward he had withdrawn the request at the suggestion of the British Government. While the negotiations were proceeding, the Albanian Minister of Foreign Affairs, Ekrem Libohova, was practically living in the Italian legation.

But when the draft text of the new Italo-Albanian treaty was submitted to Zog, he raised objections to it. The Italian Minister, Francesco Jacomoni, was then instructed by Ciano to withdraw from the negotiations, which were entrusted on the Italian side to General Alfredo Guzzoni, commanding the Italian expeditionary force. But it was Jacomoni together with Libohova who actually drafted the Albanian memorandum for a closer union.[1]

The Italian troops met with no opposition to speak of, for the small Albanian army was largely commanded by Italian officers, and the country was organized mainly on Italian lines. There were riots due to the entrance of some of the mountain tribes into Tirana, but all trouble ceased with the arrival of the Italian troops. The King then fled from his capital, and the Italian Minister saw to it that his departure was not interfered with in any way. His departure caused few regrets on the part of the Albanians.

The great majority of the people accepted the new situation willingly, and Jacomoni showed great tact in handling public affairs. The problem now was what form should be given to the closer relations between Italy and Albania. Italy had no wish to set up a colonial regime in the country; and after various discussions with Albanian leaders, Jacomoni's idea of a common citizenship between the two nations was agreed upon.

On April 12th an Albanian Constituent Assembly met and voted a resolution offering the crown of Albania to King Victor Emmanuel III of Italy, thereby establishing a personal union between the two kingdoms. An Albanian Cabinet and Parliament were instituted, and the King was represented by the then Italian Minister at Tirana, Jacomoni, as *Regio Luogotenente* (Viceroy).

Jacomoni's conception of a common citizenship was a most ingenious one, Italians in Albania enjoying the rights of Albanian citizens, and Albanians in Italy those of Italian citizens. Albania had its own Parliament, and some Albanians were appointed by the King to be members of the Italian Senate. The Albanian army was incorporated in that of Italy, the Italian Ministry of Foreign Affairs was jointly that of Albania, Albanians were eligible for Italian diplomatic and consular appointments, and an Albanian Fascist Party was created.

The system worked satisfactorily for all concerned, largely owing to Jacomoni's ability and to his great personal affection for the Albanian people and his popularity with them. Italy invested ever larger sums in Albania, thus developing its resources, which proved more important than had been believed before, especially in iron and other minerals. Important drainage and land reclamation plans were carried out, anti-malarial measures were introduced, and the Albanian people enjoyed a prosperity such as they had never known before.[2]

In Rome an undersecretaryship for Albanian Affairs was created to deal with all these various public works: it was entrusted to the Italian deputy and manufacturer, Zenone Benini.

The British and French Governments professed to be shocked by Italy's action in Albania, but they were chiefly annoyed by the strengthening of the Italian position in the Balkans. Winston Churchill in his *The Second World War* states that Albania was to be a springboard for Italian action against Greece and for neutralizing Yugoslavia.[3] But Greece raised no objection whatever, and Yugoslavia, which might have been expected to react violently, took the move quite calmly. Indeed, for the first time for many years Yugoslav relations with Italy seemed to have become quite cordial.

Secretary Cordell Hull, quoting the United States Ambassador in Rome, states that Italy's object was to bring Yugoslavia into the orbit of the Axis and that the occupation had been decided on at Hitler's suggestion. He further denounced Mussolini's occupation of Albania as "an additional threat to the peace of the world." [4] But Ciano, who was in a better position to know, asserts that it was actually inspired as an anti-German action, or at least by a desire to effect a counter-stroke to Germany's ever-increasing domination over Central Europe.

[1] From data supplied to the present writer by Sig. Jacomoni himself.

[2] All this prosperity came to an end after the second World War. Albania was reduced to slavery under Soviet domination, and the people are literally starving. Not even under Turkish rule was there as much misery and poverty.

[3] *Op. cit.,* p. 274.

[4] Hull, *Memoirs,* Vol. I, pp. 618-619; see also Tansill, *op. cit.,* p. 517.

CHAPTER TWENTY-THREE

From the Steel Pact to World War II

After the occupation of Albania, Italy was considered by the democratic governments (which were busily preparing for war) as the international danger No. 2. On April 14, 1939, President Roosevelt sent a message to Mussolini and to Hitler asking them for a guarantee that for at least ten years they would not attack any of the states mentioned in a list which included Nicaragua, Siam, Palestine, and, I think, the Republic of Andorra. Mr. Roosevelt could hardly have expected to promote peace, good-will and mutual confidence, for on that same day he made a provocative speech in which he compared the methods of Hitler and Mussolini to those of the "Huns and Vandals."

No reply was sent by the Duce to this surprising document, but on April 29th he answered it indirectly in a speech delivered in the Rome Capitol. The fact, he said, that Italy was busy preparing for a world exhibition in Rome to be held in 1942 and was erecting large and handsome buildings for the purpose implied that it had no intention of going to war: "It is time to reduce to silence the disseminators of panic, the anticipators of catastrophe, the professional fatalists who often cover with a huge banner their fear, their insensate hatred, or their defense of more or less avowable interests. . . . The universal Exhibition in Rome is destined to be the consecration of the efforts all civilized nations are making along the path of progress, and not only of material progress."

But these words of appeasement failed to appease. Mussolini earnestly hoped that the situation would be cleared up, but he did not intend to submit to the humiliation of Italy. Nor did he wish to get tied up indissolubly with Germany. But Great Britain and France were driving him daily further towards that connection. As Paul Gentizon writes: "While imagining that they were triumphing over Italy, they were working for their principal enemy, Germany." [1] In Great Britain it was still the ultra-imperialists who saw in Italy's new position in East Africa a danger to the route to India, and the League partisans (many of them still existed) were incensed at Italy's anti-League attitude. In France it was, as usual, the poisonous ideology of the *Front populaire* that instilled hatred against Italy as an anti-democratic nation and anti-"*Immortal Principles*." Germany represented a far greater danger for them, but Great Britain was coquetting with Germany—and neither Britain nor France had ever made a really effective gesture to Italy that might have enabled it to break away from Germany. When at last they tried to do so, they did it awkwardly, incompletely and too late.

Mussolini's original idea of the Axis was not a bellicose conception or one destined to detach the two powers from the rest of Europe. He saw it as part of a system wherein all the really peace-loving powers might operate in collaboration. But gradually it developed into an alliance of two powers having the same political, social and economic systems, of the two *non-habentes* nations, determined to make good their aspirations in the face of the *habentes,* demanding of them only parity of status and justice, whereas the *habentes,* having secured all that they wanted, rejected any idea of change.

When the first discussions took place for an alliance between Berlin and Rome, the instrument was intended to be of a tripartite nature—Germany, Italy and Japan. Japan insisted that it should have a definite and almost exclusively anti-Russia character, namely, the conversion of the anti-Comintern Pact into a real alliance. When von Ribbentrop suggested such a plan at the end of 1938, Mussolini agreed. On February 2, 1939, Ciano informed von Ribbentrop that the Duce's reasons for approving the idea were the now proved existence of a military pact between Great Britain and France, the predominance of warlike tendencies in France, and the renewed military preparations of the United States "with the object of providing the Western democracies with men, and above all, with material means in case of necessity." [2] Ciano continued to insist on the essentially defensive character of the Axis in order to insure "the possibility of working in tranquillity for a fairly long period." [3]

The bonds between Italy and Germany were extending to the field of economics and labor. As far back as 1937 some 30,-000 Italian farm workers had gone to Germany for agricultural employment, and trade between the two countries was becoming ever more important.

From 1936 to 1939 the climate of the Axis was specifically German. But the original idea had been Italian, dating as far back as 1922, or even earlier; and it was Mussolini who first gave it a practical shape, inspired as he was by the similarity of conditions in the two countries. Later on he saw in Hitler a pupil, even if in its later developments German National Socialism became very different from Italian Fascism. What conferred a more active character on the Axis was the fact of the Franco-British military pact, announced by the semi-official news agency *Informazione politica* on February 10, 1939. On March 5th the *Voce d'Italia* stated that, as soon as the British military magazines were once more filled with war material, "The melodies of the peace flute will be supplanted by a very different kind of music."

Beginning on April 8, 1939, the two Western Powers had been making desperate efforts to draw Soviet Russia into their fold for action against Germany and Italy. The crafty Stalin was not yet sure on which side his bread was buttered. He asked himself whether he could not secure by agreement with Hitler something better than what Great Britain and France had to offer him. We should not forget that Russia has always suffered from an inferiority complex with regard to the Germans, which it has not lost even today, owing to the long period during which Russia had been more or less under German influence;

and in 1939 Germany seemed a more solid ally than the Western Powers. Hitler at first had tried to get Poland to coöperate with him. This would undoubtedly have been the wisest plan for both. But when the attempt failed, largely owing to Roosevelt's pressure on Poland, England and France, Hitler approached Russia.

The nature and extent of Roosevelt's pressure on and assurances to Poland are detailed, among other places, in the so-called *German White Paper,* composed of Polish documents captured by the Germans during the invasion of Poland. They were published in the United States in 1940 by Howell and Soskin, with a Foreword by the able American scholar and publicist, C. Hartley Grattan. Their authenticity was denied vehemently by Secretary Hull and has been questioned by Dr. H. L. Trefousse in his *Germany and American Neutrality, 1939-1941.* But their genuineness and accuracy have been confirmed by informed and responsible Polish authorities who were in office at the time.

In the meantime, Japan had raised difficulties of various kinds, and the idea of a tripartite alliance gradually gave way to that of a dual alliance between Germany and Italy alone. Both Mussolini and Ciano were somewhat perturbed, fearing (among other things) that Hitler might extend his ambitions to Croatia, but they were reassured by the Führer's definite statement; in a letter of March 20th von Ribbentrop again informed Ciano that "in all Mediterranean questions the policy of the Axis must be decided by Rome." [4]

At a later period Ciano professed that he had always been opposed to the German alliance; but when the King had expressed doubts as to its opportuneness, and both the great airman, Marshal Italo Balbo, and Marshal Emilio De Bono, showed themselves not too enthusiastic at the prospect, it was Ciano who took up the defense of Hitler. It is not clear what his real opinions on the question were, but they probably varied from time to time, according to circumstances and to his own instability of character.

In a letter from Mussolini to Hitler, written just before the outbreak of the war (August 25, 1939) the Duce referred to a conversation he had had with Göring in the previous

April. After a long talk with the Marshal, Mussolini asked him in view of the disputes between Germany and the Western Powers: "But why don't you come to an alliance with Russia?" From this seed dropped into the brain of Göring we find the origins of the agreement between Hitler and Stalin of August 23rd. It was Mussolini who first suggested to Hitler that Bismarck's master principle of avoiding a war on two fronts was thoroughly sound even in 1939.

The letter to Hitler states: "As far as concerns an agreement, with Russia, I approve of it. H. E. Göring will tell you that in our conversation last April I stated that to avoid encirclement by the democratic powers a rapprochement with Russia was necessary." Indeed on the eve of the Pact with Russia a German diplomat told the Italian Ambassador in Berlin: "We have accepted Mussolini's suggestion."

About the Steel Pact there are many legends, and it has often been stated that Mussolini agreed to it in a moment of irritation against the press of the Western countries. But the reasons are far deeper. He agreed to it only when he realized that not Italy alone but all Europe was no longer in a position to escape from the dynamic policy of Germany, and that in alliance with Italy Hitler's Reich and Hitler's policy might be less dangerous to the rest of the world.

On May 4th, when the Pact was about to be signed, Mussolini prepared a note that was to serve as a directive for Ciano at his coming meeting with von Ribbentrop. It stated among other points:

It is my definite opinion that the two European Axis Powers need a period of peace of not less than three years.

It is only from 1943 that a warlike effort can have the greatest chance of success. A period of peace is necessary for Italy for the following reasons:

(a) to settle Libya and Albania militarily and to pacify Ethiopia, where an army of half a million men must be recruited;

(b) to finish the building or reconstruction of the six battleships now proceeding;

(c) for the renewal of all our heavy and medium-calibre artillery;

(d) to carry out autarchic plans calculated to avert all attempts at a blockade by the wealthy democracies;

(e) to hold the Exposition scheduled for 1942, which, besides presenting a record of what Italy has achieved in the last twenty years, may secure for us a reserve of foreign currency;

(f) to secure the repatriation of Italians from France, a serious problem of a military and moral nature;

(g) to complete the transfer, already begun, of many industries from the Po valley to Southern Italy;

(h) to strengthen ever more firmly the bonds, not only between the Axis Governments, but also between the various peoples to which a détente between the Church and Nazism would undoubtedly contribute, a détente also greatly desired by the Vatican.

For all these reasons Fascist Italy does not desire a premature war of a European character, although convinced that it is inevitable. It may also be possible that within three years Japan will have brought the war in China to an end.

This memorandum, which Ciano handed to von Ribbentrop on May 4, 1939, was submitted to Hitler on the eve of the signing of the Steel Pact. On the 23rd of that same month Hitler —as was not learned until the Nuremberg trials—presented the situation to the Berlin Chancery in very different terms, terms to which Mussolini never agreed. Here are some of the points of the Führer's statement:

At the present moment we are in a state of patriotic fervor shared by two other nations—Italy and Japan.

After six months the situation is today the following:

The political-national unity of the Germans has been fully realized save for minor exceptions; further success cannot be secured without bloodshed.

Danzig is by no means the cause of the dispute.

Poland will not resist Russian pressure.

It is not a question of sparing Poland, and we have decided to attack Poland on the first occasion.

We must not expect a repetition of the Czech business. There will be war. Our task is to isolate Poland. The success of isolation will be decisive.

Consequently the Führer will reserve for himself the right of giving the final order to attack. There must not be a simultaneous conflict with the Western Powers (France and Great Britain).

Bernardo Attolico, one of the ablest ambassadors Italy has ever had, had the great merit of grasping many things. He was not present at this meeting in the *Reichskanzlei,* but he had a thorough understanding of events that enabled him to guess some things the Germans did not say. It was his information that enabled Mussolini to submit to Hitler through von Ribbentrop the May 4 memorandum on the Italian situation, and also another (May 30th) brought to Berlin by General Ugo Cavallero that Filippo Anfuso (Ambassador in Berlin from 1943 to 1945), considered most important for the judgment the Italian people must deliver on these events. In addition to repeating what he had communicated through Ciano on May 4, Il Duce added:

Now that the alliance between Italy and Germany is concluded and will at every moment according to the letter and the spirit of the Treaty receive full application, I deem it advisable to set forth what I think of the present situation and of its probable future developments:

(1) War between the plutocratic and therefore egotistically conservative nations and the densely populated and poor nations is inevitable. Given this premise, we must be prepared.

(2) With the strategic positions conquered in Bohemia and Albania, the Axis Powers have in their hands a basic element of success.

(3) I have explained in a memorandum to von Ribbentrop at the time of the Milan meeting the reasons why Italy needs a period of preparation, which may go on to the end of 1942. They are:

The two European Axis Powers need a period of peace of not less than three years. It is only from 1943 onward that a war effort may have the greatest chances of victory.

He then made this further statement:

The war the great democracies are preparing is a war of attrition. We must, therefore, start from the hardest hypothesis, which is 100 per cent probable. The Axis will receive nothing more from the rest of the world. This hypothesis would be serious, but the strategic positions conquered by the Axis greatly reduce its gravity and the danger of a war of attrition. With this end in view we must take advantage of the first hours of the war and gain possession of the Danube basin and the Balkans. We must not be satisfied with declarations of neutrality, but we must occupy those territories and exploit them for war supplies, for foodstuffs and for industrial products.

With this operation, which should be carried out with lightning speed and extreme decision, not only would the *guaranteed* states— Greece, Rumania and Turkey—be put out of action, but our rear would be safeguarded. In this game we can count on two favorable elements—Hungary and Bulgaria.

These documents show that Mussolini, far from being a mere firebrand, advised against war on two fronts, considered war at that moment premature and finally advised that when war did come, it should begin on a basis of limited liability where all risks would be eliminated, as the eminent British military critic, Liddell Hart, always advises.

Indeed Hitler, on learning of Italy's decision to remain in a state of *non-belligerency*, said, "The Italians are repeating the game of 1915." [5]

In view of the very dangerous international situation Pope Pius XII on May 5, 1939, made a new appeal for peace and for the summoning of a peace conference, adressing it to all the Great Powers. This attempt might have succeeded, but the French Prime Minister, Daladier, on receiving the appeal, informed the Papal Nuncio that France "would not participate in any conference under the threat of German guns." The French refusal caused even this attempt to fall through. [6]

When the alliance was about to be definitely contracted, it was to have had at that time, in the opinion both of Mussolini and of Ciano, a non-military character. Its military aspect was to be left to a future period. Ciano, while preparing to visit Berlin for the signature, intended to bring with him as military advisers only two majors. The Germans, on hearing of this intention, were much surprised, as their delegation comprised generals of the highest rank; and so they asked that Italy should do likewise. Ciano then agreed to have a general in his suite, and the one most obviously indicated was General Alberto Pariani, the Undersecretary for War. But for reasons of his own, he did not wish to take Pariani, and had General Cavallero, then in retirement, recalled into service for the purpose. Ciano took him to Berlin. There on May 22, 1939, Ciano and von Ribbentrop signed the instrument that became known as the *Steel Pact* with a ceremony of great solemnity. In the text a certain measure of freedom of action was allowed to the two partners, for the alliance was by no means automatic. In Mussolini's view it remained always more political than military. Only in case of danger did each power undertake to lend support to the other, the Pact being definitely defensive.

Mussolini had written some notes on the treaty when it was about to be signed, and they are mentioned by Ciano.[7] Forced as he was into this situation by the attitude of the two Western Powers, Mussolini saw no safety except at the side of Germany whose military power and organization he could not help admiring. He thought that in view of the new Pact the Western Powers might be induced to alter their attitude, and that he himself might be called upon once more to play the part of mediator, as he had done in Munich and as he was to attempt to do again a few months later.

In his speech of April 20th (already quoted) the Duce hinted at the possibility of a new peace conference—not the *superconference* (*conferenzissima*) about which the press had spoken,[8] but another conference of the Four Powers, like the one that had led to the Four-Power Pact in 1933. He saw in the Steel Pact a means for diplomatic pressure in favor of a more just international situation. But for Hitler it was rather an instrument of intimidation and perhaps of war—but war in the East, as it was there that his ambition lay, not in the West. Churchill himself, on May 22nd, described the Pact as "the challenging answer to the flimsy British network of guarantees in Eastern Europe." [9]

Whatever its real nature may have been, the true authors of the Pact were Eden, Vansittart & Co. in Great Britain and Blum and the *Front populaire* in France with their respective camp followers, third-rate politicians, shady financiers and the cheap journalists of the reptile press in those and other countries.

On May 30th Mussolini sent General Cavallero to Berlin to explain Italy's military position and its need for a long period of preparation, and to make plain to the Führer that the Duce did not believe war with the Western Powers to be unavoidable. In his note to Hitler, he ended, as we have noted, by saying: "The war which the great democracies are preparing is a war of attrition. We must then start from the hardest hypothe-

sis which is 100 per cent possible: the Axis will receive nothing
more from the world." [10] He then set to work to prepare the
country for all possibilities—the fighting services, economic
autarchy, financial consolidation.

As soon as the Pact was signed, Hitler raised the Danzig ques-
tion. The political position of that city was quite preposterous,
and every German, from the most extreme Nazi to the Reddest
Communist, had long realized that it could not be maintained.
On June 17th Goebbels declared that Germany was determined
to recover the city, but the Polish Government, encouraged by
Great Britain and France, both warmly supported by President
Roosevelt, refused to consider any idea of surrendering Po-
land's rights in it. Hitler said that it was, above all, Great
Britain's guarantee that rendered the Poles intractable.

Italy's attitude in the German-Polish crisis at first was somewhat uncertain. Its relations with Poland had traditionally been
friendly, and Mussolini had always advocated the necessity of
a strong Polish state. But he realized that the permanent maintenance of the free city of Danzig and of the corridor was impossible, and he urged the Poles to come to a settlement with
Germany. Had it not been for the persistent encouragement
of Poland by the Western governments, a peaceful solution
might have been found.

On July 22nd Mussolini proposed an international conference
to settle the problem. But Hitler was not favorably inclined to
this idea. Mussolini then proposed a meeting between Ciano
and von Ribbentrop with the object of convincing Hitler that
at that moment war would be folly.[11] "Never," Ciano wrote,
"had Mussolini spoken with more warmth and sincerity on the
need for safeguarding peace."

Ciano met von Ribbentrop at Salzburg, where they were
joined by the ambassadors, Attolico from Berlin and von
Mackensen from Rome, on August 12-13th. Ciano also saw
Hitler at Berchtesgaden. He at once detected Germany's decision for immediate action, in spite of his own assertion that a
long period of peace was necessary. Von Ribbentrop, he wrote,
was determined on war but would give no details of specific
plans. Hitler, too, seemed uncompromising and demanded
Italy's coöperation.

On receiving Ciano's report, Mussolini mentioned that Article 3 of the Pact (providing for consultation before any drastic decision was taken) was not being respected, and he thought that in view of Hitler's attitude even a German attack on Italy was not out of the question. Indeed he then issued orders for erecting fortifications along the Italo-German frontier; and in due course this was done.

As even General Marshall states in his final report, Hitler, far from having a plan for world domination, had not even worked out a scheme for coöperation with his Axis ally in a limited war.

At this moment a surprise was sprung on the world. On August 21, 1939, a non-aggression pact between Germany and Russia was announced. While the British and French military representatives were negotiating with their Russian opposite numbers in Moscow for a military agreement, the Russians apparently passed on all the British and French information to the German representatives in the next room.[12]

This agreement totally altered the political situation, and Great Britain immediately concluded an alliance with Poland. France now made suggestions for Italian mediation, but Mussolini could no longer act with perfect freedom on account of the Steel Pact. Nevertheless he undertook to submit to the British and French Ambassadors in Rome a new solution whereby Danzig should be restored to Germany, after which an exchange of views and a general peace conference would follow.

On August 25th Hitler wrote to Mussolini, explaining Germany's situation with regard to Poland and the nature of the agreement with Russia. That same day Mussolini wrote to Hitler that if Germany attacked Poland, Italy would give the Reich full political and economic support. If the Allies attacked Germany, he suggested "the advisability of not assuming the initiative in warlike operations, in view of the actual state of Italy's military preparations, repeatedly communicated to you and to von Ribbentrop." The next day he sent Hitler a list of the supplies Italy needed, adding that Italy could not intervene and again proposing a political solution. Hitler replied that Germany could meet only a part of these requirements. Ciano wrote in his *Diary* that "Mussolini's military instinct and his sense of honor are drawing him towards war, but his reason holds him back." [13] Hitler then asked Mussolini not to announce his decision not to intervene "as long as it was not necessary" and to continue making such preparations as would immobilize the Franco-British forces. This Mussolini agreed to do.[14]

The French Government was tending to come around to the idea of a possible agreement with Italy, but it always found obstacles in the British attitude. Another factor that contributed to the difficulty of arriving at a real *détente* was the activities of the former Italian Minister of Foreign Affairs, Count Carlo Sforza. In his own book[15] he confesses that on August 29, 1939, he told two of the most important members of the French Government (Bonnet and Daladier) that the war was only a question of days and that they should ask Mussolini, "Are you with us, or against us?" They should tell him that "It is not your fault if you are obliged to take precautions against a regime that has publicly demanded French territories . . . If Mussolini tries to gain time with formal promises of neutrality, answer him (and let Italy know your answer): 'We cannot believe you . . . Fascism has so often broken its word, that we must, with regret, demand pledges.' Either Mussolini accepts, and he is lost—all Italy will vomit him; or he refuses, and this is what honest and gallant generals tell me: Italy has never been so disarmed and so incapable of fighting as at the present moment. In both cases France is saved, Italy is saved, and perhaps European peace, for Hitler will be disturbed at this sudden return of French virility. But if you go on caressing Mussolini, as de Monzie and one or two other French Ministers do, maneuvered by Italian intrigues, you are lost." He added that of all the statesmen whom he had known Beneš alone "had always shown himself ready to collaborate, realizing that Fascism was the supreme danger." Sforza repeated these statements in his speech at the Eliseo Theatre in Rome on August 20, 1944.[16] His attitude in August, 1939, is confirmed by the French statesman, Anatole de Monzie. In his book, *Ci-devant,* under an entry of August 28, 1939, he says: "I have not been wrong about the activities of the *fuorusciti* [Italian self-exiles], of whom Count Sforza is the leader. They are thinking about war with Italy. They would, therefore, overthrow Fascism and set themselves up amidst its ruins. One might count on the Italy of Count Sforza." [17] These treacherous intrigues undoubtedly contributed to restrain the French from coming to a decision to collaborate sincerely with Italy in working for peace.

On August 29th the Italian Ambassador, Attolico, stated that Hitler was skeptical about British suggestions, but was prepared to negotiate with Poland direct.[18] The next day Poland mobilized her army and there were incidents at Danzig. By the 31st the situation was well-nigh desperate. But Mussolini was determined to make yet another effort for peace. Knowing Hitler's dislike of general conferences, he thought that if he were promised Danzig in advance, he might agree to a limited meeting. He therefore made the suggestion to the British Government, but was met with a refusal. He then took it upon himself to propose a conference between the delegates of Italy, Great Britain, France and Germany to be held on September 5th "to examine the present difficulties arising from the Versailles Treaty."

During that day no answer was received. Then Chamberlain and Halifax declared that before such a proposal could be accepted, both Germany and Poland must demobilize; but the French Government decided that the Italian proposal might be accepted, provided that Poland were also invited to the conference and that all European problems should be discussed at it "so as to ensure a lasting peace." In order to harmonize the British and the French points of view, the answer to the Italian proposal was adjourned to the next day, September 1st. Germany had only given Poland time to agree to the negotiations until midnight of August 31st.

As negotiations had not begun by that time, German troops moved into Poland. The Germans claimed that there had already been fourteen violations of the German frontiers by Polish troops. The British Government, after ordering a general mobilization, agreed to accept Mussolini's proposal, but only on condition that all German forces were withdrawn from Polish territory; and France accepted on the same condition.

Mussolini realized that Hitler would never agree to this condition, but he implored the British and French Governments to await Germany's answer until the following day. Paris agreed to this, but London, now determined on war at all costs, declared that negotiations were impossible as long as German troops were on Polish soil. Consequently, at 9 a.m. on September 3rd the British Ambassador in Berlin asked von Ribbentrop if Germany would withdraw its troops from Poland. On receiving a negative reply, he informed the German Foreign Minister that Great Britain would consider itself at war with Germany as from 11 a.m. on that same day. At noon, the French Ambassador announced that hostilities would begin on the part of France at 5 p.m.

The second World War had thus begun. In a sense, it is still going on. While President Roosevelt had opposed military action against Germany on the part of Britain and France at the time of Munich, he pressed Britain, France and Poland to stand firm against Hitler in the crisis of 1939. By this time, with the Czechoslovak army immobilized and with Russia in a pact with Hitler, it seemed apparent at the time that a European war would continue long enough for Roosevelt to bring the United States into the conflict. Yet, had Hitler followed up his defeat of Britain, France and the Low Countries vigorously in 1940, it might not have turned out that way.

In the face of his encouragement of a firm stand by Britain, France and Poland against Germany, his pledges to Britain in the event of war, and his knowledge that the American people, on the other hand, were strongly against involvement in another European war, Roosevelt had to be extremely careful about the American diplomatic "record" in the 1939 crisis. Hence, he sent a number of pleas for peace in late August, 1939, for the sake of the "record," just as he dispatched a plea to the Japanese Emperor on the morning of December 7, 1941, *after* he knew that an attack on Pearl Harbor was almost certain before sunset on that very day.

All this explains Roosevelt's excessive sensitivity toward his "record." On the eve of Pearl Harbor, when Roosevelt and Hopkins were awaiting the attack on the next day, Hopkins observed that it was too bad that the United States could not strike the first blow and avert disaster. Roosevelt's reply indicated that he regarded the protection of his formal or apparent diplomatic "record" as more important than the protection of American lives.

[1] Gentizon, *op. cit.*, p. 310.

[2] Toscano, *op. cit.*, p. 19.

[3] *Ibid.*, p. 20.

[4] *Ibid.*, p. 37; Ciano, *L'Europa verso la catastrofe*, p. 420.

[5] Documents quoted by Filippo Anfuso in "I Rapporti italo-germanici," in *Nazionalismo sociale*, April 15, 1952.

[6] See Tansill, *op. cit.*, p. 523.

[7] Ciano, *op. cit.*, pp. 428-432.

[8] *Scritti e discorsi*, Vol. XII, p. 176.

[9] *The Second World War*, p. 294.

[10] Gentizon, *op. cit.*, p. 327.

[11] Ciano, *Diario, 1939-1943*, Vol. I, August 9, 1939.

[12] Statement made by Ciano.

[13] August 26, 1939.

[14] *Hitler e Mussolini*, Milan, 1946, pp. 6 and 7.

[15] Carlo Sforza, *L'Italia dal 1914 al 1944 quale la vidi io*, Milan, 1945, pp. 160-161.

[16] *Ibid.*, pp. 212-227.

[17] de Monzie, *op. cit.*, p. 144.

[18] *Hitler e Mussolini*, p. 10.

PART IV

THE SECOND WORLD WAR AND THE FALL OF FASCISM

CHAPTER TWENTY-FOUR

Non-Belligerence

Italy had done everything in its power to avert war, but from March, 1939, onward Mussolini found himself ever confronted by Hitler's impatience and by Great Britain's obstinate determination to go to war against Germany. The British and French Governments had bound themselves if Poland were attacked, even if there had been provocation on its part, to intervene on its behalf by force of arms. But they did not move a finger to assist that country. When Russia invaded Eastern Poland, thus doing exactly what Germany had done, but without Germany's excuse, the British and French did not declare war on Russia but merely said: "How very dreadful it all is!"

All that they could promise Poland was that when the proper time came, they would liberate it—after Poland had been completely flattened out. Later on, as the published Yalta documents prove, under the pressure of President Roosevelt, they handed Poland over, body and soul, to a tyranny infinitely worse than that of Nazi Germany.[1]

I remember talking with a British official in Rome connected with his government's propaganda services. He asked me at the beginning of the war what could be done to make the British cause more popular in Italy. I replied: "If you can explain

satisfactorily why you have done absolutely nothing to help
Poland after Germany invaded her, and why you have not declared war on Russia when she invaded Poland (with which
Russia was not at war), you will have done the trick." No answer to either query was forthcoming.

The Italian Government announced that it was not intervening in the war, and both Chamberlain and Daladier
"rendered homage to the noble efforts of the Head of the Italian
Government" to avert war.

In Italy public opinion, while deeply anxious at the turn
the situation had taken, was much relieved that the country was
not involved in the conflict, at least for the present. The chief
of the political police at the time, Dr. Guido Leto, in an interesting volume of reminiscences[2] gives an account of the
reports received by his office at the time from inspectors in all
parts of the country and all grades of society. These reports
showed that at that time the great majority of public opinion
was wholly opposed to Italy's intervention, and the reports were
submitted to Mussolini by the Chief of Police, Dr. Arturo Bocchini. Leto wrote: "Among the circumstances, unknown to myself, that determined Italy's declaration of non-belligerence, it
is not too much to include the arguments Bocchini courageously
submitted to the Duce in writing and orally, and I think it is
not an exaggeration to claim for the police this small or great
merit." [3]

The Italian leaders and public realized that a German victory
might mean German hegemony over all Europe, while an
Anglo-French victory would have equally undesirable effects.
Then it was asked whether, in spite of Hitler's declaration
that "he did not intend to appeal for outside help," he might
not end by invoking the *casus foederis* whereby Italy was bound
to assist Germany, and what would be the consequences of an
Italian refusal. On the whole, however, there was trust in Mussolini's skill in piloting the nation's policy in the best possible
way in those very difficult circumstances. For some time the
press abstained from all polemics concerning the war and Italy's
attitude towards it.

Italians were greatly shocked at Russia's unprovoked invasion
of Poland, for they had always been opposed to any Russian

advance westward. In spite of the agreement between Hitler and Stalin, they regarded the complete suppression of Poland as most undesirable from every point of view. The press generally advocated the restoration of a purely Polish Poland, without Danzig or the German, Ukrainian and Lithuanian provinces. The brutal Russian attack on Finland was strongly condemned, and there were many pro-Finnish demonstrations in Rome and elsewhere. But there was a feeling of satisfaction that no military operations were being undertaken on Germany's Western front, and it was still hoped that this fact indicated that the war might soon be brought to an end.

Relations with Russia were somewhat peculiar and by no means cordial. In December, 1939, the new Russian Ambassador, Ivan Gorelkin, came to Rome. He had submitted his credentials to the King of Italy, also as Emperor of Ethiopia and King of Albania, and to the Ministry of Foreign Affairs, where they were found to be quite in order. But the day before the one fixed for his audience at the Quirinal, he suddenly departed for Moscow. It seems that Stalin, irritated at the pro-Finnish demonstrations and the anti-Bolshevik articles in the Italian papers, decided to show his resentment by recalling his Ambassador without definitely breaking off relations with Italy. The Italian Ambassador in Moscow, Augusto Rosso, was likewise recalled.

Italy did not declare its neutrality, but defined its attitude as one of non-belligerence, as laid down in a resolution voted by the Fascist Grand Council on December 7, 1939—a status unknown in international law. It meant that Italy did not intervene in the war because its interests were not at that moment at stake; neutrality would have implied a determination to keep out of the war altogether. Italy by no means repudiated its alliance with Germany, and it refused to repudiate the anti-Comintern Pact, which Germany had tacitly dropped owing to her non-aggression pact with Russia. Italy's action aroused some resentment in German military circles, where there were reminders of Italian conduct in 1914-1915, but Hitler never encouraged these feelings.

In French circles it was recognized that Mussolini's policy had been of great value not only to France itself but to Europe generally, for it helped to localize the war and keep it out of the Mediterranean and the Balkans. In certain British quarters Italian non-intervention was at first regretted, for on the outbreak of the conflict it was hoped that Mussolini and Hitler might be crushed together once for all.

In a speech in the Chamber of Deputies on December 16, 1939, Ciano summed up Italy's whole foreign policy since Versailles and her relations with Germany, stating that the Axis, the result of sanctions, had been conceived as an instrument of order and of resistance to Bolshevik aggression. He admitted the inopportune character of Germany's action against Poland. He said that at Salzburg he had warned Hitler that his proposed Polish policy would lead to a general European war, but that Hitler did not believe him. It was thus clear that when war broke out, the two partners in the Axis did not see eye to eye and were following different if not divergent lines. But Italy had no intention of supporting the Western Powers which ever since 1918 had shown themselves ungrateful for Italy's collaboration in the first World War. The path of Italy was thus still uncertain, but it was determined not to take up arms unless its interests were gravely menaced.

On January 1, 1940, Mussolini wrote to Hitler explaining Ciano's speech and the effect produced by the Russo-German agreement, while assuring him that Italy's relations with the Western Powers were correct but cold. He considered that the existence of a small purely Polish Poland would be desirable even for Germany, and that any further intensification of Germany's relations with Russia would have disastrous effects in Italy, where "anti-Bolshevik unanimity is absolutely rock-bound and unbreakable," for Russia could never be a friend.[4]

We come now to the much-debated question of the letters exchanged between Mussolini and his old friend and admirer, Winston Churchill, during this period. This correspondence has often been mentioned, and the Italian press repeatedly stated that Churchill's various visits to Italy after the second World War—the most recent in the summer and autumn of 1951— had for their object an attempt to recover these letters. Others have denied their existence.

In 1954, *Oggi* and other weekly papers published a number

of letters purporting to have been written by Churchill to Mussolini, but even a cursory examination of their contents by any well-informed person was enough to convince any sensible reader that they were forgeries. The statement made to me in 1951 by one Tommaso David, formerly an N.C.O. attached to a police office in Mussolini's Government in 1944-1945, that he had the Churchill-Mussolini correspondence in his possession and would publish it when Churchill again became prime minister, proved equally unreliable.

Much more important is the statement of Count Vanni Teodorani, a son-in-law of Mussolini's brother Arnaldo and at the time head of the Duce's military secretariat at Gargnano. He told me that he had actually seen and read the correspondence, which began a considerable time before the war and ended with two letters written by Churchill to Mussolini during the period of Italy's non-belligerence.

Besides containing many expressions of admiration for Fascism and its leader, there is an interesting suggestion as to what the British statesman thought should be Italy's policy of Mediterranean expansion. Taking for granted the continuance of Italy's non-belligerence, which he had publicly advocated in various speeches, Churchill wrote that if in a second phase of the war Italy decided to take an active part, this could only be in the Balkans, where Germany might be tempted to expand in her new *Drang nach Osten* policy to the prejudice of Italy. Churchill believed that the phony war might be stabilized indefinitely along the Siegfried line. On the other hand, having decided to block the eastward path of the Reich, he actually condoned the Ribbentrop-Molotov agreement of August 21, 1939, and he egged Italy on to attack Yugoslavia and, above all, Greece. In the two letters there are, in fact, very definite hints at the necessity for Italy in the further development of the war to consolidate its position in the Balkans, where its presence in Albania and eventually, if it became necessary, in Greece would not be opposed by Great Britain.

Thus it was the then First Lord of the Admiralty and afterward Prime Minister of Great Britain, who suggested an Italian campaign against Greece, thereby trying to promote Ciano's policy of the *horizontal Axis*. Before the *Anschluss* this would have comprised Austria, Hungary and Yugoslavia; but after the events of March, 1938, it was displaced further to the south. The advance both of Germany and/or Russia toward the Balkans would have been blocked by Italy to the satisfaction of Great Britain.

As a compensation for a continuance of her non-belligerence, Italy would be rewarded with strategic bases and other territories in French North Africa. This suggestion was by no means incompatible with the policy of Churchill and not a few other British statesmen, ever generous with what belongs to others. The extreme manifestation of this in the case of Churchill was revealed by the publication of the Yalta documents.

That Churchill should have made these suggestions without the knowledge and approval of his own Prime Minister and of the other members of his Government on the face of it might seem unlikely; but in view of Churchill's secret correspondence with Roosevelt before Churchill became Prime Minister, and his actions on various other occasions, it is far from impossible.[5]

Teodorani believes the letters (or photostatic copies) are in safe hands and there is mention of them in General Cavallero's unpublished papers. It is probable that there were several copies or photostats of them. In any case Teodorani's evidence cannot be ignored. Up to the present no denial of the existence of this correspondence has been made, except in one Italian paper which remarked that Mussolini was always in the habit of handing over all documents of a public nature to the proper government department. But it is very likely that, in view of their extreme importance, he kept these letters for future use. The ex-Minister, Araldo di Crollalanza, who served under Mussolini until the very end, told me that the Duce had often shown him a brief case that he kept on his desk. Mussolini assured him that it contained full materials for justifying his policy but gave him no further particulars.

Italy's economic situation on the outbreak of the war to some extent explains its general policy. At first the conflict brought Italy large profits, especially through her mercantile marine, for her vessels, practically free from foreign competition, were able to ply safely between European and American ports and thus do an excellent business.

Very soon, however, Great Britain and France began to impose serious handicaps on Italian sea-borne trade. In the early period of the war Great Britain had continued to sell coal to Italy. But subsequently these exports were strictly limited, and Italian importers had to secure from Germany by sea *via* Rotterdam coal amounting to about seven million tons a year, which was almost two-thirds of German exports to Italy. Italian ships were held up, delayed and otherwise interfered with. These difficulties applied to trade in other commodities besides coal.

In February, 1940, the British Government offered Italy a deal: If it would sell war materials to Great Britain, British coal would be sent to Italy in exchange. But the Italian Government could not agree to this proposal. In the first place, in view of its own requirements, Italy dared not export war materials because it had insufficient quantities and had to take precautions against future risks. In the second place, such exports would have aroused violent indignation in Germany as a form of treachery to an ally and might have actually provoked a German attack on Italy. Mussolini made it a question of honor, and rejected the proposed deal.

The result was a blockade of all export by sea of German coal to Italy. The first Italian colliers were seized on March 6th, and this meant increasing paralysis for Italian shipping and other industries. Italian ships were frequently held up, forced to go into ports controlled by the Allies and delayed for weeks on end on any pretext or no pretext. An Italian official report, signed by Count Luca Pietromarchi of the Ministry of Foreign Affairs, set forth in detail the intolerable situation imposed on Italy by these measures, which reminded him very strongly of sanctions.

On the occasion of von Ribbentrop's visit to Rome an agreement was concluded (March 15th) whereby German coal was to be forwarded to Italy overland, and 500 trucks of coal crossed the Alps every day.

But the restraint of Italy's maritime trade continued until it became almost impossible for any Italian ship to ply the Mediterranean. The press was full of protests against these vexatious measures which threatened the country with economic starvation.[6] They exercised considerable influence on Mussolini and contributed to mold his foreign policy although, of course, many other factors were involved.

Public opinion remained confused. While Great Britain was accused of anti-Italian policy during sanctions and with having broken the Stresa front, Germany was accused of using Italy for purely German interests. It was, indeed, a tragic situation, largely due to the incredible short-sightedness of British and French politicians who, although terrified at the thought of German hegemony, were deliberately breaking down all the barriers opposed to it.

Throughout this period Mussolini rarely spoke in public, and he told the Fascist leaders in Bologna that he would address the Italian people from Palazzo Venezia only when he had a historic decision to announce. He was harassed by uncertainties, but he still hoped to get the situation settled by a conference.

With regard to the Steel Pact, General Mario Roatta, then Assistant Chief of the Staff, tells us that throughout the period of non-belligerence there were few direct contacts between the Italian and the German military authorities. Mussolini was always anxious about a possible German attack on Italy.[7] All that he could do was to strengthen the country's armaments, which were still in a backward state, and to improve the economic situation by intensifying the policy of autarchy, which was necessary in view of the great difficulties in international trade. The navy and the air force were adequately equipped, and their personnel was excellent. The army was in a less satisfactory condition; trained reserves were few, the regimental officers were good, but the General Staff and many of the generals of higher rank left a great deal to be desired.

In February, 1940, the American Assistant Secretary of State and one of President Roosevelt's *Missi dominici,* Sumner Welles, came to Italy to explore the situation. From what we now know, Roosevelt had for over two years past been preparing for war and wished the United States to intervene in the struggle at the earliest opportunity. But possibly Sumner Welles was not aware of it at the time and believed that the President merely wished to ascertain the actual possibilities for concluding peace. Welles, himself, may have been ignorant of the real state of affairs, and he seemed ready to accept all the commonplaces current in the more unreliable press. But the evident object of his mission was the best means of supporting the Western Powers.

In his book, *The Time for Decision*,[8] Welles admits that Ciano made a better impression on him than he had expected. Instead of being overbearing and full of his own importance, Welles says, Ciano was cordial, unaffected and simple. On February 26th Welles was received by Mussolini, who had not admitted any foreign ambassador or envoy since the outbreak of the war. He, too, made a very favorable impression on Welles and answered his questions very clearly and definitely. The Assistant Secretary of State admitted that Italy's detachment from Germany would not have deflected Hitler from his purpose, and he adds that "only the sure knowledge that the power of the United States would be directed against him if he attempted to carry out his intention of conquering the world by force would restrain him." Hitler, as even General Marshall admits, had no such intention, but Welles may have believed that he did. He goes on to say that "not only the vast majority of the Italian people, but also the key figures within the Government itself—save those notoriously under the Nazi influence and, of course, Mussolini himself—were totally and even violently opposed to the entrance of Italy into the war." [9] As we have seen, Mussolini at that time was far from being definitely in favor of intervention. We shall see later how his attitude and that of public opinion was to change, and why.

Welles submitted to Mussolini a message from President Roosevelt emphasizing his wish that Italy should remain neutral. By this Roosevelt really meant and hoped that Italian neutrality would weaken Germany which he was determined to see crushed at all costs.

The question of autarchy also was raised, and the Duce pointed out that Italy had been the last important country to embark on such a policy. The British Empire at Ottawa and the United States by its high tariffs and other countries by similar measures had forced Italy into that system "as a last resort and in self-defense."

Speaking of Poland, Mussolini told Welles that "the Polish people are entitled to their untrammelled independence and sovereignty, and I shall support them in their endeavor. But this does not mean that Poland should again become a crazy quilt of diverse nationalities. The real Germans of Danzig, of the Corridor and of Posen should remain in the Reich. The real Poles should have their free Poland with access to the sea." [10] He further insisted that there could be no true peace so long as Italy could not have free entry into and exit from the Mediterranean.

In a second interview in March, 1940, after von Ribbentrop's visit to Rome, Mussolini told Welles that Hitler would not consider any solution other than a military victory, that he was preparing a new offensive, and that for the moment negotiations were excluded. He set forth his own attempts to induce Hitler to suspend the offensive and to open peace negotiations to assure for Germany a living space. Mussolini said that he saw a future Europe formed by a federation of the Great Powers (the Four-Power Pact again) which would insure the integrity and independence of the smaller powers. Europe today, he concluded, cannot stand the outbreak of a *real* war; it is not in a condition to face great struggles every twenty years.

Welles phoned to Roosevelt, asking to be authorized to undertake a new peace initiative, but the President refused to commit himself.

On March 18th Mussolini met Hitler on the Brenner. Hitler told Mussolini again that Germany had no peace negotiations in view, and that he was determined to pursue his course by military action. He said that Mussolini must now decide whether to intervene or not. The Duce might still refuse, but he then risked a German attack on Italy. Hence, he ended by agreeing to intervention in principle, but he insisted that it was up to himself to choose the moment. If intervention was to come, it must be at moment in full harmony with Italian interests. He still hoped that Italy's intervention might be merely formal, without entering the fiery furnace; and later events were to show that this idea was then by no means impossible.

On April 7th the phony war came to an end when Germany invaded Norway to frustrate a British expedition against that country already on its way.[11] Then followed the invasion of

Holland, of Belgium and of France, where the famous Maginot Line crumbled without much resistance. The British expeditionary force was completely routed and forced to re-embark at Dunkirk for England, after suffering heavy casualties and losing all its artillery and equipment. Neville Chamberlain then resigned the premiership and was succeeded by Winston Churchill, who as First Lord of the Admiralty had really been responsible for the British defeat in Norway.

Secretary Cordell Hull in his memoirs reports various measures and suggestions by the United States Government to prevent Italy from intervening, not of course in the interest of Italy or of peace in general, but for the benefit of Great Britain and France. The United States Ambassador in Rome, William Phillips, cabled on April 12th that "Mussolini cannot make any new move until he is convinced that the Germans will come out victorious." [12] He and Myron Taylor[13] asked the President to make a last appeal to Mussolini, and Roosevelt did make two such appeals. Ambassador William Bullitt in Paris proposed to Roosevelt that he should request the Pope to threaten the Duce with excommunication if Italy should enter the war, that the Atlantic Fleet should be sent on a "courtesy visit" to Greece, that the remittances of Italian immigrants in the United States should be held up, and that these immigrants should be invited to pass resolutions against Italian intervention. All this, of course, for the benefit of Great Britain and France.

Germany now began to bring stronger pressure to bear on Italy in favor of intervention. The navy was the Reich's weak point (except in submarines), and on the water Italian help would be invaluable.

On the other hand, the British press began to lavish compliments on Italy, to remind its readers of Italy's attitude in 1914 (which it seems to have only just then discovered), of Mussolini's generous outburst about Belgium at that time, etc., etc. To all this the semi-official *Voce d'Italia* retorted: "Against the *words* of 1914 there are the *facts* of 1919, of 1935 and of the subsequent years."

Mussolini's own viewpoint, however, was, as usual, based only on the interests of Italy and on her position in the Mediterranean and in Africa.

In France, certain statesmen now began to make strenuous efforts to establish true friendship with Italy. Laval, above all, came out very strongly in favor of negotiations for an understanding, for which he had always honestly striven, and he criticized Daladier for not having accepted Italy's offer of mediation in the summer of 1939. Daladier was then forced to resign, but the President of the Republic, instead of sending for Laval, which would have been the obvious course to follow, preferred Reynaud. The new Prime Minister at once summoned the Italian Ambassador, Raffaele Guariglia, and assured him that if France won the war, Italy would have nothing to fear. Guariglia replied that the trouble was the presence of British janitors at the two exits of the Mediterranean. On April 24th Reynaud wrote to Mussolini that war between France and Italy would be sacrilege; the Duce's reply was somewhat chilly.

On May 1st Roosevelt sent Mussolini an oral message to the effect that an extension of the conflict (through Italian intervention) would have world-wide reactions. To this the Duce retorted: "America for the Americans is good enough for the United States, but Europe for the Europeans is good enough for the Old World." Churchill wrote to Mussolini that he had never been opposed to Italy's greatness, but Mussolini reminded him of Great Britain's recent policy of sanctions and of Italy's state of servitude in its own (and only) sea: "If it is only to honor your signature that your Government has declared war on Germany, you will understand that the same sentiments of honor and respect for obligations undertaken with the Italo-German treaty guide Italy's policy today, and will guide it tomorrow in the face of any event." [14]

The French Ambassador in Rome submitted to his Government on May 20th a suggestion that the Italian Government be informed through the Pope of the sacrifices that France was prepared to make to secure the prolongation of Italy's non-belligerence: a modification of the status of the Italians in Tunisia, concessions at Jibuti and French pressure on Great Britain in favor of concessions in the Mediterranean. Reynaud did not appear keen about such a proposal, but in France's desperate situation he felt that something must be done. He, therefore, went to London to consult Churchill, Halifax, Chamberlain

and Attlee. Halifax was prepared to agree, but Churchill and
Attlee were not. Nevertheless, a message was sent to Roosevelt
asking him to appeal to Mussolini once more; and on May 26th
the President sent another message to the Duce, stating that if
he would define Italy's specific grievances, he would communicate them to Great Britain and France, undertaking that Italy
would be admitted to the Peace Conference on terms of equality with the belligerents. Ciano replied simply that Italy must
fulfill its treaty engagements. A further message from Roosevelt
(May 31st), to the effect that Italy's intervention "would result
in an increase in the rearmament program of the United States"
and that the United States had interests in the Mediterranean,
was countered by Mussolini's retort that they were "the same
as Italy's interests in the Caribbean." [15]

In France the surrender of Belgium had produced deep consternation. At last, on May 27th, the Government decided to
make a further effort to satisfy Italy's aspirations. But before
doing so, Reynaud felt that he must again consult Churchill;
and on the 28th the British Premier replied that in view of the
disasters to the Allied arms it was not the moment to enter into
negotiations, expressing himself as flatly opposed to any concessions to Italy.

Nevertheless, Reynaud, under the pressure of some members
of the Cabinet, especially de Monzie and Chautemps, decided
to make a final effort to preserve Franco-Italian collaboration
in the Mediterranean. A vague plan was communicated to the
Italian Ambassador, who passed it on to Rome, but the Duce
considered it too indefinite. Even now, it was again Great Britain that opposed all real concessions by France. The British
Government either hoped to secure Italy's help for nothing, or
perhaps preferred to have it as an enemy to be flattened out
along with Germany, or even to have it as a mediator at the
peace table.

In Italy itself a change was now coming over public opinion.
As we have seen, according to the police reports at the time of
the outbreak of the war, virtually all Italy was opposed to intervention. But now the further reports sent in told a different
tale. The general feeling was one of anxious but not terrified
expectation. The war industries had spread prosperity in many

circles, and it was hoped that the amazing German victories would soon bring the conflict to an end. But, as Leto expressed it, there was now the fear that if Germany won the dread struggle unaided, "we, although ideologically allied to her, might remain deprived of any benefit with regard to our national aspirations. That on account of our prudence—the responsibility for which was attributed to Mussolini—we might perhaps even be punished by the Germans, and that if we are to be in time, we must drive ahead and enter the war at once." [16] This argument had been originally presented with the object of shaking the country's confidence in Mussolini and formed part of the spate of rumors spread about from day to day by the anti-Fascists for propaganda purposes. But it extended to ever wider strata that feared Italy's intervention might take place too late. In anti-Fascist circles, it was hoped that Italy's intervention would end in defeat and in the collapse of the Fascist regime, for an Italian defeat, it was considered, would be a cheap price to pay for the overthrow of Fascism.

The fear of entering too late emanated even from circles connected with the Court. The King, himself, who at first had been by no means an interventionist, feared that through the temporizing attitude of his Prime Minister Italy risked arriving "when the table was cleared." [17]

According to the chief of the political police (already quoted), this state of public opinion, if it was not the determining cause of Italy's intervention, was certainly one of the most important of the contributory causes: "Responsibilities for the final decision should then be equally distributed between the Crown, the Government and the people." [18]

Mussolini thus found himself faced with the gravest crisis of his life and in the whole history of his country. If things went well, that would assure Italy's position and his own triumph as the maker of the new Italy. If they went ill, it would mean disaster for his country, the end of the Fascist regime, ruin and perhaps death for himself—this last was the least of his considerations, for it was the country, above all, about which he was most deeply anxious. He would have been glad to to see Italian aspirations realized in an atmosphere of friendship with Great Britain and France, but during the preceding five years and more he had found in those quarters nothing but suspicion, hostility and petty jealousy, veiled or open, and he had become ever more convinced that the two Western Powers were determined to keep Italy in a state of permanent subjection. Evidence of this was seen in the guarantees given to (though not asked for by) Rumania and Greece, in the Anglo-Turkish treaty and, above all, in the Anglo-French military alliance. The strangling methods lately applied to Italian sea-borne trade put the lid on. Great Britain, he fully realized, never forgave an injury and would not forget its diplomatic defeat over Ethiopia. Now that France seemed ready to make concessions to Italy, it was still the British Government that held up any attempt of the kind.

We may ask ourselves what was the alternative for Italy except to throw in its lot with Germany and intervene on Germany's side in the war. Italy might, it is claimed, have remained neutral to the end of the conflict or else have joined the Western Powers.

Had Italy chosen the first course, it would sooner or later have been subjected to ever-increasing pressure by both sides; in the end owing to its geographical situation it would have had an ultimatum from the Allies and/or from Germany to join one side or the other, or at least to allow the Allied or the German armed forces to make use of its territory. If Italy refused, it would have been invaded and devastated by the victors, whoever they were, as a vanquished, cowardly and contemptible nation, and been deprived of all its colonies and perhaps of a large part of its metropolitan territory.

Had Italy chosen the second alternative, its fate might well have been that of Poland: an immediate German invasion with all its disastrous consequences, and as much help as Poland had received from the Western Powers—exactly none at all. Then in case of a final German victory, Italy would have been reduced to the status of a German colony. In case of a final victory of the Western Powers, it would have been "*liberated*" by them with the infliction of another devastating occupation, and what little would have been left after the German occupation would have been wiped out by the "liberators." In the end Italy would have been a pensioner or a poor relation living on the alms of the rich man's table; and as the rich man would no longer be very rich, the alms would be meagre indeed.

A third possibility suggested, is that if Italy had never shown any friendship at all for Germany, Hitler would not have gone to war, and all would have been well. The answer to that is very simple. As I think I have proved again and again, it was the Western Powers that forced Italy into the German camp. Italy was not strong enough to stand alone and had to seek alliances somewhere, for respect for the weak is no longer the fashion anywhere. All of Italy's advances to the West had been rejected with scorn, but German friendship had been offered and had proved useful, indeed. Moreover, from all that we now know, even if Italy had not accepted an alliance with Germany, Hitler's aggressive plans would not have been altered one jot.

The true solution rested with the Western Powers. If they had agreed to the revision of the Versailles treaty and had given Germany a free hand in the East, Germany would have settled its own Eastern frontier and sooner or later would have come into conflict with Russia. It was in Russia alone that Germany could find the raw materials it needed; and either in open conflict with Russia or by taking a hand in the development of that country's resources without war, it would have been kept busy for fifty years, leaving the West and Italy undisturbed.

But this solution was too obvious, too simple, too wise for the great political minds on both shores of the Channel and on both sides of the Atlantic.

Just as Mussolini in 1915 had advocated Italian intervention on the side of the Entente, he was now at last ready to intervene on the side of Germany, convinced as he was that this was the only course possible for his country. He was entering not a German war but an Italian war together with Germany.

There is yet another point to be considered in connection with Italian intervention in the war and with the actual character of that intervention, at all events at the beginning.

It has often been asked: why at the very outset of Italian intervention was no attack delivered on Malta, or a rapid advance made on Egypt, or even a vigorous offensive started against France? The defenses of Malta were in a very backward condition, with few warships and only a half-dozen aeroplanes, so that

an attack delivered within an hour of the declaration of war
would undoubtedly have been successful. In Egypt there were
less than 20,000 British troops, compared with much larger
Italian forces in Libya and Eritrea, and the Italian navy and
air force were more than a match for the British in the Mediterranean.

An explanation suggested by one of the most distinguished,
intelligent and gallant officers in the Italian navy, whose name
is still one to conjure with, is that at that time the Italian and
German governments were convinced that the war was very
nearly at an end, with victory assured for the Axis, and that the
British Government was of the same opinion in spite of anything that Churchill has since written or may write to the contrary. Churchill, himself, actually seems to have been anxious
that Italy should intervene in the war, so that Mussolini could
sit at the table of the coming peace conference and exercise a
moderating and restraining influence on Hitler in favor of a
compromise peace. The French, too, were convinced that all
hope of their victory had vanished, as was proved soon afterward by their own armistice. We know that Hitler at this time
favored a soft policy toward Great Britain in order to promote
his peace plans. It was this that led him to halt his army and
air force and allow the British to escape from Dunkirk.

There may have been yet further correspondence between
Churchill and Mussolini, in addition to the letters to which I
have already alluded. The Duce, at all events, entered the war
without intending to strike too hard at the British, hoping thus
to make it easier for them to come to terms, which would certainly have been infinitely more reasonable than those afterwards imposed at the end of the war by the victors—including
the French, who were only camouflaged as victors.

That this was probably the real situation is proved by the
fact that for the first eighteen months after Italian intervention
Italy enjoyed full superiority in the Mediterranean, even though
decisive action against Malta was no longer possible. Admiral
Cunningham writes in his book that at that time no British ship
could leave Alexandria without being at once heavily and dis-
astrously bombed by the Italian airforce, the accuracy of whose
action was most alarming, and he was constantly requesting the

Admiralty for more reinforcements.[19] It was only when the United States entered the war that the situation was radically altered to the detriment of the Axis—just as happened on the Russian front.

At any rate, it was surely the soft policy of Germany and Italy toward Britain in 1940 which cost the Axis the war and Hitler and Mussolini their lives. Vigorous action by Germany and Italy through the last half of 1940 would certainly have put England out of the war and made it impossible for President Roosevelt to enter any European conflict. Hitler might have tangled with Russia later on, but American public opinion would hardly have countenanced Rooseveltian intervention in such a struggle on behalf of Russia.

This is only a supposition, but the data available seem to bear it out, and there is no doubt that if the war had ended in July or August, 1940, with an Axis victory, as nearly everyone believed probable at the time, Mussolini's influence would have been cast on the side of moderation, in view of his well-known views in favor of peaceful European coöperation. He has been accused of not having understood that Great Britain's powers of resistance were still very strong, and that the resources of the British Empire were then far from having been exhausted. His real fault was that he saw too far ahead; the break-up of Great Britain's power and of its Empire was inevitably approaching, but not as soon as Mussolini thought. He foresaw in 1940 what was not to happen until after 1945. One may be too far-sighted as well as too short-sighted.

Exchanges of Pleas and Responses on the Eve of War.

Shortly before Italy's entry into the war in June, 1940, Pope Pius XII, Winston Churchill, President Roosevelt, and Paul Reynaud addressed letters to Mussolini, urging him not to intervene in the conflict. These appeals, together with Mussolini's answers, have now been published by Professor Mario Toscano, Vice-President of the Commission for the Publication of Public Documents. They are of unusual interest as contributing to our knowledge of the Duce's reasons for not agreeing to the requests then addressed to him.

The Pope's letter was as follows:

April 24, 1940

Well-beloved Son:

We send you Our greetings and Our Apostolic Benediction.

True to the mission of pacification, which is one of the chief duties of Our pastoral mission, we deem it desirable, while fears of a further extension of the conflict are growing, confidently to open out Our soul to you.

We know, indeed, having carefully followed them and commended them to God, the noble efforts with which you have striven, first to avert and then to localize the war; and while grieving that your solicitations have not achieved full success, We were happy indeed that your high merit in having contained the scourge within certain limits has been recognized. Nevertheless, the conflagration having spread and being today ever more active in its tragic developments, these fears, while the clouds of war seem to be threatening more than ever peoples hitherto immune from them, are justified.

While not doubting your persevering efforts along the line of conduct which you have undertaken, We implore the Almighty to assist you in an hour of such grave import for the peoples, and of such responsibility for those holding the reins of government in their hands.

In view of the universal fatherhood which pertains to Our office, we express from Our innermost heart the ardent wish that, thanks to your initiative, to your firmness, to your spirit, as an Italian, vaster devastations and numerous sorrows be spared to Europe, and that from Our and your own beloved country so great a calamity may be averted.

In full confidence that the Almighty will continue, in His Divine liberality, to grant you light and strength in these anxious hours, for the good and the safety of the Italian people, with deep feeling I commend you to Him, and in the meanwhile, in the hope of Divine favor, I impart to you Our Apostolic Benediction.

Pius PP. XII.

On May 16th, Churchill addressed an appeal to Mussolini, in which he stated:

Now that I have taken over the duties of Prime Minister, and meditate on our Roman meetings, I wish to address words of hope to you, who are the Head of the Italian Government, while we are on the edge of an appalling abyss . . . Doubtless, we may inflict terrible injury on each other and cruelly strike at each other, casting a deep shadow over the Mediterranean with our conflict.

Throughout the centuries the appeal that the joint heirs of Latin and Christian civilization be not driven against each other in deadly strife, rises up above all others. Give heed to that appeal, I invoke of your honor and your dignity, before the awful signal be given.

The French Prime Minister, Paul Reynaud, on April 23rd, addressed to Mussolini a lengthy and obsequious message, in which he said, among other things:

Responsible as I have been for the French Government during the last few weeks, I write to you independent of all ceremony, as to one of those leaders, so rare in history, who have held in their hands the destinies of millions of human beings. I believe in Democracy. You believe in Fascism. But neither the one nor the other disowns our past, and both affirm on the basis of facts that they are two glorious aspects of a Mediterranean civilization which cannot fail today, as yesterday, to inspire the future of the world, and this civilization rests on both our countries . . . You and I should without hesitation attempt to build a bridge between a traditional regime such as ours, and a new one, such as yours.

On behalf of Roosevelt, the American Ambassador in Rome addressed a *Note verbale* to Mussolini on May 1st, of which the following are excerpts:

President Roosevelt is happy to be able to realize that Italy's non-belligerence has contributed to keep the peace in the Mediterranean area, and that it is due to this decision of Sig. Mussolini that two hundred millions of people have not been dragged into war.

He concluded by reasserting that Italy and the United States had, as neutrals, the possibility of exercising a deep influence on the events of the world and on the restoration of a just and equitable peace "as soon as conditions will enable us to perceive the possibility of negotiations."

Here is Mussolini's reply to the Pope's message:

April 28

Most Holy Father,

I beg you first of all to accept my deep gratitude for the letter which You have deigned to address to me, and for Your expressions concerning myself therein.

Your recognition, most Holy Father, of the fact that I have sought by all means to avert a conflagration, fills me with the most legitimate satisfaction. It is my conviction that, without the absurd demands of the French and the British that the German armies, already on their forward march, should withdraw to their points of departure, the conference, suggested by myself, might have been summond to face and solve not only the Polish problem, but the other problems which await solution.

I understand, most Holy Father, your wish that Italy be enabled to avoid War. This has been the case up to the present day. But I cannot in any way guarantee that such a state of affairs will last to the end. We must also take into account the wishes and intentions of third parties. The history of the Church, as You, most Holy Father, may well teach me, has never accepted the formula of peace for peace's sake "at any price," of "peace without justice," of a peace which might, in given circumstances, irreparably compromise, for the present and for the future, the fate of the Italian people.

I wish to add that within the framework of the Italo-German alliance it has been possible for Italy to assume the attitude of non-belligerence.

Of one thing alone do I wish to assure You, most Holy Father, that if tomorrow Italy should have to enter the war, that would signify in the clearest possible manner, evident to all, that our honor, interests, our future have absolutely imposed intervention upon us.

It is consoling to me to feel that in both eventualities, God will protect the efforts of a religiously-minded people such as that of Italy.

On May 18th, Mussolini replied to Churchill. After reminding him of Italy's obligations of honor in connection with the German alliance, of the growing British hostility to Italy, he asked why Great Britain continued obstinately to persecute her, adding:

Without reference to more distant times, I may remind you of the initiative taken by your Government in 1935 at Geneva to organize sanctions against Italy, then engaged in trying to secure a little space under the African sun, without any prejudice to the interests and territories of your country or to those of others. I also remind you of the state of veritable slavery in which Italy finds herself in her own sea.

If it was to honor your signature that your Government declared war on Germany, you will understand that Italian policy must be guided yesterday, and today, in the face of any event whatsoever, by that same sense of honor and respect for the engagements undertaken under the terms of the Italo-German treaty.

He presented to the American Ambassador in Rome the following reply to be forwarded to President Roosevelt:

1. If two nations, Denmark and Norway, have been involved in the war, the responsibility rests not with Germany, but with the actions of her enemies.

2. Italy's non-belligerence has indeed assured peace for two hundred millions of people, but nevertheless Italian trade is subjected to constant, vexatious and injurious control.

3. As far as I am aware, Germany is opposed to any further extension of the conflict, and so too is Italy. It is a question of knowing what are the intentions of the French and the British.

4. The only European nation dominating a large part of the world and enjoying a monopoly of many basic raw materials is Great Britain. Italy has no program of this kind, but states that no peace is possible unless the fundamental problems of Italian liberty are solved.

5. As for the reactions which an extension of the war fronts may produce in the three Americas, I call attention to the fact that Italy has never interfered in the relations of the American Republics between themselves or in those between them and the United States—out of respect for the Monroe doctrine—and that she might well invoke reciprocity with regard to European affairs.

6. Should conditions allow of it, and always taking recognition of real and accomplished facts as starting points, Italy is ready to contribute to a better settlement of the world.

Mussolini sent the following reply to Paul Reynaud, on April 26th, always with reference to the alliance with Germany:

Allow me, in the first place, to state that I find that the point which gave rise to your letter is wholly without justification, viz.: the telegram with which I expressed my wish for the victory of German arms. This fact should not surprise you nor should it make you forget that Italy is and intends to remain politically and militarily the ally of Germany, according to the treaty of May,

1939, a treaty which Italy—like all nations attaching value to their honor—intends to respect.

Mussolini communicated the texts of these various letters to Hitler, who acknowledged them at once.

[1] A. B. Lane, *I Saw Poland Betrayed*, Indianapolis: Bobbs-Merrill, 1948, passim.

[2] Guido Leto, *Ovra*, Bologna, 1951.

[3] *Ibid.*, p. 205.

[4] *Hitler e Mussolini*, 19.

[5] During the Paris Peace Conference Churchill was constantly intriguing behind Lloyd George's back to promote a war against Soviet Russia. See Lloyd George, *The Truth about the Peace Treaties*, London, 1938. Before he became Prime Minister, Churchill began a series of secret messages and correspondence between himself and Roosevelt. He tells us in his war memoirs that the most important phases of Anglo-American diplomacy from 1939 to 1945 were handled in these secret dispatches which numbered nearly 2,000. For retaining a copy of some of the earlier of these, the decoding clerk in the American Embassy at London, Tyler Kent, was sentenced to several years in prison by the British Government. Roosevelt waived Kent's diplomatic immunity in order to keep him and his information safely away from American shores during the War.

[6] See *e.g.*, the *Corriere della Sera*, May 12, 21, 1940.

[7] See Roatta's book, *Otto millioni di baionette*, Milan, 1946.

[8] New York: Harper, 1944.

[9] Welles, *op. cit.*, p. 85.

[10] *Ibid.*, pp. 84-89.

[11] The British were the first to plan and to start an aggressive attack on Norway. See Lord Hankey, *Politics, Trials & Errors*, Oxford, 1951, Chap. IV. This is now fully admitted in the official British history of the second World War.

[12] Hull, *Memoirs*, Vol. I, p. 777.

[13] The President's personal representative at the Vatican.

[14] Gentizon, *op. cit.*, pp. 396-397.

[15] Hull, *op. cit.*, Vol. I, p. 782.

[16] Leto, *op. cit.*, p. 212.

[17] *Ibid.*, p. 213.

[18] *Ibid.*, pp. 212-213.

[19] Admiral of the Fleet, Viscount Cunningham, *A Sailor's Odyssey*, London, 1951.

CHAPTER TWENTY-FIVE

In the War

The combination of all these conditions and circumstances, mentioned at the end of the preceding chapter, finally led Mussolini to take the fateful step. At 4:30 p.m., June 10, 1940, he announced in a short speech from Palazzo Venezia that Italy had declared war on Great Britain and France.

The decision might well have seemed foolhardy, but it was not without antecedents in Italian history. Had not Carlo Alberto, King of the tiny state of Sardinia, without a single ally thrown down the gauntlet before the mighty Hapsburg Empire in 1848 and again, after a first defeat and the Salasco armistice, in 1849? Had not Cavour, Prime Minister of a state that had been beaten ten years before, again defied that same and not less powerful Empire, this time, it is true, with a powerful ally, but one who could seldom be relied upon? Did not Antonio Salandra intervene in the first World War on the side of the Entente at a moment when the cause of his new allies was at the lowest ebb? Mussolini's action in 1940 was no more foolhardy than that of his illustrious predecessors.

One of the most bitter charges against Mussolini is that by his declaration of war he had "stabbed France in the back." On the night of June 10, 1940, President Roosevelt said at the

University of Virginia: "The hand that held the dagger has struck in the back of its neighbor." Secretary Hull wrote: "Few episodes in history have seemed so cynical to me as Mussolini's declaration of war against Britain and France. He had virtually declared war a month before he actually entered it . . . He consulted none of the 40,000,000 Italians he destined to disaster." [1] Evidently history was not Hull's strong point, and his knowledge of contemporary facts even less so.

The hypocrisy involved in the high moral attitude taken by Roosevelt and Churchill relative to Italy's entry into the war, and in their "dagger-in-the-back" charge, is best exposed by a reminder of what they did at Yalta with less need than Mussolini had for entering the war. Here, they even gave Stalin a fatally large political bribe to stab defeated Japan in the back—a Japan that had faithfully respected its non-aggression treaty with Russia and thereby had saved Russia, and perhaps the Allies as a whole, from defeat.

A more honest and realistic point of view is that expressed by the courageous Scotch minister, Rev. Peter H. Nicoll, in his notable book, *Britain's Blunder,* in which he writes: "Britons, following Churchill's lead, have repeated *ad nauseam* the charge of basely stabbing France in the back when she was already down. But is it not pertinent to ask why should Mussolini, as an admitted friend and ally of Germany, have attacked France only when she was strong? Did Britain or any other power always refrain from attacking an enemy when she was weak and always wait for her to be strong before launching the attack?"

With regard to France, for the reasons given above, only the old plan was applied, a plan which provided for merely defensive operations on the Alps. Marshal Badoglio, Chief of the General Staff, had ordered the troops not to attack the enemy, whereas the Germans were penetrating into the heart of France by forced marches.[2] The "stab in the back" was to prove a most benevolent occupation, the most peaceable coëxistence.

The coincidence of Italy's intervention and the crumpling up of the French armies did confer on Mussolini's action an appearance of meanness, and Italy was covered with obloquy in many quarters. But there is this to remember. According to the German plan of operations, an Italian army ten divisions strong was to have joined the German invasion of France through the Burgundian Gate and descended the Rhone valley to the Mediterranean. The plan had been prepared (on the Italian side) by General Mario Roatta and Colonel Emilio Canevari; but at the last moment Mussolini suspended its execution, and the operation was limited to a sector of the Alpine front, where it lasted three days (June 21-23). It was expected that France would immediately ask for an armistice, and it did so on June 24th.

At the time of Italy's entry into the war, public feeling was far more bitter against Britain than against France, many of whose eminent statesmen had just shown themselves really eager at last for an understanding with Italy, and the French Government had only been prevented from achieving this result by Churchill's intense pressure. The character of those first Italian operations against France is evidence of it.

Mussolini, himself, replied some years later to the "stab in the back" charge (December 2, 1942). Italy's intervention had been set for June 5th, but the German GHQ for technical reasons had asked that it be adjourned to the 10th, and "no one," as Mussolini said, "thought that the end of the war in France was so imminent, and least of all Churchill who, a few months before, had admiringly reviewed the French army on July 14, 1939, and had proclaimed it the most powerful and capable army in the world. But the breakdown was complete and when we attacked the Army of the Alps was intact, as were the air force and the navy . . . And then, even if we admit that we stabbed France in the back, it would have been only one stab in contrast to the hundred that France had inflicted on us from Talamone[3] to Mentana (from 225 B.C. to 1867 A.D.)."

What he did not say was that if he had not gone to war against France, German divisions might have poured into Italy from Nice and through Trieste. Moreover, Italy's intervention in the war was expressly laid down in her treaty of alliance with Germany drawn up in 1939 and well-known in all official circles.

The war in France lasted only a few days. With the conclusion of the armistice, French territory was divided into two parts—occupied and unoccupied. Most of the former was held by the Germans, the rest by the Italians. It is now recognized that leaving half of France unoccupied and failing to land Axis troops in French North Africa were two grave political and military blunders, due largely to Hitler's hope of establishing close coöperation with France, which, owing to his great admiration for Pétain, he believed possible for a time.

On the declaration of war Italy had, of course, withdrawn its diplomatic and consular representatives from France (the Italian ambassador at the time was Raffaele Guariglia). After the conclusion of the armistice Italy was represented, at first, by its military authorities alone. But the armistice terms imposed on France were extremely moderate. Indeed, Italy's whole policy towards the defeated country was inspired by full comprehension of the conditions of the French people and of their real unwillingness to be drawn into the conflict, which was almost exclusively the result of British pressure; and nothing was done to prejudice future Franco-Italian relations.

The headquarters of the French Government were removed to Vichy under Marshal Pétain, but Germany appointed an ambassador (Herr Abetz) to remain in Paris. In December, 1940, a meeting between Ciano and the French Foreign Minister, Admiral Darlan, took place at Turin to settle the question of Italy's representatives in France. In January, 1941, an Italian ambassador was sent to Paris in the person of Gino Buti, and the Counsellor of the Embassy, Vittorio Zoppi, resided at Vichy. The consulates were reopened as armistice delegations in the occupied zone. The only other meeting between Italian and French statesmen was that between the Italian Undersecretary for Foreign Affairs, Giuseppe Bastianini, and the French Minister, Laval, in the spring of 1943.

Throughout the Italian occupation no measure was taken to press any Italian claims on France. Neither the Italian Government, the Italian Embassy in Paris, nor the office of the Italian Counsellor at Vichy ever attempted to intervene in the policy of the French Government (a line of action very different from that of the German Government and its Paris Embassy), and the conduct of the Italian occupying forces aroused little or no resentment among the French people. The interests of Italian citizens were adequately protected, but no vexatious economic or other measures were imposed on France. In the Jewish question, also, the attitudes of the two governments were entirely different. Whenever the Germans applied their anti-Semitic measures in France, the Italians not only abstained from any action of the kind, but, when it was possible, they gave assistance not only to Italian Jews but also to French Jews, whom they often protected against deportation to Germany or other punitive measures.

Hitler and the Germans generally expected to establish close and friendly collaboration with France, for in their eyes it was destined to become an integral part of the new order in Europe.[4] The majority of the French continued to be as hostile to the Germans as before, but a large number of Frenchmen did collaborate with the Germans, because they believed it to be inevitable or from a sincere desire to come to an understanding. Later on, when Germany's military situation deteriorated, the number of collaborators diminished.[5]

It has often been said that Italian dislike of the Germans made full coöperation between the two Axis partners impossible. But this is only partially true. The Italian soldiers who fought side by side with the Germans in North Africa got on very well with them, and there was a good deal of reciprocal admiration. Each had certain qualities the other lacked. The one great obstacle to full coöperation was the inadequacy of Italian war materiel, which Germany was very niggardly in supplying in spite of the constant requests of the Italian Government.

The question of Italian aspirations did not lead to serious disagreements, at least in the first years of the war. In his note to the Italian High Command after his meeting with Hitler on June 18, 1940, Mussolini said that he had told the Führer that Italy wished to occupy the area between the Alps and the Rhone valley, Corsica, Tunisia, and Jibuti; but later he dropped the claim on Tunisia.[6] In letters to Hitler in July and August, Mussolini asked that Italy should take part in the air attacks on Great Britain, but this participation was to be of a merely token nature, as the Italian air force was not strong enough to detach a large number of planes from the Mediterranean.[7]

In conversations with von Ribbentrop in Munich in June, 1940, Ciano took up the question of Italian aspirations. In addition to requests for Nice, Corsica and Tunisia, he advanced claims to a part of Algeria and Morocco where there were many Italian settlers. Mussolini, he added, demanded a position for Italy in Egypt like that then held by Great Britain, and he insisted that Gibraltar be returned to Spain. Von Ribbentrop agreed to all these points, except with regard to Egypt, which, he said, required further study. In general, however, it was clear that the Germans, especially Hitler, did not attach sufficient importance to the Mediterranean, not realizing its supreme value. For Germany the return of the former German colonies and some control over the Belgian Congo were demanded.

Ciano was convinced that Hitler then believed that the existence of the British Empire was necessary for order and stability over a large part of the world, and that he demanded only that Great Britain should surrender certain positions. Indeed, he actually made peace proposals to Great Britain on July 19, 1940, after Dunkirk. He seems to have then been inspired by the memory of Bismarck's attitude towards Austria after Sadowa in 1866. To Ciano's query whether he preferred peace or the continuance of the war, von Ribbentrop unhesitatingly answered, "Peace."

Indeed, as Captain B. H. Liddell Hart has shown, Hitler not only told his astonished generals after Dunkirk that he believed the preservation of the British Empire to be indispensable but even went so far as to say that, if Britain would make peace, he would place German military might at the disposal of Britain to protect the Empire. If Britain had made peace in 1940, the fate of the Empire might have been far different than it eventually turned out to be as the outcome of Churchill's invincible determination to continue the war at all costs.

The editors of *The European* have pointed out the fatal inconsistency between Churchill's claim that he could not morally make peace with Hitler and his almost frantic efforts to seek peace with Russia during his last years in office: "His desire for peace at the end of his days . . . was his best deed, but it deprived him of the last justification for all else that he did. He might otherwise have claimed that even if the last war was against the interests of the British Empire and all Europe, it was a moral necessity; that was the line of argument implicit in Nüremberg. But none can begin to deny—least of all Sir Winston Churchill—that the Soviet leaders, in undoubted fact, have committed crimes against humanity which have surpassed anything even suggested against the Nazi leaders. So Churchill's moral desire for peace today removes his last moral excuse for war yesterday. No one can say that peace with Nazi Germany was morally impossible while he clambers up the 'throne of skulls' to seek peace from the Soviet 'monsters' at yet another vodka banquet."

In July Ciano visited Hitler in Berlin to discuss war plans. At Ciano's request the Führer promised to contribute long-range bombers for the Italian forces in North Africa, and he reiterated that all questions concerning the Mediterranean and the Adriatic were to be dependent on Italy's wishes. But vital Italian requests for supplies were only partially met.[8]

The conversation next turned to Yugoslavia. Hitler said that both the Regent and the people were anti-Axis and agreed that the question must be settled according to Italian views. Mussolini then evidently had in mind Churchill's suggestion of a "horizontal Axis."

The Duce was now beginning, indeed, to be exercised about Italy's position in the Balkans. He agreed with Hitler that it was advisable to keep military operations out of that area, but he was anxious about Germany's plans. Hitler evidently wished to gain control of the Rumanian oil wells. As far back as March, 1940, he had asked the Hungarian Government for a right of way for his troops through to Rumania, but the request had not been pressed further for the moment. In a note to Hitler on August 27th Mussolini hinted at possible Italian military measures on the Greek and Yugoslav frontiers.

Suddenly on June 29th Russia demanded of Rumania the restoration of Bessarabia, which had been under Russian rule before the first World War, and also claimed Northern Bucovina, which had never belonged to Russia but contained a Slav (Ukrainian) minority. Rumania appealed to Hitler for help, but he advised it to agree to everything *for the present* ("vorläufig Alles annehmen").

It was then that Hungary demanded the restitution of Transylvania by Rumania, and Bulgaria requested the return of the Southern Dobrudja, wrested from it in 1913. Both Mussolini and Hitler deemed it advisable that these disputes should be settled amicably by compromise. In a conversation in Rome with the Rumanian Prime Minister, Ion Gigurtu, on July 27th Mussolini told him that these reductions of Rumanian territory would give the country greater homogeneity and enable it to carry out the internal reforms that Gigurtu himself and other Rumanian statesmen desired. As a true friend of Rumania, Hungary and Bulgaria, and as an ardent advocate of treaty revision, Mussolini was undoubtedly the man best qualified to arbitrate between those countries. Rumania, he assured Gigurtu, had always been very popular in Italy, despite the errors of certain Rumanian statesmen (he was evidently alluding to the intrigues of Titulescu) and their tendency to trust too much in the League of Nations and in Great Britain's guarantees. He suggested a compromise solution, to which Hungary, Bulgaria and eventually Rumania itself, agreed. Negotiations followed in August; and after various difficulties had been overcome through the intervention of Mussolini and Hitler, Transylvania was partitioned between Hungary and Rumania. Although the arrangement did not completely satisfy either side, it was preferable to an extension of the war or to the perpetuation of the dispute. Bulgaria also secured the part of the Dobrudja it had lost in 1913.

Negotiations were now undertaken to bring about the intervention of Spain on the side of the Axis. General Franco then seemed ready to agree, but he insisted on the promise not only of Gibraltar, but also of French Morocco and on the assurance of large supplies of war materiel. The question was discussed with the Spanish Foreign Minister, Serrano Suñer, in Berlin on September 27th and again at a meeting of Hitler and Mussolini on the Brenner (October 4th). But Franco refused Hitler's request for naval bases in Spain; and although at a meeting between the Führer and the Caudillo at Hendaye on October 23rd a vague agreement was arrived at, nothing definite was settled.

In the meantime, Hitler had decided to send a military mission to Bucharest and to entrust the defense of the Rumanian oil wells to the German air force. These decisions impressed Mussolini unfavorably, for he saw in them an attempt by Hitler to re-inforce his own position in the Balkans to the detriment of that of Italy. This was one of the reasons for the Duce's decision with regard to Greece. Ciano, himself, was strongly in favor of the idea of an action against that country, believing that Great Britain was using it as a base for future operations in the Adriatic and the Near East, and Mussolini may again have had in his mind what Churchill suggested to him during the period of Italian non-belligerence.

There were substantial reasons for action in Greece, for that country was tending more and more to become a satellite of British policy. But from a military point of view it was undoubtedly one of Mussolini's gravest errors. On October 15th he summoned a meeting at Palazzo Venezia, attended by Ciano, Marshal Badoglio, the Italian Viceroy in Albania, Jacomoni, and others. Jacomoni stated that, while there had at first been a great deal of enthusiasm in Albania over the idea of an action against Greece, which occupied the Tchamuria, a province regarded as an Albania *irredenta*, that enthusiasm had now waned. He said that the port of Durazzo would be in danger of being bombed, thereby seriously compromising the sending of reinforcements and supplies to the forces in Albania, while the Greeks, who, at first, had been inclined to offer no resistance, were now ready to resist vigorously. He was opposed to recruiting Moslem bands in Albania, since they would probably wreak vengeance on the hated Greeks.[9] Moreover, Bulgaria, which was expected to carry out a demonstrative action on the Thracian frontier, was now no longer willing to do so, and this fact would enable Greece to concentrate the whole of her forces on the Albanian frontier.

Nevertheless, Mussolini decided to open the campaign on October 28th, and he informed Hitler of the fact. The Führer, who did not approve the plan, asked the Duce to postpone operations to a more favorable season, but the original date was maintained. The ultimatum was presented to the Greek Premier, General Metaxas, on October 28th according to plan. While Metaxas at first seemed willing to accede to Italy's demands, after a conversation with the King he changed his mind and decided to resist.[10]

On the whole, it seems that Ciano was chiefly responsible for the decision to attack Greece, in order to set up a barrier against further German penetration into the Balkans and against British action in that area, or because he believed that it might lead to an understanding with Great Britain, in view of Churchill's letters.

The season was undoubtedly the worst possible time to commence a campaign in a mountainous and roadless country. While the Italian troops at first penetrated deep into Greek territory from Albania, they soon found themselves opposed by the whole of the much more numerous Greek army and were forced to fall back with heavy losses. But the gravest error lay in the fact that the Italian divisions marooned in Albania, few as they were, would have made all the difference in the world to the course of the operations in North Africa, where their presence might well have proved decisive at that time. Hostilities with Greece should have been postponed to a later date.

During the winter of 1940-1941 the Italian forces met with great difficulties, some reverses and heavy losses on the Graeco-Albanian front. But gradually as more reinforcements and supplies arrived, the situation improved and an Italian counter-offensive finally proved successful, helped by the German action on the extreme eastern end of the front. This last move was the result of events in Yugoslavia.[11]

At a meeting between Ciano and von Ribbentrop at Schönhof on November 4, 1940, the question of Russia's relations with the Axis and with Japan was raised once more. The German Minister was eager to secure a new agreement with Russia for fuller collaboration and friendship. A secret protocol was to be signed directing Japan's expansion toward the south, that of Italy toward the Mediterranean and the Red Sea, that of Germany toward Equatorial Africa. A second protocol was intended virtually to abolish the Montreux agreement and make of the Black Sea a Russian lake with freedom of transit for Russian ships through the Straits. This last concession, von Ribbentrop believed, would induce Russia to abandon any idea of establishing itself territorially and militarily in the Straits area. Once the agreement with Russia was concluded, an attempt would be made to bring Turkey into the war on the side of the Axis.

On November 12th Molotov went to Berlin to discuss these matters, but no agreement was arrived at, although Hitler made almost incredible concessions to the Russians. The Russians made unacceptable demands about Hungary, the Balkans and the Straits, and they offered nothing in exchange. We have here the beginnings of the break between Germany and Russia that was to come to a head seven months later. There is good reason to believe that Stalin instructed Molotov to make outrageous demands on Hitler in order to provoke the Führer to make war on Russia while the latter had a good chance of receiving English and American aid. If Stalin was surprised or disconcerted in June, 1941, it was probably only in regard to the speed with which Hitler picked up the gage of battle.

Events in the Balkans raised the question of Yugoslavia. While Italy was engaged in the Greek campaign, Yugoslav public opinion on the whole was very hostile, and the military leaders thought that it would be a good opportunity to attack Italy. On the other hand, Hitler was determined to make every effort to bring Yugoslavia into the Axis fold. He considered such a move important for a joint Italo-German operation in the Balkans. Mussolini, who at first was not too keen on the idea, ended by agreeing to it so as not to leave the initiative entirely to Hitler. There was a party in Yugoslavia favorable to Germany, if not to Italy, and the Regent adhered to it. On March 26, 1941, the Yugoslav Minister of Foreign Affairs in the Zvetkovich Cabinet, Milan Stoyadinovich, met von Ribbentrop and Ciano in Vienna, where a pact between the three countries was concluded. Yugoslavia was to receive an outlet to the Aegean at Salonica, in exchange for various facilities for the Axis but without being obliged to take any part in military operations.

But before the ink was dry on the signatures of the agreement, a revolt, organized by General Simovich and other Yugoslav air-force officers, broke out in Belgrade, upset the Zvetkovich Cabinet and forced the Regent to go to Greece, where he was eventually held by the British.

The German reaction was immediate. On April 6th the *Luftwaffe* bombed Belgrade, German troops occupied the city directly afterwards, Italian troops entered Yugoslavia from Dalmatia, and Hungarian troops re-occupied the Banat of which Hungary had been deprived under the terms of the Trianon treaty. The Yugoslav army broke up, its remnants offered but little resistance, and very soon the whole country was occupied by Italian and German forces. The young King Peter, although only eighteen years old, proclaimed himself of age and undertook the role of a king in exile, settling in London under the protection of the British Government as his ally. He left General Draža Mihailovich behind to organize guerrilla formations to fight against the Axis forces, but Mihailovich received virtually no help from the Western Powers.

Yugoslavia, as such, had ceased to exist, but the Reich consented to the formation of a government for Serbia presided over by General Milan Nedich, which was recognized by the Axis as legitimate. The German Minister in Belgrade essentially fulfilled the duties of civil governor; and Italy, because of her large interests and many cultural and commercial institutions in the country, retained a Legation with the Minister, Giorgio Mameli, in charge. Montenegro was occupied by Italian forces, and it was intended eventually to re-establish an independent Montenegrin government, which had always been the aspiration of the Montenegrin people since their forcible annexation to Yugoslavia in 1920.

Von Ribbentrop now proposed the formation of an independent Croatia, to include also Bosnia, Herzegovina and a large part of Dalmatia. Slovenia was to be divided between Germany and Italy. Mussolini attached a good deal of importance to Dalmatia on account of its geographical position and the highly civilized Italian element in the coast towns. Ciano insisted on this point with von Ribbentrop, who suggested that Italy should settle the question with the Croatian Government, proclaimed on April 10th. The head of this Government was to be the Ustashi[12] leader, Ante Pavelich, who had until then been residing clandestinely in Italy. Ciano's Chef de Cabinet, Filippo Anfuso, now conducted Pavelich to see Mussolini in Rome. Pavelich appeared willing to collaborate with Italy, but Dalmatia constituted a difficulty, for the Croatians demanded it as a part of their new state. But Pavelich proposed some form of Italo-Croatian union, in which case, he said, the Dalmatian question would lose significance.[13] But Mussolini was particularly keen on getting the problem solved before the Germans intervened. He therefore sent Anfuso to Zagreb to obtain from Pavelich, who assumed the title of *Poglavnik* (Duce or leader), a public and solemn declaration binding him to define the frontiers of the new State, taking Italian interests into consideration, before the official recognition of the new Croatian state.[14]

After various conversations between Pavelich and Anfuso, an agreement was reached at Monfalcone on May 7th, and no serious difficulties were encountered. Dalmatia was so divided as to leave to Italy those parts of the province which had been under the old Venetian Republic, *i.e.*, the northern half as far as a point just south of Spalato, plus the Bocche di Cattaro; and the territory of the former Slav republic of Ragusa was to be assigned to Croatia. A customs union was provided for, and it was finally agreed that the cousin of the King of Italy, Aimone of Aosta, Duke of Spoleto, should be King of Croatia.

The creation of an independent Kingdom of Croatia, in harmony with Mussolini's revisionist policy and also with historic tradition, was undoubtedly a sound measure. The Yugoslav state, like Czechoslovakia, a crazy quilt chiefly conceived by a group of second-rate British journalists, had developed into what was essentially greater Serbia, with a Serb minority dominating and oppressing millions of far more civilized non-Serbs, and was an artificial contraption without any racial, linguistic, historical or economic unity. The events of 1940-1941 showed how loose were the bonds linking these heterogeneous elements together.

Unfortunately, even the new Croatian state was not homogeneous, for while the majority of the inhabitants were Croatian and Catholic, there was a strong Orthodox Serb minority even in Croatia proper; and, by incorporating Bosnia and the Herzegovina, minorities were further increased by the addition of a large Moslem element.[15]

Had the new state been created in peace-time, it might have consolidated itself in time; then Serbia, corresponding to the territory of the old Serbian kingdom, with a homogeneous population, would have had a chance of normal development, although it would have been wiser had Bosnia and the Herzegovina been added to it, with an outlet to the sea at Metkovich.

Instead, the settlement was made during the throes of a bloody war, and the first consequence was to revive the ferocious antagonism between Croats and Serbs. The Croats, although more civilized than the Serbs, had been Balkanized during more than twenty years of Yugoslav thraldom; and, embittered by the persecutions to which they had been subjected, they now avenged themselves by massacring a very large number of Serbs.

Fighting went on between the Axis forces (in collaboration with the Croatians) and the guerrilla bands, led at first by General Mihailovich. But one of the difficulties facing the Italian and German forces was to prevent the pro-Axis Croatian and pro-Axis Serbian bands from fighting each other. The Western Allies were constantly urging Mihailovich, in the name of his King, to undertake a vigorous anti-Axis offensive, but they sent him no supplies,[16] saying that they had none to send. But when another rising broke out under the Communist partisan leader, Josip Brož, better known as Tito, unlimited supplies were sent to him to please the Russians.

One drawback of the operations in Croatia and Bosnia, as in the case of the Greek campaign, was that they immobilized many Italians and German divisions that would have been far more usefully employed elsewhere, especially in North Africa.

Spain now came to the fore again. Ciano visited von Ribbentrop at Berghof on January 19, 1941, and reported to Mussolini that relations between Germany and Spain seemed less cordial than before. As the Italian Ambassador Guariglia (transferred from Paris) wrote, the Spanish aristocracy, the upper business classes, and the remnants of the Reds were Anglophile, whereas the Falangists and many other Spaniards, who remembered the horrors of the civil war, were supporters of the Axis.[17] Franco was believed to be approaching the British in the hope of securing the material assistance which his country urgently needed. Von Ribbentrop then suggested a meeting between the Caudillo and Mussolini, owing to the Duce's great personal prestige in Spain. A meeting did take place at Bordighera on February 12, 1941, when Mussolini set forth the general situation, expressing his full confidence in the victory of the Axis even if the British should still continue to resist for a long time. He pointed out that if Spain intervened and seized Gibraltar, the victory would be greatly hastened. "It is" he said, "the destiny of the world that is being decided for many years to come by this war. Spain cannot remain aloof, for the problem concerns her too." He assured Franco that Hitler had undertaken to give Spain what it required.

Franco replied that he regretted that Spain had not intervened at the beginning of the war, but that its conditions after the terrible civil war had made it impossible. He believed that with heavy artillery Gibraltar could be reduced. But in the meantime Spain needed a large supply of wheat from abroad, for the population was starving. He added that Hitler had sent Admiral Walther W. Canaris to Spain, and that Canaris[18] had guaranteed that if Spain permitted German forces to pass through the country without opposition, they would capture Gibraltar. But Franco had replied that the Gibraltar enterprise must be a Spanish move and not a German venture, and that in any case Spain could not intervene until its desperate food situation was relieved. He told Mussolini that Germany would not give full satisfaction to Spain's colonial aspirations, and that Hitler was so eager to conciliate the French that he was ready to sacrifice Spain. France, Franco contended, was Spain's hereditary enemy and with Great Britain had contributed to Spain's decadence. Mussolini then asked whether, if Hitler should satisfy Spain's requests, the country would intervene. To this Franco replied affirmatively. The Duce informed Franco that two months previously Hitler had hoped to secure the collaboration of Pétain, but that hope had now vanished.[19] In conclusion, he promised to use his influence with the Führer in favor of the aspirations of Spain.[20]

At a subsequent meeting between Mussolini, Hitler, Ciano and von Ribbentrop on the Brenner (June 2nd) the German Foreign Minister said that he was continuing to exercise pressure on Franco, but that he did not altogether trust him, Serrano Suñer or the other Spanish leaders. On June 3rd Ciano referred to this conversation in a letter to Suñer, but evidently nothing was concluded.[21]

After the end of the war, Spain was publicly stigmatized at the United Nations as "an enemy of peace." Because she had refused to intervene in the war on the side of the Western Allies she could not qualify as a "peace-loving nation."

[1] Hull, *Memoirs,* Vol. II, pp. 784-785.

[2] Emilio Canaveri, *Graziani mi ha detto,* Rome, 1947, p. 34.

[3] A battle took place at Talamone (Telamon) between the Romans and the Gauls in 225 B.C.

[4] Much information concerning Franco-Italian relations during the war was kindly supplied to me by Ambassador Buti.

[5] Nevertheless the most ruthless persecution was administered to all non-Communist collaborators after the end of the war, with over 100,000 executions and hundreds of thousands of prison sentences. See Sisley Huddleston, *France: the Tragic Years, 1939-1947,* New York: Devin-Adair, 1955, especially Chaps. 18, 22, 23; and *Terreur, 1944,* Paris, 1945.

[6] *Hitler e Mussolini,* p. 52.

[7] *Ibid.,* p. 54.

[8] Enno von Rintelen, *Mussolini als Bundesgenosse,* Tübingen, 1951, p. 93.

[9] Mentioned in the decision of the Court of Cassation on Jacomoni's appeal against the sentence pronounced against him by the Court of Assizes, March 6, 1948.

[10] *Hitler e Mussolini,* 71.

[11] For the Greek campaign, see Ugo Cavallero, *Commando Supremo,* Bologna: Cappelli, 1948.

[12] *Ustashi* was the name given to the Croatians in revolt against the Belgrade government.

[13] Filippo Anfuso, *Roma, Berlino, Salo,* Milan, 1950, p. 188.

[14] *Ibid.,* p. 191.

[15] In those provinces there is a large number of Serbs who have been converted to Islam. They form a separate community.

[16] It is said that the only war materials sent to him by the British were some cases of whisky dropped from the air.

[17] Raffaele Guariglia, *Ricordi*, Naples, 1950, p. 478.

[18] Head of the German military information service.

[19] Nevertheless Pétain was condemned to death by a French court as a collaborator. The sentence was later commuted to life imprisonment. See Sisley Huddleston, *France: the Tragic Years*, pp. 282 ff., 347 ff.; and Maître Isorni, *Souffrances et Mort du Maréchal*, Paris, 1952.

[20] Ciano, *L'Europa verso la catastrofe*, pp. 631-643.

[21] *Ibid.*, pp. 661-662.

CHAPTER TWENTY-SIX

The War Goes On

The course of the war was closely associated with the increasing necessity for close coöperation between the German and Italian peoples, but certain cultural differences between them often made this coöperation difficult. The rise of National Socialism had strengthened the friendly feelings toward Germany of Italians, and not only among the Fascists. It made public opinion realize that totalitarianism was not an accidental contingency peculiar to Italy but a movement of wider significance, common to many countries and arising out of the grave problems left unsettled by the first World War that the old democratic liberal systems had seemed incapable of handling. To many Italians the German movement appeared a sort of homage to the originality of their own country. The personal friendship between Hitler and Mussolini had strengthened the bonds between the two countries.

But Nazi methods seemed to many Italians excessively and unnecessarily harsh, marking the difference between the Latin spirit, realistic, well-balanced and moderate, and the uncompromising doctrinairism of the Teuton. This contrast drew many Italians—at one time even Mussolini himself—toward the British, who seemed inspired by a greater measure of common

sense and moderation in the face of the hysterical and unreasoning French hatred of Germany and of the more extremist
attitude of the Nazis. It was only the short-sighted jealousy of
certain British statesmen and groups that had driven Italy reluctantly into Germany's arms.

On the 10th of June, 1940, all Italians should have gathered
round the national flag and given full and unquestioning support to the Government, even if many were opposed to some of
its policies or doubted the wisdom of the German alliance.
Few, indeed, were in a position to judge the wisdom or otherwise of the Government's foreign policy, being without the
necessary knowledge of the facts.

The bulk of the Italian people at first did give the Government full support, and the soldiers, sailors and airmen did
their duty valiantly. But there were hostile tendencies among
many factious politicians who did not look forward with favor
to an Italian victory, and even hoped that through defeat in
the field Fascism would be destroyed. Others went even further
and deliberately sabotaged the nation's war effort; and a few
actually betrayed their country, as is proved by the many published revelations and confessions of politicians and generals and
of one admiral. Men such as Count Sforza, Alberto Tarchiani
and Randolfo Pacciardi, then living abroad, conducted an active
propaganda in the interest of Italy's enemies—and boasted of
it. These men, although hated and despised by every patriotic
Italian, are now (or were) in the seats of the mighty.

These various circumstances contributed to weaken and undermine the war effort of the Government and to render vain
the bravery of Italy's armed forces in innumerable engagements.

The Germans were fighting desperately on many fronts, including that of North Africa, and they coöperated loyally with
their Italian comrades. Hitler, however, as I have said before,
never really understood the vital importance of the Mediterranean for Germany as well as for Italy, and he often failed
to send his ally the indispensable supplies he had promised.[1]

On June 15, 1941, Ciano met von Ribbentrop in Venice and
learned from him that Russo-German relations were becoming
very strained. The Soviet Government was concentrating

large forces on the German frontiers and had defaulted on many of its commercial pledges under the agreement. Hitler might be forced, von Ribbentrop added, to put certain questions to Stalin in the nature of an ultimatum. The German Minister's tone left no doubt in Ciano's mind about the Führer's intentions, although he was not given any inkling as to when action would be taken or how.

It was on June 22nd that Hitler struck. For this decision there were no doubt many valid reasons, and sooner or later a Russo-German conflict was inevitable. But, as in the case of Italy's Greek campaign, the attack on Russia at that particular moment was most unwise and in the end was to prove disastrous. It is true that, until the open intervention of the United States, the Germans soundly defeated the Russians, putting their huge armies to flight, taking hundreds of thousands of prisoners, and reaching within 22 kilometers of Moscow, where they were halted by winter and fresh Russian armies. It was already evident that American intervention was being rapidly prepared and in a sense had already materialized in the sending of unlimited supplies to Great Britain and its allies. There is no doubt, however, that one-quarter of the German forces concentrated against Russia would have produced an absolutely decisive victory in North Africa and perhaps even succeeded in an invasion of Great Britain. Even if a complete victory was not achieved, a negotiated peace might have been concluded, which would have been better for all concerned.

At 3 a.m. on June 22nd, the Counsellor of the German Embassy in Rome, Prince Bismarck, brought Ciano a message for Mussolini from Hitler announcing the attack on Russia. Italy, thereupon, also declared war on that country, and Great Britain, in turn, concluded an alliance with Russia.

The United States Ambassador in Rome, William Phillips, was convinced that his own country was nearer to intervention than ever, and he told Ciano that he had always hoped that it would be limited to war against Germany, which he hated, and that he deeply regretted that it would inevitably mean war also against Italy, for which he felt great sympathy.[2]

An Italian expeditionary force was sent to the Russian front to coöperate with the Germans, and it distinguished itself in the campaign. The Italian soldiers, indeed, proved hardier than the Germans in resisting the terrible cold of the Russian winter. Whether it was advisable for Italy to have taken part in the Russian campaign is doubtful for the same reasons that I have given with regard to the Greek and Yugoslav adventures. But the great mistake, as I have said, was Hitler's; and his decision having once been taken, it would have been very difficult for Mussolini to avoid sending forces to coöperate with him. Moreover, it had been Mussolini who had first realized the Bolshevik danger, and it was hardly conceivable that when Hitler followed suit, Italy should not have taken a share in the campaign. It was, indeed, considered necessary that Italy should be present on the front when Germany might secure possession of half the world.

According to Ciano, Mussolini was at that time beginning to feel a certain irritation against the Germans, but the Foreign Minister's *Diary* is not always to be relied on. Although it was written down day by day, there is reason to believe that he touched it up at a later date to justify his own action, and that when Germany was losing ground, he tried to make it seem that he himself had always been anti-German. Mussolini often indulged in outbursts against the Germans for not sending Italy the necessary supplies which he demanded, but he never showed himself actually anti-German.

On August 25th the Duce visited the Führer at his G.H.Q. on the Russian front. Hitler admitted that the Russian armies were better organized and equipped than he had been led to believe by his information services, but he was absolutely certain of a German victory, and hundreds of thousands of Russian prisoners of war were serving in the German army. The German advance was continuing vigorously, although at a somewhat slower pace than at first. One satisfactory feature of the situation was that the German forces had secured the Ukranian wheat crop.

With regard to Italian participation in the Russian campaign, Hitler's views were subject to frequent alterations. On the occasion of Mussolini's visit he expressed the wish that Italy should play an important part in it, and he suggested that some Italian divisions should relieve German units so that they could be sent temporarily to rest camps. His general intention was to annihilate Russia's armed forces so as to liberate Germany from the ever-recurring Russian menace. The Italian corps in Russia was afterwards raised to an army under the command of Field Marshal Giovanni Messe.

On October 25th it was Ciano's turn to visit Hitler, to discuss both the Russian situation and the treatment of Italian workers in Germany, which was far from satisfactory. On this later point, Hitler undertook to see that the situation would be improved. In general the German labor organizations and the military command regarded foreign workers, even if from allied countries, as impersonal instruments to free as many German citizens as possible for military service.

Ciano saw Hitler again on November 26th and 27th in Berlin together with Göring and von Ribbentrop. Hitler talked a great deal about European solidarity, showed special consideration for the Italians and expressed great admiration for what they had done in the North African campaign. He asked Ciano to be present at a meeting with Serrano Suñer, then in Berlin, to discuss the Spanish situation, but on this point no agreement was reached.

Both Hitler and von Ribbentrop repeatedly continued to affirm that nothing would be done in the Mediterranean area without Italy's approval. When Ciano complained that German agents were intriguing in Croatia to undermine Italian influence in that country, Hitler insisted that Croatia was definitely within the Italian sphere. The increase of Italian forces in Russia was discussed, but this time Hitler did not seem very keen that this should be done, except in so far as it concerned the Alpine divisions, for they would be very valuable in the Caucasus, which was to be included within Italy's sphere of influence. As a matter of fact, one excellent Alpine division was sent to Russia, but instead of being employed in the Caucasus, it was allowed to waste its resources on the Russian steppes.

On returning to Rome, Ciano learned that the tension between the United States and Japan had reached an acute stage. The Japanese Ambassador in Rome told Mussolini that his Government had done everything possible to arrive at an ami-

cable settlement with that of America, but Roosevelt was determined to place every obstacle in the way of the formation
of the new order in the Far East, as he was also doing with
respect to the creation of a new Europe sponsored by Germany
and Italy.[3] Relations between Japan and the United States
would never be cordial so long as Japan was associated with
the Axis Powers in the Tripartite Pact. The American Government, he said, was demanding that Japan should withdraw from
the Pact and give no assistance to Germany and Italy. "It is
evident," the Japanese diplomat continued, "that the United
States Government, together with those of Great Britain,
Australia, Holland and China, regards Japan with the same
hostility as Italy and Germany."[4] He considered war between
Japan and the United States and (consequently) Great Britain
as imminent. He requested, on the basis of the Tripartite Pact,
that Italy's declaration of war should follow immediately on
that of the United States against Japan, and that an agreement
be signed whereby the two governments should undertake not
to conclude an armistice or a separate peace with the United
States or Great Britain. He added that a similar request had
been addressed to Germany.

Mussolini replied that this did not surprise him, for he had
followed the extended conversations between the Japanese
diplomats in Washington and the members of the United States
Government, and that the Italian Ambassador in the American capital, Don Ascanio Colonna, had expressed the conviction that the President's determination to go to war at all
costs made it impossible for a satisfactory adjustment to be
reached. American plutocracy, Mussolini added, regarded Asia
as a territory for exploitation, and he declared his readiness
to sign the requested declaration and to assist Japan in every
way.[5] Italy, he considered, was practically at war with the
United States; indeed, some American officers had already been
taken prisoners in North Africa.

Ciano states in his Diary[6] that Roosevelt had succeeded in
his maneuver; being unable to intervene against Germany at
once and directly, he was entering into war through the back
door by getting himself attacked by Japan. This hunch of
Ciano's has been confirmed with great learning by the famous

American diplomatic historian, Charles Callan Tansill, in his book, *Back Door to War,* the definitive work on the policies and acts which led the United States into war in December, 1941.

The United States Government had, indeed, for a long time instituted a series of measures against Italy almost tantamount to war. Certain foreign consulates in Italian ports were suspected of furnishing the British with information about the movements of Italian ships; and this was particularly the case with the United States consulates. On February 12, 1941, the Italian Government had requested that the consulates in Naples and Palermo should be transferred to Rome or, at all events, away from the coast. The United States Government retaliated on the 28th by ordering the closing of the Italian Consulates at Detroit and Newark.[7] On March 30th the United States Coast Guard took into protective custody all German, Italian and Danish ships in American ports, "following evidence that the German and Italian ships were being sabotaged." The State Department sent a note to the German and Italian embassies stating that the crews in damaging the ships had committed a felony under United States law.[8]

On June 14th the President issued an order freezing all German and Italian assets in the United States, and a few days later he ordered the closing of all consulates and certain other agencies of the Axis Powers in the United States. These were unquestionably war measures, calculated to defend the integrity and interests not of the United States itself but of Great Britain.[9]

The story of President Roosevelt's futile efforts to incite the Germans and Italians to respond to his acts of war, such as the above and many others—giving munitions, warships and airplanes to Britain, convoying Allied shipping containing munitions of war, and the like—by declaring war on the United States has been told by the American scholar, Dr. H. L. Trefousse, in his book, *Germany and American Neutrality, 1939-1941.* How Roosevelt then decided, in conjunction with Churchill at Newfoundland, to enter the Pacific "back door" to war has been described by American writers, notably George Morgenstern in his *Pearl Harbor.* The details of the American provocation of Japan and the failure to warn the American commanders at Pearl Harbor have been revealed by two leading naval officials, Admiral Robert A. Theobald in *The Final Secret of Pearl Harbor,* and Admiral Husband E. Kimmel in *Admiral Kimmel's Own Story.* Perhaps as good a summary of the background of Pearl Harbor as will ever be set down was that given by the eminent British official, Captain Oliver Lyttelton, Minister of Supplies in the Churchill Cabinet, in June, 1944: "America provoked Japan to such an extent that the Japanese were forced to attack Pearl Harbor. It is a travesty on history to say that America was forced into the war."

On December 7, 1941, the Japanese attack was launched on Pearl Harbor, and war between the United States and Japan broke out at last. Italy and Germany, thereupon, also declared war against the United States, but both Roosevelt and Hull stated that a distinction should be made between the Italians, on the one hand, and the Germans and Japanese, on the other. The American people, according to Hull, had always been friendly to Italy, in spite of their hostility to Fascism. While Mussolini, he said, had dragged his people into war without consulting them, both he and the President believed it possible to get Italy out of the conflict before the surrender of Germany and Japan.[10] But the later course of events does not seem to prove any particular friendliness toward Italy on the part of either the President or his Secretary of State.

The declaration of war on the United States by Germany and Italy, in conformity with the anti-Comintern Pact, was a great diplomatic and strategic mistake. Japan had not informed either Germany or Italy of its intention to *attack*. Hitler could easily have expressed surprise and indignation and Mussolini would have had to follow suit. Under these circumstances, it would have been very difficult for Roosevelt to have put American forces into the European War for, perhaps, many months. The "back door" plan would have failed for the time being and the outcome of the European war might have been quite different. The German and Italian declarations of war played directly into the hands of Roosevelt and Churchill and, from that time until the collapse of Germany in May, 1945, the Far Eastern War occupied only a very secondary rôle in the war efforts of the United States. The European War dominated American interests and efforts, and General MacArthur had to beg for even inadequate supplies to conduct the Pacific campaign.

During the course of the year 1942 the military situation of the Axis underwent sundry variations. In the early part of the year it progressed satisfactorily. The capture of Tobruk on June 21st by German and Italian forces commanded by General Rommel, when 25,000 prisoners were taken, proved one of the most remarkable strategic exploits in the whole war.

But in the second half of the year the situation of the Axis began seriously to deteriorate, both in Africa and on the Russian front. The Germans, after penetrating deeply into Russian territory in all parts of that front, reaching as far as the Caucasus in the Southeast, were held up and forced to fall back with heavy losses, owing in part to the enormous mass of American war materiel supplied to Russia and in part to the appalling weather conditions. With the German defeat at Stalingrad, January 1943, a general retreat began. In Cyrenaica, the German and Italian advance proceeded toward Alexandria and had nearly reached it, while the British command fled to Palestine, and nearly all the ships left the port. But in spite of the great valor and ability displayed by the troops, they were held up at El Alamein in November 1942, largely because the needed supply of gasoline could not reach the advancing forces. Treachery seems to have been responsible for this, as many of the tankers were sunk almost as soon as they left Italian ports.

In East Africa the Italian forces, cut off from all supplies or reinforcements from Italy or Germany, made a gallant and protracted resistance but were gradually driven back from post to post, until the whole of the Empire was lost, and the heroic Commander in Chief, H.R.H. the Duke of Aosta himself, was taken prisoner. He died in an internment camp in Kenya.

On November 7-8, 1942, a large convoy of Anglo-American ships landed a force in Algeria, an operation made possible by Hitler's failure to occupy that French colony immediately after the armistice of June, 1940, and by his persistent failure to understand the importance of the Mediterranean. From that moment the fate of all North Africa was sealed, although the

Axis forces continued to hold out for many months. It was the overwhelming superiority of American war materiel—armored cars, aeroplanes, battleships, submarines and every other kind of new weapon—that proved decisive.[11]

Trouble now broke out in Yugoslavia. On May 22nd Hitler informed Mussolini that the High Command considered it advisable to exploit the antagonism between the *Cetnitzi,* led by General Mihailovich and faithful to the King, and the partisans under the Communist adventurer, Tito. It seems that the German and Italian commands in that area were not always acting in full harmony, and Hitler wrote to Mussolini that a common plan of action must be devised.

In the meantime the aerial bombings of Italian towns increased in intensity day by day; in most cases the objectives hit were not of a military character, and the numbers of civilians killed or maimed was far larger than that of soldiers, sailors or airmen. Mussolini told Ambassador Guariglia that Myron Taylor (President Roosevelt's personal representative to the Pope) had gone to London "and suggested that terrorist bombings in Italy should be intensified, as they would thus assure the Allies of the country's speedy collapse." In the case of Italy these bombings can in no way be regarded as reprisals, for the Italian air force had never indulged in similar operations against enemy cities, limiting itself to purely military objectives.

The deplorable sequel of events in the military field, added to the aerial bombing of Italian cities, inevitably reacted on the internal situation. While most Italians still felt it their duty to hold out to the end, others began to think only of how best to provide for themselves if the Western Allies should win and the Fascist regime should fall in consequence. Among these were many disgruntled politicians, who saw in the defeat of their country the only possibility for a comeback, and a certain number of intellectuals, such as Benedetto Croce, whose personal ambitions and prejudices overcame such patriotism as they still retained.[12] Even among the Fascists there were many who were preparing to "rat," especially those who had received the greatest benefits from the regime but hoped to secure yet others from its successor.

Hitler now tended to attribute the unfavorable course of events to his Allies—the Italians, the Hungarians, the Rumanians. But in Italy, the Germans were regarded as responsible: (1) on account of Hitler's strategy, imposed by him on the German armies against the advice of his ablest generals; (2) owing to his failure to understand the importance of the Mediterranean front and to send the maximum amount of supplies to it; and (3) because of his treatment of the inhabitants of the occupied territories, such as the Ukrainians, who had at first welcomed the Germans as liberators from Soviet tyranny, only to find that Russian or pro-Russian officials were left in charge by the liberators.

In Italy the insufficiency of war materiel was being felt ever more acutely, especially in the air force. On April 30, 1943, Mussolini sent Hitler an urgent request for more planes to resist the enemy's overwhelming aerial superiority. Hitler replied that he had sent 574 machines in March and 699 in April, besides those of the German units transferred to Italy and those used for transportation purposes.[13]

The situation in North Africa was deteriorating, and the Italian and German forces were being slowly driven back into Cyrenaica, then into Tripolitania, until on January 23, 1943 Tripoli itself was evacuated. The Italian troops now fell back on Tunisia, where they met further enemy units. After a series of violent engagements, in which both Germans and Italians resisted vigorously, their forces found themselves surrounded by British and other armies. After a hard-fought battle on the Marteh line in Tunisia the Italian First Army, commanded by General Messe, was forced to surrender on May 13, 1943. Only a small number of Germans and Italians succeeded in withdrawing to Sicily.

[1] *Hitler e Mussolini*, 154, 155.
[2] Ciano, *Diario, 1939-1943*, Vol. II, p. 48.
[3] Text in Ciano, *L'Europa verso la catastrofe*, p. 694.
[4] All this is confirmed by C. A. Beard, *President Roosevelt and the Coming of the War, 1941*, New Haven: Yale University Press, 1948; George Morgenstern, *Pearl Harbor*, New York: Devin-Adair, 1947; C. C. Tansill, *Back Door to War*, Chicago: Regnery, 1952; F. R. Sanborn, *Design for War*, New York: Devin-Adair, 1951; and H. E. Barnes *et al.*, *Perpetual War for Perpetual Peace*, Caldwell, Idaho: Caxton Printers, 1953.

[5] Ciano, *L'Europa verso la catastrofe*, p. 697.

[6] December 5, 1941.

[7] Hull, *Memoirs*, Vol. I, p. 296.

[8] *Ibid.*, Vol. II, p. 941.

[9] *Ibid.*, p. 945.

[10] *Ibid.*, p. 1548.

[11] *Hitler e Mussolini*, 156.

[12] It will be remembered that during the first World War Croce's sympathies were openly on the side of Germany and Austria. In the second World War he shifted to the side of the Western Powers. In a public address in Rome, he openly stated that he had been glad to see his country defeated in the second World War, since that defeat had insured the downfall of Fascism. A more ignoble confession is hardly conceivable. He afterwards ingenuously admitted that he had believed blindly in the promises of the London radio that, if the Italians got rid of Mussolini and Fascism, they would be treated with the utmost generosity, and that he was painfully surprised when he found that not one of these promises had been kept.

[13] *Ibid.*, 154-155.

CHAPTER TWENTY-SEVEN

July 25, 1943: The Dismissal of Mussolini

By the spring of 1943 all North Africa was lost. On June 11th the island of Pantelleria to the east of Sicily was occupied after one of the most formidable air-bombings of the whole war; and on July 10th Anglo-American forces landed in Sicily. Fighting went on for several weeks longer in the island, which had already been subjected to extremely heavy air-bombings, destroying a great part of all the chief cities and lines of communication. By August 17th the last Italian and German forces evacuated Messina for the Calabrian coast, leaving the whole of Sicily in enemy hands. The invasion of the peninsula was now expected at any moment.

These events naturally reacted on the domestic situation, but Mussolini was determined to make every effort to hold out. A meeting took place at Feltre in the province of Belluno on July 19th attended by Mussolini and several of his Ministers, Hitler, the German Ambassador in Rome, von Mackensen, General Keitel, the German military attaché in Rome, Colonel von Rintelen, and others. Again the Duce insisted that more supplies be sent to Italy to defend the country against invasion, but the Germans replied that they had sent all that they could, and this produced a sense of consternation even among the most optimistic.[1]

According to von Rintelen, there were at that time very few troops in the metropolitan area of Italy. Some 36 badly equipped divisions were scattered about the Balkans, 5 were in France, 4 in Sicily (before the enemy occupation), 4 in Sardinia and Corsica, and only 12 in the peninsula, largely due to the insufficient supplies provided by Germany.[2]

It was at this moment that Roosevelt and Churchill issued a joint message to the Italian people (July 16th), stating that the "sole hope for Italy's survival lies in an honorable capitulation to the overwhelming power of the military forces of the United Nations.[3] If you continue to tolerate the Fascist regime, which serves the evil purposes of the Nazis, you must suffer the consequences of your own choice." [4] There was no mention as yet of applying to Italy the Casablanca "unconditional surrender" formula, casually concocted by Roosevelt at a luncheon party in that African port.

While it is true that Roosevelt did invent the specific term, "unconditional surrender," inaccurately attributing it to General Grant at Appomattox, the British have unfairly accused Roosevelt of having been the author of this policy. It was specifically of British origin. Chamberlain started it in his blank check to Poland in the spring of 1939 and continued it when he rejected Hitler's generous offer of peace after the Polish campaign. It was continued unchanged by Churchill when Hitler's peace offers after Dunkirk were unceremoniously turned down. If Britain suffered grievously as a result of this policy through the complete destruction of Germany and the rise of Russia to the hegemony of Europe, its people cannot fairly blame Roosevelt; their own prime ministers must bear the main responsibility. This is pointed out at length and repeatedly by Nicoll in *Britain's Blunder*.

Over many months, plans and plots for getting Italy out of the war had been brewing in several quarters. According to Ambassador Filippo Anfuso, as far back as 1942 the King had contemplated what was called the "uncoupling of Italy from Germany." [5] Ciano, too, for some time had begun to profess anti-German sentiments, or at least he said afterwards that he

had professed them; and Anfuso, himself, who was to stand
by Mussolini to the very end, had written to Ciano from
Budapest, where he was then Italian Minister, that it was time
to examine the possibility for Italy to withdraw from the conflict with dignity and honor.

After March, 1943, Ciano was no longer Minister of Foreign
Affairs, having been appointed Ambassador to the Holy See;
Mussolini himself had once more taken over the Foreign
Ministry, with Giuseppe Bastianini, the last Italian Ambassador in London before the war, as Undersecretary. Ciano,
bitterly disappointed at being no longer at the Palazzo Chigi,
began to intrigue actively with the Vatican, with certain dis-
credited generals, with factious and ambitious politicians and
with ladies of the Roman aristocracy.[6] He was generally believed to be aspiring to succeed his father-in-law as head of
the government.

The leading conspirators were: Marshal Badoglio; the
former Minister of Foreign Affairs, and afterwards President
of the Chamber and Minister of Justice, Dino Grandi; the
Princess of Piedmont (Marie José of Belgium, daughter of
the king of the Belgians); the Chief of the General Staff, General Vittorio Ambrosio; and the Minister of the Royal House-
hold, Duke Acquarone. But the various plotters, although all
aiming at the removal of Mussolini from the Premiership,
did not conspire together, for each individual or group played
a different game. The most sinister figure was that of Marshal
Badoglio. As far back as 1925, Marshal Enrico Caviglia, one
of the most distinguished Italian generals in the first World
War, had warned Mussolini not to trust Badoglio, as he would
prove the ruin of Fascism, of the Monarchy and of Italy.[7] But
the Duce, who in many respects was truly ingenuous, had
loaded Badoglio with honors and emoluments, granting him
all that he asked and believing blindly in his judgments and
merits.

But according to Anfuso, the chief figure who unseated
Mussolini was General Eisenhower, for his aerial bombings
of Rome and other Italian cities affected a far larger number
of people than did the plots and gossip of politicians, generals or ladies of fashion. As one observer remarked, "his

bombs were the salt which seasoned the Roman plot." The
one man whom Anfuso regarded as really sensible was Er-
manno Amicucci, Undersecretary for Corporations, who said
to him: "I do not know what they are up to, but from what
I do know of them [the plotters], they are fixing up something
big. It is easy to say that they are idiots, but you will see
that they are leading us to ruin."

Rumors now began to go around that Mussolini's political
position was no longer invincible. Although the German
Ambassador in Rome reported that the Duce and the Fascist
party were as strong as ever, the German Consul, E. F. Mölhausen, told Dörtenbach of the German Embassy that when he
was at Cortina, he had heard that Fascism was *in extremis*.[8]

In view of the ever graver military situation, Mussolini decided to summon the Fascist Grand Council. This body, consisting of the members of the Government, some of the Undersecretaries and other prominent political men, had purely
advisory powers (except in the drafting of lists of candidates for
Parliament), but it was entitled to be consulted by the Prime
Minister whenever a decision of national importance was
about to be taken, although he was not legally bound to follow
its advice.

The Council met on the afternoon of July 24, 1943, and sat
until the early hours of the 25th. No full report of that fateful
meeting has yet been published, but a spate of documents,
memoirs and reports concerning it has been pouring out during the past twelve years. Although it was primarily a meeting
on domestic political policy, it had a direct and serious bearing
on the international situation of Italy as well.

The origin of the events that resulted from the meeting
must, of course, be sought in the unfavorable course of the
war, for although there had always been tendencies opposed to
Mussolini and to Fascism, they would never have come to a
head if the military situation had continued to be as satisfactory as it had been in the beginning of the conflict. Indeed,
it has been rightly said that Mussolini's one unpardonable
offense was that he had been defeated.

For some time before July 24th Mussolini himself had been
reflecting on the advisability and possibility of bringing the

war to an end by uncoupling Italy from Germany, but in an open and loyal manner, avoiding all that savored of treachery to an ally. Some authorities claim that he himself wished for a solution such as that which materialized on July 24-25th, although not of course in the manner it actually worked out. Others assert that he was then already convinced that the war was lost. Still others, relying on his own words, maintain that he continued to believe in victory. But it seems that after the Feltre meeting when Hitler had refused to give Italy the supplies it needed, Mussolini had told the King that he was prepared to withdraw from the Alliance before September 15th. On the other hand, the Germans were beginning to doubt whether he could still continue to rule the nation and to think that another man might more usefully take his place.

That the King wished to break away from the alliance is proved by his notes on the subject published by the *Vita Italiana*.[9] On May 15, 1943, he wrote: "We must consider very seriously the possible necessity of detaching Italy from Germany whose internal breakdown might be as sudden as that of the German Empire in 1918."

Some days before July 24th Mussolini had a conversation with the Rumanian Assistant-Prime Minister, Mihai Antonescu, who complained that von Ribbentrop never gave a definite answer to the query about the war aims of the Tripartite Pact. Antonescu further insisted on the necessity for close coöperation between Rumania and Italy, to which Mussolini cordially assented.

On the 17th the Undersecretary, Giuseppe Bastianini, had written to the Papal Secretary of State, Cardinal Maglione concerning the Pope's alleged intention of trying to bring the conflict to an end. He added that Italy would never assume an initiative of her own in this connection. If the military situation should deteriorate still further, the only man capable of inducing the Germans to withdraw from Italian territory was Mussolini himself. Hence, the necessity that Great Britain and the United States should not insist on Mussolini's resignation and on setting up an entirely new government in Italy, which would lead to a disastrous civil war.[10]

On the other hand, the Italian Ambassador in Berlin, Dino

Alfieri, had written to Bastianini, on July 14th that Germany could not undertake any serious resistance and still less launch a counteroffensive in Italy, as it must prepare for a new Russian offensive and for an Anglo-American attack on the territory of the Reich. Germany regarded Italy merely as a bastion to hold up and wear out the enemy forces as long as possible, "thereby preventing them from menacing areas more directly connected with the territory of the Reich." As a matter of fact, the Germans under General Albert Kesselring did hold up the far more numerous Anglo-American forces in Italy for nearly two years longer.

The Grand Council met, as we have seen, on the 24th of July. There was much recrimination and bitter wrangling during the meeting; and Grandi and Luigi Federzoni violently attacked Mussolini. Finally a resolution drafted by Dino Grandi was put through by 19 votes against 7 and one abstention, that of Roberto Farinacci.[11] The Grandi resolution stated that in view of the present situation, "the immediate restoration of all state functions was necessary, and the tasks and responsibilities laid down in our fundamental and constitutional laws should be assigned to the Crown, the Grand Council, the Government, Parliament and the Corporations;[12] the Head of the Government is hereby requested to beg His Majesty the King, to whom the heart of the nation addresses itself faithfully and with confidence, to take over, for the honor and security of the nation, together with the effective command of the armed forces on land, on the sea and in the air, in accordance with Article 5 of the Constitution of the Realm, that supreme initiative of decision which our institutions attribute to him, institutions which have always been, throughout our national history, the glorious heritage of our august Savoy Dynasty." [13]

This resolution was, of course, an invitation to Mussolini to submit his resignation to the King, although, as I have said, he was not constitutionally obliged to do so, in view of the purely advisory powers of the Grand Council. The resolution was the result of a double plot to oust Mussolini from office. One was inspired by Grandi himself, who aimed at setting up a new Fascist Government with himself as Prime Minister and

with the support of Ciano, although the latter retained a
mental reservation that he should be the successor of the Duce.
The other was inspired by the King, Badoglio and other generals, with Duke Acquarone as the *éminence grise,* to create an
entirely new government of a military character, devoid of all
Fascist personnel or affiliations, with the object of breaking
away from Germany and concluding a separate peace with
the Western Powers, although this last intention was kept
strictly secret at the time.

Mussolini, himself, does not appear to have been greatly
concerned by the resolution as it was voted. In fact, at 11 a.m.
on the 25th it was he who asked for an audience with the
King, which was fixed for 5 p.m. on that same day. At noon,
he received the Japanese Ambassador, Hidaka, and insisted on
the necessity of concluding peace with Russia, suggesting that
Japan, not being then at war with that Power, should take the
initiative, while Italy would make a similar proposal to Germany. Otherwise, he said Italy, in its present situation, would
be forced to alter its relations with its Axis partner.

At 5 p.m., according to plan, Mussolini was received by the
King, in his private residence, Villa Savoia. His Majesty at
once said that things were going very badly and that the soldiers would no longer fight for Mussolini. "You are now," he
affirmed, "the best-hated man in Italy. You can count only
a single friend—myself." He added that he considered that
the most suitable successor was Marshal Badoglio, who would
form a Cabinet of officials to administer the country and continue the war. "Within six months we shall see," Mussolini
replied; "You are taking a very serious decision. The [Govern-
ment] crisis means making the people believe that peace is in
sight. That the soldiers do not wish to fight for me is of no
consequence, provided that they are ready to fight for you.
This crisis will be regarded as a triumph for the Churchill-
Stalin combination, especially for Stalin, who will see in it the
withdrawal of an antagonist who has fought against him for
twenty years[14] . . . In any case I wish good luck to the man
who will take over the situation."

There are other versions of this conversation, but this one,
Mussolini's own, is the most reliable.

At 5:20 p.m., the King escorted the Duce to the threshold of his Villa, and it is certain that he departed with no ill feeling towards his sovereign—indeed he was still as devoted to him as before, not knowing, as he then did, the existence of a palace plot. The King, himself, admitted in a letter to a friend, published by the journalist, Paolo Monelli, that the initiative, which had developed through the dark ways of a military conspiracy, was his own. He knew that several of the Fascist leaders were plotting against Mussolini; and although the only man in whom he had confided was Acquarone, he had found support among some of the generals, especially the Chief of the General Staff, Ambrosio, who was bitterly anti-German and incidentally a soldier of very limited military abilities. The King trusted Badoglio, who, although professedly Fascist and devoted to Mussolini, from whom he had received every possible favor,[15] was ready to betray him, as he believed himself destined to be the Duce's successor. Badoglio had also plotted with two ex-Premiers, Ivanoe Bonomi and Vittorio E. Orlando, who had likewise formerly supported Mussolini, but now "ratted." On July 15th Badoglio had been received by the King, who then informed him for the first time of his intentions and asked him if he were prepared to take over the premiership.[16] Badoglio at once replied affirmatively but disagreed with the King about the composition of his future Cabinet; he wanted one composed of politicians. The King insisted on one formed of non-party officials, and it was this plan that was carried out.

On quitting Villa Savoia, Mussolini was at once arrested, in consequence of a decision taken by Badoglio himself, by Generals Ambrosio and Castellano and by the Chief of Police, Carmine Senise. The King seems not to have originally had that intention. The Duce was conveyed in a motor ambulance, first to one of the military barracks and then to the police barracks, on the pretext that his life must be protected, although he was not actually in any danger.

The King at once entrusted Badoglio with the formation of the new government, as arranged. The King's action for the first time in the whole of his reign was completely unconstitutional: in the first place, because the powers of the Grand

Council were, as we have seen, purely advisory, and there had been no hostile vote in Parliament or at a general election; and in the second place, because he had no right to confer full powers on Badoglio, this being the prerogative of Parliament alone. Moreover, he agreed to summon to the various ministries men who represented no party or other important influences. There is, indeed, every reason to believe that, by this time, the King's mental powers had suffered a decline, for his actions both then and during the subsequent period were in sharp contrast to the whole of his previous career when he had always acted in a thoroughly constitutional, straightforward and patriotic manner. It was said that he on this occasion had defaulted on the tradition of monarchy in general, on that of the House of Savoy and, actually, on that of Victor Emmanuel III, himself, as all his own previous actions prove.

Both the King and Badoglio now issued proclamations to the nation. In that of the Field Marshal it was declared that "the war continues," and that "Italy will keep faith with her plighted word," which implied that the alliance with Germany was to remain unchanged. Badoglio telegraphed to Hitler to the same effect, but his real intentions were radically different.

Hitler, who had never swerved from his admiration and affection for Mussolini, was most indignant at the news of the Duce's removal and arrest; and he began to talk of an immediate intervention to liberate him, to seize the person of the King and to punish the enemies of Fascism. German public opinion was greatly concerned, fearing that the change of regime meant the collapse of the Italian state. The military authorities at once began to send more troops into Italy. Had they done so before, the situation might well have been different.

Badoglio's first actions were to arrest many of the Fascist leaders, to suppress the Fascist party and to remove all Fascist emblems from public buildings.

From the police barracks Mussolini was transferred to the island of Ponza. As this was not considered a sufficiently safe place of detention, he was sent to Maddalena, an island off the coast of Sardinia. In a diary written there, of which only a few pages exist, he says:

In due time Fascism will once more shine on the horizon. First, in consequence of the persecutions to which the "liberals" will subject it, proving that liberty is that which each man reserves for himself; second, because of a nostalgia for the "happy days" which will come to corrode the Italian spirit. From this all those who have fought in all the European and especially the African wars, will suffer. The *mal d'Africa* will prove devastating.[17]

From Maddalena he was again transferred to the summit of the Gran Sasso, in the province of Aquila, where there is a large hotel, Campo Imperatore, for winter sports.

[1] *Hitler e Mussolini,* 165, 174.

[2] Von Rintelen, *op. cit.,* p. 197.

[3] They were already so called.

[4] Hull, *op. cit.,* Vol. II, p. 1548.

[5] Anfuso, *op. cit.,* p. 330.

[6] It is believed that through one of these ladies who had relations in London and elsewhere military and other information communicated by Ciano was passed on to the enemy via Switzerland.

[7] Saverio Cilibrizzi, *Pietro Badoglio,* Naples, 1948, p. 244.

[8] E. F. Mölhausen, *La carta perdente,* Rome, 1949, p. 534.

[9] December 1944.

[10] Which actually did happen as soon as he had been eliminated.

[11] Member of Parliament and journalist, Secretary of the Fascist party until 1926.

[12] Economic guilds of manufacturers, landowners, industrial and agricultural workers and professional men.

[13] Mussolini said at the meeting that he had taken over the supreme command of the armed forces at the request of the King on a proposal made by Badoglio in a letter of May 3, 1940.

[14] Mussolini was the only important European statesman who had consistently opposed Bolshevism.

[15] Mussolini had made Badoglio Chief of the General Staff, conferred on him the Order of the Annunciation and the title of Marquis, made him Viceroy of Ethiopia, a position which he held for only a month, but received its emoluments for life, and also had induced the King to make him head of the National Research Council.

[16] In his memoirs Badoglio claims that he first learned of the King's intention to offer him the premiership on the afternoon of the 25th; but even apart from the Royal audience of the 15th he had heard of it on the afternoon of the 24th and again on the morning of the 25th.

[17] Attilio Tamaro, *Due anni di storia,* Rome, 1948, Vol. I, p. 282.

CHAPTER TWENTY-EIGHT

The Armistice of September 8, 1943

Negotiations for an armistice with the Western Powers, unbeknown to Germany, commenced as soon as Badoglio came into power; and the Ambassador, Raffaele Guariglia, Minister of Foreign Affairs in the new Cabinet, sent his private secretary, Marquis Blasco d'Ajeta, to Lisbon to make contact with the British Ambassador in that capital, Sir Ronald Campbell. The latter, after hearing d'Ajeta's account of the state of Italy, declared that the country must accept unconditional surrender, the disastrous formula which had been casually excogitated by President Roosevelt at Casablanca for Germany, and prolonged the war for two more devastating years.[1]

I need not enter into details of the intrigues and negotiations for the conclusion of the armistice between various Italian generals and diplomats and the representatives of the Western Powers, as these questions did not concern Mussolini's foreign policy, the Duce being no longer in power. But they did, of course, react on that policy and molded its course. It has been rightly said that if a hundred of the most intelligent men in Italy had been entrusted with the task of concluding an armistice in the worst possible manner, they could not have acted more preposterously than the negotiators actually did.

Throughout the negotiations the Allied bombings of Italian cities continued unabated, even after the armistice had actually been signed on September 3rd, at Cassibile in Sicily by General Giuseppe Castellano on behalf of Badoglio and by General Bedell Smith on behalf of General Eisenhower. There were two documents—the *short* armistice and the *long* one.[2] General Eisenhower himself stated that the armistice was "a crooked deal."

On September 8th the King received the new German Ambassador in Rome, Dr. Rudolph Rahn—an audience which Duke Acquarone and the Foreign Minister Guariglia should have prevented at all costs, knowing that the armistice was already signed and that the King would have to deny its existence. Rahn met with a very cordial reception and was assured that Badoglio's word was wholly to be trusted.[3]

Eisenhower now telegraphed to Badoglio ordering him to carry out his task of defending Rome against the Germans and adding that if he and his followers did not keep their word, his Government and his nation would be dissolved.

A Reuter message announcing the armistice had now been distributed, but the Secretary General of the Ministry of Foreign Affairs, Augusto Rosso,[4] who knew nothing of the fatal decision, on receiving Rahn assured him that the statement was untrue. A Crown Council was held on September 8th at 6:30 p.m. In the meantime General Eisenhower had officially announced the armistice. Marshal Badoglio then went to the E.I.A.R. (the official transmitting wireless station), and issued the following communiqué at 7:15 p.m.:

The Italian Government, realizing the impossibility of continuing the unequal struggle against the overwhelming hostile force, with the object of sparing the nation further and graver disasters, has asked General Eisenhower, Commander-in-Chief of the Allied Anglo-American armed forces for an armistice. It has been granted. Consequently, all acts of hostility on the part of the Italian forces against the Anglo-American forces must cease everywhere. The Italian forces will resist eventual attacks whencesoever they may come.

Rahn was now summoned by Guariglia and informed that in view of the desperate military situation Badoglio had been forced to sue for an armistice. "This is treachery to the plighted word," Rahn indignantly exclaimed. When Guariglia protested against the word "treachery," Rahn retorted: "I do not accuse the Italian people, but those who have brought it to this unworthy situation. I fear that this decision will be a grave burden on Italy's future fate." [5] According to another version, Rahn added: "The King told me again today that Italy would continue the struggle, true to her plighted word. Now we see what the word of the King and of the Marshal are worth." He left the room without even saying farewell to Guariglia.[6]

Badoglio then sent a note to the Italian Legations in Budapest, Bucharest, Sofia, Zagreb and Bratislava, stating that Italy, being no longer able to defend herself against invasion, had been forced to sue for an armistice.[7]

This statement was wholly misleading, for while Badoglio declared Italy was absolutely unable to go on fighting, he was actually preparing to go to war against Germany. He might, indeed, have decided on a strict neutrality for Italy, pointing out that as Germany had not given it the support that had been promised, Italy was no longer bound by its conventional obligations. Mussolini himself had said more or less the same thing. But Badoglio's conduct in this connection was inexcusable.

The error on the side of the Western Powers was even greater. A systematic and well-prepared collaboration by Italy, grossly immoral as it would have been, might have facilitated their task from a military point of view. Although they had already landed forces on the South Italian mainland by September 3rd, it was to take them another nineteen months of very hard fighting with enormous losses to overcome the small German forces, aided by the still smaller Italian forces in the North, before they brought the war to an end. As Mussolini wrote, "the unconstitutional surrender of September 1943 was the greatest material and moral catastrophe in the thirty centuries of our history!" [8]

At that moment many Italians, exhausted by the long struggle, the atrocious air-bombings and all the incredible hardships and lack of food and of all other necessaries, expe-

rienced a sense of relief at the news of the armistice, believing
(wrongly, as it happened) that it meant the end of the war.
When the consequences were realized, they deplored the decision and were filled with bitter hatred not only for its Italian
authors but for the enemy who had taken advantage of the
treachery of Badoglio and of his handful of fellow-conspirators
and had flagrantly broken every promise they had made to the
Italian people. Few, indeed, were the Italians who were not
utterly heartbroken at the situation, even if some of them
afterwards took advantage of it for their own purposes.

Typical of the general state of mind was the speech pro-
nounced on that fatal September 8th by a poor workman,
Giuseppe Bentivoglio, from the balcony of the town hall of
Molinella, ever a centre of advanced Socialism:

I cannot share in the general gladness, nor can you do so, you
who were brought up in the school of Giuseppe Massarenti.[9]
Socialists cannot be satisfied when the country is humiliated by
an armistice of surrender such as the one announced by Marshal
Badoglio. To be a Socialist means to wish the fatherland to be
great and strong, so as to enjoy authority and be capable of safeguarding the interests of the workers at home and abroad. One
cannot be a Socialist and yet rejoice that the army should be breaking up, for when there is no army, the nation has no backbone. We
cannot be Socialists and not feel shame for what is happening.[10]

An eminent Swiss personage, who had been in Italy at the
time, said on his return from Rome that "unpopular as the
War may have been, when the hour of surrender arrived,
the majority of the people felt that it would have been better for the honor of the country to fight to the bitter end. A
woman of the people, whose son was in Greece and who had
had no news from him for many months, indignant against
a lady who visibly showed satisfaction at the armistice, said to
her: 'But, Madam, do think: This is the end of Italy, the breakdown of all we have lived for.' Tears rolled down from her
poor eyes." [11]

On September 10th Roosevelt and Churchill sent a joint
message to Badoglio and the Italian people, "urging them to
strike hard alongside of their American and British friends to
drive the Germans out of Italy." [12] In order to conciliate the

Adolf Hitler

Field Marshal Rodolfo Graziani, Marquis of Neghelli

Italo-American voters, Roosevelt said in a propaganda speech in favor of a new war loan, that the armistice was "a great victory also for the Italian people." This was a statement which, like some others made by the late President, can only be called, to say the least, a "terminological inexactitude."

The first consequence of the armistice was the immediate occupation by the Germans of the whole of Italy, except Sicily and the small area of the peninsula where Allied forces had landed. The Germans took possession of the principal cities and imposed their authority everywhere.

Then the King was told by Badoglio that he and his family and all the members of the government must depart from Rome and from any part of Italy occupied or likely to be occupied by the Germans. To this the King agreed. The fact that he left the capital without any government or proper authority has been severely condemned, even by many sincere Monarchists, on the ground that the captain should *always* be the last to leave the sinking ship. This action on his part seems to confirm what I said before as to his being no longer master of himself and perhaps not even of his personal liberty. His departure for Pescara and thence for Brindisi had been practically forced on him by Badoglio. Prince Humbert seems to have tried to dissuade him from leaving.

No systematic attempt to defend Rome against the German occupation was made by Badoglio or anyone else. There was some sporadic fighting on the outskirts of the city and elsewhere between small isolated German and Italian units, but no serious operations. The greater part of the Italian troops, finding themselves without their generals, who disappeared without leaving orders or substitutes, disbanded and returned to their homes, or they surrendered to the Germans. This was particularly the case in North Italy, where hundreds of thousands of men were deported to Germany as prisoners of war. Allied forces landed at Salerno, but the Germans in that area reacted vigorously, defeated them repeatedly and held them up for a long time.

The King with his shadow government at Brindisi was devoid of all authority and was treated by the British with the utmost discourtesy. On September 10th Eisenhower sent Badoglio a message ordering him to prepare the nation for war against Germany—after Badoglio had declared that Italy was absolutely incapable of continuing to fight. Eisenhower assured him that the whole future and honor of Italy depended on what her armed forces were prepared to do. Eisenhower was, no doubt, quite sincere, but he was asking for the impossible. The message to the King from Roosevelt and Churchill to the same effect, inspired by less good faith, was equally futile.

Badoglio assured Eisenhower that he had made all the necessary arrangements for the Italian army to operate strenuously against the Germans; but he had done nothing of the kind, nor could he have done anything of the sort.

In accordance with the terms of the armistice, the fleet surrendered to the Anglo-Americans at Malta. But Admiral Carlo Bergamini, the naval Commander-in-Chief, raised his flag on the cruiser *Roma* and sailed forth from Spezia. His ship was struck by German bombers (who were not aware of his attitude) and sunk, and he and 1,500 of the crew of 1,800 were drowned. Several other officers, including Admirals Legnani and Galati, also refused to surrender and were afterwards regarded as having violated their oath to the King.

Hull quotes Churchill as having said that "Badoglio, from the time he had safely delivered the fleet into our hands, has been a useful instrument." [13] It will be many years before Italians forget this surrender and those responsible for it, however *useful* they may have been to the Allied cause.

The break-up of the army was the result not merely of the cessation of the war, but also of the attempt of the Western Powers, with the complicity of Badoglio & Co., to force on it a new war against the Germans. If a good deal of ill-feeling had grown up in certain circles against the Germans, whose want of tact was often very marked, there was no wish to fight against them. Many officers and men preferred not to fight at all, but those who did would have preferred to fight against the Western invaders. The myth created by Badoglio and kept up by his successors down to the present rulers of the country that in September, 1943, all Italy was bitterly hostile to the Germans as the nation's hereditary enemy is pure bunk.

Many charges were levelled against the generals and other

officers for the collapse of the army, but the guilt for what happened, apart from the course of events, lies chiefly if not solely with a handful of ambitious, unscrupulous and selfish generals, the least competent in the army. What the failure to create and execute a wise policy toward Italy from 1943 onward, instead of the "unconditional surrender" formula, cost the Allies, can be seen from the fact that the United States alone poured over four billion dollars into Italy between 1945 and 1955 to keep its anti-Fascist Government afloat.

[1] On this point see Lord Hankey, *op. cit.*, Chap. II; and F. O. Miksche, *Unconditional Surrender*, London, 1952.

[2] Tamaro, *op. cit.*, Vol. I, p. 332.

[3] Rudolph Rahn, *Ruheloses Leben*, Düsseldorf, 1949, p. 229.

[4] Formerly Ambassador in Washington and then in Moscow.

[5] Rahn, *Ibid.*

[6] Note by the *Deutsche Nachrichten Bureau*, but not quoted by Rahn.

[7] Joseph Goebbels, *Tagebücher*, Zurich, 1948, p. 401. (English translation, *The Goebbels' Diaries*, New York: Doubleday), 1948.

[8] Benito Mussolini, *Storia di un anno*, Milan, 1944, p. 221.

[9] A prominent Socialist leader and for many years mayor of Molinella.

[10] Carlo Silvestri, *Contro la Vendetta*, Milan, 1948, pp. 183 ff; Tamaro, *op. cit.*, Vol. I, pp. 529-530.

[11] *Journal de Genève*, October 24, 1943.

[12] Hull, *Memoirs*, Vol. II, p. 1549.

[13] *Ibid.*, p. 1564.

CHAPTER TWENTY-NINE

The Return of the Duce: Institution of the Italian Social Republic

Mussolini spent his days at Campo Imperatore in perfect quiet, but his health was much impaired. Thin, pale and often suffering from a duodenal ulcer, he had heard from the Algiers wireless that his surrender and that of his chief supporters to the Allies had been provided for in the terms of the *long* armistice. But Lieutenant Faiola of the escort guarding him assured him that he would see to it that he escaped in due time. Mussolini told the officer that if the armistice had not been concluded, Italy could not have suffered more than she had. He said, further, that for some time past he had tried to induce Hitler to make peace with Russia, once in February and twice in March 1943, and that he had talked to him on the subject at Klessheim, but always in vain. He expressed himself with great bitterness against Badoglio and the King, but while he longed to get away from Campo Imperatore, he only wished to retire to his castle at La Rocca delle Caminate, not thinking of any possible return to power.

Suddenly, only four days after the signing of the Armistice on September 8th, the German wireless announced that Mussolini had been liberated from Campo Imperatore.[1]

The German G.H.Q. had ascertained his whereabouts and despatched a party of eight parachutists under Major Skorzeny, who had landed on the mountain eyrie' on September 12th. Here were stationed many carabinieri on guard with Lieutenant Faiola and a police inspector named Gueli, who had orders to shoot Mussolini if he tried to escape. The Chief of Police in Rome, Carmine Senise, had confirmed this order to Gueli. When the inspector replied that he was no murderer, Senise assured him that the execution had been entrusted to the carabinieri. Nevertheless, when Badoglio had fled from Rome, Senise began to have qualms of conscience and feared that if Mussolini were murdered, the Germans and the Fascists would exact fierce reprisals on himself and his friends. Senise then phoned to Gueli ordering him to "act with prudence," which was tantamount to saying "do not kill him." On the 12th he phoned again, after consulting General Count Calvi di Bergolo (the King's son-in-law, then commanding the Rome garrison), enjoining Gueli to "act with the *greatest* prudence."

When Skorzeny and General Soleti of the Italian police corps (whom Skorzeny had brought with him to Campo Imperatore) landed on the mountain, two of the carabinieri asked them what they wanted, but Faiola ordered them not to fire. Skorzeny and Faiola drank to each other's health, and the Duce was flown first to Pratica di Mare near Rome and then to Vienna.

From Vienna he was conveyed to the German G.H.Q. After two conversations with Hitler he decided that it was his duty to take up the burden of power once more—to save what could be saved, as he said, for Italy in her desperate condition.[2]

Hitler insisted that Mussolini should proceed at once against "the traitors of the Grand Council" by whom he had been ousted from power, but for a long time Mussolini refused to admit that there had been any treachery. As usual, he showed himself ingenuous and did not realize the character of certain men by whom he had earlier been surrounded and could not believe that those on whom he had showered unlimited benefits could betray him. Hitler at last succeeded in convincing him that Grandi, at least, had been a traitor, although the Führer's personal *bête noire* was Ciano. He considered that Italy was already practically at war with Germany although no declaration had yet been made, and that it was up to Mussolini to alter the situation, insisting that he should become the head of a new republican Fascist state. Italy without Fascism, he said, was Germany's enemy, and Fascism without Mussolini was not Fascism. Only by resuming power could he avert the many dangers to which Italy was exposed. Germany for strategic and moral reasons could not evacuate Italy, and Mussolini must undertake to collaborate with the Reich and trust in its power to resist indefinitely and achieve ultimate victory.

According to Goebbels, Hitler then did not believe that Mussolini had tried to break away from Germany but was furious against Ciano and his wife, Edda. Indeed, Hitler attributed to Edda a disastrous influence on her father, who consequently for a long time had rejected the idea of treachery, so as not to involve his daughter's husband.[3]

For Mussolini it was a great humiliation to return to power with German help. But Italy had to be withdrawn from any dependence on Badoglio and his group; and this, Hitler said, could be done only by Mussolini himself. Goebbels disliked the idea of a reinstatement of Mussolini, for it would prevent Germany from having an absolutely free hand in Italy. He wrote, in fact that "so lange der Duce nicht da war, war für uns die Chance ganzen Italien *tabula rasa* zu machen" (as long as the Duce was not there, we had the opportunity of making *tabula rasa* of all Italy).

At first Mussolini seemed unwilling to have anything more to do with Fascism, for so many prominent Fascists had let him down. The new state would be called the Italian Social Republic, in which the word Fascist did not appear. But the Fascists then in Germany who adhered to Mussolini and were supported by Hitler insisted on the reconstitution of the Fascist party, now to be called the Fascist Republican Party. The proclamation of an Italian Republic was certainly a grave mistake on Mussolini's part, for it alienated many patriotic Italians—Fascists and non-Fascists who were Royalists—and prevented them from lending support to the new regime which was to reconstitute Italy and exonerate it from the shame of the armistice. The institutional question should have been adjourned until after the end of the war when it could have been settled by a popular referendum.[4] A provisional government would have been the best solution in the meantime.

We can well understand Mussolini's indignation against Victor Emmanuel for his conduct on July 25th and for agreeing to the abominable armistice, but the person of the King was independent of any judgment on Monarchy as an institution.

On September 15th Mussolini issued five wireless messages from the German G.H.Q., announcing that he had resumed the leadership of the Fascist Party, appointed Alessandro Pavolini the party secretary, ordered all officials to return to their duties, re-established the various Fascist institutions, including the Volunteer Militia with the ex-Minister of Corporations, Renato Ricci,[5] as its commander, and freed all officers of the fighting services from their oath of allegiance to the King.[6]

Until the first German wireless message of September 12th came through announcing the liberation of the Duce, no one in Italy knew what had happened to him or where he was, and many did not at first believe that message. But his voice was heard once more, and although it was weaker and his words less hammerlike than before, there was no mistaking its authenticity.

Mussolini then proceeded to Munich and sent Pavolini to Rome to form a new Cabinet. Several ex-ministers and other important leaders now came to Munich to wait on the Duce and place themselves at his disposal. But one prominent figure was missing. What had become of Field Marshal Cavallero?

Count Ugo Cavallero had had a long and brilliant military career. He had been in G.S.O. 1 Operations under General Diaz in the last year of the first World War, and had planned the victorious battle of Vittorio Veneto (October-November 1918). Since then he had held various high appointments and collaborated with Mussolini in the reform of the army organization. After the unfortunate beginning of the Greek campaign in the autumn of 1940, Cavallero had been sent to Albania, where he succeeded in pulling things together and eventually in achieving success. While still in Albania, he was appointed Chief of the General Staff, and he took part in the operations in North Africa. But after the loss of Libya, he was deprived of his command and was succeeded by General Ambrosio, a man of far inferior caliber.

In 1942, while holding no actual command, he had more than once considered the possibility of Mussolini's resignation, although still admiring him in many ways, and had actually suggested Badoglio as a successor, in spite of past dissensions with him. But when Badoglio became head of the Government on July 25th, he at once had Cavallero arrested and interned in the military prison of Forte Boccea just outside Rome. Two days later, apparently on the King's intervention, he was liberated. But on August 23rd he was arrested again, also on the order of Badoglio, who professed to believe that he was organizing a Fascist plot to restore the fallen regime—a wholly fantastic charge.[7]

After the armistice, when the Germans were in occupation of Rome, they had Cavallero liberated once more (September 12th) and conveyed to the German Embassy. Cavallero feared that he might have trouble with the Germans because Badoglio, on his flight from Rome had left only one document on his desk, a memorandum by Cavallero criticizing Germany's policy, which now had fallen into German hands. But General Kesselring, commanding the German forces in Italy, showed every consideration for his Italian colleague, invited him to dine at his G.H.Q. at Frascati and placed a villa at his disposal, where he went to spend the night. The next morning Cavallero was found dead in the villa with a bullet through his head.

According to one version, he had been put to death by the Germans, but there is no reason to believe this rumor. It is, indeed, claimed that Kesselring had informed Cavallero that he wished him to be appointed commander-in-chief of the new Italian army under Mussolini's reconstructed government. But even this statement is very doubtful, for on September 12th Mussolini had only just been liberated and had not yet even considered the reconstruction of his government or his army. There is every reason to believe that Cavallero committed suicide out of sheer despair at the disaster that had come to his country.[8]

On September 18th Mussolini delivered a speech over the German wireless, telling the story of his recent vicissitudes. He accused the Dynasty of having been defeatist during the war, of having acted as the agent of anti-German propaganda and of organizing the *coup d'état* of July 25th with the complicity of Badoglio and some other generals. He was now, he continued, determined to take up arms once more on the side of Germany and Japan, to reorganize the armed forces of Italy, to eliminate the traitors, to destroy parasitic plutocracy and to make labor the basis of the state.[9]

Badoglio's reply was hopelessly feeble, and it reacted against himself and the King as jointly responsible for the catastrophe. He declared that the Italian people had not betrayed Italy, and that only the Fascists and Nationalists had done so. He claimed that Italian soldiers had fallen in Africa solely for German interests, quite forgetting that Libya and East Africa were Italian and not German colonies. He subsequently issued a second proclamation that was such a medley of nonsense that little attention was paid to it.

A German command was in possession of Rome, but it was Count Giorgio Carlo Calvi who, in the absence of the vanished ministers, placed commissioners chosen from among the highest-ranking civil servants in charge of the various government departments.

The liberation of Mussolini altered the attitude of the Western Allies towards Italy. So long as there was no regular Italian government, in the parts of the country occupied by the Germans, there needed to be none in those occupied by the Anglo-American armies; the carabinieri and the fire brigade were sufficient. But now that a new Italian Government under Mussolini was being formed in the North, it was deemed necessary to create something of the kind in the South with at least an appearance of autonomy. In his speech of September 21st Churchill sang the praises of Badoglio, but the recognition of a real Italian government was adjourned.

The only men available for the purpose were a few third-rate politicians, who had been out of office for decades, and others, who had been so long absent from Italy that they had forgotten what it was like and who had learned nothing and forgotten everything.[10] All these men, responsible for the deplorable conditions of Italy in 1919-1922 and consequently for the advent of Fascism, were now inspired only by savage vindictiveness against those who had deprived them of the joys and spoils of office. These returned refugees made innumerable Italians, regardless of party, look to the restoration of a Mussolini government with relief and hope as representing, at all events, an improvement on the regime that these nonentities were trying to set up under the aegis of British, American, French, Yugoslav, Indian, South African, Brazilian, Australian, Russian and other bayonets.

It was by no means easy for Mussolini to find the right men for his new Cabinet, but he did succeed in securing a certain number of valuable lieutenants—Angelo Tarchi, Piero Pisenti, Domenico Pellegrini-Giampietro and some others—who proved thoroughly competent for the technical departments, and Ferdinando Mezzasoma was an excellent choice as Minister of Popular Culture (propaganda services). For the Ministry of Foreign Affairs with himself as nominal head his choice fell on Count Serafino Mazzolini, as Undersecretary, an excellent appointment. Mazzolini was a fine character and a man experienced in foreign relations, who for many years held important diplomatic posts with success. Guido Buffarini-Guidi, appointed, it is said, under the pressure of Himmler, as Undersecretary of the Interior, was a much less fortunate selection.

Whom to appoint Minister of Defense was a difficult problem. The army, navy and air force were practically non-existent and would have to be entirely reconstituted. Marshal Rodolfo Graziani was undoubtedly a first-class soldier of long experience, but he had been on bad terms with Mussolini owing to the failure of the North African campaign, although the defeats were chiefly due to causes other than Graziani's possible shortcomings. But on September 22nd the Duce offered him the appointment, and the German Ambassador Rahn warmly supported the proposal. Graziani replied that, in view of the grave situation of the country, he accepted the burden "to reduce the shame of the surrender and of the act of treachery towards Italy's allies."

A conflict now arose between the German civil authorities in Italy and the German military command. The former advocated the formation of an Italian Government complete in all its departments and of an Italian army, but the latter were averse to an autonomous Italian army, for they distrusted the majority of the Italian generals and demanded a free hand in the conduct of all military operations in Italy. Mussolini insisted on the creation of a real Italian army and justified the appointment of Graziani. On September 25th Graziani delivered a fiery speech in Rome to 4,000 Italian officers, attacking the King and appealing to all good Italians to fight once more for the liberation of Italy.

On September 25th Hitler informed Mussolini that he officially recognized the new Italian Government and intended to pursue the war side by side with Italy until victory was achieved.

[1] Erich Kordt, *Wahn und Wirklichkeit,* Stuttgart, 1948, pp. 363 ff.

[2] For the details of Mussolini's rescue see Tamaro, *op. cit.,* Vol. I, pp. 553-567.

[3] Goebbels, *op. cit.,* p. 466.

[4] It should, of course, have been a genuine referendum held with full freedom, not like the bogus referendum of June 2, 1946—Monarchy or Republic?—which was one of the most colossal swindles in history.

[5] One of the ablest and most faithful of the Fascist leaders.

[6] This measure has been much criticized even in some quarters not hostile to Mussolini. But when the King left his capital without a government and placed himself, legally bound hand and foot, at the disposal of the country's enemies, could the oath still be regarded as binding?

[7] Cavallero's Fascist sentiments had never been more than lukewarm.

[8] Giuseppe Braccianti, Preface to Cavallero's *Commando Supremo.*

[9] We have here a reminiscence of Mussolini's old Socialist mentality dating from before the first World War and never quite forgotten.

[10] Like the French and Spanish Bourbons after 1815.

CHAPTER THIRTY

The New Government at Work

Mussolini's new regime was called the Italian Social Republic, and it was undoubtedly only a *de facto* government. But some Italian government in the parts of the country under German occupation was better than none at all; had there not been such a government, most of the country would have been in German hands, as Southern Italy was in those of the Western invaders. As it was, Northern and Central Italy were governed by Italian ministers and officials, according to Italian law, even though the German authorities exercised a certain measure of control over it, especially in military matters, for the armed forces at first were almost entirely German. The government of General de Gaulle was surely only a *de facto* government, but it was recognized as the only legitimate government of France by the Allies because it suited their interests.

In the South the imposition of the long armistice (the text of which was not published until much later) made of the Italians truly a conquered nation without a vestige of national sovereignty and without any rights whatsoever. But in spite of this situation Badoglio chose this moment (October 11th) to send instructions to the Italian Ambassador in Madrid to inform his German colleagues that Italy would consider itself at war with the Reich as from October 13th. He then communicated this decision to General Eisenhower, where-upon the United States, Great Britain and Russia recognized Italy as a "co-belligerent."

This expression, in the situation of Italy at the time, meant exactly nothing at all, as Badoglio was not in a position to wage war, having no autonomy and no army with which to fight. His decision was made even more ridiculous, inasmuch as in the armistice of September 8th Badoglio had declared that Italy surrendered because it was unable to go on fighting. In any case, the Western governments declared that they had given no pledges to the King or to Badoglio, and that the political situation of the part of Italy occupied by their forces was un-changed. Thus the act of treachery of September 8th did not even receive a reward.[1]

In the meantime the occupiers proceeded to operate in every department of Italy's internal life. At the Moscow Conference (October 19-30) it was agreed: that all Fascist institutions must be destroyed (down to maternity and child-welfare institu-tions); that all Fascists or pro-Fascists should be expelled from all political and administrative offices and from the manage-ment of all public or private economic and industrial organiza-tions and firms; that scores, indeed hundreds, of thousands of them, should be arrested; and that only anti-Fascist political parties or associates, *i.e.,* those under the control of the Allies or of the Communist Party (which was, of course, sacrosanct) should be allowed to exist. Full freedom of speech and of the press was granted, provided that not a word was written or spoken that was not agreeable to the Allied Powers and their Italian supporters.

Badoglio's Italy was henceforth to be governed not by Badoglio but by an Allied Control Commission, composed of British, American, French, Russian, Greek and Yugoslav mem-bers. The American member represented the predominant partner, but he almost invariably allowed himself to be in-fluenced by his British colleague, whose only object was to vent the vindictive feelings of his government on the Italian nation, to treat its nominal rulers, from the King downward, with the utmost contempt and the people as *taillable et cor-*

véable. American observers frequently deplored the subservient attitude of their representatives in Italy to those of Great Britain. The Communist leaders who re-entered Italy in the wake of the Allied armies were left free to do their damnedest —which they did.

Mussolini set up his Government at Gargnano on Lake Garda, but many of the departments were scattered about elsewhere; some were at near-by Salò, others in Brescia, Verona, Milan, Padua, Venice, etc., and branches of many of the various ministries remained in Rome until the city was occupied by the Allies in June, 1944.[2]

Such of the Italian troops in the Balkans and the Venezia Giulia as had not been disbanded or deported to Germany were withdrawn from those areas, and their place was taken by German units. One of Mussolini's first causes of anxiety on resuming office was the penetration of German authorities, some of them civilian, into the frontier provinces. He hastened to send a letter brought by Marshal Graziani to Hitler (October 4th), protesting against the action of German *Gauleiter* (provincial high commissioners) in the Venezia Giulia and in the Alto Adige and against the impositions of some of the German military authorities in other parts of the country. Sometimes there were even conflicts of authority between the different German commands. We do not know what Hitler's reply was, but certain improvements were subsequently made. Throughout the whole life of the Italian Social Republic Mussolini and his ministers never ceased to protest against the actions of the German military or civil authorities when they behaved in a manner contrary to Italian sovereignty, and very often they did so with success. No action of the kind was ever attempted by the Italian Government in the South, under either Badoglio or Bonomi, who succeeded Badoglio June 8, 1944. Both these premiers and all their ministers and subordinates seemed to be inspired by a veritable lust for servility towards every officer, N.C.O. or civil servant of the Allied Powers.

The military situation in the territory of the Italian Social Republic was better consolidated by the setting up of a single German command under General Kesselring, one of the ablest of Hitler's officers. When the new Italian Government had

been recognized officially by that of Berlin, Rudolf Rahn
ceased to be the German plenipotentiary and became the regular Ambassador to Italy, invested with more authority, even
with regard to the German military commands. Being a level-
headed and intelligent man, he proved a useful element in the
situation, although at times even he had disputes with Mussolini.

On November 14, 1943, a congress was opened at Verona,
under the chairmanship of the Fascist Party Secretary, Pavolini.
Here a new program of social legislation was drafted. Many
of its provisions were of a semi-Socialist nature and somewhat
immature; but they were a mere outline that would have been
completed and improved had the Government survived.[3]

Several other reforms were introduced, and the general conditions of the country were rendered more regular and satisfactory. The mass of the people were undoubtedly far better
off under the Italian Social Republic, in spite of German requisitions and the actions of certain German police officials and
Fascist extremists, than the Italians in the South, where no
man's life or property and no woman's honor were safe from
the Allied soldiers (including Negroes) or from native criminals with whom the Allied authorities never interfered. In Sicily
the Mafia had been completely wiped out under Mussolini's
regime, and its leaders had been imprisoned or forced to go
abroad. When the Allies landed in the island, they brought a
number of escaped *Mafiosi* in their wake, posing as political
exiles, and they liberated those in the local prisons. The Mafia
at once proceeded to resume its old activities—and is still to
some extent continuing to do so.

Hardly had the new Government been set up when a series
of outrages against prominent officials and others were committed. These crimes in many cases were the result of instructions issued by the Allied commands in the South by
wireless to anti-Fascist groups or to their own paid agents. One
of the first victims was the Fascist leader in Ferrara, Igino
Ghisellini. Reprisals were committed, and several hostages
known to be anti-Fascists were executed without trial. These
actions were stopped by Mussolini's express orders. But other
actions of the kind were occasionally repeated, and they be-

came more numerous as soon as the partisan movement developed greater strength and received arms and money from the Western Allies. One of the worst outrages was the murder of the distinguished philosopher, Professor Giovanni Gentile, in Florence on April 15, 1944, committed by partisans, but acting under the direct suggestion of the British Eighth Army Command, transmitted by wireless a few days previously.

With regard to the Jews, the Fascist racial laws had been enforced only to a limited degree, but now under the German occupation many Jews were arrested and deported. The German Commissioner in Rome, General Stahel, was opposed to these measures, but the S.S. groups, not under his authority, insisted on their rigorous application. In December, 1943, the German authorities in Rome and some other places proceeded to rope in large numbers of persons—Jews and non-Jews—for work on the lines of communication or on defense projects, or to deport them to Germany. This policy had been organized by the *Gauleiter* Sauckel. Von Ribbentrop, himself, was opposed to it and appealed to the German Commander-in-Chief, Kesselring, who finally succeeded in terminating the deportations.[4]

An all-important question was the reconstitution of the armed forces. That there should be two Italian armies opposed to each other was a deplorable tragedy, and no one realized it more keenly than Mussolini himself. On both sides, there was a yearning to see Italy freed from all foreign armies, but while the Duce and his followers aimed at driving the Western Armies out of the country and hoped to contribute to this consummation, the Italians in the South wished to expel the Germans, but could do nothing about it.

On both sides it was hoped that liberation could be achieved without relying exclusively on foreign arms; and on both sides the advocates of a reconstituted Italian army found the foreign commanders skeptical and diffident. But there were differences between the two Italys. The followers of Badoglio and then of Bonomi were completely subordinated to the invading forces and were allowed to create only very small military units, to which for a long time only rearguard activities were permitted. The Western Governments tried to incite the Italians to take an active part in the war and demanded that a large Italian people's army be raised, but Marshal Alexander and Admiral Cunningham said that they preferred not to use Italian forces. General Eisenhower finally authorized the formation of one division (the *Legnano*), but it was not adequately equipped or utilized, and all proposals for the formation of other large units were rejected.

In the North, on the other hand, some large military units were gradually formed and proved good material. About the middle of November, 1943, the first Fascist unit—the "M" battalion—appeared on the British front near Mondragone, and it inflicted heavy losses on the assailants. The Western Powers now decided that Italian troops must appear on their side too, because for them an Italian civil war was most desirable. Accordingly, a motorized group was sent to the front. The soldiers themselves were not by any means very keen on fighting for their ex-enemies against their ex-allies, and still less against their own fellow-countrymen. Finally, however, 5,500 men were raised and attached to the 36th U.S. (Texas) division and sent forward to attack at Montelungo. They fought well and reached the position assigned to them as their objective. But finding their flanks unsupported by the American forces and having lost 40 per cent of their effectives, they were forced to fall back. Some days later, they were again sent forward, again they recaptured Montelungo, but they were repulsed by German counter-attacks. They were finally withdrawn, and many of the men deserted. Other attempts at creating a Badoglio army failed except for some very small groups; and fortunately they never came into conflict with the Italian forces from the North.

In the territory of the Italian Social Republic military organization encountered many difficulties, but of a different nature. There was far more willingness on the part of the people to join up than in the territory under Allied occupation; but the German authorities were not disposed to grant adequate equipment and armament. They had seized most of what had belonged to the old Italian army; and until the Italian industries began to produce a large output once more, it was very difficult to arm the new units. The skepticism of the Germans after what had happened on September 8th was not surprising, but in view of the willingness of the Italians to answer the call to the colors, it should have been overcome. What Mussolini wanted was a really autonomous Italian army, to be employed in Italy's interest and to represent "the truest and best expression of the Italian people, which refuses to accept the surrender and wishes to fight to the last man for independence."

Marshal Graziani as Minister of Defense now set to work to create this army; and though some of the Fascist leaders wanted a new Fascist militia, Graziani's plan was finally accepted. He proceeded to Germany in October and concluded an agreement with the German authorities for training five new Italian divisions there, whence when trained they would be sent to fight the invaders. Mussolini wished these divisions to be recruited from the Italian soldiers interned in Germany after September 8th, but Hitler refused to agree to this plan, for his generals did not trust the internees. In the end the great bulk of the recruits were sent from Italy to Germany as volunteers for the new units. The training imparted in Germany was of the highest quality, and the new divisions proved models of their kind.

On returning to Gargnano from Germany Graziani found that Mussolini had issued decrees (October 27th) calling to the colors all young men born in 1924 and 1925; and it was decided, in spite of the opposition of Pavolini and others, that the army should be strictly non-political. As a result of the insistence of Renato Ricci, Mussolini agreed to the formation of the *Guardia Nazionale Repubblicana,* composed of members of the former Fascist militia, the carabinieri and the police forces from Italian Africa, but with purely police duties.

The number of recruits answering the call varied from one area to another; but, on the whole, it proved unexpectedly large. In some districts only 40 per cent joined up, but in others, including Emilia, the percentage was as high as 98.[5] The number of volunteers for the units in Germany rose from 30,000 to 150,000.

Graziani's Chief of Staff was General Gastone Gambara, a fine soldier who had commanded the Italian legionaries in

Spain and had distinguished himself in the Balkan campaign. For the navy, Commander Ferruccio Ferrini was made Undersecretary, and Commander Valerio Borghese,[6] one of the most gallant and competent officers in the service, revived the *Decima Mas*, a naval unit which during the War had utilized the secret assault craft and weapons of the Italian Navy and had accomplished exploits of an almost legendary nature. It now became a large unit operating chiefly on land (the whole Italian navy having been shamefully handed over to the enemy), and it was divided into many small groups scattered all over the country. In these duties, too, it performed many admirable exploits. The courage and resourcefulness of its officers and men and, above all, of their commander, almost pass belief.

A small air force was created, but it was handicapped by lack of material, and Germany now had very little to give it.

Mussolini thus succeeded in creating a small but efficient fighting force, which distinguished itself in action, and it would have done better had it not been handicapped by the restraint of the German High Command, which was never wholly overcome.

---

[1] This declaration of war against Italy's ally, however futile from a practical point of view, was morally criminal. It induced many Italians, including the present writer, to give allegiance to Mussolini's new government.

[2] The Italian Social Republic was usually spoken of as the Salò Government from the name of the principal town in the district.

[3] See the texts in Tamaro, *op. cit.*, Vol. II, pp. 249-253; and in Francesco Galanti's *Socializzazione e sindacalismo nella R.S.I.*, Rome, 1949, *passim*.

[4] Mölhausen, *op. cit.*, pp. 146-148.

[5] Rodolfo Graziani, *Ho difeso l'Italia*, Milan, 1948, p. 439.

[6] His exploits at Alexandria and Gibraltar were quite astounding. After the war he was interned in a British concentration camp and treated with the utmost brutality.

His book on the exploits of his force, *La Decima Mas*, is an extraordinary record of patriotic daring. It was published also in English under the title, *Sea Devils*, and was favorably received and widely read in England and the United States.

CHAPTER THIRTY-ONE

The Foreign Relations of the Italian Social Republic: Germany and France

The foreign relations of Mussolini's new Government were of a somewhat peculiar nature, very different from those of any state under normal conditions, and were closely associated with many problems of a primarily domestic character.

The first problem for Count Mazzolini was to create a Ministry of Foreign Affairs—surely no easy task. A certain number of members of the Italian diplomatic and consular service then in Rome agreed to remove to Lake Garda, where the new headquarters were established, and a few were left in Rome at the Palazzo Chigi. Some officials refused to join the new Government, because they still considered themselves morally bound by their oath to the King, and because they disapproved of Mussolini's policy and the German alliance, while others did not wish to be inconvenienced by moving from their comfortable quarters in the capital and running unpleasant risks and discomforts in the North. Several of those who were really governed by this consideration professed to be acting for moral reasons in refusing to go to Lake Garda. It is not too much to say that, with very few exceptions, those who did give allegiance to the new Government were the best men in the service, and those who had received no special favors from the old Fascist Government. Having served the regime in its palmy days, they felt morally obliged to support it in times of storm and stress. This was also the case with officials of most other government departments.[1]

It was thus possible to set up a Ministry of Foreign Affairs with all the indispensable departments but with reduced staffs. Of course, in view of the peculiar situation, only a part of the diplomatic services could function normally. The Ministry was ready to take over Italian diplomats and consuls in the Axis countries and in those occupied or controlled by Germany in Europe and by Japan in Asia. Many of them accepted the situation, regardless of their political leanings, as they were not expected to take a new oath of allegiance or to join the new Fascist Party, and as they considered it their duty to continue to serve the country.

In addition to Germany, the governments of Japan, Manchukuo, Rumania, Hungary, Bulgaria and Denmark had official relations with the Italian Social Republic. The German Embassy was located at Fasano on Lake Garda, and the other embassies and legations were situated in Venice.

Relations with Germany were, of course, the most important, but they had undergone many changes since July, 1943. About the middle of that month the Italian Ambassador in Berlin, Dino Alfieri, had left the capital to attend the meeting of the Grand Council in Rome on the 24th, and he never returned. On August 3rd Count Delfino Rogeri di Villanova, minister plenipotentiary, reached Berlin as chargé d'affaires, to await the arrival of the new ambassador.

On the very eve of September 8th General Alberto Pariani, formerly Undersecretary for War and Chief of Staff and known to be a friend of Germany, had been appointed Ambassador. But before his departure the news of the armistice came, and he never went to Berlin.

As soon as the armistice was announced, the German Ambassador in Rome, Dr. Rahn, prepared to leave the capital with his whole staff, and he proposed an exchange between the German and Italian diplomatic and consular personnel.

It seemed necessary that Italian interests in Germany should
be entrusted to a neutral power, for although the two countries
were not actually at war, diplomatic relations between them
had practically ceased. In Germany there were some hundreds
of thousands of Italian workmen, whose situation would now
be very precarious, and their interests and safety would have to
be provided for in some way. Count Rogeri had conversations
with the Swiss Minister, who would probably have been entrusted with the task, if Switzerland had been chosen as the
Schutzmacht (protecting power). Several Italian diplomats and
consuls wished to leave the country at once, but Rogeri and
some others felt it their duty to remain at their posts until
protection of Italians in the country had been provided for.
Rogeri made arrangements for the departure of such of his
colleagues as wished to leave, and he ordered the Italian
workers' syndicate to remain, eventually to be under the protection of the neutral power, to be selected, in order to assist
their compatriots until they could be repatriated.

As the situation was extremely difficult and not without
danger, the diplomats and consuls showed uncommon courage
in remaining at their posts. The Embassy could no longer communicate with Italy, for the *Wehrmacht* had cut off all railway,
postal, telegraph and telephone connections for civilians with
that country.

But on September 11th it was learned that the exchange of
diplomats and consular officials would not take place, as it had
been decided that Italy was not at war with Germany. On the
same day the German press issued a premature communiqué
announcing the formation of a new Italian Fascist Government,
and the *Auswärtige Amt* (German Foreign Office) stated that
the protection of Italian interests would be entrusted to that
Government exclusively. But the Italian Embassy had not yet
heard of its existence; and the Italian diplomatic and consular
officials in Berlin were asked by the *Auswärtige Amt* to abstain
from all activities outside the embassy building. The Italian
representatives could get no news of any sort from the Royal
Government, and did not even know its whereabouts.

It was not until the 13th that news of Mussolini's liberation
reached Berlin, and Count Rogeri was informed officially by

the *Auswärtige Amt* that a new Government had been formed in Italy and would assume responsibility for the Italian diplomatic and consular staff in Germany. Rogeri replied that he would make no engagements with a foreign government, but must wait until he could communicate with an Italian Government, in view of his task of protecting Italian citizens and interests in Germany. The new Italian Government then being constituted seemed to offer the best protective agency for those interests, because only a regime under Mussolini, Hitler's personal friend, could hope to mitigate the severity of German control over Italy after the armistice. But until contacts were established with that Government, nothing could be definitely settled.

In view of the lack of any instructions from the Royal Government as to how Italian representatives were to face the conditions of the armistice, Rogeri and some other diplomatic and consular officials came to the conclusion that it was up to them to carry on their indispensable duties toward their fellow citizens in Germany. Otherwise, the latter would have been at the absolute mercy of the German authorities, inspired by bitter indignation against them on account of events of September 8th, or they would have been entrusted to irresponsible local Fascist groups, devoid of all legal or diplomatic status or experience. The other Italian officials, who felt no anxiety about the fate of their fellow countrymen, preferred to leave Germany; and Count Rogeri proceeded to make arrangements for their departure. A special train was provided in which they left for Italy. But they were held up by the German authorities and interned for some weeks at Garmisch-Partenkirchen until the Embassy at last succeeded in getting permission for them to proceed to Italy.

Filippo Anfuso, then Minister at Budapest, who had from the very first adhered to Mussolini's new Government, was now appointed Ambassador in Berlin, and he arrived there at the end of September. The Embassy and the consulates were now able to resume their normal activities for the protection of Italian citizens, although the German atmosphere was still cold toward them, if not openly hostile.

The problem of looking after the masses of Italian workers

who had emigrated to Germany during the war, attracted by the high wages offered, and who had been obliged to remain there after the armistice, whether they wished to or not and under conditions of practically forced labor, was a very grave one for the Italian diplomats and consuls, but they faced it with the most ceaseless and untiring efforts amid the appalling air bombings to which Berlin and other German cities were subjected.

The armistice created other and greater difficulties, owing to the rapid and chaotic influx of hundreds of thousands of Italian soldiers whom the German troops in Italy had disarmed, made prisoners and deported to Germany, along with a small number of civilians, Jews and non-Jews, who had been deported for political reasons. The soldiers, contemptuously dubbed *Badoglio-Truppen* by the Germans, were exposed to harsh treatment from the internment camp guards and other authorities and to the detestation of the local population. They were forced to work under the most difficult and dangerous conditions.

Anfuso and Rogeri were particularly suited to the task entrusted to them by their perfect knowledge of Germany and the German language and by their friendly relations with the leading personalities of the Reich.

The armistice had created a sort of *modus vivendi* between Italy and the Western Powers, but it had abrogated the treaty relations between Italy and Germany. It was a very complicated and delicate problem, and the German Labor Front authorities saw here the possibility of fully exploiting Italian workers without any of the impediments imposed by the various Italo-German syndical agreements. The *Auswärtige Amt* ultimately recognized the validity of these agreements, but it was far more difficult to make sure that they would be respected and applied by the local authorities. In October, 1943, when the Government of the Italian Social Republic was officially recognized by Germany, Italy itself became the *Schutzmacht* of her own citizens, internees and others, in Germany, and the Embassy was thus the only juridical authority on whom the three chief Italian activities in the country devolved—consular action in general, the protection of Italian civilian workers, now practically converted into forced laborers, and assistance for the military and civilian internees.

One of the many difficulties was that when any action concerning Italian citizens was taken by the *Gestapo*,[2] the other German authorities, to whom the Italian representatives were duly accredited, were themselves often impotent, especially with regard to persons interned in the *Konzentrationlager* (concentration camps). But little by little, by patience, pressure and diplomatic tact, improvements were slowly effected.

Other Italians, numbering scores of thousands, who had been deported from the various Balkan countries which the German forces were evacuating, now drifted into Germany. These, too, had to be provided for. Altogether there were about 600,000 military internees in the *Grossreich*, and another 100,000 or 120,000 in Croatia and the Balkans.

It was not until the Bellagio agreement was concluded in the autumn of 1944 that the Reich Government and the Labor Front undertook to abolish any further forced recruiting of Italian workers.

The most difficult problem was that of the military internees deported to Germany, where air-raids and other war conditions made proper provision for their reception impossible. But when the I.S.R. was recognized as the protecting power, Italian organizations were created to assist these men. After protracted negotiations, Mussolini at his meeting with Hitler on July 20, 1944 (the day of the attempt on the Führer's life) succeeded in obtaining the liberation of the internees. It began during the following August and was gradually completed. By January, 1945, there were only 13,000 of them left, mostly officers and men employed in German war industries.

Italian diplomacy had to deal with still other questions. One of them was the situation in the Venezia Giulia and in the Trentino-Alto Adige, which was a cause of particular concern for Mussolini. The Italian officials in those two areas were more or less subordinated to the German *Gauleiter;* and Mussolini was never free of the anxiety lest Germany should end by absorbing both into the Reich. It is a curious fact that the two *Gauleiter* and most of the other officials whom the German Government appointed in those districts were not German nationals, but natives of the Austrian provinces, who were much keener on getting control over the two districts than were the *Reichsdeutsche*. This was a cause of increased anxiety. Finally at the Salzburg meeting Hitler assured Mussolini that Germany had no intention of altering the national status of the provinces or the frontier line; and at the end of 1944 an official statement to that effect was issued. No attempt was ever made by the South Italian Government to prevent the filching of Italian territories by the Western governments. In fact, the Peace Treaty of 1947, imposed by the Allies and accepted without protest by the De Gasperi Government, deprived Italy not only of all her colonies, but also of important districts in her metropolitan territory (the Venezia Giulia to the East, Briga and Tende to the West).

Another question dealt with both by the Ministry of Foreign Affairs and by the Berlin Embassy was that of the German operations against the partisans in Italy and the reprisals against the civilian inhabitants who were (rightly or wrongly) accused of aiding and abetting the partisan bands.

The Allies had attempted to create a large partisan movement to coöperate with their armies against the Germans and the Italian Social Republic, a movement organized, armed and financed by them. These partisans were mostly Italian soldiers who had deserted after the armistice, men with criminal records, many Communists, and a small number of sincere anti-Fascists. The great majority of the last group, however, merely wished to remain in hiding and avoid fighting on either side, and the attempts by the Allies to organize them into units of military value generally proved fruitless. The partisans who did operate at all limited their activities to acts of sabotage on the lines of communication, and the murder of officials, of isolated soldiers, of persons designated to them by the Allied wireless as undesirable or, in many cases, of well-to-do persons of all political persuasions who could be profitably plundered. In all, there were never more than 50,000 partisans during the War, and most of them remained in hiding in the woods and mountains until all military operations had ceased.[3] In the Venezia Giulia some Italian partisans of Communist sympathies joined up with the Yugoslav bands, and under orders of Moscow (where Tito was still in the odor of sanctity) they tried to secure the annexation to Yugoslavia not only of the whole of the Venezia Giulia, but even of a large part of the Friuli as far as the Tagliamento or the Livenza.[4]

The Germans treated the partisans, whenever they caught them, as bandits, without recognizing their rights as belligerents, but this was in conformity with the Hague Convention, which accorded belligerent rights only to those who wore uniforms or bore some distinctive signs and were incorporated in regular units under recognized commanders. The partisans who qualified under these conditions were few in number; the rest were merely *franc-tireurs* and liable to be treated as such. The Germans were rarely lenient with regard to these partisan activities, and they imposed punitive measures often of a very extreme nature on the local inhabitants accused of supplying the partisans with food and shelter. In many cases where German soldiers were fired upon by partisans, the whole population of the nearest village would be executed by way of reprisal, or at least their dwellings blown up.

Mussolini and his officials had, of course, no sympathy for the partisans, but they were constantly trying to restrain the Germans from their ruthless reprisals and punitive measures, especially those against the civil population which merely served to make both the Germans and the Fascists unpopular. Through his Embassy in Berlin Mussolini did succeed in getting orders for greater moderation issued to the military commanders in Italy, but they were not always respected, as the *Gestapo*, the S.S., and the various other police organizations often acted independently of the military commanders.

Other troubles arose in connection with the interference of the Germans in the purely internal affairs of Italy. Hitler protested, for instance, at the absence of the word *Fascist* in the title of the Italian Social Republic, for he feared that it meant a gradual falling away from the Fascist character of the new regime, the chief guarantee of fidelity to the Axis. He was also annoyed by Mussolini's program of social legislation as set forth in the Verona decrees, which conferred on the

workers the right to share in both the profits and the manage-
ment of the industries. Hitler did not consider this to be in harmony with the *Führerprinzip*.

There began to be a good deal of opposition to some of
Mussolini's subordinate leaders, especially to the Undersecretary and virtual Minister of the Interior, Buffarini-Guidi. At
the end of February, 1944, the Duce dismissed him and appointed in his place Giorgio Pini, one of the most level-
headed, intelligent and moderate of the younger leaders of
the Fascist Party. The German Ambassador Rahn protested at
this change, for Buffarini-Guidi was regarded as a close friend
of Germany, and Rahn tried to prevent the Italian radio from
issuing the communiqué on the dismissal. This aroused Mussolini's anger, and he declared that he would make the announcement himself over the wireless. Owing to the German's
objection to Pini, Paolo Zerbino was appointed Minister of
the Interior. But the S.S. leaders, Generals Karl Wolff and
Herbert Kappler, by way of reprisal for the dismissal of Buffarini-Guidi, had Eugenio Appollonio, a member of the Duce's
secretariat, and the ex-Chief of Police, Tullio Tamburini,
arrested on apparently bogus charges of intriguing with the
enemy.

Mussolini at once sent Alberto Mellini, then acting for
Count Mazzolini, who was seriously ill,[5] to Rahn to protest
against these intolerable interferences in Italian domestic
affairs. Rahn replied that many of the men around Mussolini
were definitely anti-German, and that the Duce himself was very
suspicious of Rahn and of Wolff, who were doing their best
for Italian interests. The fact is that Mussolini found himself
ever oscillating between the necessity of leaning on Germany's
military support, in view of the insufficiency of the Italian
forces (chiefly due to the failure or inability of the Germans
to supply the necessary equipment), and the yearning to insure
the independence of his own Government and country. Rarely
has any statesman been in so tormenting and inextricable a
dilemma.

Rahn was sincere in his friendship for Mussolini and for
Italy, but he was handicapped by certain German interests and
tendencies and by those German officials who saw Italy merely

as an instrument of German policy. Hitler, himself, oscillated between his real personal friendship and admiration for Mussolini and the sinister memories of the September armistice, of which he was perpetually reminded by many of his ministers and generals.

On top of all this turmoil was the ever-increasing pressure of the enemy forces, American and British on one side, Russian on the other, plus the satellites of both, while Germany's only allies were Italy, divided by internal feuds, with her armed forces only beginning slowly and painfully to be reconstructed and reorganized, and Japan, now a mass of wreckage.

One of Mussolini's nightmares was the number of different police forces and organs cropping up in various parts of Italy, both Italian and German, under no known or responsible control. Some irregular groups committed illegal and brutal actions, although the reports about them were no doubt often exaggerated by popular rumor and hostile propaganda.

The Archbishop of Milan, Cardinal Ildefonso Schuster,[6] who was to play a prominent and none too creditable part in the last act of the Italian tragedy, communicated to Mussolini a memorandum on the activities of the Koch group (one of the irregular self-appointed police units), and he sent a copy of it to Switzerland for anti-Fascist and anti-Italian propaganda purposes; but he never said a word about the outrages committed by the partisans. The Cardinal further complained of the arrests and ill treatment of priests accused of connivance with the partisans, but he said not a word about the priests, arrested, tortured and put to death by partisans. Mussolini had the members of the Koch band apprehended, but they were set free by the German authorities. On the other hand, Mussolini liberated a number of men accused by the Germans or the Italian Fascists of subversive activities, including Ferruccio Parri, the future Premier.[7]

The Communists, independently of those who were taking part in partisan stunts, continued to conspire in the hope of promoting a general uprising, and they were encouraged in these attempts by the Allies, especially by the Russians. But they never attained any notable success, and their numbers were greatly exaggerated. We do not know exactly how many there were altogether in North Italy; but in Turin the clandestine Communist bulletins claimed that there were 5,502 in the city out of a total of some 200,000 industrial workers. In the city of Milan out of 5,935 tramwaymen only 104 were Communists; in the Milan province 6,000 out of many hundreds of thousands of industrial workers; in Biella 400 out of 40,000. According to that same Communist source, there were some 60,000 throughout the whole territory of the Italian Social Republic, or 0.33 of one per cent of the population. A prominent Communist in Milan stated openly that the workers were ready to act on economic questions but took no interest in purely political agitation.

In March, 1944, a general strike broke out in Milan and other industrial centers of North Italy, organized by the Communists and Russians. The Red leaders claimed that one million workers took part in it, but the figure is undoubtedly exaggerated, while that given out by the Government, 208,549, is probably an understatement. In any case, it was an economic movement even if it had a political background, and only a small percentage of the workers took part in it. It began in some cities on March 1st, and its last remnants came to an end on the 8th. Mussolini took no repressive measures, but let the strike peter out of itself.

In the meantime, attempts were being made within the territory of the Italian Social Republic, and with the approval of the Duce himself, to bring about an understanding between Fascists and anti-Fascists on a patriotic basis, among others by Professor Edmondo Cione, a Neapolitan scholar and author, who then professed himself an anti-Fascist but was attracted by the personality of Mussolini.

With regard to Italy's relations with countries other than Germany, those with France presented interesting features. After July 25, 1943 the German authorities in that country began to be suspicious of the attitude of the Italian officials in France. Shortly after that date Ambassador Buti was summoned to Rome by the Badoglio Government. Some time after the announcement of the armistice Mussolini's new Government entrusted the Embassy to a Chargé d'Affaires, the Consul-General at Bordeaux, Manfredo Chiostri.

After the armistice the Italian situation in France became somewhat critical because the majority of the diplomatic and consular officials preferred to quit their posts, and only five remained in the country. The German authorities at first did not interfere with the movements of those who refused to adhere to the new Italian regime. But later on they were interned in a large hotel at Vittel and subsequently at Salsomaggiore, where the Italian authorities, on the orders of Count Mazzolini himself, provided for their comfort and convenience, and eventually they were permitted to return to their homes. New consuls were appointed in some French cities.

Before September 8, 1943, although the German authorities had deported many Frenchmen to Germany to be employed as industrial workers, the very numerous Italians in France had been exempted from deportation. But after the fatal date this privilege ceased, and the French themselves were only too glad to get Italians sent to work in Germany instead of themselves. Many were thus deported, having been denounced by Frenchmen. The Italian representatives reacted energetically, and eventually they came to an understanding with the Germans whereby the great majority of the Italians were exempted from labor conscription in Germany, although some of them were recruited for work in industries in France operating on behalf of Germany or for coast defense work. The Embassy and the consulates did all they could, often successfully, to protect the Jews, both Italian and French.

When the Badoglio Government declared war on Germany, the hostility of the French towards the Italians, far from being lessened, expressed itself more openly than before, in the hope that the Germans would cease to protect their "faithless" allies. The French courts and police and the fiscal authorities did all in their power to make the lot of the Italians intolerable, although the Italian representatives did eventually succeed in getting some of the more oppressive measures withdrawn or modified through the effective intervention of the German authorities.

But the situation of the Italians in France continued to remain most unsatisfactory. With the landing and the advance in France of the Anglo-American invading forces the representatives of the Italian Social Republic were forced to repatriate.[8]

---

[1] Most of these men were arrested at the end of the war and dismissed from the office for having faithfully served their country. But after appealing to the Council of State, nearly all of them have been reinstated.

[2] *Geheime Staatspolizei* (Secret state police).

[3] After the war the number of partisans rose to 200,000 and later to 400,000, but most of them joined mainly to secure the practical advantages of that status when no personal danger was involved. A comparable situation developed in France. See Sisley Huddleston, *France: the Tragic Years*, Chaps. 18, 22, 23.

[4] These actions led to armed conflicts with the partisans serving the Yugoslav Communists, and to wholesale murders of Italian patriots and anti-Yugoslav partisans.

[5] He died soon afterwards, deeply mourned by all his associates.

[6] In the palmy days of the Fascist regime Schuster had expressed the greatest admiration for Mussolini and had shown almost servile deference to all Fascist authorities.

[7] As Prime Minister, Parri savagely persecuted the Fascists and pro-Fascists. After his resignation he was accused in the press of shady financial transactions. One of Mussolini's greatest mistakes was to regard Parri as an honest man.

[8] The story of the foreign relations of the Italian Social Republic is told in detail in my book, *Affari Esteri, 1943-1945*, Rome, 1948.

(*Milton Bracker, in The New York Times Magazine*

Walter Audisio, the Communist partisan who directed the
assassination of Mussolini at Dongo, on Lake Como, April
29, 1945. Mussolini was actually shot by another Communist
partisan, Michele Moretti. Audisio is now a Communist
member of the Italian Parliament.

MUSSOLINI IN GLORY, AND IN DEATH AND HUMILIATION

Mussolini and his bodyguard, daggers raised, review Italian troops and military police in Rome on June 5, 1939.

Bodies of Mussolini, his mistress and four aides, hung head downward from roof of gas station in Milan.

CHAPTER THIRTY-TWO

Relations with the Near and the Far East and with Neutrals

As we have seen, after the collapse of Yugoslavia at the hands of the Axis forces, the country had been partitioned between the Germans and the Italians. Germany annexed the greater part of Slovenia, and Italy a smaller part, including the city of Ljubljana (Laibach). Most of Dalmatia also was assigned to Italy and occupied by Italian civil and military authorities, and Croatia was erected into an independent state with an Italian prince as King,[1] but ruled by the Croat leader, Ante Pavelich. Serbia and Montenegro were occupied by Axis forces but not annexed, Serbia being ruled by a native government under General Nedich.

Immediately after July 15, 1943, Badoglio decided to withdraw all Italian forces from the Balkans and Croatia. On August 6th at the initiative of the Germans a meeting was held at Tarvisio (on the Italo-Austrian frontier), attended by the two Foreign Ministers, Guariglia and von Ribbentrop, and by Generals Ambrosio and Keitel. The Germans went there in order to ascertain the real Italian situation, and the Italians wished to secure permission to withdraw all Italian forces from beyond the frontiers. Although the Italians assured their German colleagues that Italy intended to continue in the war, even the far from brilliant von Ribbentrop got an inkling that the situation was not too favorable. Ambrosio asked the Germans to move their divisions further south and protested against the overbearing conduct of the German commands in Italy, saying that Italians were hardly masters in their own house. He and Keitel nearly came to a showdown, but Keitel finally asked Ambrosio to withdraw his forces from South Italy and concentrate them on a defensive line between Vasto and Minturno (in Central Italy).

Von Ribbentrop suddenly asked Guariglia if he would give him his word of honor that Italy was not negotiating for an armistice, and Guariglia gave it without hesitation. He afterwards explained this statement by saying that Italy was then not really negotiating for an armistice but only gathering information as to the possibility of doing so, and that in any case "there could be no talk of negotiations with an enemy who demanded unconditional surrender." [2]

After the Tarvisio meeting the evacuation of Italian forces from the Balkans began, at first in an orderly manner, but following the armistice it became chaotic.

After the armistice, Pavelich, by agreement with the German General Glaise-Horstenau, who was virtually the arbiter of the situation in Croatia, proclaimed the annexation to that country of the parts of Yugoslavia assigned to Italy. Mussolini's new Government protested against this decision and expressed the wish that an Italian Minister be appointed to Croatia and a Croatian Minister to Italy. Some time later, the Croatian chargé d'affaires in Berlin informed the Italian Embassy in that city that Italy must relinquish the territories named in favor of Croatia as a condition for the establishment of Italo-Croatian diplomatic relations. The Embassy replied that no such one-sided conditions could be accepted, and in any case this was not the moment for dealing with the matter. Finally, through the mediation of the German Ministry of Foreign Affairs, the Croatian Government accepted the Italian point of view; the territorial question was dropped, and a Croatian representative was appointed to Mussolini's Government.

After the collapse of German resistance, the Croatian Government also came to an end, and the whole country, including Dalmatia and part of the Venezia Giulia, was overrun by Tito's murderous gangs who committed the most grisly atrocities. In Ljubljana alone, out of a population of 50,000, all Slovenes, some 20,000 were massacred for alleged collaboration with the Italians; and in Istria large numbers of the Italian population were murdered, many of them being buried alive.

Slovakia had been an independent state since the establishment of the German protectorate over Bohemia and Moravia in 1939, and it had suffered little injury from the War. Indeed, it had prospered economically, there had been no deportations of workers, and even after the Italian armistice Monsignor Tiso's Government had taken no measures against the Italian diplomats who had adhered to the Badoglio Government, although he declared that Slovakia recognized as the only Italian Government that formed by Mussolini at Salò.

Italo-Slovak commercial relations became very active, but the German Government claimed that trade between the two countries should be conducted through Germany; and it was finally agreed that the Italo-Slovak clearing arrangement should be liquidated through the German-Slovak clearing system and thence passed on to the German-Italian account. The Slovak Government proved the most moderate of those created under German auspices.[3]

Italo-Hungarian relations had been traditionally friendly, whereas those between Hungary and Germany had been more in the nature of a *mariage de convenance,* largely maintained on account of the mutual fear of Russia. It was chiefly due to Italian influence that Hungary had secured by the first Belvedere arbitration[4] the part of Slovakia containing a large Magyar population, and by the second, a considerable portion of Transylvania, a part of that precious jewel of the Crown of St. Stephen.

As an ally of the Axis, Hungary had taken part in the Russian campaign, but, when the military situation became unfavorable to Germany, the Hungarian Government and people began to contemplate the possibility of uncoupling from the Reich.

After the conclusion of the Italian armistice, the Italian Minister in Budapest, Anfuso, realized that Italy's position in Hungary could be adequately safeguarded only by means of a close understanding with Germany. While he, himself, had openly adhered to Mussolini's new Government, he left such members of his staff as wished to quit the Legation free to do so. The Hungarian Government recognized the Italian Social Republic, but representatives of Badoglio's Government were allowed to remain in Budapest more or less clandestinely.

When Anfuso was transferred to Berlin, he was succeeded in the Hungarian capital by Raffaele Casertano, who found himself in a somewhat awkward situation. The Hungarian Premier de Kállay continued to keep some sort of contact with the pro-Badoglio diplomats and was therefore highly suspect in German eyes.

Early in 1944 the Regent, Admiral Horthy, unexpectedly issued a proclamation announcing Hungary's intention of concluding an armistice with the Western Powers, whereupon German forces immediately occupied the capital and other cities, and arrested various Hungarian politicians and officials and the members of the Badoglio Legation. Casertano did his best to prevent their deportation to Germany, but without success, except as regards their families and the subordinate personnel. He managed, however, to repatriate the disbanded remnants of the Italian forces in Hungary.

In the meantime, as the result of a *coup d'état,* a new pro-German Hungarian Government was set up under Szálássy, and certain Italian citizens, compromised with the Badoglio diplomats, were arrested, but subsequently set free, again through the intervention of the Italian Legation.

At the end of 1944, when the Soviet armies were approaching Budapest, the members of the Italian Legation removed with the Hungarian Government to Szombáthely, where they remained until March 1945, when they were able to repatriate, and all Hungary fell under the savage tyranny of Soviet Russia.

At the moment of the September 8, 1943, armistice, Rumania was in a state of complete exhaustion, owing to war losses, enemy bombings and the large amount of requisitions carried out by the Germans, and the moral spirit of the nation was utterly broken by the deep disappointment at losing a large part of Transylvania and the Dobrudja. The Head of the Government and *Conducator,* Marshal Ion Antonescu, who was still faithful to the Axis alliance, found himself isolated between the royal family, where the pro-British sentiments of Queen Marie prevailed over the German origins of the dynasty, and the Vice-Premier, Mihai Antonescu, who had now decided to detach the country from the alliance. Germany, after having forced Rumania to renounce Transylvania and the Dobrudja, was now not in a position even to guarantee Bessarabia, demanded by Russia.

On the conclusion of the Italian armistice the members of the legation proclaimed their allegiance to Badoglio. Owing to the presence of the Germans in the country they were no longer able to safeguard Italian interests.

Anfuso, who from Berlin was in a better position to size up the Rumanian situation than the Ministry of Foreign Affairs, still in formation at Salò, proposed the appointment of the Italian journalist, Franco Trandafilo, for many years resident in Rumania, as chargé d'affaires, until he was able to send Dr. Armando Odenigo, then Consul-General in Hamburg, to Bucharest as Minister. The Rumanian Government gave its approval to Odenigo but, on various pretexts, prevented him from presenting his credentials to the King, thus making it very difficult for the Italy of the Social Republic to secure wheat and gasoline from Rumania, while the Italy of Badoglio could, of course, get nothing at all.

Rumania, too, had a double set of diplomatic representatives in Italy. The Royal Legation, reflecting the anti-Axis sentiments of the Rumanian court and diplomatic circles, had not joined Mussolini's Government at Salò, but remained in Rome waiting for something to turn up. But in May, 1944, Mihai Antonescu sent a semi-official representative in the person of Dr. Alexandru Gregorian,[5] a man of letters and formerly cultural attaché to the Legation, with a message to Mussolini, to the effect that Rumania saw military disaster approaching, that there was no other solution than to enter into negotiations with Western Powers—these negotiations were already proceeding through Princess Marthe Bibescu at Constantinople and through Prince Stirbey in London—and that he hoped to pursue this course of action together with the Italian Social Republic, which, he imagined, was equally desirous of detaching itself from Germany.

Mussolini admitted the basis of Antonescu's argument but not his deductions, and rejected the possibility of following the suggested Rumanian solution. The Italian Social Republic, whose territory was now occupied by the Germans, would only be repeating Badoglio's criminal error, which had caused and was still causing such disastrous sufferings on the part of the Italian people.

On August 29, 1944, Rumania signed an armistice with the Allies and was then occupied by Russian forces. Both the Conducator and Mihai Antonescu and innumerable other eminent Rumanians were executed, scores of thousands of others were imprisoned or sent to slave labor camps. The country, where the Communists numbered only 300 in all, was placed under a Communist government composed of Moscow agents, and the population was reduced to an appalling state of misery and starvation, which grew worse for years.

The Italian Minister Odenigo, Trandafilo and other members of the diplomatic and consular staff were quite illegally arrested by the Russians and imprisoned in Moscow, where they were kept incommunicado until early in 1951, when they were at last liberated. Odenigo's wife, who had insisted on following her husband to Russia, was interned in a different prison, where she died a year later; her husband never heard of her death until he was liberated.[6]

The Italian Minister in Yugoslavia at the outbreak of the war was Mussolini's former Chef de Cabinet, Giorgio Mameli, but in June, 1943, he was transferred to Sofia, his place being taken by Emanuele Grazzi, formerly Minister in Greece.[7] After September 8th he and his staff and the teachers at the Italian Cultural Institute were interned in the Legation by the German authorities. On the 16th Grazzi addressed a note to the German Chargé d'Affaires, asking him to inform the Italian Government—he did not say which one—that his most ardent wish was again to serve his country in this most critical moment of its history. This somewhat peculiar communication could not be regarded as an effective declaration of allegiance to Mussolini's new Government, and the internment of the Italians in the Legation continued.

Grazzi himself was now offered the post of Minister in Budapest on behalf of the Italian Social Republic, an appointment which he accepted. He departed for that city in October, leaving his First Secretary, Giorgio Spalazzi, as chargé d'affaires at Belgrade. Subsequently, Spalazzi was summoned to Salò by Count Mazzolini, and the Marquis Giorgio Gozzi took his place in the Serbian capital. Grazzi, after definitely accepting a post under the Italian Social Republic at Budapest, withdrew his allegiance and went to Venice where he remained until the end of the war.

Gozzi had to face an appalling task at Belgrade, looking after the thousands of Italian soldiers who had disbanded after the armistice, as well as the innumerable civilians, either residents in Serbia or persons coming there from other parts of the Balkans, half starved, wholly without resources, despised by the Germans and hated by the native population. Gozzi, with his reduced staff and very limited funds at his disposal, provided food, clothing, lodging and assistance of all kinds. In the end he succeeded in repatriating all those who had survived starvation and hardships.

General Mihailovich, fighting for the exiled King—the ally of the Western powers—continued to hold out against Tito and his Communist supporters; but he was let down by those same Allies at the behest of Russia, was captured by Tito and was executed as a traitor. This was the climax of the tragic civil war in Yugoslavia, where after Tito's triumph a million persons were massacred, a holocaust which was falsely attributed by the Allied Powers to the German and Italian occupying forces, and for which these Allied Powers themselves were largely, if indirectly, responsible.

Montenegro had been occupied by Italian forces in the spring of 1941 and was promised independence. An anti-Italian revolt broke out but was temporarily overcome, until, with the defeat of the Axis Powers and the withdrawal of the Italian forces, the country fell once more under Yugoslavia's yoke as represented by Tito.

Bulgaria never actually intervened in the war but was allied to the Axis, whose policy it followed closely, although it continued with Germany's permission to maintain diplomatic relations with the USSR even after June, 1941. This peculiar position enabled certain Bulgarian statesmen and officials to cultivate a policy friendly to the Allies, but relations with Italy always remained cordial.

On the announcement of the Italian armistice, the Bulgarian press inveighed against Italy, the King and Badoglio; and the Italian residents were regarded as accomplices of treason. But on September 27th the Cabinet Council under German pressure decided to recognize the Italian Social Republic; on the 28th the Sobranje (Bulgarian parliament) ratified this decision. Relations with the Badoglio Government were broken off, and the Minister Mameli, who had adhered to it, was invited to leave the Legation, which was handed over to the representatives of Mussolini's Government. Mameli and part of his staff were interned in Bulgaria, two other secretaries resigned but without giving allegiance to the I.S.R., and six consular officials and the press attaché remained at their posts and served the I.S.R. in the interests of the local Italian community. The Legation, now in charge of men faithful to Mussolini's Government, succeeded in preventing measures of persecution from being taken against the few Italian residents politically compromised as hostile to the Germans, and it was able to provide for the disbanded soldiers interned by the Germans.

At the end of the war the members of the Legation staff repatriated, with the exception of a naval officer who was arrested and interned by the Russians, together with the Italian diplomats and consuls in Rumania.

Greece was occupied by Italian forces, and later an Italian department for civilian affairs was set up. A pro-Axis Greek Government was formed, and it had friendly relations with the Italian authorities, while commercial intercourse between the two countries was very active.

After September 8th the Italian soldiers in Greece were nearly all deported to Germany. The exceptions were some detachments of Blackshirts who took service under the German command, a few men who joined the anti-German partisan bands and some others, who remained concealed in the houses of Greek friends. Italian civilian residents were subjected to petty persecutions or placed under house arrest, and Italian economic interests suffered severe handicaps.

After the institution of the I.S.R., an Italian engineer, Vittorio Sandicchi, was appointed head of the civilian services in Greece and was able to create a sort of diplomatic and consular representation that operated satisfactorily until the end of the War, when Sandicchi succeeded in repatriating such Italians as were politically compromised.

Italian relations with the Far East underwent many vicissitudes. For geographical reasons communications between Italy and the Far East were practically impossible during the war, and the various Italian representatives had to act on their own initiative.

On the news of the armistice, Italian ships in the Pacific were sunk by their own crews, and the Japanese authorities acted with considerable severity against the Italian communities and interests until the recognition of Mussolini's new Government led to some mitigation of these measures. The Italian Ambassador in Tokyo refused to serve under the I.S.R. and was interned with a part of his staff. But by the summer of 1944 a temporary Embassy and several consulates, entrusted to career officials adhering to the I.S.R., were able to function. A part of the Italian properties in Japan and in the Tientsin concession were restored to the Italian authorities, and negotiations were set on foot to secure the liberation of the Italian internees. But the end of the war in Europe deprived the Italian representatives of all authority.

Siam had somewhat unwillingly contracted an alliance with Japan, and as soon as the news of the Italian armistice reached Bangkok, the Italian Legation was occupied by the Siamese police, and its members were placed under house arrest. The Italian Minister, Guido Crolla, remained at his post and tried to get into touch with the Badoglio Government through the

Swiss Consulate in Bangkok; but, having received no instructions whatever, he ended by adhering to the I.S.R. in order to safeguard Italian interests. In Siam there was a curious rivalry between the Germans and the Japanese, as both tried to gain possession of Italian properties. Crolla, with great ability and tact, succeeded in saving the situation by collaborating with the Siamese Government.

The neutral countries recognized no official Italian representatives except those of the Royal Government already on the spot.

In Madrid the Italian Ambassador, Marquis Paolucci de' Calboli, who had been appointed to that position by Mussolini, with whose policy he had been intimately associated ever since October, 1922,[8] refused allegiance to the Salò Government and remained at his post as Ambassador of Badoglio's Government. The Italian Consul at Malaga, Morreale, took over the duties as semi-official representative of the I.S.R.; and in Portugal a similar position was held by the former military attaché, General Terragni.

In Switzerland the majority of the population was anti-German and consequently anti-Italian. After the armistice the small band of friends of Italy was still further reduced. The Federal Government did not wish to appear openly hostile to the Germans, by whom the country was then wholly surrounded, and it was anxious to safeguard some very important Swiss interests in Northern Italy. But it did not wish to compromise itself by appearing too friendly to the enemies of the Western Powers, especially when the latter seemed likely to win the war. It never recognized the I.S.R., but it kept open and active its consulates in I.S.R. territory and appointed a Commercial Delegation in Milan to maintain relations with Mussolini's Government. It also consented to the setting up of a similar Italian Commercial Delegation in Zurich.

A group of Italian anti-Fascists tried to browbeat the Italian official and semi-official representatives in Switzerland and to gain control of the many flourishing Italian economic, welfare and cultural organizations. Another group of Italian residents gave open allegiance to the I.S.R., while the great mass of the Italian citizens in Switzerland admitted the advantages secured under the new political incarnation but kept itself detached from either group.

The Commercial Delegation succeeded in enabling the Italians who were natives of the territories controlled by the I.S.R. to keep in touch with their relatives in Italy and to secure such official documents, legal papers, affidavits, etc., as were necessary for relations with the Swiss authorities. As soon as the war in Italy came to an end, the officials of the Commercial Delegation and of the consulates closed their offices and handed over all the records, money, valuables and other property to the consuls of the Royal Government.

---

[1] The Duke of Spoleto never actually ascended the throne.

[2] Tamaro, *op. cit.*, Vol. I, pp. 229-231.

[3] Nevertheless, after the end of the war, Monsignor Tiso and his chief supporters were hanged by the re-instated Czechoslovak authorities.

[4] So called because it was concluded at the Belvedere Palace in Vienna in 1940.

[5] Now living in exile abroad.

[6] Diplomats of enemy states, always exempt from arrest according to international law, were frequently seized, imprisoned or interned after the second World War in violation of all the accepted rules of international law. The Russians were by no means the sole offenders in this matter.

[7] Previously he had been Consul-General in New York City.

[8] He had been the Duce's Chef de Cabinet for five years (1922-1927).

CHAPTER THIRTY-THREE

Verona and Rome

The trial of the members of the Fascist Grand Council who on July 25, 1943, had voted for the Grandi resolution, which was the immediate cause of the fall of the Fascist regime and of the appalling disasters which followed, was held in Verona in January 1944. Most of the members who voted against Mussolini had escaped abroad, including Grandi himself, or had remained in concealment in Italy. But Ciano, Marshal De Bono, the ex-Ministers, Luciano Gottardi and Carlo Pareschi, the ex-Under Secretary, Tullio Cianetti, and the Administrative Secretary of the Party, Giovanni Marinelli, were under arrest.

The extreme Fascists and the Germans demanded that they be prosecuted. Mussolini had at one time declared the trial necessary, but he had many hesitations, not only because Ciano was his daughter's husband but also on account of moral scruples. In October, 1943, he said to the Prefect Dolfin, Director of General affairs at the Foreign Ministry: "I do not believe, as you know, I never have believed that the condemnation of these men will be of advantage for our country and for the restoration of internal order." [1] But there is no doubt that the German authorities were determined to have them tried and executed, and both the Undersecretary for the Interior, Buffarini-Guidi, and the Party Secretary, Alessandro Pavolini, were of the same opinion.

From a strictly legal point of view, the guilt of the accused men is doubtful, considering the limited powers of the Grand Council in which a majority or even a unanimous vote need not have been followed. But its decision had wrought such disastrous consequences to the country that the punishment of those responsible for it, if not the imposition of the extreme penalty on them, appeared justifiable on moral grounds. That Ciano in his unlimited ambition aspired to succeed Mussolini is unquestioned, and this was known to many of the people with whom he associated—indeed he made no secret of it. His attitude toward his father-in-law, to whom he owed his own astonishing career, varied like so many other aspects of his conduct and was always openly expressed, whether favorable or not.

Mussolini, himself, realized his son-in-law's defects but was restrained from expressing his opinions, possibly out of love for his daughter, Edda.

One of Ciano's outbursts, reported by Guido Leto, then the Chief of the Political Police, is truly amazing. The Chief of Police, Arturo Bocchini, was in the habit of reporting to Ciano every week on the general situation of the country and on the state of public opinion. One day, on returning to his office after one of these meetings, he told Leto and a few other intimates that Ciano, in a fit of rage, had asked Bocchini to procure for him a poison of undoubted potency which left no trace, as he was determined to liberate Italy from "the tyrant." He had further suggested that Bocchini should ask Himmler for such a poison. Bocchini replied evasively, not having the courage flatly to refuse although, of course, he had not the slightest intention of doing anything of the kind. In reporting the request to his friends, he spoke with shocked indignation against Ciano. The latter repeated the request some months later; and again Bocchini reported it to Leto and others, adding that this time he had answered in no measured terms, flatly refusing to have anything to do with the matter.

Leto himself says that he cannot make up his mind whether

Ciano's outburst implied a definite intention to eliminate the Duce or was merely one of his frequent expressions of violent temper.[2]

Ciano had certainly made himself unpopular in many quarters, owing to the high position he had achieved through his marriage with Mussolini's daughter rather than by exceptional personal merits, and on account of his excessive love for outward display and extravagance and his weakness for fashionable and snobbish society. He was far from unintelligent or uncultivated, and the charges of financial corruption leveled against him, which even Sumner Welles, who had otherwise been favorably impressed by him, repeats in his preface to the Ciano *Diaries,* proved devoid of foundation. He no doubt enjoyed large emoluments and may have obtained useful Stock Exchange tips from insiders; but he spent freely and generously, and the amount of property he left at his death proved to be very small. Nor is there the slightest evidence that he was responsible for the murders of several enemies of the regime; Welles suggests this, while admitting that he had no conclusive knowledge of the facts.[3]

What does seem evident is that Ciano was a sort of Dr. Jekyll and Mr. Hyde—on the one hand, a capable, intelligent and brilliant diplomat who rendered valuable services to his country, and on the other, a man of such inordinate ambition and vanity that these defects were to lead him into courses disastrous to Italy from every point of view.

Grandi was far more culpable because, while he was more level-headed and acute in his perceptions than Ciano, he was inspired chiefly by personal ambition. But he, too, cannot be rightfully accused of having availed himself of his position to secure illicit gains; and the same may be said of most of the defendants at the Verona trial. These charges, leveled against many other prominent Fascist leaders, although of a purely domestic nature, had international reactions, inasmuch as the colossal fortunes which they were accused of having accumulated constituted one of the main criticisms expressed against the regime in the foreign press. Against many of the statesmen of the countries opposed to Italy in the late War, these charges might well be directed with far greater reason; and perhaps the same may be said of some of the members of the various post-Fascist governments of Italy.

Of the defendants at the Verona trial, Marinelli was the most open to criticism. Marshal De Bono, Gottardi and Pareschi seem to have had no full understanding of the real meaning of the Grandi resolution when they voted for it.

The trial was held in the Castel Vecchio at Verona before a special tribunal of nine judges presided over by the jurist Vecchini; five out of nine demanded a capital sentence for all except Cianetti, who had withdrawn his vote after July 25th and who was therefore let off with 30 years imprisonment. The others were condemned to death by a majority of the judges. The other four judges were in favor of more lenient sentences. Capital sentences were pronounced against the absent members of the Council who had voted for the resolution.

The question of an appeal for pardon then arose. The condemned men all applied for it. But after protracted discussion over which authority was competent to present the plea to the Duce, it was never allowed to reach him at Gargnano; and the sentence was carried out on the morning of January 11, 1944. All the condemned fell honorably and bravely, except Marinelli, who gave way to despair and terror.

There is no doubt that the German authorities did bring pressure to bear on the court, but the text of the sentence, as Attilio Tamaro writes, shows that "they [the men executed] had been scapegoats or propitiatory victims, sacrificed, as it were, in a fatal decision to placate the furies of a blood-stained tempest which tormented everyone." [4]

Rome, although part of the I.S.R., was leading a life of its own at this time, virtually cut off from the rest of the country, for railway communications with the North had been completely suspended, and roads, telegraphs and telephone lines were constantly interrupted by enemy bombings. Food supplies were intermittent and always insufficient, and the population was suffering, if not from hunger at least from a very acute scarcity. The Germans were fighting desperately on the Cassino front. Although they were far less numerous that the variegated armies of the Allies, they held them up for many long months, inflicting terrible losses on them.

The *Wehrmacht* [5] needed labor for defense works and for repairing the roads, and its patrols frequently raided cinemas, theatres and other public places, seized the sturdiest youths, apparently idling away their time, and carried them off to work. The population was in a general state of apathy and despair, its chief anxiety being how to get the next meal through the black market, but no one was eager to work on the roads or defenses.

Rome had been unofficially recognized as an open city by the Allies through an agreement with the Vatican, and the Germans had withdrawn their forces from it, leaving only police units so as to spare it from air raids; but nevertheless air attacks occasionally took place in spite of the Pope's protests. [6]

While the seat of government of the I.S.R. was in the North, there were still, as we have seen, sections of the various ministries in Rome. The diplomatic representatives of the Axis or pro-Axis Powers were also in the North, and only those of the neutrals and those accredited to the Vatican remained in the capital.

Frequent curfew orders were issued by the German authorities, and many restrictions were imposed on the daily life of the people, often because of the bombings which damaged the aqueducts and the electricity supply, while gas and coal for heating were almost unobtainable, but also because of the occasional murder of German soldiers by persons unknown.

In the meantime the anti-Fascists and other opponents of the I.S.R. and of the German alliance, more or less grouped under the so-called National Liberation Committees (*C.L.N.*), were constantly plotting to overthrow the regime. But their chief activities consisted of conferences in secret or semi-secret hiding places in Rome and elsewhere, and of constant bitter wranglings and exchanges of invectives between the various factions over political and personal ambitions. They never succeeded in inflicting any serious harm on the Government or on the German authorities.

One episode occurred which deserves mention on account of its sensational nature and its bearings on the general situation. The Rome Fascists intended to hold a public demonstration to celebrate the 25th anniversary of the Fascist movement on

March 23, 1944, but the German authorities very wisely forbade it. The anti-Fascists then decided to commemorate the date in a very different way.

A truck filled mainly with soldiers unfit for front-line services, nearly all of them natives of the Alto Adige, but serving under a German command and employed on police duties, passed every day through the Via Rasella (near Via del Tritone), conveying the men to their various duties. The so-called military giunta of the C.L.N., of which the ex-deputy, Lussu, Pertini, and Bauer, were members, decided upon a sensational outrage in the vain hope of terrifying the Germans into behaving like lambs. The order was issued by Giorgio Amendalo to the Partisan Action Group, and Carlo Salinari organized the deed. The actual executors of the violence were to be Bentivegna, Calamandrei and Marchini, and the object was to hurl a bomb at this truck. Explosives were concealed in a garbage cart and when the truck entered Via Rasella, Bentivegna gave the orders and then fled to a safe place, while others threw the bomb. The result was that 32 soldiers and several civilian passersby, including a child, were killed and many others wounded. The plotters all went into hiding.

The German authorities were violently incensed at this wholesale slaughter, as well they might have been, and as usual they did not know how to restrain their indignation or moderate their reaction. So they committed acts of reprisal that reacted against themselves. At first they intended to blow up every house in Via Rasella,[7] but this they did not do. An order came from Hitler to have ten Italian hostages shot for every soldier killed. Reprisals were, no doubt, legitimate in the circumstances, even under the provisions of the Hague agreements.[7] Indeed, the British and Americans in Italy shot a great many Italians for real or alleged infractions of military regulations.

Kappler, the S.S. Commander, demanded of the warden of the Regina Coeli prison 350 prisoners under death sentences or charged with offences punishable with death (the number demanded actually exceeded by 5 that of 10 to 1). As this number was not available, others charged with less serious offences and a few Jews were added to make up the total. On March 24th they were conveyed to the Fosse Ardeatine near

Rome and executed. Among them were Colonel Cordero di Montezemolo, a gallant officer who had been in communication with the invading forces and was, therefore, liable to the death penalty under the laws of any country in wartime; the diplomat, de Grenet, who was much less guilty; and others, none of whom was in any way responsible for the Via Rasella outrage. The actual authors of the deed had taken good care to save their own skins. They re-appeared only after the arrival of the invaders in Rome.

The Ministry of Foreign Affairs at Salò, as soon as it heard of the decision to carry out reprisals, did all it could to save de Grenet, but even Rahn's intervention came too late. Mussolini, himself, was deeply incensed at the whole affair, as he was, for political as well as for moral reasons, at all the acts of violent reprisals committed by the Germans.

The victims of the Fosse Ardeatine were afterwards commemorated as martyrs, and tablets were placed on their dwellings, but the provocation which had brought about the deed was forgotten, and its real authors, the murderers of the C.L.N., were awarded medals for military valor and patriotic merit for their outrage.[8]

The Germans, after a protracted and heroic resistance on the Cassino front and at Anzio, where the Anglo-Americans had landed a force some time previously, gradually fell back, while continuing to inflict heavy losses on the enemy. Finally on June 4, 1944, they evacuated Rome, which was at once occupied by the invaders. At first, the Anglo-Americans were received as liberators, but the population very soon found that they were nothing of the kind. Innumerable arrests were made of Italians suspected not only of being friendly to the Germans or of giving them information, but also of merely being supporters of the Fascist regime. Scores of thousands were apprehended and interned in the Rome prisons or in the internment camps at Padula (province of Salerno) and elsewhere, on any pretext or no pretext, without any definite charges against them. They were detained for long months or years without trial, in violation of every accepted principle of international law or ordinary justice. To quote but one instance, Professor Giulio Quirino Giglioli, one of the most eminent archeologists in Italy with a world-wide reputation, was imprisoned for many months at Padula for having written some articles on Malta in which he dwelt on the Italian character of the island's civilization.

Nothing was done to improve the food situation of the city or its water, electricity and gas supply, and the issue of an unlimited amount of worthless paper currency produced inflation to a degree never known before in Italy.

The British appointed a mayor of their own choice for Rome, naming Prince Filippo Doria, a worthy gentleman and one of the richest landowners in Europe, but wholly lacking in the most elementary knowledge of administrative affairs. He was selected for this position because he was known to be pro-British and to have said that no Italian was to be trusted. Rome took years to recover from the chaos he made of the city's administration in the short period of his mayoralty.

After the occupation of Rome, Badoglio resigned the premiership and was succeeded by a former Prime Minister, Ivanoe Bonomi.

[1] Giovanni Dolfin, *Con Mussolini nella tragedia*, Milan, 1948, p. 139.

[2] Leto, *op. cit.*, pp. 188-189.

[3] Actually, the only political enemies killed during the Fascist regime were Matteotti, Amendola and the Rosselli brothers, and for these killings neither Ciano nor any other member of the Government was responsible. Medical evidence actually proved that the deaths of Matteotti and Amendola were not due to murder.

The total of political enemies slain during the Fascist period was not greater than those murdered in the average democratic country from 1922 to 1943, and a mere drop in the bucket compared to the wholesale murder of the enemies of the Nazis from 1933 to 1945, or even from 1933 to 1939, or to the purging of tens of thousands by Stalin following 1936.

[4] Tamaro, *op. cit.*, Vol. II, p. 457.

[5] The Axis troops in Central Italy were mainly Germans, the Italian units being nearly all in the North.

[6] Among the buildings partially destroyed was the famous basilica of San Lorenzo (now repaired). A few bombs were even dropped on the Vatican City.

[7] An American prisoner of war in Rome at that time stated that, in comparable circumstances, his own countrymen would have carried out more severe reprisals.

[8] Not all Italians, however, regarded them as heroes, despite the medals conferred on them, and most honest and patriotic citizens shunned them after the award.

CHAPTER THIRTY-FOUR

The End of the Italian Social Republic and the Assassination of Mussolini

We do not know very definitely how Mussolini really sized up the situation during the last months of the War. At times he seemed full of hope and believed that the new arms which Hitler often mentioned would produce a miracle. Here again he saw too far ahead; the arms did exist, but time for their production on a large scale was lacking. At other times he felt that the end—defeat—was approaching. At others again he hoped for a compromise solution. Often he seemed to be thinking not of the fate of the Axis or of Italy alone, but of the new world which was to emerge from the War, however it might end, and he seems to have risen far above mere personal and political considerations.

His health, which had been very bad for a long time, had greatly improved after he had settled at Gargnano, under the treatment and regimen applied to him by his doctors, especially by Dr. Georg Zachariae, a celebrated German physician sent to him expressly by Hitler. Afterward the doctor published a very valuable account of the Duce's last months as seen by a medical man. With Zachariae Mussolini was very outspoken.[1]

While he believed in the possibilities of new and more lethal weapons, he shrank from the effects of their indiscriminate use, and he wrote two letters to Hitler imploring him not to resort to means of which the appalling consequences could not be calculated.[2]

Above all, he felt that he must go on with his task to the bitter end as best he might, and not leave Italy wholly in the hands of the Germans. They regarded Italy merely as a field of battle and would spare the country and the people no suffering or destruction if it was necessary for military purposes; but for Mussolini Italy was his country and the Italians his people.

Anfuso continued to report from Berlin on the grave difficulties facing the Germans in spite of assurances from official circles about the new weapons shortly to come into action. In one report he said that there was hope that through the use of these weapons better peace terms could be secured from the Western Powers, and that the divergences between the latter and Russia would prove favorable to the Axis. This report irritated Mussolini against von Ribbentrop, of whose intelligence he had the lowest opinion. These divergences did undoubtedly exist, but like the new weapons, they came too late to be of any decisive advantage to the Axis. All the favorable elements in the situation were foreseen by Mussolini, but they failed to mature in time.

The various C.L.N.'s, known in North Italy as the C.L.N.A.I. (*Comitati di Liberazione Nazionale Alta Italia*), were busily plotting, but thinking chiefly of the vengeance which they hoped to wreak on their opponents as soon as they could safely do so when the invading armies occupied all Italy and the Fascist regime was definitely overthrown. The Communists, openly supported by Russia and to a large extent by the Western Allies as well, looked forward to dominating Italy and carrying out a wholesale slaughter of all their opponents.

The partisan organizations ended by accepting as their commander General Raffaele Cadorna, unworthy son of an eminent father, but not too willingly, for the Communist elements were always predominant in their ranks and showed greater allegiance to the Communist leader, Luigi Longo. The latter and Ferruccio Parri, representing the almost non-existent Party of Action,[3] were second in command. But the only military operation of any importance they achieved was the occupation of Domodossola near the Swiss frontier, which they held for a few weeks until they were dispersed and put to flight by an Italo-German force.

There was much talk of the menace to Italian industries, which the Germans wished to destroy as they fell back before the enemy advance, and the partisans afterwards claimed that the salvation of the plants was due to their activities. But as a matter of fact it was the ceaseless efforts of the technical Ministers of the I.S.R., especially Angelo Tarchi and Domenico Pellegrini-Giampietro, aided by Count Cantonimarca of the Economic Section of the Ministry of Foreign Affairs, that finally induced the Germans to abstain from wholesale destruction and to cease transferring to Germany the machinery of the various industries, as they had begun to do. That is why after the war nearly all the Italian factories were found to be almost intact, the aerial bombings having hardly ever touched them.

The situation was now further complicated by a plot for concluding an agreement between the Anglo-Americans, the Germans, the Committees of National Liberation, the partisans and certain Swiss personages. The moving spirit in this was the Archbishop of Milan, Cardinal Schuster, acting quite independently of the Vatican, while Mussolini was kept absolutely in the dark about it. The first move was made by the Cardinal, the second by certain individual Germans supported by some of the German authorities in Italy but not by the Reich Government.[4]

Schuster's initiative was carried on with the German Ambassador Rahn, that of the Italians and the Swiss with the S.S. Commander in Italy, General Karl Wolff. The loyal Germans were chiefly eager to protect the retreat of their army, while Wolff, knowing that he was on the list of "war criminals," hoped to save himself by rendering services to the Western Powers. Rahn seems to have been sincerely eager to save Italy from further disasters and bloodshed.

A new figure now appeared on the scene, the somewhat mysterious Luigi Parrilli. Parrilli's record was not too good. He had been in the Italian Political Police, the British Intelligence Service and the German Secret Service at different times, or at the same time, and had been involved in some rather curious financial transactions. He knew the S.S. leaders, Dollmann and Kappler, personally, a German officer named Zimmer, head of a counterespionage organization, and some Swiss citizens.

According to his story at the time, Parrilli hoped to bring the Germans and the Allies into contact in order to save Italy from further devastation. He explained his project to one Husmann, a Swiss of Russian-Jewish extraction living in Zurich, who put him in touch with Major Waibel, a collaborator of Colonel Mason, head of the information section of the Swiss General Staff. Waibel undertook to talk to Allen W. Dulles, Roosevelt's confidential agent in Switzerland. Parrilli suggested a meeting between Dulles, Zimmer and Dollmann; and Dollmann was authorized by Wolff to go to Switzerland for this purpose, both being convinced that the United States wanted an agreement with Germany against Russia.

Rahn had given Mellini, then acting as Mussolini's Chef de Cabinet for the Ministry of Foreign Affairs, a hint that he and Wolff were contemplating a policy in Italy independent of that of Berlin, but he said nothing of the negotiations with the Western Allies.

When Dollmann went to Switzerland and was told by Husmann that the end of the war must be hastened by the surrender of the German army in Italy, he pretended to protest; but talking to Dulles's representative, one Blum, he ended by agreeing to everything. As evidence of his good intentions, Blum asked Dollmann to get Wolff to liberate Parri and Usmiani who were in prison. Dollmann then appealed to Wolff who agreed at once, but it was Mussolini who had Parri liberated, although he knew nothing of the negotiations.[5]

On March 8, 1945, Wolff saw Dulles and agreed not to destroy the Italian industries,[6] to guarantee the lives of all hostages in German hands, to abstain from further attacks on the partisans and to prepare the surrender of the German forces in Italy, without Hitler's knowledge.

On returning to Italy, however, Wolff received orders from Germany to break off all negotiations with Roosevelt's agent and to have Parrilli arrested. He did not obey but, instead, sent Parrilli again to Switzerland to confer with Dulles. The latter asked him whether Wolff could carry out his plan and whether, if Marshal Kesselring were supplanted by another commander in Italy, the new man could be brought into the scheme, or, if not, whether Wolff could act without him. Wolff undertook to carry out his engagements and summoned all his subordinates, enjoining them not to allow any acts of violence against persons or the destruction of buildings.

Mussolini had at last got wind of the negotiations with the C.L.N.A.I and Cardinal Schuster. On March 6th, Mussolini sent Mellini to Rahn to secure further information. Rahn replied that nothing definite was in preparation, but that in any case Italy's interests, Mussolini himself and the Fascists would be properly cared for. He said not a word about the negotiations in Switzerland.

On March 19th, Wolff, Zimmer, Waibel, Husmann, Dulles, Gaevernitz, General Lemnitzer, the British General Airey and Parrilli met at Ascona in Switzerland. Wolff agreed to contact Kesselring's successor, General Heinrich von Viettinghof, and he gave the Allied representatives plans of the German front in Italy, which were to prove of great value to them in the coming final offensive.

President Roosevelt's death retarded the negotiations, and the Russians, when they heard of them, expressed opposition to anything of the kind.

Wolff in the meantime had a wireless transmitting set installed in Zimmer's room to communicate to the Allied G.H.Q. at Caserta the exact position of the German G.H.Q. at Recoaro (province of Vicenza), which was heavily bombed in consequence.

On April 19th the new German Commander-in-Chief in Italy, General von Viettinghof, and his Chief of Staff, General Rottiger, called officially on Mussolini and assured him of their determination to hold out to the end. Immediately after this, they went to see Wolff and Parrilli to make preparations for surrender. On his part, Cardinal Schuster was continuing the talks with Wolff's agent, Colonel Rauff.

While all this was going on, the Allies did not wish the

surrender to be arranged through the C.L.N.A.I. and ordered Cadorna and the partisan leader Valiani to keep the partisans out of the negotiations.

In the meantime the invading armies were advancing slowly and painfully along the Adriatic and the Tyrrhenian coasts, but the French attempt to break through on the Alpine front was repulsed by the Italian *Littorio* and *Folgore* divisions and some German units. Von Viettinghof could get no further reinforcements from Germany, now occupied from east to west, and he had to rely solely on the forces he had in Italy, which were much reduced, his air force being almost non-existent. Valerio Borghese's *Decima Mas* was the only Italian unit still fighting vigorously, but he actually had to buy arms from the Germans to continue the struggle. Mussolini complained that the Germans refused to allow the other Italian divisions, although in full efficiency, to defend the Apennine front.

Bologna was occupied by the Anglo-Americans on April 21st, but they were received by the population in icy silence; on the 22nd they reached the river Po, and that same day the Yugoslavs entered Fiume.

In the wake of the Allies came the partisans, mostly recruited at the last moment, and they at once proceeded to murder a number of Fascists and other personal enemies. The Allied commands, although they would not allow them any political authority, left them free to rob, murder and rape.

Von Viettinghof had agreed to Wolff's plan on the 21st. On the 22nd Wolff, himself, with his own German, Italian and Swiss followers and von Viettinghof's delegates, Colonel von Schweinitz and Major Wenner, went to Switzerland. On the 25th Wolff returned to Italy and informed Cardinal Schuster that he would arrange the surrender of the German forces to the C.L.N.A.I.; he signed the agreement at the archepiscopal palace. That same day General Meinhold at the head of a large force surrendered to the partisans at Genoa, apparently on Wolff's orders. On the 27th two German officers went to the Allied G.H.Q. at Caserta to arrange the details of the surrender.

Mussolini had still been kept in ignorance of all these activities. But when he came to Milan on April 17th, Rahn told

Mellini, under promise of secrecy, that the Germans were negotiating with the Allies to save the Duce from the Communists and that he was to be conveyed to Spain. In Milan the Duce had been enthusiastically welcomed by the crowds, and the members of the Government, also transferred to that city, continued to attend to business as usual. In spite of the chaotic political and military situation, the administration of the I.S.R. proceeded normally and efficiently down to the very end, and the finances were conducted in an orderly manner. This was certainly not the case in the area occupied by the Allies, where the population was almost starving; the finances were conducted on the basis of a colossal inflation caused by the issue of unlimited quantities of Allied paper currency guaranteed by nothing at all; and all public business was operated with the most wholesale corruption, in which the officials of the Bonomi Government and those of the Allied commands vied with each other as to who should perpetrate the most flagrant swindles.

Rahn saw Mussolini on the 20th, advised him to return to Gargnano and continued to keep silent about the German negotiations with the Allies. Mussolini refused to return to the Lake and held his last Cabinet Council, at which he ordered his ministers to disband.

As far back as February 13, 1945, Mussolini had told Count Mazzolini that he would have preferred to make his last stand at Trieste, which was threatened by the Yugoslavs, but he was prevented from going there by the Germans. Marshal Graziani had later proposed to defend Milan, but Mussolini did not wish to expose the population of the city to the terrible devastation that would have ensued. Now he proposed to withdraw with the whole Government to the Valtellina, Pavolini having assured him that there were in that area some thousands of volunteers ready to hold out to the last. As a matter of fact, the alleged preparations in the Valtellina did not exist.

Before quitting Milan for the Valtellina, the Duce thought at one moment of handing power over to the Socialists,[7] still harking back to his early affiliations and to the socialization plans of the Verona program. But this idea was soon dropped.

By the 25th of April the Government departments had

ceased to function, the German army was in dissolution, and the police forces had faded out. The C.L.N.A.I. members, still in concealment in a convent, did not proclaim the general uprising, as they awaited orders from the Allies—this they had been told to do by a certain Max Salvadori, an Italian renegade, acting as a British agent.

Mussolini's secretary, Luigi Gatti, had proposed a flight to Spain by air, but the Duce refused to leave Italy. He had at last heard rumors of the German negotiations for surrender. He asked Colonel Rauff about them, but Rauff indignantly denied that there was any truth in the story,[8] and so did the German Consul-General in Milan, who actually demanded of the Italian Finance Minister, Domenico Pellegrini-Giampietro, an advance of 8 milliards (billions) of lire for the month of May. The Minister refused. After the Consul-General's threats he phoned to Mussolini, who entirely approved of his refusal and instructed him to order the Finance Guards to fire if any attempt was made to seize the money by force.

Mussolini now made up his mind to negotiate with the C.L.N.A.I., in order to avert a general massacre, and one of the Committee's members, Marazza, advised him to conduct negotiations in the archepiscopal palace. He assured Mussolini that his fate would be settled by Bonomi's Government, then in Rome, in agreement with the Allies, to whom he would be handed over as soon as their forces reached Milan. Mussolini then went to the palace to discuss the situation with Schuster and Cadorna, accompanied by Marshal Graziani, Barracu, the Prefect of Milan, Bassi, and the Minister Zerbino.

At the palace, it was expected that the surrender of the *Wehrmacht* to the C.L.N.A.I. would take place in the presence of the Cardinal himself. But the Allies, who had been informed of the plan, had no intention of accepting this procedure. In fact no German representative came to the palace at all.

The Cardinal addressed Mussolini as a guilty man coming to confess his sins.[9] He implored him to spare further massacres for Italy and to agree to surrender, to which Mussolini replied that he would disband his remaining forces in Milan and retire to the Valtellina, where he would continue to resist for some time longer before surrendering. In a whole hour's con-

versation the Cardinal never said a word about the negotiations with the Germans. Then Cadorna, with Marazza and
Lombardi of the C.L.N.A.I., arrived, and Bassi, who had heard
of the negotiations, proceeded to tell Graziani about them.
Marazza asked Mussolini if the Fascists were ready to accept
the conditions which the C.L.N.A.I. proposed, viz., that they
would be concentrated in an area between Milan, Como and
Lecco, when they would enjoy full immunity, except in the
case of such of them as were charged with specific offenses, and
that these would be tried before regular courts of justice. Their
families would be undisturbed, and the diplomats would be
treated according to the rules of international law.[10]

Graziani thereupon communicated the news of the imminent
surrender of the German forces. Mussolini showed violent indignation at having been kept in ignorance of this fact. The
Cardinal, his subterfuge being thus exposed, appeared greatly
embarrassed. Graziani exclaimed that the German commanders
by this action had forfeited all claims to Italy's loyalty, and
Mussolini added that by initiating negotiations without informing him they had been guilty of treachery and thus given him
full liberty of action. He then left the palace, saying that he
would give the C.L.N.A.I. an answer within an hour's time.

The Cardinal waited for his return and for the arrival of
the German delegates, but neither came. He rang up the Duce's
headquarters at the Prefecture, but learned that he had already
left Milan.

Mussolini had set out for the Valtellina, deceived by Pavolini's fictitious statement that he would find a body of faithful followers assembled there to support his last stand.

On the night of April 25-26th, when the Government of the
I.S.R. had ceased to exist, the German army was in full disintegration, and its units in Milan had shut themselves up in
their barracks. The C.L.N.A.I. had at last received authority
from the Allied command to order a general uprising—when
there was no longer anyone or anything to revolt against.
The Allied troops suspended their entrance into Milan and
other cities for several days, probably in order to allow the
C.L.N.A.I. and the partisans to murder as many Italians as possible who might afterwards have caused trouble—*i.e.,* those who

were inspired by any patriotic feelings. For the wave of atrocities committed between the last days of April and the month of May the Russians were largely responsible, as they hoped in that way to eliminate all Italians who might oppose a Communist Government for Italy. But the Western Allies had their own share of responsibility for their subservience to the Russians in all the bloodshed they demanded.

Mussolini, on leaving Milan, was accompanied by the Ministers, Ferdinando Mazzasoma, Ruggiero Romano and Pavolini, and by various officials. At Menaggio the party joined a column of thirty German cars on their way to Merano. At Musso the column was held up by the partisans; the Germans were allowed to continue their journey undisturbed, but the Italian party was forced to stop at Dongo on Lake Como.[11] Mussolini, himself, was conveyed thence to Germasino and there locked up in the customs house. Claretta Petacci, who had long been devoted to Mussolini, asked to be allowed to join him, and her wish was granted. The two were then escorted to a small house at Giulino di Mezzagno. They reached it at 3 a.m. and were interned there for the rest of the night.

The capture of Mussolini was communicated to Como and Milan. Commander Dessy and Dr. Guastoni seem to have been charged by the Allied Command to recover him for them; and his nephews, Vito Mussolini and Count Teodorani, tried to join him, but they were prevented from proceeding beyond Cernobbio. Other attempts to get hold of the Duce also failed. There is every reason to believe that the Allies were none too eager to save his life, for, if he had survived and been tried, he might have made revelations extremely awkward for the leading statesmen of the Allied Powers.

The Dongo partisans received a telegram—it is not known who had signed it—ordering them not to allow Mussolini to be harmed, adding that if he attempted to escape, he was not to be prevented from doing so.

A Communist functionary named Walter Audisio ordered Colonel Francesco Malgeri, with a party of customs guards, to escort the Duce back to Milan. But later, this same Audisio and another irresponsible Communist, Guido Lampredi, went to see General Luigi Cadorna and told him that the C.L.N.A.I.

had ordered them to execute Mussolini. This was untrue, and no such order had been issued, inasmuch as the C.L.N.A.I. then represented the Rome Government, which was bound to respect the clause in the armistice according to which Mussolini was to be handed over to the Allies alive.

Subsequently Audisio said that he had received the order to murder Mussolini and all the other Fascist leaders from "all the members of the General Command." [12] That Command consisted of Ferrucio Parri and Longo, to whom Lampredi was afterwards attached in some unspecified capacity. But that day both Parri and Lampredi were absent, and Cadorna claims that he had learned of this order from Audisio as one coming from the C.L.N.A.I. Audisio was obviously lying. Still later he said that he had received the order from the C.V.L. (Liberation Command of Volunteers), but this also was untrue, for that committee had never been invested with any such authority.

The real fact seems to be that the order had been given to Audisio by a Communist member of the C.V.L.—either Longo or his substitute and successor, Lampredi. It is strange that Cadorna accepted the statement without troubling to verify it, or at least to ask for a written communication. The fact is that Palmiro Togliatti (the head of the Communist Party), Longo, Lampredi and others all aspired to secure for the Party the honor of having taken a decision of such an admirably Russian and Bolshevik nature.

Audisio was given one pass by the C.V.L. and another by the Americans, was "promoted" to "Colonel Valerio," and went with Lampredi, Gementi and a dozen men, first to Dongo on the Lake, and then to Giulino with Lampredi, Michele Moretti and Canali, political commissars of the 52nd partisan brigade. Audisio gave five different versions of his final conversation with Mussolini, each contradicting the others on many points and all of them being obviously untrustworthy.

In any case, he summoned Mussolini and Claretta Petacci to follow him, giving them to understand that he had come to liberate them. He conveyed them instead by car to a place chosen by himself and made them both get out of the car. There Moretti shot them dead (April 29, 1945). According to an eye-witness account, the first two weapons used by Moretti failed to fire and he was compelled to get a third to consummate the foul deed.

Audisio, full of sadistic delight over the murder, returned to Dongo, where the other members of Mussolini's party were under arrest, conveyed them to a spot on the shore and lined them up with their backs to the lake. They were: Francesco Barracu; Nicola Bombacci; air-captain Calestri Casalinuovo (Mussolini's A.D.C.); the eminent Greek scholar and President of the University of Bologna, Goffredo Coppola; Ernesto Daquanno, director of the Stefani News Agency; Mussolini's secretary, Luigi Gatti; the Minister of Popular Culture, Mezzasoma; the Minister of Public Works, Ruggiero Romano; Pavolini, Zerbino and four others. None of these men had been guilty of any offence whatsoever, nor had any sentence been pronounced against them even by a sham tribunal. A priest who was present asked permission to grant them absolution, but the assassins refused his request, and he was only able to give them a collective blessing. They were then all shot dead. As they died they shouted "Viva l'Italia!"

To the assassinated was also added Marcello Petacci, the brother of Claretta, but the other prisoners refused to have him with them, for they considered him a traitor; and he was shot separately—the only favor granted to the murdered men.

The arch-assassin, Audisio, is now a member of the Italian Chamber of Deputies and is esteemed in Communist circles.

The local inhabitants, the partisans and the Communists seized all the money and valuables found on the murdered men, partly their own private property and partly the funds of the various government departments that were to have been conveyed to safety. All this loot was divided up among the murderers and their friends. The chief looter, as appears from the investigation conducted by General Zingales, was Moretti, Mussolini's murderer.[13]

The bodies of Mussolini and the other murdered men and of Claretta Petacci were brought to Milan, hung up in the Piazzale Loreto, and exposed to the contumely of the scum of the local mob. Cardinal Schuster was asked by an aged priest to go to the Piazzale and insist that an end be put to this spectacle. But the Cardinal refused to do anything about it. The burial place of Mussolini has long been kept secret, even from his widow and children, owing to the fear that too many wreaths would be placed upon it. It has been stated, however, that he is buried in the famous Certosa of Pavia.

The occasion of Mussolini's murder afforded an excellent illustration of the sportsmanship and consistency of Winston Churchill. When the news reached him, Churchill rushed into his dining-room and exultantly exclaimed to his guests: "Ah, the bloody beast is dead!" This of the man whom, a short ten years before, he had described as "so great a man, so wise a ruler." And, only eight years before that, he had proclaimed that, if he had been born in Italy, he would have been "wholeheartedly with" Mussolini in the service of the Fascist regime.

The partisans and other Communists also wished to murder Marshal Graziani, but an American captain saved his life, and he voluntarily surrendered. He was taken first to a hotel in Milan, then to the San Vittore prison in that city and next to the headquarters of the American Fourth Army corps, where he countersigned the surrender of the Italian army of Liguria. From San Vittore he was conveyed to Florence, where he transmitted the surrender order to all his other forces. He was detained a prisoner by the British for many months at Algiers and then was handed over to the Italian authorities, who imprisoned him in the spring of 1946 on the island of Procida, where the present writer had the great honor of making his acquaintance. In 1950 he was tried, first by a civilian court and then by a military tribunal, which condemned him to 19 years imprisonment, but with a sentence so worded as to allow of various reductions in the term; and in August of that year he was set free.

Note on the Death of Marshal Graziani.

Marshal Graziani died in January, 1955, and the American magazine, *Time,* felt impelled to write an obituarial notice of some length in its issue of January 24th, designed to charge or imply that Graziani was a combination of a fakir, coward and sadist. This calls for some comment to set the record straight.

The *Time* correspondent stated that the family motto of Graziani was "An enemy forgiven is more dangerous than a thousand foes." Actually, the motto is *Ensis et aratrum* (the Sword and the Plough), since there had been many soldiers and farmers in the Marshal's family.

At the end of the first World War, Graziani was by no means "jobless," as the *Time* correspondent alleged. He had been promoted to the rank of Colonel (the youngest in the Italian army), and he continued to carry out his duties as commander of the 61st Infantry Regiment.

Later, Graziani volunteered for active service in Libya under Field Marshal Badoglio, then Governor of the Colony. He was entrusted with the pacification of Cyrenaica, where there was an endemic rebellion of a few thousand Senussi bandits in the pay of the British authorities in Egypt. Since the Senussi forced the local inhabitants to help and feed them, Graziani removed the latter to the coastal area where they were adequately provided for by the Italian authorities. The "electrified wires" mentioned in *Time* were a precaution taken only along the Egyptian frontier to prevent British and Senussi agents from entering the colony. The reference to captured Senussi "hung in bags from tall trees" is hard to believe, as there were then no trees at all in Cyrenaica. The allegation that rebels were dropped from airplanes savors of the Arabian Nights.

In the Ethiopian War, Graziani once more served under Badoglio as commander-in-chief. His advance from Somaliland was carried out by a relatively small force—two divisions, with no tanks and only a small number of caterpillar trucks, ordered (and paid for) by the Italian Government from the U. S.

The Addis Ababa outrage was the outcome of a plot organized by a group of "Young Ethiopians" in the pay of the British Intelligence Service. It had as its object the wiping out of not only Graziani but all the other Italian military and civil personnel then attending a meeting during which Graziani distributed alms to the poor of the city. At least 18 bombs exploded, two of which struck Graziani and about 300 fragments lodged in his body. He did not "fall down," but held himself erect, and later drove around the city in his car. When I saw him, in 1946, he was still having fragments of the bombs extracted from his body every few weeks.

At the end of the War, Graziani was not "caught by the partisans," as the *Time* article states. He surrendered voluntarily to Major Fiske of the American Army in Milan, and was handed over by Fiske to the British. They conveyed him to Algiers and put him in an internment camp where he was most brutally ill-treated. Later on, the British handed him over to Italian authorities who detained him in various prisons until his trial in 1950 before a military tribunal. He was condemned to 19 years imprisonment but the court stated that he "had acted from higher motives of a social character," which was tantamount to acquittal. His sentence was, in fact, reduced by amnesties and extenuating circumstances to four months.

At the time of Graziani's funeral, there was an impressive gathering and demonstration of some 200,000 persons. This fact presents the truest verdict on the sentiments of the Italian people concerning their foremost national military hero since the first World War.

---

[1] Dr. Georg Zachariae, *Mussolini si confessa*, Milan, 1948.

[2] Carlo Silvestri, *Contro la vendetta*, Milan, 1948, pp. 306 ff.

[3] This Party of Action, which adopted all the old slogans of conventional democracy, acquired a certain measure of prestige when it was supported by the Banca Commerciale. When the managers of the Bank became fully aware of the nature and activities of the Party, financial support was withdrawn, and the Party faded out.

[4] For the events of this last act of the tragedy, see Ferruccio Lanfranchi, *La resa degli Ottocentomila*, Rome, 1948; E. F. Möllhausen, *op. cit.;* I. Schuster, *Gli ultimi tempi di un regime*, Milan, 1946; Ernst Berger, "Oberitalien in der Geschichte der deutschen Kapitulation," in the *Frankfurter Hefte*, IV, February, 1949; and Tamaro, *op. cit.*, Vol. III, pp. 553-664.

[5] Mussolini, in agreeing to Parri's release, said that he was an honest man. The Duce was often strangely ingenuous.

[6] This had been, as we have seen, the work of the Italian authorities.

[7] Carlo Silvestri, *Turati mi ha detto*, Milan, 1946, pp. 99-106.

[8] *Ibid.*, p. 230.

[9] In the past Schuster had glorified Mussolini as "the splendor of his age."

[10] Not one of these promises was kept.

[11] It was reported in many papers that Mussolini was on his way to Switzerland, but Dongo is located far to the north of the last road leading into Switzerland.

[12] *Unità*, November, 1945.

[13] The investigation of the plundering at Dongo, entrusted to the military magistrate Zingales by the De Gasperi Government, was later held up and prevented from reaching a final conclusion lest certain high personages who had got rich on the proceeds might be compromised. The records of the investigation, so far as it went, were published by E. Saimi in *Italia Nova*, March and April, 1948.

Epilogue

What judgment can be passed on Mussolini's foreign policy as a whole?

Some aspects of it will, no doubt, form a subject of polemics among future historians, but on others some conclusions can, I think, be established even at the present moment.

In the first place, as has been made crystal clear in this book, the judgment passed on Mussolini's foreign policy has been based chiefly on the reaction at home and abroad to his *domestic* policy. The opposition of British imperialists to his Ethiopian venture is the only prominent exception. Liberals and radicals everywhere were vigorously opposed to Fascism as a political system, whatever the benefits conferred on the Italian people. Even conservatives who admired Mussolini did so mainly because he suppressed Communism and radicalism in Italy, "made the trains run on time," and the like. Those foreign liberals and radicals who did sincerely wish for peace were unable to overcome their prejudices against a totalitarian state sufficiently to give Mussolini any credit for peaceful intentions, even though his demand for financial, political and territorial Revisionism after 1919, and his proposal of a Four-Power Pact, were the most realistic suggestions looking forward to permanent peace between the two World Wars. One could the better excuse the prejudices of liberals and radicals against totalitarianism if they had been logical and consistent. But, while they denounced the relatively mild totalitarian regimes of Hitler and Mussolini, they professed great admiration for the much more drastic and brutal Soviet totalitarianism, and many of them held it up as a model for the future of political and economic life. Conservative foreign financial interests "soured" on him mainly because he refused to support his system extensively by foreign loans.

Mussolini was condemned for his Ethiopian foray because he imitated in a very slight and modest degree what England, France and Belgium had already done on a vast scale and with far less justification. And, in the Spanish Civil War, he sought to block the advances of Communism a decade before the "Free Nations" came to recognize the need for such a policy when they launched the Cold War in 1947.

Secondly, there is little doubt that Mussolini's conduct of Italy's foreign relations conferred on the country a position and prestige such as it had never enjoyed before. No Italian Minister of Foreign Affairs ever achieved such success since Cavour, and never before had Italy been so greatly respected abroad. Not only did its diplomats realize this, but even its humblest emigrants felt at last that they could hold up their heads with pride and say *"Civis Italicus sum."*

Thirdly, the two main principles, the keynotes, so to speak, of his foreign policy, viz., a timely revision of the Peace Treaties of 1919-20 and the creation of a Four-Power Pact, if they had been accepted and applied by the other Great Powers, would undoubtedly have contributed very materially to the maintenance of world peace for a very long time.

Mussolini has been severely condemned in many quarters for his alliance with Nazi Germany, and on this point his policy may be open to criticism. But we must remember that what drove Italy into that alliance was: (1) the refusal of Britain and France to accept the two aforesaid proposals; (2) the vindictiveness and jealousy of Great Britain (or at least of certain leading British statesmen), and (3) the absolute failure of France to comprehend Italy's position and requirements due, no doubt, to its perpetual panic fear of Germany.

The blocking of Italy's population expansion by the closing of all gates to its emigrants, and the ever-increasing customs tariffs that strangled its export trade contributed to force Italy to follow such courses as autarchy, which would otherwise have been unnecessary.

Mussolini's chief fault perhaps was his excessively outspoken frankness in dealing with foreign countries. If he had followed even a Berlitz school course in international hypocrisy—and he could easily have found admirable teachers in certain countries that shall be nameless—he might have secured much of what Italy needed under the guise of rendering services to the League of Nations, to international justice, to humanity, and to other things of the kind, and thereby he might well have competed for the Nobel Peace Prize. But like Theodore Roosevelt, he never lost the habit of calling a spade a spade, and he always said exactly what he thought and with the most uncompromising frankness.

In dealing with foreigners, and especially with the British, he failed to attach sufficient importance to what a witty Spanish publicist defined as the *vegetarian* aspect of their mentality, which is so largely inspired by sentimental considerations. These, however foolish they may appear, do influence an immense number of British and even American citizens. The statesmen of those countries, even if they do not themselves believe in such idealistic principles, cannot fail to take them into account, in view of their electioneering value. Mussolini regarded all that sort of thing as bunk—and he said so, which was often unwise.

We must also remember that Italy was not a sufficiently strong power to impose its policies, even if they were sound ones, on other countries, and that it had to seek alliances where it could find them. Mussolini, himself, would have preferred other alliances than those which he chose, but circumstances over which he had no control compelled him to follow the path he did.

Finally, as I have often said in the course of this book, Mussolini was too far-sighted. He foresaw future events and counted on their coming to pass at a particular moment, whereas they did not materialize until later—when it was far too late for them to influence the situation decisively. Thus he predicted the break-up of the British Empire and the inevitable conflict between the Western Powers and Russia; both were bound to occur and did occur, but after the end of the second World War and not before.

The following material, taken from the German edition of the Memoirs of Franz von Papen, indicates how much more clearly Mussolini and Franco foresaw the future of Europe, than did Winston Churchill.

On February 21, 1943, when the War was about to enter its decisive phase, General Francisco Franco, head of the Spanish Government, sent a memorandum to the British Ambassador in Madrid. This dealt with the dangers inherent in a Russian victory in Europe, and Franco asked that it be sent to the proper persons in the British government so that they might consider the situation likely to arise after the War. Franco wrote:

Our anxiety on account of Russia's advance is not only shared by other peoples, but also by all Europeans who have not yet lost their capacity for clear discernment. Communism is an enormous danger for the world, and now that it is supported by a victorious army, all those who see clearly are alarmed. If the war goes on like this, it is obvious that the Russian armies will penetrate deeply into German territory. If this happens, the danger will arise for England of a Soviet State in Germany who will supply Russia with her own military secrets, her engineers, her science, her specialists and will thus enable Russia to create a monstrous power, extending from the Atlantic to the Pacific.

Will there any longer exist in Central Europe, in that mosaic of nations, without cohesion, ruined and devastated by war and occupation, any Power capable of opposing Stalin's ambitious plans?

We appeal to the sound instinct of the English people; if Russia gains possession of Germany, no one will be in a position to hold up her advance.

Franco's statement of the potential Russian menace was precisely what Mussolini had held to be the facts for two decades before Franco submitted his memorandum and particularly after June 22, 1941. Indeed, Franco's presentation of the situation could fairly be regarded as a paraphrase of Mussolini's interpretation of the issues of the second World War. But Churchill took exactly the opposite view of the outlook.

He composed the following answer and rejoinder to Franco on February 25, 1943:

I hope I can prove to you that your fears are devoid of foundation. You say that Communism constitutes the only real danger for Europe, that a Russian victory will have as its consequences the progress of Communism in other parts of Europe, and that this will mean the destruction of European civilization and of Christian culture.

Our point of view is diametrically opposite to this! Do you really believe that a single nation is strong enough to dominate Europe after this war? And that it will be actually Russia, who is forced, more than other nations, to devote herself to large-scale reconstruction, and who for this purpose will have need of England and the United States? I venture to prophesy that, after the war England will be the greatest military Power in Europe. I am sure that England's influence will be stronger in Europe than it has ever been before since the days of the fall of Napoleon.[1]

The trend of events since 1945 show how much more clearly and accurately Mussolini and Franco discerned the inevitable results of an overwhelming Russian victory than did Churchill. Churchill's lack of realism was truly appalling. As Captain Russell Grenfell has pointed out in his book, *Unconditional Hatred,* Churchill was so obsessed with military victory that he gave little thought to the responsibilities and consequences of victory. Before the year 1943 was over, he was suggesting at Teheran that Germany be dismembered after the War, a policy which probably contributed more to the increase of Russian power and influence than "unconditional surrender," or the Stalin-White-Morgenthau Plan to destroy the industrial life of the Germany that survived the War. Russia has become the most powerful nation in the Old World, if not in the whole world, and Britain has sunk to the level of a second-class military and naval power with less prestige than at any time since the close of the War of the Roses, and it lies under the perpetual shadow of destruction by atom bombs and guided missiles dispatched by the Russians.[2]

History will hold Churchill mainly responsible for these disasters to England, although probably the deeper responsibility was that of Eden's foreign policy in the 1930's. Aneurin

Bevan satirically but correctly observed that: "Sir Winston Churchill's superlative personal gifts have eased the passage of Britain to the status of a second-rate power." The editors of the British periodical, *The European,* thus concisely assessed the final outcome of Churchill's policies for Britain and its future: "He found a great Empire and he left a small dependency."

With the defeat of Italy and the elimination of Mussolini himself in such monstrous circumstances, and with men and parties radically opposed to all his ideas now in power, what will remain of his foreign policy? It is difficult to say, but we must not forget that the good as well as the evil that men do lives after them. In a future world, less maniacal than that of today, many of Mussolini's better principles in the international field will finally, I am sure, be generally accepted and applied—unless a new and yet more devastating catastrophe occurs that will reduce our present civilization to a state of complete and irreparable wreckage. Perhaps the day will come when a new account of Mussolini's foreign policy will have as its motto the words: "I told you so."

[1] Interestingly and instructively enough, this exchange of letters between Franco and Churchill was omitted from the English edition of von Papen's Memoirs, and only appears in the German and Italian editions.

[2] See Emrys Hughes, *Bomb over Britain,* London, 1954.

INDEX

Index

40-3, 53, 182-95, 213; British culture abroad, 58-9; necessity for understanding with, 96; and Ethiopia, 126; Anglo-Ethiopian Commission, 128-9; report on Ethiopia, 132-4; full support of the League of Nations, 135; encouragement of Ethiopia, 139-40; anti-Italian attitude on Ethiopia, 143-52; anti-Italian propaganda in Spanish Civil War, 170-1; Amritsar atrocities, 183; relations with Germany, 184; effects on, of Second World War, 195; hatred of Italy, 224; military pact with France (1939), 225; alliance with Poland (1939), 233; peace proposals to (1940), 269

See also Four-Power Pact

Greco-Turkish War (1897), 20

Greece, 255, 270, 272, 346-7; relations with, 20; conflict with Greek claims in the Near East, 20-5; attack on, error by Mussolini, 272-3

Gregorian, Alexandru, 343

Grenfell, Captain Russell, Unconditional Hatred, 377

Gringoire, 152

Guardia Nazionale Republicana, 324

Guariglia, Ambassador Raffaele, 252, 267, 277-8, 290, 303-5, 339-40

Gueli, Police Inspector, 311

Gunther, John, Inside Europe, 178-80

Guzzoni, General Alfredo, 220

Hácha, President Emil, 214

Hague Court, 23, 89

Hailé Selassié. See Ethiopia

Halifax, Lord, 184, 191, 192, 235, 252; visit to Rome, 213

Hapsburgs, 116, 117

Hart. See Liddell-Hart

Hassell, Ambassador Ulrich von, 104, 185

Hatred of Italy in Great Britain and France, 224

"Have and have-not" nations, Italy and Germany, 224, 229

Hegel, Georg Wilhelm Friedrich, 195

Held, President, 37

Henderson, Ambassador Sir Nevile M., 208, 236

Henlein, Conrad, 205

Herriot, Premier Edouard, 103, 104

Hervé, Gustave, 8, 9

Herzegovina, 275, 277

Hidaka, Ambassador, 299

Himmler, Heinrich, 316, 351

Hitler, Adolf, 27, 39, 91, 101, 103, 134, 135, 162, 184-5, 187, 195; violent revision of Versailles Treaty, x; ex-

pansion policy, xi; advent to power (1933), 92, 94; pupil of Mussolini, 93; meeting with Mussolini (1934), 113; visit to Rome (1938), 193; opinion of, by Sisley Huddleston, 193; death, 193; anti-Semitism, 198-9; intentions after the Anschluss, 204; Berchtesgaden meeting, 207; at Munich Conference, 207-9; views, after Munich, on other countries, 210; extension of power, 214; message from Roosevelt, 223; letter from Mussolini, 226-7; not bent on conquering the world, 249; meeting with Mussolini at the Brenner (1940), 250; visit by Ciano, 270; meeting with Mussolini, Ciano, and Von Ribbentrop, 279; visits to Mussolini and Ciano (1941), 284, 285; meeting with Mussolini (1943), 293; talk with Mussolini at Klessheim (1943), 310; talks with Mussolini, 311; attempt on life, 331; meeting with Mussolini (1944), 331

Hoare, Ambassador Sir Samuel, 14, 145, 148, 150, 151, 155, 196; resignation, 156

Hoare-Laval Plan, 153-6

Holland; invasion by Nazis, 251

Holy See. See Vatican

Hoover, President Herbert, 84; proposed moratorium on war debts and reparations, 84-5

Hopkins, Harry L., 236-7

Horthy, Admiral Nicholas, 342

Huddleston, Sisley, on Edenism, 196; on Hitler and Mussolini, 193; on the Spanish Civil War; In My Time, 170, 196, note; France: The Tragic Years, 1939-1947, 218, note; 280, note; 338, note; Popular Diplomacy and War, 25, note; 196, note; Terreur, 1944, 18, note

Hull, Secretary Cordell, 113, 140, 152-3, 155, 187, 209, 222, 226, 265, 288; memoirs, 113

Humbert, Prince, 307

Hungary, 211, 241-2, 271, 275; division after the First World War, 5, 89; relations with, 46, 54; rearmament, 103; commercial agreement with, 115; subjugation by Soviet Russia, 342

"Immortal Principles" of Western democracy and socialism, 9, 42, 90, 210, 217, 224

In My Time, by Sisley Huddleston, 170, 196, note

India, route to, 13; Amritsar atrocities, 183

Voce d'Italia, 225, 251
Volpi, Count Giuseppe, 53
Volta Congress, 97, 98
Volunteers, Liberation Command of, 368

Wal-Wal episode, 127-9, 137-9
Wales, Prince of. *See* Windsor, Duke of
Wallachia, 46, *note*
Walters, Frank, 147-8
War; views of Mussolini, 85-6; Cold, 175; new weapons, 358-9
   See also Briand-Kellogg Pact
War debts and reparations. See First World War
Wars. *See* names of wars
Washington Naval Treaty, 16-7, 80
Weimar Republic. *See* Germany
Welles, Sumner, 186, 248-50, 352; *The Time for Decision,* 248
Wellington, Duke of, 189
Weygand, General Maxime, 98
What Price Israel, by Alfred Lilienthal, 198
William of Wied, Prince, 47
Wilson, Sir Arnold, 156
Wilson, President Woodrow; objections to Pact of London, 3; anti-Italian, 4; fanaticism and ignorance, 41
Windsor, Duke of (formerly Prince of Wales; King Edward VIII), 146
Wolf, General Karl, 334, 360-3
Workers; unemployment, 70; problem of Italian workers in Germany, 328-30; conscription by Nazis, 354
World Economic Conference, 98
World War I. *See* First World War

World War II. *See* Second World War
Writings and Speeches of Benito Mussolini, 12, *notes*

Yalta Conference, and documents, 241, 246, 265
Young, Eugene, *Looking Behind the Censorships,* 180
Youth Organization (Balilla), 64
Yugoslavia, 111, 118, 270, 274-5, 290, 339, 340, 344-6; differences with, 3; relations with, 4, 17-9, 26-32, 55; Serbia, 10, 48, 339; in the Little Entente, 44-6; and Albania, 48-50, 221-2; treaty of friendship with France, 49; Slav terrorism, 84; oppression under Tito, 96; conflicts with, 115-20; hatred of Italy, 119, 120; agreements with, 184; government for Montenegro and Serbia, 275; heterogenous state, 276-7; Marshal Tito, 290, 333, 341; triumph of Tito, 345-6; Slovenia, 311, 341
   See also Little Entente

Zachariae, Doctor Georg, 358
Zaharoff, Sir Basil, 23
Zaldumbide, Gonzalo, 158
Zara, 17, 18
Zeeland, Paul van, 161
Zerbino, Minister Paolo, 334, 365
Zionism. See Jews
Zog I, King, 49-51, 219-20
Zoppi, Vittorio, 267
Zvetkovich, Dragisha, 274, 275